Manna Gathering

Fresh Insights Into The Heart Of The Gospels

Jean Allen

Cover Artist

Brian Allen lives and works in Calgary, Alberta, Canada. He's an art director, a closet illustrator, and a devoted Husband and Dad. He can be contacted at brian@digitalbrian.ca

Scripture Permissions

DISCLAIMER

This book details the author's personal experiences with and opinions about scripture and spirituality.

The author and publisher are providing this book and its contents on an "as is" basis and make no representations or guarantees of any kind with respect to this book or its contents. The author and publisher disclaim all such representations and guarantees including spiritual direction for a particular purpose. In addition, the author and publisher do not represent or warrant that the information accessible via this book is accurate, complete or current.

Except as specifically stated in this book, neither the author nor publisher will be liable for damages arising out of or in connection with the use of this book. This is a comprehensive limitation of liability that applies to all damages of any kind, including (without limitation) compensatory; direct, indirect or consequential damages; loss of data, income or profit; loss of or damage to property and claims of third parties.

You understand that this book is not intended as a substitute for consultation with a professional pastoral counselor. Before you begin any change your lifestyle in any way, you will consult a licensed professional to ensure that you are doing what's best for your situation.

This book provides content related to spiritual topics. As such, use of this book implies your acceptance of this disclaimer.

Acknowledgments

When I think back over the years during which I was writing the Manna Gathering Reflections, what strikes me is that I was not writing in isolation. I always had faces in my mind, faces of men and women who shared with me that the reflections were meaningful to them. They accompanied me through the writing of every reflection and reminded me at every new paragraph that I was writing for real people desiring to live in the heart of God within their very real lives. There are some faces I especially want to thank.

The original Manna Gathering was not a set of reflections but a small group. Michelle La Grange Holmes, Patti Dansereau and Pat Bakker have been with me from the beginning even when distance separated us. In my mind's eye, they were always epitomes of those I write for: holy people hidden within ordinary lives – if any life can be defined as ordinary. I thank them for their incredible humor, their absolute dedication to spiritual growth and their openness to life.

Much gratitude goes to Fr. William Hann, Melani Fricot and Theresa Robinson who have been especially supportive of Manna Gathering. I am honored by the gracious words they wrote for the cover of this book.

My son, Brian Allen, a professional in the creative design industry, designed the profound cover for this book. His art often gives me a sense that I am being invited to go beyond to discover wonder. These are reminders of Kingdom reality that I treasure.

Dedication

I dedicate this book to my husband, Charlie, my blessed companion on this incredible path to the heart of God, who supports and sustains me. No matter what I need, he is there to give it, build it or procure it in whatever way possible and he does so with immense love and generosity.

He is a man with a Magdalene heart.

Manna Gathering

Fresh Insights Into The Heart
Of The Gospels

Table of Contents

Preface

Welcome to Manna Gathering: the book version. Many of you have been faithful and exceedingly encouraging readers for the whole time I posted the Manna Gathering reflections online. I completely agree with those of you who expressed the desire to have a hard copy of the reflections. There is something undeniably good about a book that's yours, that you can hold in your hands and put wherever you wish, that can be underlined or highlighted and where it's easier to flip back and forth to find favorite sections. A book is a wondrous thing and I am honored that many of you thought Manna Gathering worthy to be put into book form.

This book of reflections is based on a three-year cycle of the Catholic Lectionary readings. Please note that I said *'a'* three-year cycle, not *'the'* three-year cycle. The Catholic lectionary is complex and the schedule of Ordinary readings changes from year to year, depending upon which Sunday Easter falls. Some Ordinary Sundays may be included or omitted that weren't included or omitted in another cycle. Also, every year, some Feast days that normally fall on a weekday will fall on a Sunday and will replace the regular readings for that Sunday. For the most part, the reflections will follow the Church calendar, but there will definitely be times when they won't be in sync.

You may note that I have not included the full Gospel reading for each reflection. Instead, I have given the scripture reference plus a short synopsis of that reading. This is to avoid copyright infringement of any one translation of the scriptures. You may want to keep a bible handy in case you prefer to read the entire scripture passage rather than a synopsis of it. There are times when I summarize only the part of the reading that I am focusing on.

You may also note that I have not included a separate reflection in every year for Christmas, Ash Wednesday and the Feast of Mary the Mother of God. There is one reflection for each of these Feast days at the back of the book. Ash Wednesday, of course, never falls on a Sunday, and Christmas and Mary the Mother of God only occasionally fall on a Sunday. However, they are major Celebrations in the Church Year and therefore it felt right to include a reflection for each.

The best way to approach this book is not as a definitive Lectionary companion, but simply as a series of reflections based on Gospel passages that are so familiar that we often don't pay as much attention to each one as we should. In each reading I covered, I endeavored to open a door to the Kingdom. Sometimes I focused on the theme that the Church has assigned for a particular Sunday, but very often I went on my own journey of finding and opening little doors hidden in that particular Gospel. My focus is never in opposition to the theme chosen by the Church. The Gospels are layered with teaching and significance and never mean just one thing. We've all had experiences where we've read a scripture passage, gleaned something from it, then revisited it later and found a totally different implication.

Manna Gathering is simply a small contribution to a community meal that has an abundance of appetizers, full courses, desserts and fine wines.

May it provide satisfying nourishment for your journey.

YEAR A

Is Everyone Present?

Matthew 24: 37-44
On being prepared because Christ will come at an unexpected time.

Pay attention!

Advent is here and the first thing the readings and the Church tell us is pay attention! "Be ready," says Jesus. For what? For the mother of all natural disasters? For our co-worker to suddenly disappear before our eyes? For Jesus to come one last time? There is no healthy reason to wake up every day expecting it to be the last one before the world implodes, and there is no great spiritual benefit to keeping fearfully awake wondering if every bump in the night of our souls is a thief or if it's Jesus coming to take us away. So, what should we be paying attention to? How does this Gospel apply to us every day and not just in Advent? How can it further our spiritual growth and relationship with the Lord?

Advent: the arrival of a notable person, thing or event. We're called to pay attention to the arrival of this notable person and naturally, at this time of year we immediately think of Christmas as the notable event that heralds the arrival of the notable person, Jesus. We think Advent is the time of preparation for this arrival. But advent does not mean 'preparation'; it means 'the arrival'. However, we are encouraged to use this season to make ourselves mindful of the advent of Jesus and, in terms of our everyday life, he is coming all the time. Pay attention. Jesus comes. *Now.*

Yesterday has gone and tomorrow never comes. Yet, where do our minds most often dwell? We tend to live predominantly in either the past or in the future. We are rarely in the present moment or wholly attentive to it. Part of us is usually engaged in remembering things that happened in the past (usually the worst things) while another part of us is constantly exploring the possibilities of the future, good and bad. A very small part of us is in the present dealing with the demands of the moment and, for most of us, that small part is very small indeed. If the task of the moment is dull routine, our minds try to find stimulation in the past or the future. If the present moment is demanding and stressful, our visitations to the past and the future actually increase the stress of the moment because our experiences of similar stress shoot us into anxious expectations of future consequences.

The problem with spending time in the past or in the future is that you are not spending time in God's reality; you are living in your own past memories and in your future imaginations, which are rarely, if ever, based on the present reality of God. Even when you are remembering how he blessed you at one time or answered a prayer, that memory usually pushes you into thoughts of the future, hoping that he will bless you or answer your prayer in the same way again. If he didn't bless you or answer a prayer in the past, your future expectations are muted and maybe even hopeless. Meanwhile, God is in the present moment saying, "Look at me. I'm here. The past belongs to me and the future is actually none of your business. Be with me here...*now.*"

So hard, isn't it? It's especially difficult when the present moment is extremely dull and lonely or else full of maximum stress. It's so hard to stay present and pay attention because, for some odd reason, when we spend time in the past or in the future we feel we're more in control. Or at least we feel there's more potential for control if we can get it all together and figure out exactly what should be happening and then make it happen. Staying in the moment is an act of supreme trust. It means that we give up control. We leave the past in his hands and assume that he can and will create our future according to his word, not according to our expectations.

We need to pay attention to the present moment because that's when and where he comes. Every moment is an advent of our God and every moment we spend in being attentive is a season of preparation for a full awareness of his presence. I totally believe that all of us continually miss a multitude of quiet but astounding advents simply because they are quiet and don't fall within our set expectations. It's difficult to hear a gentle whisper when your mind and heart are filled with the raucous clamor of the past and future, a clamor that forms your ideas of how God should come.

The times when I have learned best the beautiful and powerful mystery of staying in the present moment have been during some times of extreme pressure and stress where it seemed like there was far too much to accomplish in the time given, where there was no leeway in terms of deadlines and where it felt like everything could go very badly. During these times, as long as I stayed in the present moment, focused only on the immediate task at hand and spoke to the Lord only about what I was doing in that moment, even if that task was something mundane, I was fine. As soon as I allowed my mind to latch onto all that was left to do or onto all the possibilities of disaster, everything inside of me would fly apart. I would immediately become overwhelmed and filled with a need to get everything under *my* control. Then all my energy seemed to be sucked out of me.

When I stayed in the moment, not only was I much more calm but I would continually be amazed at the orderly manner in which things progressed and how minor miracles kept happening. The present moment with God has its own particular power.

The Advent/Christmas season is chaotic in itself and just because it's the Christmas season, it doesn't mean that all the other heavy expectations, wounds and struggles you've been dealing with can be put aside so you can concentrate on the demands of Christmas. Don't berate yourself or the world for the pressures and demands of Advent and Christmas. Embrace them. Remember that it was into a world of wounded and materialistic chaos that Jesus was born very unobtrusively and in a way that met no one's expectations. This Advent season, try to remember that every moment is an Advent of our God and commit to trying to stay in the moment. Simply focus on the task right before you in the moment while you watch and wait for God.

And remember that God is in the present moment also watching and waiting for the appearance of a notable person.

You.

The Desert

Matthew 3: 1-12

John the Baptist appears out of the wilderness preaching repentance and foretelling the coming of Christ.

In the last reflection, I wrote about paying attention and staying in the present moment and because this is a topic that I believe is so important for our spiritual growth, I am going to make it my Advent theme.

When you reflect on John the Baptist, do you ever wonder what happened when he was out in the desert? What we read in scripture is that he ate locusts and wild honey and wore clothing of camel's hair with a leather belt. But something happened out there that formed and shaped him to become the forerunner of Jesus, a voice crying out in the wilderness, *"Prepare the way of the Lord, make his paths straight."* What was it?

My guess is that he had to learn to be in the present moment.

Have you ever experienced a spiritual desert? This is a time when your heart is arid and your spirit thirsts for God but it feels more like he's an isolated idea rather than an active presence in your life. It's a time when scripture holds no comfort and seems to be trite words, a time when spiritual disciplines that once fed you and comforted you now feel senseless and uninspiring. You worry that you've lost your way and you wonder if it's your fault. You speculate that perhaps you're praying the wrong prayers, thinking the wrong thoughts or reading the wrong books. It's a harsh and dry time.

Welcome to John's desert. It would be safe to assume that John felt deeply called to head out into the wilderness and to take very little with him. He probably even went out with a great sense of adventure and a lot of expectations of meeting his God. He most likely went out filled with certain precepts, laws and principles he strongly believed in and within which he expected God to show himself. For the first while he perhaps did not notice that he wasn't sensing God's presence at all as he kept himself busy with his prayer disciplines and was occupied with acquiring the basic necessities of life in the desert but eventually the starkness and emptiness of that desert wilderness must have begun to seep disturbingly into his soul. Prayers that were so comforting in the old community started losing relevancy. Spiritual disciplines that used to speak to his heart began to feel empty and lonely as the sun beat down on him and the wind blew sand in his eyes. The sense of adventure and joy diminishes rapidly in the desert.

Did John doubt himself? Did he doubt the call that drew him out there? Did he wonder if he had made a mistake and God was hiding from him until he figured out what he was really supposed to be doing? I think he did. John was human and in order to come face to face with God and hear his voice with clarity we humans have to lose much. We have to lose the idea that anything we do can guarantee that God will act in certain ways or make him love us more. We have to lose distorted perceptions of who God really is. We have to lose our idea that the more we know *about* God, the more we know him. There is so much we all need to lose. John had to lose all his preconceived ideas of God before he could find the pure voice of God, a voice so life shifting that, once heard, it recreates the one listening to it.

John had to lose all he knew and expected, and in that unforgiving desert he found that the past was long gone and the future was a vast expanse of sand. What was left? The present moment. At first, that present moment seemed as empty as his dry aching spirit but as he persisted in focusing on what he was called to do in the moment he began to be more and more aware of the simplicity of God. What was he called to do in the moment? Probably find some locusts and gather some honey so he wouldn't starve. He needed to gather some firewood for the cold nights. He had to build a shelter against the sudden windstorm. He had to find water. Basic stuff. Unexciting stuff. He had to apply himself to tedious tasks that seemed to have very little to do with great spiritual revelations. And he was called to speak to his God within and through these seeming trivialities of life – not outside of them.

These kinds of activities don't seem to carry a lot of spiritual potential until we pay attention, until our minds stop racing to the past or to the future and until we realize that all we do is holy mystery when we seek God within it. When we learn the art of bowing down before the God of the present moment something begins to happen. Where we would once only see dreary tasks, we begin to notice beauty within the ordinary. Where we would once have dismissed certain situations and people as unimportant to our spiritual growth, we begin to realize that in God's kingdom, nothing is unimportant. He engages with his angels, with us and with grains of sand with equal delight and individual attention. He is powerfully present in the ordinary and the humble. We need not and should not look anywhere else.

God pays deep attention to us in the present moment and it is there that he calls each of us by name. When John had lost everything that God had called him into the desert to lose, John became attentive and quieter. He became less anxious and less self-conscious. Then he heard his Name:

"John...listen! You are not just John. Listen to me. Listen to *me*! The One whom you seek is coming. Cry out to my people!

Listen to me! You are 'My Voice Crying Out in the Wilderness'. Cry out to my people!

Listen to me! You are 'The Preparer of the Way for my Chosen One'. Cry out to my people!

Listen to me! You are 'My Baptist'. Cry out to my people!

Listen to me! You are my 'Leveler of Mountains'. Cry out to my people!

Listen to me! You are my 'Straight Highway'. Cry out to my people!

Listen to me! You are my 'Filler of Valleys.' Cry out to my people!

My son, listen to me!"

In the stillness of his spirit, John heard all this. He heard it on the wind of the present moment. He saw it reflected in the well as he drew water. He saw it written in the stars on the cold clear nights. He heard it in the whir of the locusts' wings and he tasted it in the honey he swallowed. *He knew who he was*. He knew who he was called to be. He knew his God. Everything he had known before that moment of hearing could not in any way have prepared him for this encounter. Everything had changed – except God. God was right where he had always been. John could not contain the presence of his God or the name God called him by and was compelled to cry out to the very wilderness itself, *"Prepare the way for the Lord!!"*

Do not rebuke yourself for the desert you are in. Welcome it and seek Christ, the One Who Comes in all of our drearily ordinary or stressful moments. In this desert world, in the desert of your heart, be here now and pay attention. Listen for your ancient name, a name that will come to you in the desert emptiness. Listening and watching is a way of preparing the way of the Lord and making his path straight.

He is coming. He is here. He is calling your Name.

3rd Sunday of Advent A

Of Gaudete and Prophecy

1st Reading: Isaiah 35: 1-10.
The desert blossoming and rejoicing

Gospel: Matthew 11: 11
Christ saying that the least in the kingdom of heaven is greater than John the Baptist.

In the last reflection I wrote about John learning to be in the present moment in the desert – a spiritually romantic idea until you try it. How hard it is to be in the moment when many of your present moments are far from gratifying. But in this season of Advent, a time when we are called to open ourselves to the coming of the Lord and to being changed, we need to understand that it is in the present moment that we need to stop, pay attention, ponder and allow ourselves to be changed enough to be open to what is right in front of us. The present moment can redirect us, transform us, simplify us and teach us the mystery of the kind of quiet joy an unrecognized newborn infant in a manger can offer.

It is in the present moment that we are called to discover how rejoicing is both a strong perspective and a persevering attitude, not necessarily a reaction and not necessarily an emotion. Being rejoicing people doesn't mean we are never sad, angry, overwhelmed, frustrated, afraid or grieving. It means that after honestly experiencing the emotions that assail us, there is a determined turning to the truth that God is present in every moment of every day. This is metanoia: turning from self-focus and self-effort to watch for and anticipate the coming salvation of God.

This is Gaudete Sunday. The entrance antiphon says, *"Rejoice in the Lord always. I will say it again: Rejoice! The Lord is near."* Elsewhere in scripture the psalmist says, *"This is the day that the Lord has made, we will rejoice and be glad in it."* Today is the day...not tomorrow, not yesterday but today. This day, this moment, is when you should be watching and not just during the four weeks before Christmas. In the antiphon, Paul was exhorting the Christians to *always* rejoice because every day is the day of the Lord and the Lord isn't just near, he is here!

Even in the desert? Yes, even in the desert. Isaiah prophesies, *"The wilderness and the dry land shall be glad, the desert shall rejoice and blossom ... Strengthen the weak hands and make firm the feeble knees. Say to those who are of a fearful heart, 'Here is your God.'"* (NRSV)

Notice that he didn't say gladness, rejoicing and blossoming would happen once one is out of the desert. The desert itself was the place that would be transformed in Isaiah's prophecy. So making great efforts to get out of the desert may cause you to miss metanoia: transformation, change and going beyond your limited mind. Stay awhile. Pay attention. Repent. Rejoice.

We are all called to be consecrated members of the Royal Priesthood and here's something else we are all called to be: prophets. Prophets don't necessarily foretell anything; they are simply those who speak God's word as God gives it to them to speak. It is in the desert wilderness that you will learn about the God who desires to speak through you. Are you unsure that you could possibly be called to be a prophet? In the Gospel this week, Jesus says that nobody born of a woman is greater than John, but in the Kingdom of heaven, the least are greater than John is.

John was the last prophet of the Old Testament and Christ's death on the cross ushered in a new age and a new covenant. Jesus was saying that in the new order of things, in the Kingdom of Heaven, every one of us is called to be a prophet and because we have received the baptism of Christ and the blood of Christ has redeemed us, we have a greater ministry than John the Baptist. This is pointed out so that we will begin to get an inkling of the powerful mystery we have been called to participate in. This is not tame stuff. This is wildly real if we could only accept the truth of who we really are.

We are called to be messengers and prophets to a dry and barren world but first we need to experience the wonder of prophesying to our own deserts and wildernesses. How? By strengthening our weak hands, making firm our feeble knees and saying to ourselves within that wilderness, "Be strong. Do not fear. Here is your God." This is a great prayer for the present moment: "Be strong. Do not fear. My God is here." This is real prophecy. It doesn't matter if you can't see him and can't feel him yet. Metanoia means going beyond the world-based mind and into the mind of the Kingdom. This is the prophetic word; this is the word of God, which is not a feeling, an emotional response or an intellectual conclusion. It is truth. Prophesy to your wilderness. Prophesy often. Eventually you will sense a creeping gladness and eventually you will witness the first of many tiny blossoms opening up. One must persevere and be very still and patient to actually see a flower in the act of blossoming but once witnessed, it is never forgotten.

On this Third Sunday of Advent and always: Rejoice! Prophesy with joy and singing; prophesy to your wilderness and announce to it that the day of the Lord is here. Proclaim to your land, "Sing and rejoice O Child of Zion for, behold, he comes!"

He may come like a raging wind in the wilderness or he may come like a single blossom in the desert sand, as delicate as a newborn child.

However he comes, your desert will become a land of plenty.

Earthen Vessels

Matthew 1: 18-24

Mary is found to be with child from the Holy Spirit. The angel appears to Joseph to tell him not to be afraid to take Mary as his wife and reminds him of the prophecy that the virgin will conceive and bear a son whose name will be Emmanuel.

When we wait in our present moments and watch for the coming of the Lord, we probably have this image of Jesus traveling from somewhere else in order to arrive in our lives and our circumstances. This image isn't an easy one to dispel when our waiting and watching seems to be fruitless in the moment and when there is no sense of his presence at all. The natural conclusion is that he is not here yet; he is coming. He has not yet arrived on the scene to display his blessing and his love. We wait like an anxious lover in a train station watching the arrival of every train, hoping that the next train will be the one that the Beloved arrives on.

Mary shows us a different way of waiting. She, too, had to wait for the coming of the Savior but she wasn't just watching the far horizons and mountains as she waited for the voice of her beloved. She had to wait for his appearance but she also knew the Savior was within her. As soon as the angel announced to Mary that the Holy Spirit would overshadow her and she would conceive a son, Mary entered into the mystical and contemplative journey of fully believing the Lord was with her in the present moment while she waited and watched for his coming.

Scripture says that Mary held all these things in her heart and pondered them. For her, the appearance of Jesus in all his fullness was the journey of a lifetime where she was called to let go of her natural expectations in order to allow the coming of the Savior to be manifested within God's timing and in the way God has chosen. From the moment of conception, Jesus was completely present with Mary, yet she still had to wait and watch for signs of that presence. A pregnant woman is not completely aware of every infinitesimal stage of development of the child within the womb, especially at the beginning. She pays attention, waits and watches. She watches for clues and indications of the presence within. She waits for arrival, yet the child is always there.

This is our waiting and watching. He is not coming from afar. He is here within. We cannot totally depend on our senses and limited understanding to tell us that. We can only wait in joyful hope for the coming of our Savior. Joseph was also called to enter into the contemplative journey of trusting in the Word of God and believing that it was 'God With Us' who was indeed developing in Mary's womb. Our journeys are very parallel to the journeys of Mary and Joseph, as they trusted that God was with them as they waited for his coming.

The psalm this week gives a great picture of the kind of waiting we enter into:

The earth is the Lord's and all that is in it, the world and those who live in it.
You are the earth. Everything within you is God's. You pray all the time for God's kingdom to come and his will to be done on earth as it is in heaven just as Mary prayed, "Be it done to me according to your will," and "All the ends of the earth (and my earth) have seen the salvation of God."

Who shall ascend the hill of the Lord? And who shall stand in his holy place?
The hill of the Lord and his holy place is within each of us. Jesus said, "The Kingdom of God is within you." It is not in some faraway place or time. It is as near to you as Jesus in the womb was to Mary.

Those who have clean hands and pure hearts, who do not lift up their souls to what is false,
It's not hard to bring to mind definitions of clean hands and pure hearts or the false things we all lift our souls to but please include in that definition the way we lift our eyes and souls to what we fear will happen in the future and the things we regret or are angry about from the past. To remain in the present moment is to enter very much into a purity of heart – a letting go of all that has gone before and that which is yet to come. Focusing on and obsessing about past injuries and future problems is truly lifting the soul to what is false. It is a beautiful spiritual exercise of the heart to lift it up to what is true: Emmanuel or God With Us right now.

They will receive blessing from the Lord, and vindication from the God of their salvation.
After waiting and watching, a child will be born to you. It's easy to miss if you are waiting for blaring trumpets, earth shaking mightiness and huge changes. The birth of an infant is wondrous indeed but after the miracle of birth you are called to be very present to care for the child, the small blossom in the desert. That child is your vindication but you must be very present to him from the beginning and willing to nurture and protect the small beginnings of new life, just as Mary and Joseph did.

Such is the company of those who seek him, who seek the face of the God of Jacob.
We are a company of seekers, watchers and waiters struggling with the tension of a God who is indeed present and who is yet to come. He dwells within yet we constantly seek his Face. He is the God of Jacob, the seeker who wrestled through the night in the desert and who struggled like a woman in labor to bring forth the Blessing and the Vindication. (Excerpts from Psalm 24. NRSV)

We are all called to be Mary. We are all Christopher, which means 'Christ Bearer'. We are all Joseph, trusting in the face of a situation that was a messy enigma to him. If the watching and waiting becomes wearying or you feel like you're losing your way, ask Mary to comfort and mentor you on this journey that she knows everything about. Ask Joseph to uphold you through the doubt for he, too, had much to fear from the future and resent from misunderstandings of the past. Yet, he walked daily in trust that the dream was true: God With Us was present and was to come.

May the blessings of the Just One within you bring you and your families to the rain of wonder-filled appearance. May your hearts exult and cry out with joy, "He is here! Emmanuel is here! He is with us and always was!"

Picture Perfect

Matthew 2: 13-15, 19-23
Joseph is warned that Jesus' life is in danger and he takes Mary and Jesus to Egypt until Herod is dead.

When I posted this reflection on my blog, I put together a picture of Mary, Joseph and baby Jesus traveling on a donkey through Egypt. Joseph is looking up at Mary a little anxiously and Mary looks just a little disgruntled. She is thinking, "If he says one more time that I'll just love the pyramids, I'll scream."

I hope that doesn't offend you. I put the 'cartoon' together for the purpose of creating a bit of a jolt. We just don't see Mary and Joseph as real people dealing with real life. For most people, they are simply a diorama, a tableau or a set of frozen images depicting perfection in the middle of unusual circumstances. "Such a perfect family," we think. They probably were a good little family...but perfect? What does that mean? Never a cross word? Never a troubled moment? Never a time when the directions and perceptions of one partner made the other uncomfortable or worried? What is our cultural and theological idea of a perfect family? Is there any such thing?

Any priest, spiritual director or counselor would agree that a lot families that appear whole and happy on the outside are often struggling, aching, crumbling and dying on the inside. Appearances can be deceiving. So the next time you gaze upon what looks like a perfect, functional and happy family and wonder why your own family is so full of cracks and fissures, hold that thought. Actually, don't hold it. Throw it out. Life is just not that simple.

The Holy Family of the Gospels did not wander peacefully off to Egypt with halos around their heads as a sign that they were the epitome of ideal family life. They were scared and confused. They were tired and homeless. They were facing huge unknowns and heading to a country full of strange customs and stranger gods. They had very little money and a need to acquire more. They were stretched beyond their limits.

In other words, they were human.

What happens when you are weary, deeply anxious and are in unfamiliar surroundings facing unknown possibilities? Sometimes you snap in irritation at someone who doesn't deserve it. Often you find it's more difficult to fight fearful imaginings. You feel out of control of the big stuff so you become over controlling in the small stuff. You resent more easily and forgive less readily. You want to be full of faith and peace but deep inside you yell at God, "What the heck is *this*? I've been as obedient to your will as far as I know it, I've put up with some really hard and challenging issues, I've tried to trust you completely and now...*this*?"

This. This betrayal. This anxious situation. This person who threatens your family and you (who could even be a family member). This extra burden of responsibility. This journey into the unknown. You want so badly to return to normal, to a life where you are secure and problems are easy to deal with and now God is taking you further from that home base than you've ever been before. When you wanted simple you got convoluted. When you ached for easy you got complex. When you desired relief you got chaos. What is the matter with you?

Holiness is the matter with you. Mary, Joseph and their baby were not The Holy Family because they were perfect and their lives reflected a media generated idea of ideal family life. They were holy because they were God's. They were consecrated and set apart for God's purposes. Just like you, they were committed to God, listened for him and struggled to believe and trust when their lives were turned upside down.

The holiness of family binds us to the earth when we ache to fly. The holiness of family is the soil of our self-death. It is where we grind against one another, struggling and reaching through the darkness to find the light. The holiness of family calls us to open doors we'd rather keep shut. It pushes us on to Kingdom glory and then pulls us into the depths of the hell called Egypt. Family holiness calls us to accept gifts from those we would prefer not to receive from and to be receptive to those who challenge us at our deepest levels. Family is the rising and the falling of us all. If we try to escape family, we will escape into a formless wilderness where it becomes all about self and self-need, where there is no dying or resurrection, only fractured comprehension and scattered dreams with no hope of fruition.

We need to stop confusing 'Holy Family' with 'Perfect Family' and get on with the consecrated journey of allowing our lives to be redeemed - not by being perfect but by being humbly open to the sacredness of imperfection.

If you struggle with family, if you feel the humiliation of the flaws of your environment, of yourself and of those you live with, if you feel like it's all gone wrong in so many ways but you still reach for God and ache for his blessing: holy are you.

The perfect picture is cracked. Alleluia!

The Door

Matthew 2: 11, 12 (Excerpt from Gospel)
The story of the Magi.

Here's another beautiful tableau in our thoughts. When we bring to mind the story of the Magi finding Jesus, we may envision the crèche at the church or on the mantle or the Christmas cards received down through the years where the Magi on camels, trekking through a desert, are sharply silhouetted against a night sky while the star blazes brilliantly in the east. We may recollect that the gifts the Magi brought were representative of the character and mission of Christ, gold for kingship, frankincense for divinity and myrrh for his death. The wise men seeking out Jesus was another confirmation that the Light for all had indeed come into the world.

But it's much more than that. We can appreciate and ponder Christ's whole life and leave it on the level of a story of how God incarnated himself into the world and brought about our redemption. Or we can recognize that Jesus' story is our own and find within it the pattern, flow and anointing of our own lives.

It's not so startling. We know we are baptized like Jesus was baptized and that we rise up out of the waters of baptism into our call and mission. We know that we go through the wildernesses of temptation where we are faced with the choice of either self-gratification or the recognition that God is God, not us. We struggle to allow ourselves to be made bread for the poor and to understand that the Spirit of the Lord is indeed upon us to set prisoners free and help the blind to see. And we too die and are resurrected, sometimes daily. Christ's life is my life and your life.

So, each of us has also received gifts of gold, frankincense and myrrh. Each one of us is anointed and gifted as a daughter or son of the King, to find our place within the divine and to experience the death that leads to resurrected life. Each one of us is an epiphany to the world. If you are not a light set high on a hilltop, how can the world know that the light it aches for is indeed here and is not just a Christmas story? If you are not a son or daughter of the divine King, who are you and why should the world care? If you are not anointed for holy death in a way that opens doors for the poor and lowly, of what use is your Christianity?

As Christians we can't pick and choose who we really are but we tend to do just that. It's hard for us to keep the whole panorama of our anointing before our eyes and what most often happens is we find the path of least resistance. The easiest thing to believe about ourselves is that we are simply ragged sinners. Yes, we are. But if God doesn't stop there, we should be careful of doing so. We keep forgetting our anointing because it's hard to believe that, like Christ, we are also dignified sons and daughters of the living God, that we are priests, prophets and gracious sovereigns, and that we are the light of the world. When we celebrate Christ's birth, life, death and resurrection we are also celebrating our own. He came to share in our humanity and that means he became one of us and one with us. He gathered us all into the story and if we separate ourselves from the story, we are separating ourselves from everything we really are. Christ's history is our mystery. It's the mystery of our full identity.

St. Paul says, *"Those who are led by the Spirit of God are sons of God. For you did not receive a spirit that makes you a slave again to fear, but you received the Spirit of sonship. And by him we cry, ""Abba," Father." The Spirit himself testifies with our spirit that we are God's children. Now if we are children, then we are heirs--heirs of God and co-heirs with Christ, if indeed we share in his sufferings in order that we may also share in his glory.* (Romans 8: 14-17 NIV)

Every event in Christ's life that we celebrate is a door that he opened for us to follow through – not peek through.

Walk through the door and receive your gold. You are a child of God and the King of Kings is your brother. This brother of yours walked in poverty on earth but he walked as one who was responsible for and responsive to all who came to him for healing, teaching and deliverance. His kingdom and his responsibilities as King are yours as well. How is this being manifested in your life?

Walk through the door and receive your frankincense. If you are a child of God then you have divine genetics. *"By the mystery of this water and wine may we come to share in the divinity of Christ who humbled himself to share in our humanity."* (The Liturgy of the Eucharist.) Christ walked humbly as one of us but was always aware of his divine nature. He offered forgiveness and reconciliation, called God his Father and invited us also to forgive, reconcile and call the Divine our Father. How is this blood relationship to the Divine being manifested in your life?

Walk through the door and receive your myrrh. If you are a child of God then you are familiar with the door to death but rather than fearing it, you know that Christ turned it from a door to the end of everything into a door to the everlasting Kingdom. Christ walked daily fully anointed for death. He experienced the small daily deaths we all experience and then took on the Death of all Deaths and made it the door of all doors. His anointing turned death into life. How is your anointing for death that leads to life being manifested in your daily existence?

Walk through the door and become light, a light that shines for everyone, not just for the ones who please you or who agree with you or who are on your side. Do you know what will block your light? Walls. Jesus walked without walls surrounding him and he walked with no fear of those who were different, who had divergent creeds, who were socially unacceptable or who were lost. In fact the only ones who could not receive Christ's light were those who surrounded themselves with the walls of religious righteousness. If we accept the light of Christ to be our own light, we are agreeing to walk without defensive walls. It's the only way our light can be seen. How far does your light shine?

Walk through the door…

…and be an Epiphany.

Walking In Water

Matthew 3: 13-17
John baptizes Jesus.

In the last few reflections we have been looking beyond the 'Christmas card' presentation of the whole Christmas story to see starkness of a kind that is often forgotten in the midst of Christmas celebrations. The mystical events of the Nativity, the Holy Family fleeing to Egypt, the Epiphany, and now Jesus at his adult baptism could in no way be construed at the time as magical. Nothing was clean, sparkly or pretty. It all took place in the muck of harsh reality and those involved in these mysteries had to pay deep attention in order to discover and have faith in the presence of the Spirit in it all.

As I noted in the Epiphany reflection, the Christmas story is, in fact, the story of our lives where the journey is often hard, dry and rocky, where life is rarely simple and clean. We have moments of enunciation and magnification where we experience beautiful grace to say yes to God's desires and where our hearts overflow with praise for his abundant life. And then we have times where the will of God leads us into journeys of hardship and spiritual poverty. We are confronted by circumstances that utterly confound us. We may experience joyful rebirth and a sense of having arrived and then just as suddenly we may feel like we have no home and grieve for what's been left behind and for what we feel we never had.

I am emphasizing once again that it is within the very fabric of our uneven, difficult and chaotic lives that Mystery appears and grows. We cannot wait until things are 'picture perfect' before we begin to watch for the manifestation of God. He comes in the midst of the mess but he often comes 'small'. Often his coming can create what seem to be complications but are really complex and intricate patterns of beauty being woven into our fabric of our own stories. In retrospect we can see those patterns of light in the Christmas story but it certainly wasn't easy to see them at the time.

The baptism of Jesus is yet another lovely vignette in our storehouse of perfect theological images. It seems so far removed from the Christmas story because now our little Savior is all grown up but it's definitely all tied together. We are looking at subtle mystery upon subtle mystery. Jesus participated in a ritual cleansing he didn't need and he did so because, as a mewling infant lying in a pile of straw, crying and pooping like any other baby, he was not just immaculately inserted into this crazy world but was immersed in the mucky depths of it in order to redeem life as it really is, not to present an unattainable ideal. Our mangers, the roads we travel in terror, our senses of being homeless and foreign to this world and our ever present grief that something has been lost but we don't know what, have all been transformed by Jesus into rich soil for the growth of his presence and mystery in our lives. He blessed the mess by becoming completely one with it all. He is one with our births and rebirths, our rising stars, our struggles to grow, mature and understand, our plunges into the waters of rebirth and, finally, our deaths. Mystery flourishes in the midst of mess. Yes, in the midst of *your* mess. Your mess is holy ground and it is there you will find him. It is there that you are plunged again and again into the waters of rebirth.

We have our sacramental Baptism and then throughout our lives we 're-member' or relive that baptism every time we make a turn around in our lives and recommit ourselves to be who God has called each of us to be. Every time we intentionally bless ourselves with holy water and every time we intentionally repeat our Baptismal promises we are reminding ourselves of our true identity. In his baptism, one of the things that Jesus showed us about our own daily baptisms is what to listen for after rising out of those waters of 're-membering' and regeneration. As he rose up, *suddenly the heavens were opened to him and he saw the Spirit of God descending like a dove and alighting on him. And a voice from heaven said, 'This is my Son, the Beloved, with whom I am well pleased.'* (NSRV)

When you come to God for inner cleansing, to tell him you are his and that your desire is to be open to the fulfillment of his will in your life, what you should be listening for are the same words that Jesus heard. "This is my son. This is my daughter, the Beloved in whom I am well pleased." You must listen for those words because in Baptism you are clothed in Christ. It is he that you have put on. God looks at you and sees the glory and beauty of his Beloved son.

Can you believe that God looks upon you with such joy? Can you believe that God eternally treasures you? The understanding that you fall and fail brings you back to your waters of baptism, to repentance and regeneration but it's not repentance that causes God to speak words of love over you. It is repentance that gives your eyes the ability to look up and your ears the capacity to hear the words he is always speaking over you. If you don't give yourself permission to listen, your eyes will remain focused on your limited false self rather than being opened to the awesome mystery of how Jesus pushed aside the walls of all our limitations and opened the way for us to assume our rightful places as priests, prophets, sovereign rulers and dignified daughters and sons of the living God.

This reflection continues next week but until then, why don't you enter into a long-term Lectio Divina. Take the following words from this week's first reading to your daily prayer time and listen to them, meditate upon them and contemplate them as words being spoken about you:

Thus says the Lord:

Here is my servant, whom I uphold, my chosen one in whom I delight; I will put my Spirit on him/her and he/she will bring justice to the nations. (Isaiah 42:1 NIV)

May this word of the Lord lead you to amazement and profound joy.

Do You Know Who You Are?

John 1: 29-34
John testifies that he saw the Spirit descend on Jesus and that Jesus is the Messiah.

As I've been saying in previous reflections, these accounts of Jesus' own baptism and confirmation are also accounts of the true beginning and continuation of your personal spiritual story. I am deliberately using the pronoun 'you' instead of 'we or us' because unless you truly personalize this event it will remain another one of those frozen theological vignettes. It is critical right now as you read this reflection that you don't visualize the baptism of Jesus and the descent of the Holy Spirit on him as an event that is separated from you by a couple of thousand years or by the idea that because Jesus was the son of God, his experiences are far removed from your realm of existence. Try not to think of this as the story of Jesus that happened a long time ago in a land far away. The sacrament of Baptism makes Christ as intimately and constantly present in the baptismal water and the oil as he is in the Eucharist. God does not deal with time lines like you and I do and even your own baptism is not just an event that took place X number of years ago. Every moment of every day Jesus is being plunged with you into the waters of your baptism and the Holy Spirit is descending like a dove upon you, anointing you with the power to become who you really are.

There is no space between what you read in the Gospels and who you are called to be right now. There is no space between you and Jesus as he rises out of the waters to hear the voice of God expressing his everlasting love as the Holy Spirit descends on his son and upon you. As it is with all sacraments, baptism is a sacrament of deep intimacy between you and Jesus. Every moment of every day, you would be speaking the full truth if you were to say, "I am being baptized in a deluge of Holy Waters and I am being anointed by the Spirit of God right this moment. I am truly God's Beloved. Here I am, Lord. I come to do your will."

Ministerial priests are God's anointed. You respect that anointing and you also have clear ideas in your head of how that anointing should define everything a priest does. You totally expect that a priest's life be lived in accordance with his anointing. You, with the rest of the world, take it for granted that a priest is anointed to serve with authority and to bring Christ to people in a special way. When it comes to the sacraments, it is totally true that a ministerial priest is anointed in a way that you are not. But your expectations of the role of a priest go beyond the sacraments, do they not? We expect much of our ministerial priests but we tend to let ourselves slide off the hook when it comes to discerning what our personal anointing means and how it defines each of us. It's easy to forget that your anointing is no less solemn and powerful than that of a ministerial priest, just different. Just as a priest's anointing defines who he is and how he responds to those he interacts with, your anointing also defines you. Within your baptism, you can discover your true identity. Everyone is desperate to know who they really are but the world and the Church are equally as desperate for the active presence of people who have discovered who they really are.

Honestly, do you see yourself as a person who walks daily in the powerful anointing of God? Do you stop and ponder your own priesthood and what it means? Do you continually ask the Lord, "What have you anointed me to do? Here I am. I want to do your will. What is it? Who am I?" If you seriously ask those questions with desire and a real belief in your own anointed priesthood, he will seriously answer you. The answer will be meant for you and you alone and the answer will astound you. God does nothing small or inconsequential. We are the ones who think of ourselves in small and inconsequential terms, not God.

You actually have a choice as to whether you are going to exist in a small confined Christian walk or whether you want to walk wide and large, side by side with Christ, touching when you see him touching, speaking when you hear him speaking, listening with respect and compassion when you observe him listening with respect and compassion. The anointing on you is a call to walk with Jesus in a way that allows you to echo what he said about his relationship with his God, "I do nothing except I see the Father in heaven do it first." Now that is an intimate relationship! And that is what you are called to: "I do nothing except I see Christ doing it first." That means more than just knowing the Gospel stories. It means seeking Christ every moment of the day. It means having an intimate relationship.

For that kind of a walk and that kind of relationship, you must believe in your anointing and endeavor to live within that anointing every moment of every day. Without the belief in who you really are it is not possible to walk with Jesus in such intimacy. He will always love you, bless you and be completely available to you but without the conviction of your anointing, you will always feel self-conscious about your position in the kingdom and be a little anxious that you might start 'thinking too highly of yourself'. Go back to Jesus and see how it is to really walk as the Beloved of God. He knew who he was, he didn't need anyone else to affirm his position or his ministry but 'full of himself' was the last thing he was. What he was full of was the voice of his Father saying, "You are my Beloved in whom I delight. I am so pleased with you. You are beautiful." That's why he was so attractive to others. That's why the people said, "He speaks with authority and not as the scribes." He spoke and acted with the authority of one who knows he is loved and is called to transmit that love without stint. This is exactly what you are called to. This is your anointing.

Will you fail sometimes? Naturally. Will you often choose not to walk as an anointed one? If you're human, you will find yourself making that choice more often than you wish. But the more you choose it and the more you consciously believe in it and seek it, the less you will want to live without it.

Carlos Carretto, a Little Brother of Charles De Foucauld, once wrote that if we are having trouble believing the truth about ourselves or about God, then we should simply "act as if..." Act as if you are the Beloved. Act as if you are a dignified daughter or son of God. Act as if you have been given the authority to dispense mercy and compassion like oil on wounded hearts. Act like a pastor. Act as if Isaiah 61: 1-3 was written about you and repeat it to yourself daily:

The Spirit of the Lord GOD is upon me; because the LORD has anointed me to preach good tidings to the poor; he has sent me to bind up the brokenhearted, to proclaim liberty to the captives, and the opening of the prison to them that are bound; To proclaim the acceptable year of the LORD, and the day of vengeance of our God; to comfort all that mourn; to appoint unto them that mourn in Zion, to give to them beauty for ashes, the oil of joy for mourning, the garment of praise for the spirit of heaviness. (KJV)

Act as if you are anointed from on high. It will show you exactly who you are.

Through Chaos To The Still Point

Matthew 4: 12-23
Jesus hears that John has been arrested.

There are people we all know who are grieving deeply right now. In the middle of fresh grief there is very little one can say that will bring real comfort. Sudden and tragic death can never 'make sense' and even time cannot completely heal the wound; it will always be a wound that opens easily, often when least expected, bleeding out the bitter knowledge that this one deep desire, to behold the beloved alive and well again, is one that will never be met on this side. Death has said, "No."

Grief can come from so many situations other than physical death. The death of a marriage can be an awful grief. The loss of the ability to live independently is a huge grief. Deep, tearing, large and small grief can overwhelm us at every corner of life and, as Christians, we reach insistently to find a way to cope that brings us more clarity about who God is, who we are and where our hope lies. We don't always realize it but what we desire is a way to make grief itself a holy place. Otherwise, there is no point.

In this week's Gospel, John had not yet been put to death but hearing the news of John's arrest must have been a time of terrible grief for Jesus. Herod was not known to be a merciful man. He was a proud, cruel man and John had shamed him publicly. Jesus probably knew that John's death was a certainty. Death had not yet arrived but death was certainly coming.

Jesus withdrew to Galilee. The Gospels make it sound like Jesus was a chess piece being physically moved into a certain area in order to fulfill Isaiah's prophecies about the regions of Zebulun,

Naphtali, the Jordan and Galilee. However, the parts that we really need to pay attention to are, *"He withdrew to Galilee"* and *"the people living in darkness have seen a great light, and for those living in the shadow of death a light has dawned."* (Matthew 4: 12, 16. NIV)

Jesus withdrew. He didn't only head off into other physical lands; he withdrew into the land of grief, the region filled with the shadows of death. Jesus experienced grief so profound that he went off on his own to a place where only those who have experienced deep grief have ever gone. He went into the canyons of crying out for the loss of one who was too young for the finality of death. He ached until his bones felt crushed for John who was alone, uncertain and frightened. He was stunned by the finality and cruelty of harsh death. And, like all who have ever grieved for someone who has died or is facing death, he encountered the stark reality of his own death and had to grapple with his own faith that the promise he received was real, the promise that he would indeed rise again after his own death and this rising again would become John's salvation and would bring John into the arms of the Father. Being comforted by the belief that someone we love is in the arms of a loving Father only brings full comfort if we truly believe that we too will encounter those same arms when we die. Everyone's death is in some way our own.

John's arrest and finally his death was Jesus' as well. This was not a Lazarus event. This was Jesus pushing into the human condition and confronting it in all its pain, reality and apparent futility. This was Jesus forging through to the crushing center and pushing all the pain, grief and sorrow through the portals of heaven to the place where nothing is lost and all becomes life of the deepest kind. He went where we all must go at least once in our lifetime. Long before he went to the cross, he entered into our private hells of human sorrow and in doing so, created a place that was no longer the end. He made it the beginning of new life.

Then he began to proclaim that the Kingdom of heaven was near. He proclaimed these words with an authority that can only come from one who has suffered through to a point beyond what we can humanly perceive yet are invited to experience through our own grief. It is a place where we lose all that we thought we were and all that we thought was central to a happy life. It's a place where death is not a final wall we crash against but a door to the whole kingdom. It's where we find that Joy can be serious and Dignity wears simple and often ragged robes. It's a place where we lose our baggage and become increasingly able to travel light. It's a place where we begin to understand that in the kingdom, authority flows from having nothing. It's a place of immense simplicity.

One who has known grief and has struggled through to the still point of knowing nothing matters except being naked before the power of the Giver of all life, is one who can say with moving authority "The Kingdom of heaven has come near. I know this because I have gone there and I now carry it within me. It is the only thing worth carrying, the only 'baggage' you will ever need. Repent. Turn around and enter in with your grief, your pain and your wounds."

The world has a phrase that has done untold damage to our psyches: "Get over it." Just get over your pain and struggles and get on with life. Jesus never says that. Never! He says, "I have been there and I know what you are going through. I made a path through it but you still need to go through it to get to the place I have prepared for you, a place of great sanctity, a place of strong light for your darkness – a still point. You will find me there and you will find your true self there."

When we feel like we have to 'get over it', feelings and emotions are denied and trampled. Jesus holds our emotions and pain with great respect and love. They are not feelings to get over but to go through. They are the very material that God uses to create new and deeper life within us. The Spirit hovers over our chaos and prepares it for the creative Word. We must not deny our own chaos but move through it in its totality as Christ did, respect it as much as Christ does and love ourselves through it in the same way Christ does.

There is a door on the other side. It's open and the light of dawn is visible. It has been opened to you – and for you.

Because You Are Blessed

Matthew 5: 1-12
The Sermon on the Mount. The Beatitudes.

What intrigues me about this Gospel is what may have been taking place in the disciples' minds in the days before the Sermon on the Mount. Jesus had traveled to Galilee, chosen several of his disciples and then proceeded to go *"throughout Galilee, teaching in their synagogues and proclaiming the good news of the kingdom and curing every disease and every sickness among the people. So his fame spread throughout all Syria and they brought to him all the sick, those who were afflicted with various diseases and pains, demoniacs, epileptics, and paralytics, and he cured them."* (Matthew 4: 23, 24 NRSV)

What a wild time for the disciples.

I'm thinking that they had to be one group of extremely discombobulated and confused men. They're going about their lives thinking about nothing much more than making a living and then Jesus appears and calls them to follow him. Against all common sense, they are strangely drawn to do just that and immediately they are witnessing healings and deliverances while this compelling man preaches about Good News and Repentance. They are suddenly engulfed in the chaos of crowds of suffering and spiritually hungry people who have heard of Jesus and seek him out day and night.

I'm pretty sure that this explosion of bewildering activity was not part of their life plans. It wasn't something they had dreamed of doing after they finished high school. Whenever the subject of the coming of the Messiah came up, they would never have thought there was any possibility whatsoever that they could be personally and intimately involved in the plan. Yet, he found *them* and called *them*. They had to have questions.

They would wonder if this man was the real Messiah. He seemed to indicate to them that he was and he certainly seemed to be more than just a prophet, healer or itinerant preacher. He was completely different than anyone they had ever encountered or heard of before. He was so gentle and compassionate yet so full of authority. It was hard to doubt him and harder still not to love him and yearn for his individual attention. His words were simple yet when he spoke it was as if heaven cracked open a little and hope and joy spilled through into their hearts.

So, the burning question swirling around in their heads was, "Why me? Why us? Why would the Messiah come and call us, a bunch of unknown, unimpressive, illiterate and somewhat ignorant fishermen to be in the vanguard? What's up with that? What about all the priests, scribes and Pharisees who have money, serve in the temple, know the law and have influence over the people and sometimes have access to the Romans? Wouldn't they be the ones the Messiah would and should immediately connect with in order to lead the Jews to freedom? What the heck does he think we can do? We have no authority, affluence or influence and our lives have been full of worry and trouble from the day we were born. Obviously we're sinful men and we have offended God somehow – otherwise we'd be more successful and life would be less of a hardscrabble day-to-day existence full of illness, loss and fear. It's true that we have longed and waited for the day of the Messiah as much as the priests and scribes have and maybe even more. Even though we are the scum and we maybe deserve to live in struggle and fear, our households have always served the one true God and our hope has always been that the Messiah will come in our lifetime.

So, if this man is the Messiah, the question really is, why us? What can we possibly do for him?"

Perhaps they thought these things to themselves or maybe they discussed them quietly around the campfire late at night when Jesus seemed to be asleep. And Jesus would have known of their lack of self-esteem because a people who have been downtrodden all their lives, not only by the Romans but also by the spiritual authorities, can hardly be expected to know their value and importance. He would have understood the lives they had come from, the losses they had endured and the longings of their hearts and he would have understood that the questions raging through them were valid questions that they needed answers to. As he listened quietly, a little ways away from the fire but close enough to hear them talking and wondering, he began to compose within himself a sermon, one that would teach the crowds about the true focus of the coming Kingdom but also one that would answer his disciples questions of, "Why me? Why us?"

The next day, he went up the mountain and after he sat down, his disciples came to him. Then he began to speak, and he taught them. As he taught them, he looked into the disciples' hearts and silently communicated with them through his eyes and his love. He said to them, *"Blessed are you, you who are poor of spirit, who have served the Lord your God to the best of your ability without building up little kingdoms for yourself. Blessed are you who have lost much, endured much and have hungered much for rightness in the earth of your heart and in the land. Blessed are you because you have shared mercy and struggled to keep peace in your homes and in your community. Blessed are you because you haven't justified yourselves in self-righteousness and you haven't imprisoned others through spiritual arrogance. Blessed are you because you have not sought after false authority in order to use it like a club. This is why you are chosen. This is why you qualify. This is why you received the grace to follow me – because you are the ones I can speak to and lead into the truth. You are the ones I need. Blessed are you."*

Do you qualify to be a disciple of Jesus? I would guess that you do.

The Song Of God

Luke 2: 22-40

Jesus is presented in the Temple. The prophecies of Anna and Simeon.

In this reading, God in his incarnation entered his own earthly temple for the very first time. I love this scripture because the humility of God is portrayed so profoundly. It was his temple where he was honored, worshipped and magnified. Yet, in his humble humanity, he entered in complete helplessness, totally dependent on Mary and Joseph to bring him there and present him in the manner that every first-born male child was presented. He came in a way that was not special or obvious. His entrance was neither a strident bid for recognition nor a noisy demand for homage. But two people who were deeply sensitive to the nuances of God immediately recognized that God had entered his own temple.

If Simeon and Anna had been relying totally on scripture to give them clues as to what God would look like when he came, they would have completely missed him. The psalm for this Sunday speaks of a strong and mighty King of glory and the first reading from Malachi implies that the arrival of the Messiah would be so awesome that no one would be able to stand in his presence. An ordinary baby brought to the temple by a poor carpenter and his wife would have been the last thing Simeon and Anna would have been watching for if all they had paid attention to was Logos or the inspired Word of God. However, Simeon and Anna had something else that was and is absolutely essential; they had relationships with God. They were connected to the '*Ruach* HaKodesh' or the Spirit of God who opens our eyes to see what we cannot see on our own, who shows us the reality of God which is above, beyond and around the corner from what we think we can see.

This is critical. If you think you know what everything *should* look like then you are most likely closed to *Ruach* HaKodesh and you will miss God when he manifests himself in his temple – the temple that is you. *"Do you not know that you are God's temple and that God's Spirit dwells in you?"* (1 Corinthians 3:16 NRSV)

The priests, scribes and Pharisees thought they knew what God would look like when he came. They knew all the Law. They knew scripture inside out; they had it memorized and could recite it. They literally wore the Word of God on their foreheads and arms (phylacteries or tefillins). They had mastered it all. But they completely missed God because they knew the letter of the Law and the written Word but they had forgotten the Spirit of it. They had lost the Song of God.

The Spirit of the Word, the Song of God, is easy to miss because the Spirit does not comprise the black and white keys of the instrument; the Spirit is the resonant tone - the music. If you simply looked at a piano, just saw the keys and then declared that because you had looked at the piano keys you have experienced the wonder of music, well, that would just be sad. Even if you knew that the keys themselves weren't the music, there is no possibility that you could imagine and perceive what music sounds like simply from gazing at the keys. As important as those keys are, even memorizing the name of each key will not fill you with the sound of music.

Anna and Simeon had learned to see and listen beyond the keys – beyond their head knowledge – and when the fullness of time came, they witnessed God humbly entering the temple and they heard the amazing Song of God. They didn't even stop to say, "This can't be because scripture says..." They knew the resonant tone of God so well that they recognized him immediately even though there was nothing about him that fit common interpretations and expectations.

From his conception to his death, there was nothing about the Messiah that obviously fit the common interpretation of the Word and the Law. Only those who were open to a symphonic song that they had never heard before were able to hear the Song of God.

It is the same today.

We know so little yet we often become rigid in our expectations. We see the keys, think we know the song and only look for what we think God *should* look like and what he *should* sound like. God continually enters our temples unrecognized and unheard. We look for majesty and he comes poor. We look for power and he comes weak. We look for perfection and he comes handicapped and challenged. We look for ancient and he comes new and then when we look for new he comes ancient. We listen for familiar and recognizable music when we've never heard the totality of God's Song. We seek to be right and sure and we hide from our own crumbling dead certainties.

Only two people were able to recognize that God had entered his temple.

Just two.

Salt, Light And Desire

Matthew 5:13-16
You are the salt of the earth and the light of the world.

I've got a question that I think has crossed every Christian's mind at some time or another, a question that isn't easily expressed because it seems like such a selfish question. It is the question of "Why should I?"

Why should I be salt? Why should I be a shining light? Why should I share my bread with the hungry? Why should I walk as a member of the royal priesthood in order to pastor the poor and serve the people with my gifts? What's in it for me?

Isn't that a terrible question? What's in it for me? How selfish and shallow can you get? Yet, in actuality, it's a valid question and one that we would all do well to seriously ask the Lord because if we don't get an answer to that question, an answer that satisfies our hearts, we will always find it difficult to be salt and to let our lights shine. It would be wonderful if we were all totally selfless creatures filled with a constant desire to give with no reward. It would be marvelous if all our motives were pure and holy with no thought of self-satisfaction ever entering our minds or hearts. But we're not like that. Part of the reason for this is because we are broken. We have a false self that makes us selfish and self-oriented.

However, there is another reason we need to ask "What's in it for me?"

It's because God created each one of us with a deep need and desire. This need is within every living being and every living being spends its days trying to fill up this need and desire, usually without success if there is no God in the equation. The desire is to be intimately and lovingly connected to God. As someone once said, there is a God shaped hole in each of us, and God is the only one who can fit into that hole and fill it up completely. We yearn to know God and to be known by him. We long to understand our worth and value to him. We desperately need to know our worth in our heart of hearts not just in our heads. We want to have faith that we are loved so strongly that nothing can shake or jar that knowledge. It is out of this heart knowledge that dynamic life filled goodness flows.

Consider this: if the whole world suddenly decided on an intellectual basis that all of Jesus' directions on how to be people of integrity made logical sense and laws were passed that required everybody to be kind to each other, share their goods and make sure that everyone had what was needed to live comfortably - and everyone actually obeyed those laws - the world would be a much nicer place to live. But it would lack something. What would be lacking would be salt and light. It would lack flavor and illumination. It would lack the Spirit's dynamic force that begets life. It would be missing the God filled love relationship that has creative power. Life would be nice but it would be flat.

When Jesus calls us to be salt and light, what he is inviting us to do is be intimately connected to him. Jesus didn't come to give a whole bunch of new and improved rules to live by because rules, even really good rules, aren't enough to bring inner life to people. Life under the Old Testament law proved that just following all the rules didn't create relationship with the heart of God. The Jews for the most part followed rules assiduously but they had lost their saltiness and illumination. They had lost relationship. Jesus wants a people who are so enthralled by him and so eager to spend time in his presence soaking in his love that they just can't help but reflect the light of his face and become a pungent and pleasing flavor to the world. When Jesus walked on the earth, it wasn't just the fact that he was a man who followed good rules that touched the people; it was that he was 'plugged in'. He was so intimately connected to God's love and had such a deep sense of who he was that people were astounded. People either loved him or despised him but nobody was neutral about him. He was the saltiness that the world had lost; he was the light that had come to rekindle and enliven all that had become dark, stale and two-dimensional.

Another word for the combination of light and salt is 'joy'. Joy is not necessarily a happy bubbling emotion although it can present itself like that sometimes. Joy is the manifestation of being solidly plugged in to Christ and consequently being solidly plugged in to who you really are. There is nothing in the world like that heart knowledge. It is not a precept. It is not the culmination of being obedient to a collection of rules. When Jesus says, "Be flavorful salt and let your light shine," he is not simply providing laws for being good people. He is saying, " Stay intimate with me. Then you will be able to love yourselves and each other *the way I love you.* Then your joy will be full." It's a case of cause and effect. You can't love like he does, you can't add flavor like he does, you can't illuminate the world around you like he does unless you experience his love, taste his salt and are lit up within by his light. You can't possess joy unless you experience *his* joy. Jesus is a joyful God. He is continually beside himself with delight and jubilation. This is what he calls you to experience in your relationship with him.

Possessing this joy won't mean that you will never have pain or struggles in your life again. It won't mean you'll never be stressed, disappointed, anxious or in deep grief. What joy does is give you a solid foundation so that all the hard things life throws at you become the building blocks of a higher and stronger spiritual life. Joy also becomes the cement that holds the blocks firm and creates a durable edifice that won't crumble from under you.

So, when Jesus says to be flavorful and shine, go ahead and ask, "What's in it for me? What do I get out of this?" The answer will be: a strong foundation and the fulfillment of the desires God placed within you before you were born. These are desires that he put there because it is his own huge and eternal desire to be the true fulfillment of those desires. First, you receive him. Then you receive your true self. After that you will have the strong desire and the grace to be salty like him and be light like him. This is God's desire that was planted in you. He wouldn't have put it there unless he meant to fill it.

For the next few Sundays, try not to hear the Gospel readings as a list of New Testament addendums to the old law. Try to hear Jesus saying to the Jewish people, "Come to me. *I* am the fulfillment of what the old law was trying to lead you to. *I* am the incarnation of The Relationship. *I* am the image of the heart that has always been calling you to merge with his integrity, walk in his humility, allow his love to flow through you and be one with his mercy. Instead, you just followed dead law, lost the light, lost the vision, lost the salt and lost the flavor. By losing these things, you lost yourselves. Come home. I have come that you may have life and have it to the full. I am the way, the truth, the resurrection and the light. I am the salt. I am your identity. I have come to bring you back home."

Go to him. Go home. You have to receive salt and light before you can be salt and light.

The Law of Love

Matthew 5: 17-37

Jesus says he did not come to abolish the law but fulfill it. He speaks of some of the 10 commandments and adds that even minor infringements are as serious as murder or adultery.

Jesus sounds drastically stern in this Gospel passage, especially if one is interpreting it as Jesus simply adding a bunch of subsections and small print to the Law of Moses, making it more complex and infinitely more difficult to adhere to. Who among us has not been guilty of at least one of the sins he speaks of? We could be forgiven for throwing up our hands along with Peter when he once asked Jesus in complete bewilderment, "Who, then, can be saved??"

The one statement Jesus makes that we really need to pay deep attention to is, *'Do not think that I have come to abolish the law or the prophets; I have come not to abolish but to fulfill."* How does one fulfill a law? The same way one fulfills a contract: by doing everything that is required by the law or the contract. Jesus is stating for the sake of the scribes and Pharisees that he did not come to introduce a new law that would oppose the old law. He came, instead, to satisfy every single requirement of the old law, a task that was impossible for people. In other words, he came *to do it for us*. He fulfilled the whole contract – even the small print.

The old law was even more complex and burdensome than the people suspected and Jesus was pointing this out, especially to those who were trying to adhere to the letter of the law without trying to understand the spirit of the law. He was showing how murder and adultery spring from the very same root as being angry with someone or looking at another person with desire. Sin is deeply rooted and although there are more obvious manifestations of sin, like murder and adultery, it doesn't mean that the more private sins like anger and lust are any less serious. Those who make a great show of outwardly observing the law without paying attention to the state of their inner hearts or their deeper motivations are fooling themselves.

However, even those that Jesus was addressing, who were more aware of the heart of God rather than just the letter of his law, still could not have been justified simply by keeping the law because sin makes it impossible to keep the law perfectly. There is not one being on earth who can come before God and claim righteousness just because of obedience to the law. Because of our brokenness, it is an impossible and unattainable goal.

The immense and astounding gift of Christ is that he did it all for us. In complete love he fulfilled the requirements of the *whole* law. He was a good and upright citizen of Israel as was required by the civil aspect of the law. He was sinless as was required by the moral component of the law. And in the end, he became the paschal sacrifice required by the ceremonial component of the Law. He did what was and is absolutely impossible for humans to do: he stayed pure and holy in the sight of God. Still, we often try to justify ourselves by being rule keepers and there is a great reluctance to depend on Christ's gift of himself. We need to examine this reluctance for as St. Paul says in Galatians 2: 21, if the law can do the job of justifying us, there is no point in Christ's death.

I know this is hard for us to wrap our minds around – it's almost as if we should be suspicious of a gift so huge and so freely given. Surely, it can't be that simple. Are we just let completely off the hook? Can we just act however we want, forget about being good and not worry about the consequences?

These questions are answered, in depth, by Paul in many of his letters, especially the one to the Romans and I certainly can't cover it all in a short reflection. But it comes down to one thing: an ongoing and ever deepening relationship with Jesus that is based on reverent gratitude for what he did for us. We need to open ourselves to growing closer to his heart so that our actions become less and less based on fear of breaking rules and laws (which we inevitably fail to keep) and flow more and more from being so close to him and feeling so loved by and so influenced by him that we can't help but be true reflections of him. Our behavior changes as we encounter Jesus more and more but Jesus is still the one who is our justification, not our behavior. It's so hard to keep that clear in our hearts but if we do, it leads to constant thankfulness for and appreciation of what this God of ours did for us out of sheer love. It's totally mind and heart boggling.

Some things that St. Paul says that gives us a concise idea of how we are to behave now that we are a people of the Living Spirit and not slaves of the dead Law is in Galatians 5 where he tells us to stand firm in the freedom and not to become self indulgent because the whole law is summed up in one commandment: Love your neighbor as you love yourself. Then in Galatians 5:22 he lists the fruit of the Spirit: love, joy, peace, patience, kindness, goodness, faith, gentleness and self control, and says that these things are completely in accordance with the law of God.

Right there is the heart of the whole law. Right there is the heart of Jesus. Right there is the complete fulfillment of every iota of the law. No one is 'let off the hook'. Rather, we are all called to a higher 'hook': living in communion with the heart of Jesus and, by the power of his grace, becoming just like him. Right there is your breathtaking freedom all wrapped up in the gift of Christ's love for you.

Can you accept it? No, really...can you accept it?

Mission: Completed.

Matthew 5:38-48

Jesus speaks about laws like "An eye for an eye" or "Love your neighbor but hate your enemy," and insists that God wants us to love our enemies. Be perfect because the Father is perfect.

"Perfect". Now there's a loaded word. Especially in today's North American culture, the idea of perfection has overtones that haven't done anyone any favors. We live under a lot of pressure to be perfect: to have the perfect body shape, the perfect smile, the perfect career, the perfect relationship, the perfect family, the perfect spirituality, the perfect lifestyle based on a perfect amount of money. So, when we hear Jesus' words, "Be perfect, therefore, as your heavenly Father is perfect," there's a huge possibility we can go into 'perfection burn out'.

We have allowed media and big business to define what perfection means. Standards have been set, standards that pretty much can never be achieved because even when something looks flawless on the surface, life just doesn't go along with the program. The model with the perfect face and body has been photoshopped. The family that looks perfect out in public may be wounded and dysfunctional in private life. The career that looks so great and filled with status turns out to be a grind like every other career. The perfect relationship is a myth even in a good marriage. And spiritual perfection is impossible because we are beset by original sin. Even if one starts to feel one is perfect according to all the 'shalts' and 'shalt nots' there comes (or should come) the uncomfortable realization that ugly spiritual pride has crept in. Flawless perfection in an imperfect and broken world is an unattainable goal so why would Jesus exhort us to be perfect?

There is another definition of perfect that is, perhaps, more in line with what Jesus was saying. It is 'complete'.

"Be complete, therefore, as your heavenly Father is complete."

Take another look at the rest of this week's reading (as well as the Gospel readings for the last two weeks) in which Jesus takes the letter of the law and moves it to a deeper level where life is not lived on the surface of the law but in the heart of the law. The actions Jesus talks about such as turning the other cheek, giving more than was asked for or loving one's enemies are examples of how a person who is complete in God's love would naturally live. Completed people are ones who know they are totally loved by God and have experienced his provision and unconditional love to such a degree that they can turn the other cheek not because it's a rule but because they have no need to prove their worth to other people or get into self-defensive anger. They may decide to turn a cheek or they may decide to bring justice to the situation because they see that turning the cheek is not healthy for all involved. A completed person knows that the letter of the law cannot and must not eclipse wisdom, mercy, love and justice.

Completed people can give more than is asked for because they know from experience that God is a God of amazing provision so they don't need to worry about not having enough. They can lend, share or give whatever they have because their material goods aren't what define them, give them status or show how worthwhile they are.

Completed people live as wholly Beloved Ones. The more complete they are the more they lose the need to justify or prove their value and their actions flow from being so much in communion with the Lord that they don't just 'do' God's will, they participate in it. They forgive easily because they have experienced forgiveness. They hold others with respect because they have understood that they themselves have been given the gift of holy dignity. They don't just follow the Lord; they dance with him.

The Father is complete within himself. He did not create us because his ego needed our adoration. He does not love us for selfish reasons; he just loves us period. We are made in his image and because he loves who he is and is completely at home with himself, he cannot help but delight in his creation – his whole creation. Jesus was the incarnation of Complete Love. He, too, was completely at home with himself and with his Father. Nothing he did was done because there was a rule about it and never because he needed people to be impressed, to understand him or to approve of him. Everything he did was simply Love made manifest. Sometimes he turned his cheek and other times he refused to allow others to abuse him but it was never a decision based on a broken sense of self worth, a need to please or on the letter of the law. He neither over valued himself in arrogance nor undervalued himself through low self-esteem. He simply knew who he was and he loved being himself. He knew without a doubt that the Father loved him and he loved the Father without reservation. All this pure love produced a beautiful complete third: the Holy Spirit. The dance of love's creation went on and continues to go on.

When Jesus invites us to be complete as the Father is complete, he is beckoning us to enter into an amazing journey of becoming who we were always meant to be. He invites us to participate in the love circle that is already complete and when we join in, we begin to experience the healing of being encircled by and nestled into completion. Love's wholeness permeates us and fills up the holes that we could never fill up before.

So...it is simply allowing ourselves to be loved that makes us complete.

Perfect!

Being Present To Provision

Matthew 6: 24-34

Jesus teaches the lilies of the field analogy. Don't worry; the Father knows what you need. Don't worry about tomorrow.

At first glance, this week's reading, in contrast with the readings of the last several weeks, is a bit of a relief. Instead of overtly challenging us with ultra-high Kingdom ideals, Jesus says, "Don't think about money or food or clothes or the future. Don't worry, God will take care of you, he knows what you need, he will feed you and clothe you. Don't worry about tomorrow." Such a loving God we have!

And then the discomfort starts to seep in. If we accept that the last four weeks' Gospel readings were pushing us beyond simply keeping laws and rules and were inviting us to go deeper to discover the inner heart of God's law and of his kingdom, then this week's reading is the ultimate challenge to let go of all control and lose ourselves in God's love and providence. It's direct, explicit and hard to slide over. This is the crux of our faith in God: do we trust him or not? Do we believe that he will take care of us or not?

It is truly a difficult task that Jesus sets for us in this week's Gospel. Jesus isn't saying that money itself is bad. Money is simply what it is: a currency of exchange. If I give you some money and you give me some bread, where's the sin? But ever since people learned to exchange currency for goods, it has been accepted that the wealthier you are, the more control and power you can have. But the more control and power you have of that sort, the less likely it is that you will depend upon and trust God to take care of you. The less you have to trust God, the less inclined you are to seek him, have relationship with him and experience his provision.

Do we trust God or not? Do we believe that he will take care of us or not?

Jesus is also not indicating that having any thoughts or plans for the future is bad. It's when we begin to worry and obsess about the future that the problems begin. We envision situations where the worst happens. We gnaw on these possibilities and we try to work out how we can change people and situations so that we are comfortable. We feel our ideas, visions and opinions are the valid ones and are what should be guiding the process. We work to make others see our point of view so they will admit that we are right. We want to know we are in control.

Do we trust God or not? Do we believe that he will take care of us or not?

Do we ever feel like we have enough? There is a subtle and pervading sense in all societies that the more we have, the less vulnerable we are. It's like our money and possessions are a cushion that we use as a shield. They give us a sense of being securely in control and sometimes they are symbols of power and status. We have fears about being without them and about not having enough.

Do we trust God or not? Do we believe that he will take care of us or not?

Pondering on what Jesus says to us in this Gospel reading is where we discover that it's actually much easier to try to keep laws and rules than to throw ourselves without reservation into the merciful arms of God. This is where we find out that Christ calls us to move beyond our basic human nature, a nature that wants to create rules where there were none. Don't get me wrong. People and communities need laws. Society needs laws, the church needs laws and families need laws; otherwise, anarchy would reign. But when it comes to our relationship with God, our broken human nature wants desperately to be in control. We want rules and rituals that guarantee that by our actions we can manipulate God into acting the way we want him to act, give us what we want to have or at least feel we have the power to keep him from being angry.

Have you ever had the experience of praying a certain way or praying a certain prayer and being blessed with a beautiful answer from God? Now, were you, or were you not, tempted to repeat that prayer or way of praying the next time you needed to ask God for a particular favor? Have you ever had things go wrong in your life and felt that it had to somehow be your fault, that you didn't pray properly or didn't have enough faith or weren't good enough? These feelings and questions stem from our basic need to feel we are in control. Everyone has this need; it's human nature and it is a need that can certainly be used for good. However, it can also easily become distorted, imbalanced and detrimental to the spiritual walk.

In this week's first reading, the Lord says that even if a mother could forget her nursing child or showed no compassion for the baby in her womb, he could never forget us (you!). The psalmist says that for God *alone* his soul waits in silence, for his hope is from God. God *alone* is his rock, his salvation and his fortress. He states, "I will not be shaken." Then Jesus tells us that God cares for us and provides for all our needs. He encourages us to stop our imbalanced striving and simply trust. He instructs us to stay in the present moment because when all our thoughts and energies are directed toward being in complete control of our future moments we totally miss experiencing his beautiful provision for the present moment.

God will never engage in a power struggle with us. If we decide to spend our time wrangling with what was, what is and what is to come, he will allow us to do that. It doesn't mean we will have more control over anything. It will mostly mean we will go around in endless circles: circles of anxiety, circles of confusion, circles of resentment and circles of energy spent on what fails to satisfy and will never bring us peace. 'Being in control' is rarely a desirable condition nor will it fulfill the deepest desires of our hearts.

Of all the steps Jesus encouraged us to take toward the heart of God in the last several Gospels, this week's exhortation is actually the most difficult. I often fail to trust and abandon myself wholeheartedly to God's provision. I have areas in my life where I slip so easily and begin to entertain anxious thoughts or where I allow my mind to dwell too long and too heavily in the future. But that's all right. God knows my desire is to grow in trust and freedom so all he does is send his gentle Spirit to remind me of this desire and to support me with grace so I can turn myself back to him. The point isn't to be complete all at once.

The point is to begin.

9ᵗʰ Sunday Ordinary A

Shifting Sand And Solid Rock

Matthew 7:21-27
Not everyone who calls Jesus "Lord" will enter into heaven. Jesus gives the analogy of a house built on sand versus the house built on rock.

When I was young, I was a bit confused by this scripture passage. The question I had was, if someone is prophesying, casting out demons and doing deeds of power like Jesus did, wouldn't that mean that the person had been anointed by God to do these things? How could they do them without God's blessing and if his blessing was there, wouldn't that mean they were doing his will? If success in ministry is not the indication of being centered in God's will then what is?

Eventually I came to understand there are many traps that can snare us, even if we are called to a ministry and are successful in that ministry. If we are not careful and we fall into one or more of these traps, God may continue to use us for the sake of his people but we will always have free will and we will always have choices in regards to how we develop and maintain our relationship with Christ and with the people we are ministering to. We are at liberty to endeavor to walk closely with God or to end up with empty words of "Lord, Lord..." In the kingdom walk, it is never a good thing to be tempted to rest on one's laurels.

There are many traps that can entangle us as we work for the Lord: power positions, status, territorialism and sexual abuse are a few of the more obvious ones. But I want to focus on one trap that is subtle and affects all of us. It is the trap of seeking approval from people and basing one's sense of self worth on affirmation received from others. Enjoying approval and affirmation from other people is not a sin in itself. It's lovely when someone says that you did a great job or that they really enjoyed and were blessed by something you did. That kind of praise and affirmation freely given and freely received is a building block of a healthy spiritual community and we all should express affirmation and gratitude to our sisters and brothers far more often than we do. In itself, it is a ministry not a sin.

The trap I'm speaking of is the trap of getting caught up in needing the approval of other people in order to feel we are worthwhile. We want the praise and affirmation because it says to us was that we are valuable. Who among us doesn't have the deep need and desire to know our value and worth? The only problem with entering into any ministry with a need to know your value and worth and seeking to measure it by people's praise is that even when you get the praise and approval, it is never enough.

Never. Ever. Enough.

It feels great in the moment – and it really is great in the moment. But have you ever noticed that after you receive a lot of kudos for a job well done, such as a great presentation, some funny entertainment or some music beautifully sung, the next day you are back to square one? The need for approval is still there; the yearning to see one's value reflected in the smiles and words of praise from others is still there and perhaps even stronger. It's easy to get hooked on praise if you are getting it frequently and if you're not getting it very often, it's easy to start feeling useless and as if you're a disappointment to God and to yourself.

The problem comes when we lose sight of who we really are in God's eyes. If we do anything just for human approval or simply to have our value recognized then we are absolutely building our houses on sand. As I said before, the affirmation that comes from other people is never enough to fill us up and make us happy and people can be so fickle. They may approve of you one minute and disapprove of you the next. One group might think you're wonderful while another group would like to run you out of the church. You may give hours of your time, sweat bullets and compromise your health for the sake of some church project, only to discover that no one particularly cared and didn't even realize you were involved. Human approval is like sand, continually shifting and being reconfigured by the tide. It is undependable and capricious.

The words that Jesus really wants us to build our homes on can be found in last week's Gospel: Seek the Kingdom of God first and you will be given everything you need." Seek first the heart of God. Seek first the unconditional love and approval he has for you. Seek first the One who created you as his own. *"I am my beloved's and my beloved is mine."* (Song of Songs 6:3 NRSV) When you discover that the approval you need and yearn for is all there in God's eyes, like in the eyes of a lover, you will feel your house become a home and you will know that you have been settled on a foundation of Solid Rock.

When Jesus said in last week's Gospel that if you seek the kingdom and everything you need will be given, he wasn't just talking about bread and clothes. He was also talking about the needs and deep desires of our hearts. What we seek from those around us – approval, love, recognition and praise – is all there waiting for us in the Kingdom. And what freedom is ours when we find it!

We need to understand, though, that we cannot seek God's approval through 'doing'. It may be marginally better to offer our services in order to gain God's approval instead of the approval of other people but it's still missing the point. It's still getting things backwards. What we need to do is experience God's love and approval *before* we do anything for him. Then whatever we do will come from the secure joy of being a Beloved One. This is the true source of real deeds of power, deeds that don't depend on numbers or the worldly definition of success, deeds that aren't kept in a personal ledger under the heading of, "All The Things I Have Done For God", a list that we keep in order to prove to God and to ourselves that we really are worthwhile. When we are in love and know that we are loved for who we are *before* we do anything, we stop keeping lists. We act from a secure and joyful foundation of love and we cease acting *for* God and begin to move *with* God. The difference is subtle but drastic. It's the difference between always being on an anxious quest and being on a journey of peace.

When we experience God's approval, service becomes a response in the heart of the moment, not an agenda. Effectiveness and success cease to be judged by normal standards. In fact, our effectiveness and success is none of our business. It is God's business and all we are called to do is be wherever he wants us to be, doing whatever he calls us to do. If that means being in front of groups giving spiritual talks, so be it. If it means cleaning a toilet, so be it. If it means wiping a baby's bottom, so be it. There is no 'more effective and less effective'. If what we do is done in the glow of God's approval and is done because that's what he is calling us to do in the moment, whether it has to do with toilets or retreats, then it is a deed of power. Immense power. In fact, I would say that more people have been changed by a Beloved Soul, who knows he or she is loved and appreciated by God, serving alone in a kitchen or an office, than by a talented speaker who speaks to thousands but has not yet discovered his or her own approval in God's eyes.

May God grant that we will all come to him on the last day, not to say, "Lord, Lord, I did this, that and the other for you," but to say, "Lord, Lord, I thank you for all that you have given to me, especially your love, approval and delight. I was so privileged to walk with you and participate in all that you did. You are wonderful to me and a marvel in my eyes. I am so glad to be home!"

And he will say, "So am I!"

1

Reclaiming The Garden

Matthew 4: 1-11
Jesus is tempted in the wilderness.

Love went into the desert for us. This was not a retreat; this was a mission to meet the enemy on his own ground.

The Word went into the wilderness to reclaim what had been too easily relinquished: our innocence.

The Truth went into the wasteland to draw fire and accomplish what we could not.

The First Ones, Adam and Eve, were given the kingdom and had everything they could possibly desire: fruitful trees, pure water, warm shelter and plenteous food. They had relationship with each other, with the land, with other creatures and with their God. But they wanted more.

Jesus was led into a barren rocky land and all he had were the words of his Father soaking into the foundations of his being: *"You are my Beloved Son in whom I am well pleased."* The whole Kingdom was held within those words and he wanted nothing more. He needed nothing else.

"**YOU** are my Beloved."

"You **ARE** my Beloved."

"You are **MY** Beloved"

"You are my **BELOVED**."

It was enough for the job.

The First Ones were convinced they lacked the most desirable thing of all and traded their innocence for the knowledge of good and evil – that's intimacy with good and evil, not just recognition of what is good and what is evil. When one is intimate with both, both begin to mesh and become tangled. What is innocent is judged as nakedness and naivety. What is corrupt is accepted as desirable and worthy of attainment. The false self becomes paramount: self-consciousness, self-defense, self-reliance, self-indulgence, self-determination, self-sufficiency...

The Last One walked into enemy territory desiring only oneness with the Creator and needing nothing more – he was intimate with his Father and his innocence was intact. He was complete within his true self because he was one with God's love. He wasn't selfless; he was the Word of True Self.

He had everything he needed to accomplish what had to be accomplished.

Into the wasteland he went, with nothing more than his innocence and relationship with his Abba. He entered willingly into the furnace of contaminated and defiled desires and faced them in all their guile, artifice and fury. His True Self, the Word, obliterated the habitual patterns of false promises and healed the immense chasm that shattered the world when the First ones believed the lie that intimacy with good and evil could make them anything like God. It made them *nothing* like God. All it did was create a false self that only desired to fill self up with self - a self devoid of fullness, which means nothingness. And being nothing like God is an aching, dry and formless void that continually clutches at empty promises of secrets to fulfillment.

Into the dry and rainless desert Christ went as Word. Three times, as Word, he cried, "NO!"

Three times.

Did he know that at the point of a cock crowing three times there would be three denials? Perhaps. Perhaps not. But know this: even Peter's ultimate betrayal and denial of the innocent Lamb could not overcome the beginning of redemption that Jesus accomplished in the desert. The Liar and the Seducer of False Self will try until the end of time to re-establish himself as lord of the earth and the shaper of our ends but he has no hope. None at all.

Because Love, the Word, went into the desert for us.

Lent has begun and the desert awaits us all. There may be battles in our deserts or there may be peaceful pondering, but whatever awaits us, we must go. The desert has been sanctified for our journey. We can either choose to stop, not enter and simply maintain in our present state or we can go through to the garden that was reclaimed for us. There is no going around.

May this Lenten season name you, simplify you and bring you back to innocence.

Ears Open

Matthew 17: 1-9
The transfiguration.

Imagine…

You're at Mass. Your priest is saying the words of consecration and says, "This is my body which was given up for you," and holds up the wafer for all to see. As he holds the substantially changed and mysteriously beautiful wafer of bread, a voice suddenly fills the church: *"This is my son, the Beloved. Listen to him!"* Not only is the church filled by this voice but every heart is filled as well. No one doubts that it is the Father's voice but later no one can say if they actually heard the voice with their ears. Was it authoritative words or was it an instantaneous complete inner knowing? No one can say for sure but all agree that something radical, immense, critical and utterly astounding has taken place.

What would we do with an experience like that? Form committees? Build a shrine? Organize pilgrimages? That would definitely be our inclination because the first thing we want to do with a mystical experience is somehow capture it, announce it and give others an opportunity to come close to the mystery as well. There would also be the desire to create a sacred space, a place where we could leave the ordinary chaos and confusion of the world and come to re-visit and re-member the mystery and the glorious awesomeness of it. We would want to hold this experience close to our hearts somehow, some way, in order to keep it fresh, real and alive. We would yearn to have a place of silence where we could come, recall the moment and do what the Father said to do: listen to his son.

There is nothing wrong with these very natural desires. It is a wonderful thing to have shrines and sacred spaces that are set apart from the hurly burly of the world, places that offer rare silence and a touch of peace. These are necessary spaces whether they are found in a chapel, a forest glade or on a deserted beach. But we must never forget that Jesus went *with* the disciples back down the mountain. There was no physical memorial constructed of an event of huge significance. There was no material tabernacle built.

Why? Because the Tabernacle went down the mountain with them. We do need our set aside sacred spaces but we must never ever forget that the most sacred space of all is within each one of us and that the Tabernacle of God, Jesus, comes down the mountain with us, right into the noise, chaos and, as our priest likes to put it, the messiness of real life.

God the Father says to us, "Listen to him! Every moment of every day, get into the habit of listening to my son. Speak with him. Discover that my Tabernacle is within you and that the Holy Presence, the Lamp stand is always lit and always burning in your inner room. Find that place within yourself and learn to tell me how good it is to be there. Speak to my son there and listen, listen, listen!"

Too often, we leave the tabernacle behind when we leave Mass. Most of us go out with the understanding that we have been sent and that as Christians we have responsibilities to attend to but perhaps we go a feeling a little insignificant. There can be a sense of, "I'm just one small person trying to make some difference in my corner of the world, trying to be a good disciple of the Lord." We can feel just a little bit alone and sometimes lonely. But that's not the case. Jesus is going down the mountain and out of those doors with us. He's not staying in the church in the tabernacle like an executive director, sending us out on our own to do whatever we can. He's not hanging out with Moses and Elijah while we head on down our mountains. As we are making our way back into the fray, into the crowds and into the marketplace, he's with us every step of the way as our companion. He doesn't stay behind and he doesn't go on ahead without us because he is within each of us. He is with us in the most intimate way possible. Even the most loving of married couples will never know such intimacy.

"Listen to him!" When the Father said this on the Mount of Transfiguration, he wasn't telling them to listen to what Jesus had to say *before* they went down the mountain." It wasn't a one-off instruction to just Peter, James and John. He was speaking to all of us for all time and it was his intention that there would never be a separation between us and his son and that there would never be a space that could keep us from being able to hear him if we listen. But we can keep ourselves from hearing. We can forget to listen. We can choose not to listen. We can believe the lie that we're not good enough or important enough to listen and be spoken to. We can have distorted ideas about God and think he wouldn't be interested in speaking to us. We can get discouraged and think that listening is all right for others but probably not for us.

Listening is a habit and, like all habits, it's one that develops and becomes stronger over time. Another way to say 'listen' is 'Pay attention.' We tend to spend large chunks of our time engaged in the activities of our daily lives, never remembering to simply turn to the Lord to say, "I'm here. I'm listening..." Then when we go to our prayer time, if we have one, we're all distracted, tense and harried. We try to listen but we don't know what to listen for. What we mostly hear is the chattering of our minds.

We have to build up the habit of continual listening during the course of our day and to understand that Christ can speak through everything and anything. We can't pick and choose where or how he will speak; we can only watch and be open. What better time to start building a listening habit than during Lent? All that's needed is a short and simple prayer that says something to the effect of, "Open my ears so I may hear you. Open my eyes so I may see you." I have suggested to others that a good way to remind themselves to pray often is to choose a small object, like a stone, and put it in a place where it will be seen or felt often: in a pocket, in front of the computer, at the back of the sink – somewhere that will catch your eye several times each day. You could have several stones, or whatever you choose as a reminder, left in different places. Eventually you will not need the reminder; the prayer will rise up out of you unbidden because you will have developed a holy habit of turning to the Lord in a listening mode.

One thing needs to be understood. The act of listening is not an act of simply receiving instructions or answers to our prayers and questions. The act of listening is an act of love. The act of listening is a critical part of any relationship and there needs to be a commitment to learn the language of his love. In natural relationships, learning to listen to the language of one's partner is a lifetime activity. Really listening and hearing goes beyond mere words. Committed married couples learn to read each other in many ways other than through verbal exchanges. Learning to listen to the Lord or pay attention to him is far more than waiting to hear some sort of verbal communication; it's learning to sense his whole being by paying attention to all the small expressions of his love. Those expressions are always there, coming at us all the time. We need to tune in and learn to recognize the movements that speak his love. God has a sign language all of his own. And we need to be there to get it.

May his 'voice' be like a stream in the desert for you and may your listening be like drinking cool clear water in a parched land.

Spirituality On The Right Side

John 4: 5-42
The story of the woman at the well.

Most people are familiar with the fact that our brains have two sides of operation, the left side and the right side with the right side of the brain being used for creativity and the left side for analytical, logical thinking. Often it ends up that our creative side is stifled because the left side of the brain has a tendency to over-analyze everything. It assumes it knows what things should look like, what is reasonable, what is allowed and what is acceptable. The left side of the brain can be quite the critic.

God created the functions of both sides of the brain and both are essential for balanced living. The problems arise when one side is developed more than the other side and, it has to be said, we live in a world that tends to value left brain functions over right brain functions.

Jesus knew this. Jesus himself was completely balanced in how his brain operated but he came to a world and to a religion that valued and trusted left brain perspectives. So, what did he do? Mainly he shocked and confused people because he taught "outside the box" and challenged people to see beyond what they were used to seeing. He used story, analogy, metaphor, miracles – and love.

Take the woman at the well for instance. The whole dialog between Jesus and the woman was a dialog between left and right brain points of view with the woman representing the left-brain and Jesus representing the right. The conversation began with Jesus making a request that was completely outside the acceptable code of behavior. He not only spoke to a Samaritan woman who was a social outcast but he asked her to get him a drink of water. We think this simply shows how Jesus loved and accepted everyone no matter who they were, which is true, but it also shows that Jesus valued this woman so much that he desired to communicate something of immense importance to her to let her know how loved she was and he knew the only way to get to that point of true communication was to jar her out of her preconceptions immediately and keep her from dragging the conversation into the realms of 'the way it's always been' and 'what I know in my head.'

Listen to this first part of the dialog between Jesus (right brain) and the woman (left brain) and see how Jesus refused to allow the analytic and the critic to dominate the conversation. (Scripture used is from NRSV.)

Jesus said to her, 'Give me a drink'. Jesus knew that this would shock the woman. He immediately started speaking and acting outside the parameters of acceptable behavior.

The Samaritan woman said to him, 'How is it that you, a Jew, ask a drink of me, a woman of Samaria?' (Jews do not share things in common with Samaritans.) She immediately countered with a logical analysis of the situation based on common assumptions or traditions and she was a bit critical because she didn't know how to deal with his words and actions.

Jesus answered her, 'If you knew the gift of God and who it is that is saying to you, "Give me a drink", you would have asked him and he would have given you living water.' This was a totally unexpected response. He did not enter into a debate with her about the rightness or wrongness of his request or of the law; he simply jarred her a little more and shifted the whole meaning of 'water' from the material plane to the spiritual plane by using imagery that was designed to awaken desire in her.

The woman said to him, 'Sir, you have no bucket, and the well is deep. Where do you get that living water? Are you greater than our ancestor Jacob, who gave us the well, and with his sons and his flocks drank from it?' The woman didn't 'get it' and came back with more logic and more criticism; she wanted to debate the issue. She was also slightly defensive in case he was denigrating the Well of Jacob, which held great significance for the Samaritans.

Jesus said to her, 'Everyone who drinks of this water will be thirsty again but those who drink of the water that I will give them will never be thirsty. The water that I will give will become in them a spring of water gushing up to eternal life.' Again, Jesus refused to enter into a discussion based on the prevalent accepted logic. He creatively opened her to the idea of a full life in God and again used the image of water, something essential to life, to open her ears, eyes and heart.

 I'm not going to write a commentary about the whole Gospel passage of this week's reading but I encourage you to go and read it and see for yourself how Jesus kept refusing to fit into the woman's ideas of law and logic, and kept creatively drawing her further and further out of her preconceived ideas until finally she broke through to joyful epiphany and entered into the kind of realization that doesn't come from the intellect but from the heart. She wasn't an educated woman but this didn't matter. Whether one is intellectually brilliant and knows everything there is to know about one's religion or whether one has little formal education and only knows a smattering of religious law from hearing others talk about it, God is constantly trying to shift us beyond what we *think* we know. He wants us to dive into the well of his heart to find Living Water and that experience may not always come to us the way we think it will...or the way we think it should.

In a very popular book on learning to draw, the author suggests a simple exercise. Take a photo of something you want to draw, turn it upside down and then sketch it. Why upside down? Because when it's right side up, the left-brain thinks it knows what *should* be drawn and unless one is very gifted artist with exceptionally keen observational skills, what the brain thinks should be there is rarely exactly what is really there. Turning the picture upside-down jars the left side of the brain and allows the right side to come into play.

When Jesus spoke to the people he encountered, how often did he turn their ideas of God and spirituality completely upside down, pairing images and perspectives in a way that was completely foreign to them? He knew that the only way they could see things from a fresh and living perspective was to have their whole image of God turned upside down. How often do we need to have our images and expectations totally shifted and upended in order for God to open us up to the full reality of his love? How open to this are we? How much do we cling to what we think *should* be there?

We feel comfortable when we know the rules and have all the right information. We like to know there is a logical progression that can be followed and we feel secure when there's a definite conclusion that can be reached. We feel more in control when we think that A+B will always = C. But what happens when the Lord meets us at the well and tells us that L+W=J (squared)?

Can we handle a creative God?

4ᵗʰ Sunday of Lent A

The Least Expected

John 9: 1-41

Jesus heals a blind man by spreading mud, made with dirt mixed with his saliva, onto the man's eyes. The Pharisees do not believe that he was blind and then healed by Jesus whom they consider to be a sinner.

So, what do you think you *really* know about God?

The first reading and the Gospel for this week both focus on the fact that God does not pay much attention to our common assumptions about what his intentions are in any situation. How uncomfortable for us! We surely would like to follow a God who is completely predictable and safe. But if there is one thing that is a constant in the spiritual life, it's that God is surprising and that he doesn't pay a lot of attention to what we think he should do according to who we think he is.

In the first reading, Samuel was sent by God to find the one who was to be anointed to be king. Samuel looked at Jesse's son, Eliab, and was sure this was the one God had chosen. He was the one Samuel would have chosen and Samuel was a prophet. Eliab had all the right characteristics and qualities as far as Samuel could see. Right there is where we all make our mistake: we see things as far as we can see. In other words, not very far. God told Samuel that he looks at the heart and not on the outward attributes that everyone else looks at. Samuel was open enough to listen to God's perspective and let go of his own assumptions. Are we that open?

In the Gospel, according to the Jewish law and according to the discernment of the Pharisees, Jesus was a sinner. They were

78

totally convinced that he was not God's chosen one because his actions were not in line with the common perception of righteousness. In their view he didn't look like a Messiah, he didn't act like a Messiah and he didn't talk like a Messiah. Therefore, he was not the Messiah and people faced expulsion from the Jewish religion if they accepted him as the Messiah.

Now, Jesus could have fulfilled their expectations if he had wanted to. He could have done everything perfectly according to the law and according to what everyone thought was holy and right and he would have been a lot more acceptable to a lot more people had he done that. But he didn't act in order to be acceptable to people and to fit in with prevalent attitudes about holiness or beliefs of what someone sent from God would look like. To the Jewish authorities, the prognosis was clear: Jesus was a dangerous write-off and a failure.

Another problem with Jesus was that he didn't choose followers who fit the common expectations of who should be the Messiah's right hand people. He chose the broken, the sinful and the ones who failed to live up to the mainstream holiness criteria. He chose the uneducated, the blind, the excluded and the ones with a sketchy past. He chose those who had been beaten by life, disappointed by broken dreams and beleaguered by unasked for circumstances. These were the Chosen Ones, the ones he discerned had the capacity for true holiness within them. He chose them, healed them and sent them. He never said to them, "You go change who you are and clean up your own mess and then come back to me and we'll see if you can squeak by on the righteousness scale." All he did was love and accept them, touch their wounds, open the kingdom to them and ask them if they would believe in him. He chose the ones who could simply love and accept him in return.

He has not changed. Every mystic the Church has ever known will tell you the same thing. He has not changed.

Do you sometimes feel small, inadequate and not up to the task? You are a Chosen One.

Do you feel like you made some choices or were pushed into circumstances in your life that have marked you as a failure in areas where failure really is not an option? You are a Chosen One.

Do you habitually compare yourself to others in your faith community or to the saints and feel like you're just not making the grade and maybe never will? You are a Chosen One.

He has not changed. Not one of his followers in scripture was adequate for the job and not one of them had the power to do anything about it. Every single one of them had to come before him in all their vulnerability, moral failures and spiritual poverty. When they saw not only how loved they were but also how much he valued them without them having done anything, their joy overflowed and their love for him was pure and full of gratitude. When he sent them out, they didn't go in order to earn his love for them; they went because they were passionate about expressing their love for him and bringing others to the same place of healing.

If you are like most people, you will read this and agree that in scripture Jesus seemed to be more comfortable with the failures and the poor in spirit but you won't really believe it's still the same today. It couldn't be that easy. Now that the church has been around for a couple of thousand years, we all know better and Jesus expects more of us than he did when he walked the earth, because people knew nothing about Christianity or what it is that makes us acceptable to God. Right? If we all go to Mass every week, study the bible, read spiritual books and endeavor to have a consistent prayer life, he's going to expect more from us than if we were prostitutes or rough, ignorant fishermen or people who are lost, destitute and blind. Right?

He has not changed. He did not choose the ones he chose because he had no choice. He chose the least and the poorest because they had the most capacity to receive him. He has not changed.

Do you know what the Lenten season is? It's a 'Come As You Are Party'. It's a time to drop all your assumptions and self-expectations of what a good Christian looks like and come to the Lord just as you are. Come as the prodigal child, the tax collector, the woman at the well, the blind man, the woman caught in adultery, the hungry crowd, the desperate father or mother, the lost lamb, the grieving soul, the sick at heart, the terribly betrayed, the unfairly misunderstood, the weary, the doubting and the discouraged.

He has not changed. Just come.

The Human Face Of God

John 11: 1-45
Jesus raises Lazarus from the Dead.

A couple of questions come to me in reading this scripture. The first is, why was Jesus greatly disturbed in spirit and deeply moved? The second question is why did Jesus begin to weep? Was it personal grief over his friend's death? Was it compassion for Martha and Mary, who had not only lost a brother but perhaps a provider and protector as well? But neither of those options makes complete sense since Jesus knew, from the moment he heard that Lazarus was ill, that he would be raising him up from the dead. John was very explicit about Jesus' foreknowledge of what was going to happen.

In pondering Jesus' emotional responses when he arrived on the scene, I was struck by the reception he got. Everyone had one immediate reaction to him. Reproach. No one turned to him for the kind of comfort and support that can come from a beloved friend. No one drew him into the circle of mutual grief that everyone was experiencing. No, he was rebuked for not having come sooner and for not having done something earlier.

The Lord of Resurrection and Life was rebuked. On one hand, their rebukes indicated a small measure of some sort of faith in him because they seemed to totally believe that if he had been there, Lazarus would not have died. Martha and Mary had come that far on their faith journey, but they had not yet come to the kind of faith that is not based in human circumstances that are going well. They did not yet have the faith that Jesus is the Lord of *all* resurrection and all life. *All* of it. They did not yet know that no matter what their eyes had seen, their ears had heard or what their emotions dictated, Jesus and the Father are the masters of life.

But I don't think it was the lack of mature faith that hit Jesus in his heart. John said in the gospel that Lazarus, Martha and Mary were ones that Jesus loved. This was human love and friendship. Perhaps Jesus had known them for a long time. Perhaps their home was one where he could find a place to rest, where there were some good people willing to ask him what his needs were when most of his ministry comprised interacting with crowds who just wanted him to cater to their needs. So, maybe the rebukes he received from Martha and Mary were hard for his heart to take because here were two more people expecting him to be there for them to supply whatever they thought they needed. Here were two more people not looking at him, not seeing him and not being open to allowing him to simply share their life, whatever the circumstances. I think it can come as a shock to us all that Christ doesn't just want us to share in his life; he wants to share in our lives as well.

Were not their rebukes really saying, "O.K. Lord, We believed in you and gave you the right labels. We've called you Lord and Master and listened to your teachings. If you really loved us, you would have come to us as quickly as possible and you would have kept this bad thing from happening." Martha told him that even though he had come late, God would do whatever Jesus asked him. It was as if she was keeping him at arms length. She wasn't opening herself to him as a beloved friend or someone who would share her grief. She was still making him responsible for an outcome that would be acceptable to her. That was the basis of her faith: outcomes that were acceptable to her.

It must have wounded Jesus' human heart to be rebuked, to basically be accused of not caring enough and to have snide remarks made behind his back by the other Jews who were there about how he opened the eyes of the blind so he should have been able to heal Lazarus.

We forget that when Jesus was on earth he was fully human. We focus on his Godhead and proclaim that he was and is the Resurrection and the Life. We highlight the Fire of Divinity within him – and so we should. But we should never ever forget that he suffered when friends died, could feel the sting of exclusion and be wounded by an unfair rebuke. We need to ponder the fact that Jesus experienced fear, frustration and abandonment. We need to think about what it felt like to have people crowding him all the time, always wanting, wanting, wanting. We need to stop in this particular Gospel and become deeply aware that he was weeping and that he was greatly disturbed in spirit. He was hurting.

Why should we do that? How is that going to help our faith in Christ, our Lord, and what has all this got to do with Resurrection and Life? It's because there is resurrection *before* our physical deaths. There is the Great Resurrection – the resurrection of Jesus from death, the resurrection that opened the door to heaven and eternal life for us – but this eternal life is right now, right where we are and in all the circumstances in which we find ourselves. Our eternal life began in the mind of God. *"Your eyes saw my unformed substance; in your book were written, every one of them, the days that were formed for me, when as yet there was none of them." (Psalm 139:16. ESV)*. Jesus' eternal life began well before he went to the cross; it was a reality before the world was even created. Eternal life is eternal life. It has no beginning and no end so it doesn't just begin at death. We can be resurrected and enter into eternal life the moment we say, "Yes, Lord. I believe." That's the divine part of journeying with Christ but there is another part to this eternal life: the present moment of being fully human just as Jesus was fully human and knowing that whatever we experience, he experienced it too and is now experiencing it with us. This sharing of life goes two ways but too often we don't allow Christ to be with us in compassion, which means to 'suffer with'. Instead, we hold him at arm's length, resentful or anxious because he isn't showing up in the way we think he should show up in order to accomplish what we think he should accomplish. Or else we try to bravely suffer alone, afraid that he will judge our fears and our grieving to be signs of a lack of faith.

There is great hope for us in the fact that Jesus fully lived life. He was Fullness of Life. We need to understand that all the human emotions he experienced in no way detracted from who he was or from the completeness of his whole life. He could experience fear without it meaning he was lacking in trust. He could feel burned out without it meaning he wasn't depending on his God enough. He could feel disappointment, loneliness, grief and sorrow without it meaning his Father wasn't enough for him. He didn't allow his emotions to define his relationship to God or keep him from looking his father straight in the eye. Therefore, he wasn't spending time wrestling with guilt over simply being human. He just walked with his father moment by moment in a relationship so authentic and so connected that he could live out his humanity without fear of being judged unworthy of a relationship with God.

He knew that he was completely and utterly loved *within* it all, not just in spite of it all and that's the kind of resurrected life he wants to bring to you - but he can't do that unless you open your life and share it, exactly as it is, with him.

Listen! He is calling you out of your tomb of self-denigration and guilt. He is calling, *"Come out! I want to unbind you and let you go."* He is asking to be given permission to share in your life so that you can share in his. He wants to bring you the gift of resurrection so you can be fully human and fully alive.

Sometimes it's easier to believe in resurrection and life after death than it is to believe in them right in the present moment and be willing to open up and be vulnerable to Christ in midst of all that's happening and all that you are.

Share your life with him and he will share his Life with you.

The Crux Of The Cross

Gospel Reading: Matthew 26:14 - 27:66.
The Passion Narrative.

On Palm Sunday and throughout the Holy Week we are taken to the foot of the cross through story and ritual. What we can actually do there is difficult to grasp and very often we end up as solemn observers rather than bringing our own story to the terrible hill of crucifixion. No, it's certainly not easy to participate rather than just observe.

Someone recently presented me with a pondering question that I am going to use to see if we can carve out a meaningful place for ourselves at the foot of the cross.

The question: Did Mary struggle with forgiving the soldiers and the temple authorities for what they were doing to her son?

Think...what is hurting you or challenging you right now? What are you struggling with that is with you daily? What is causing deep weariness, anxiety or grief in your soul? It doesn't matter if what you think of is a huge unbearable wound or if it's a series of small but inescapable irritations that sometimes threaten to overwhelm you. If you're not wrestling with something, I would be worried about you because suffering is part of the full human condition.

Mary's struggle at the foot of her son's cross would have been sheer agony and no one would dispute that. But have we made our image of Mary so perfect that we feel that her grief was ultra pure and didn't contain any of the negative emotions that we so often grapple with? Was she immune to furious gut reactions like tearing resentment or bitterness towards the people and conditions that were causing her son pain? Did she totally escape selfish feelings like terror and fear for her own wellbeing in the place of her son's torture? Did she not ache to run away, hide and deny the reality facing her? Did she not wrestle with survivor's guilt that she was spared the agony of the cross while her son was not? If Mary did not struggle with these emotions or emotions like them, then the foot of the cross is just a place for the pristine pure of heart, those who have the super spiritual ability to suffer with immense grace and dignity and we followers of Christ who struggle with so much have no place there.

Experiencing natural human emotion is not sinful. It's what we do with that emotion in the long run that can become the sin. If Mary had not been overwhelmed with outrage toward the soldiers and temple authorities, she would not have been human. And when Jesus cried out, "My God, my God, why have you abandoned me?" Mary's inner pain must have reached critical mass. Where could she go with her faith when Jesus himself seemed to have lost his God and felt completely abandoned? How do *you* feel when the little bit of faith you have is not enough to give any comfort at all to a loved one who is suffering and when you have absolutely no power to rescue them? You feel acutely helpless and abandoned as well. What good is your faith if it can't save you or anyone else and if it has no power to bring comfort and healing? You have been there. We have all been there.

The cross was more than the death of Jesus; it was the crux of all our hopelessly harsh and painful circumstances and every person who was present at Golgotha was there on our behalf. Only Jesus would have realized how all of humanity was represented there, not only in the ones on the cross with him but also in the people at the foot of the cross, in the ones who were nailing him there and in those who ran away because they were emotionally incapable of being there. The cross is the place of reality for the weaknesses and pains of all of us, not just of the super spiritual. And every one of those people there experienced a huge crisis of faith.

The cross *is* a faith crisis but it is the only door to the capacity to hear the voice of God in a new way – and that door is at the very center of all the agonizing situations in which we continually find ourselves. We can't avoid suffering because suffering means not being able to control the things that are happening to us or to the ones we love and there is so much in life we have no control over. Mary suffered horribly and suffering means feeling it all – the sorrow, the rage, the desperate helplessness, the resentment, the fear and the crisis of faith. Somehow, in the midst of all that pain, if we don't deny it or hide it away, we can come to a point of hearing the voice of Jesus saying, *"I know! I know how it is. It's brutal. I could save you from the pain but then I would be saving you from the portals to the very heart of God. You need to go through the pain and through the cross to find the place of stark but fiercely beautiful simplicity. It is there that God's voice is always speaking to you. You are his Beloved and you are my Beloved. I am with you through it all. You just can't see me because I am on the cross with you."*

Mary lost much from those terrible hours of watching her son die. She was stripped of more than she ever thought she could be stripped of and still live. But it is my belief that for the rest of her time on earth Mary was a full vessel of God's voice for the rest of the disciples, for the newborn church as it waited for Pentecost and for all those who were part of that early church. She was able to hear the voice of her God with new clarity and with a very different level of intimate understanding. John, too, was one who became utterly familiar with the mystical voice of God. If we cannot bring our sufferings to the cross, stand beside Mary and believe that she and Jesus are in complete solidarity with us as we struggle through the pain, it will be very difficult for us to ever hear the voice of God.

It would seem that the pain and suffering of our circumstances are the only things that can strip us of all our false ideas of God – ideas that hold us hostage, make us fearful, distort our expectations or were appropriate for a certain stage of our growth but now are ones that we need to let go of in order to move to higher ground. It's the only way we can be opened to resurrection life. Mary had to go there. She had to have Jesus, her son, wrenched from her in order that she could receive Jesus, her Lord. She had to go through the door of raw pain in order to find the grace and wisdom needed to hear the new and bigger voice of Resurrected Life.

This Holy Week, go to the cross and bring all of your sufferings with you – even the small stuff. Bring it all and stand beside Mary. Give yourself full permission to be there and to experience every nuance, large and small, of your own suffering and crises of faith. Allow Jesus and Mary to accompany you through the door of life, all three of you stripped, naked and exhausted.

And then, listen for the voice of your God.

Standing Empty At The Tomb

John 20:1-9
Mary Magdalene goes to the tomb.

When Mary went to the tomb she was a true believer. She believed in the goodness of Jesus' teachings as far as she understood them. She believed that he had been the most amazing man she had ever encountered. She had come to believe that he was the Messiah sent to bring his people freedom – and she believed he was dead and gone for good. It was that one erroneous belief that filled her with such confusion and grief. She was a believer and her belief brought her to the tomb and to more devastation.

To Mary and the other disciples who looked into the tomb, seeing the body gone but the linen cloths still there was worse than just thinking he had been simply moved. To them it looked as though he had been deprived of the last dignity of being wrapped in linen. Whoever moved him hadn't even had that much respect. It must have ripped them in shreds to see that.

You, too, are a believer. You may be a happy believer or you may be a struggling one but before you go headlong into the joy of the Easter season, be a Mary at the tomb just for just a little while. Leave all your knowledge about Jesus, your strong beliefs and your spiritual habits in a small pile on the ground and go as she did to see where they laid the Lord in the tomb. Go in aching sorrow to view him one last time. Go in despair. Go with your dreams shattered. Go stripped, broken, grieving and empty to allow yourself to be confronted by the shocking nucleus of our entire faith: the empty tomb.

When you gaze into that tomb, try to realize that what you are looking at is a stark question of belief. It doesn't matter how deeply or for how long any of us have believed in the dogma of the risen Christ, we all need to face this unembellished question and face it often. We need to look at our small pile of precepts, understandings and beliefs that we left on the ground and then look again into the empty tomb and try to grasp that unless we have come to terms with the emptiness of our own tombs and have cried out to be shown where the Lord really is, our tidy and correct collection of creeds and dogmas does very little for us. The question we have to deal with is whether we really believe that Jesus rose from the dead.

If our answer is, "Yes, I believe," then we need to ponder what that actually means.

Whoa! Hold on there! Don't go running back to that pile you left on the ground at the beginning of this exercise. I know that when you hear the question, "What does it mean to believe that Jesus was raised from the dead?" the first inclination is to run to that pile and pull out all the standard answers. They may be extremely good answers but, for the moment, just be a Mary at the tomb. As you stand there, allow yourself to soak in the emotional and spiritual state of a grief of Magdalene proportions. Everything you loved is gone. Your master and your Lord, who was your whole reason for living, is gone. You witnessed him dying horribly on a cross; now he is missing from the tomb. You just wanted to come and be near his body one last time because you never had the chance to say good-bye to him, not one on one, not face to face. You didn't know that his words about being lifted up meant literally lifted up on a criminal's cross. You didn't realize it wasn't just a disturbing parable or an analogy. All that is left is to be near his dead body but now he's gone and you don't know where.

Look again at your pile of beliefs. Mary, too, left behind her a pile of beliefs and desires when she went to the tomb. Nothing was as she thought it would be. Nothing made sense anymore. The future was a bleak empty slate and all that was left inside her was a wild, aching yearning to be with him just one more time. She didn't want to be with the rest of the community. She didn't want to discuss endlessly what happened, who did what and why. She didn't want to hear any more excuses or watch Peter huddled in a corner with his own brand of searing misery. All she wanted was a quiet space to grieve near her beautiful Lord and to not only grieve his death but also the crashing of all her beliefs, hopes and visions - her small pile of ashes left on the ground. She did not have any theology to fall back on. She didn't have anyone to whom she could go for spiritual direction, encouragement and maybe some answers. The only one who had all the answers was Jesus and he was gone. Dead is dead. Gone is gone. There is nothing more brutally final than death. Anyone who has lost a loved one knows that. Mary was empty of hope.

It was to this state of complete emptiness that the Gardener appeared. Mary probably did not recognize him at first because encountering him alive and well was the last thing she expected. It took the familiarity of him saying her name in the way he had always said it to awaken her to reality. Whenever he said her name before, she felt beautiful, loved and safe. When he said her name at the tomb, there was no mistaking who he was; his voice had been imprinted so deeply upon her soul. It was his voice, nothing else, which filled her with living hope.

Be a Mary. Hear your name and allow the dawn of full recognition to slowly light up the darkness within. Let the sound of his voice loving you, recreating you and keeping you safe be imprinted deeply on your soul. Don't be distracted by all the "shoulds and shouldn'ts" in your pile that tend to try to crowd in on your face-to-face encounter with Jesus. This needs to be a moment of pure relationship: desire answered by love, need answered by fulfillment, death answered by life, grief answered by unfettered joy. He has risen indeed!

In the joyous revelation of realizing that Jesus is alive and well, you may be tempted, like Mary, to resurrect your meager pile of beliefs that you left on the ground. Your first thoughts may be, "All is not lost! My dreams, visions and beliefs have not been in vain; they are real because he's alive!!" But pay attention to what Jesus said to Mary when she clung to him. *"Don't hold on to me, Mary. I haven't gone to the Father yet."* In other words, "Don't cling to me as if nothing has changed and everything is the same as it was before. Don't hold on to what you thought my mission was or your mission was or to *anything* you thought you knew for sure. Everything is still shifting and changing; completion has not yet taken place. Just go and tell my brothers and sisters that I am ascending to my Father and your Father, to my God and your God."

Everything had changed. EVERYTHING HAD CHANGED. Mary could not be allowed to hold on to her old ideas; they would only trip her up and keep her from fully participating in the new order of things. They would inhibit her from opening herself to the new and radical dimension of a resurrected Lord. Everything Jesus taught when he was a man walking on the earth was real and true but Mary needed to let go of her half formed perceptions and limited understanding based on the past and allow Jesus to become the door to a completely new Way based on Spirit and Life.

In our spiritual lives, we are also called constantly to move from old orders to new ones. Sometimes we, too, need to find the courage to let our old spiritual habits go, face the empty tomb and simply cry out for a face-to-face encounter of a new order with the resurrected Lord.

Be a Mary. Someone is calling your name and it's different than what it ever was before.

Rest In Peace

John 20: 19

Jesus appears to the disciples. He says, "Peace be with you" and tells them that he is sending them just as the Father sent him.

*The grace and **peace** of God, our Father and the Lord Jesus Christ be with you...Glory to God in the highest and **peace** to his people on earth...Grant us your **peace** in this life...Deliver us, Lord, from every evil and grant us **peace** in our day... **Peace** I leave with you; my **peace** I give to you. I do not give to you as the world gives. Do not let your hearts be troubled, neither let them be afraid...The **peace** of the Lord be with you always... let us offer each other a sign of **peace**...Go in **peace** to love and serve the Lord... and the **peace** of God, which surpasses all understanding, will guard your hearts and your minds in Christ Jesus...Keep on doing the things that you have learned and received and heard and seen in me, and the God of **peace** will be with you.* (Scripture from NRSV, other texts from the Liturgy of the Mass.)

O.K. Hands up: How many of you have stood in the midst of the chaos of your life and desperately wondered where this peace is that Jesus is supposed to have given to you? Do you feel that 'peaceful' is pretty much the last thing you feel most of the time? How many of you have decided that the gift of peace has not been given to you because you're doing something wrong? You don't exactly know what it is you're doing wrong but it must be your fault that this peace that Christ promised his followers is so elusive or generally unattainable.

All right, we can *all* put our hands down now. I doubt if there are too many Christian people who have never felt the sting of a lack of peace in their lives or felt like they would never be able to achieve a spirituality so virtuous that peace would never again storm off, banging the door on its way out. When we think of peace we think of and yearn for a state of absolute calm where nothing rocks the inner boat and nothing causes anxiety, stress, fear or tension. The problem is, when it comes to the peace of Christ, that's the wrong definition.

In a previous reflection titled 'Mission: Completed', I offered another meaning for the word perfection. It was 'complete'. *"Be complete even as your heavenly Father is complete."* In the reflection I wrote for last Easter Sunday (Standing Empty at the Tomb), I suggested that Mary was not allowed to cling to Jesus because he still had to ascend to the Father; his mission had not yet been completed and therefore her understanding of him and of her relationship to him was incomplete. In this Sunday's Gospel, Jesus says, not once but twice, "Peace be with you." Do you know what the Hebrew word for peace (shalom) means?

The verb 'shalam' means to make whole or complete and the noun 'shalom' means to be in a state of wholeness or to be without deficiency, or in other words, to be complete.

Also, the verb 'shalam' is used when one talking about making restitution. Whoever causes another to become deficient in some way, it is the responsibility of the person who created the deficiency to make restitution for what has been taken, lost or stolen.

When Jesus said, Peace be with you," to his disciples, he was saying, "Don't be afraid; everything is all right. I have accomplished what I came to accomplish. By my death and resurrection, I took the burden of your responsibility and I made full payment, cleared the debt and completed the transaction. I have restored you to the Father. I have completed my mission and have completed you. Be at peace."

If we define the peace of Christ as a state of undisturbed serenity and spend our energy looking for it and yearning for it, it's the same as searching through a big loaf of bread for grains of yeast and, when we can't find the yeast, saying, "I have no yeast. There is no yeast. It must be my fault that I have lost the yeast." Peace is the yeast of our bread. Christian peace is not one thing nor is it a simple state of being without stress or anxiety although it can manifest itself that way at times. Peace is the medium in which we live move and have our being. Peace is Christ and we cannot reduce Christ into any one simple thing or state because he is a whole and complex *person* – far deeper and far more complex than any human being. In the kingdom life, if you say, "I have peace," what you are really saying is, "I have Jesus and everything that he is." If you pray for peacefulness, you will be shown Christ who became the restitution for your brokenness and your exemption from the crippling and impossible responsibility of paying for all the damage the world, the flesh and devil has ever tried or will try to do to God.

Peace is the water of life in which you were baptized and in which you swim daily by the utter grace of God. Peace is the strong foundation of your faith. Peace is the spiritual air you breathe even when you're not thinking about breathing it. I'm quite aware that I'm mixing my metaphors all over the place here but my point is that Jesus is our All in All and if we used every metaphor the world has to offer, we couldn't even begin to give any sort of an idea of all that he is for us or all that he did for us. We just need to be so chuffed that he is OURS! He gave himself to us and he gave himself for us thereby creating peace between the Father and us. We are blessed beyond blessed. The angels are in awe of what we have been given.

If you really had no peace, it would mean you had irrevocably lost Christ and were completely dead to God. If you had really lost your peace, you would know it. It would be the despair to end all despair. I don't think any of us could survive a moment of truly lost kingdom peace.

The disciples genuinely thought they had lost their peace. They thought Jesus was dead and gone, vanished forever, and they were feeling the edges of real despair. Jesus had been with them for three years and I'm sure they were in agony as they considered that they had squandered, wasted and betrayed a treasure beyond all treasures, the Pearl of Great Price. They were lost in the torment of knowing their actions had incurred a debt so impossibly huge that they could understand the despair that caused Judas to hang himself.

Jesus walked right through the closed doors of despair and entered that room full of crushed and hopeless men and women. He, who had the right to condemn, immediately and lovingly ministered to their pain. *"Peace be with you,"* he said. *"Peace is with you. See? I am here with you. Look at my wounds. They are the new covenant signed in blood, a covenant that says your debts have been paid in full so that you can have complete and free access to our Father. My peace isn't easily understood with the mind; it surpasses understanding. It is the peace that comes from having lost everything and then having it all restored to you better than it was before. The world does not understand this kind of peace and has no ability to attain it. But you have it because you have me. I paid the price and I did it because I love you so much."*

Isaiah 53:5 says, "But he was pierced for our transgressions. He was crushed for our iniquities. The punishment that **brought our peace** was on him; and by his wounds we are healed." (NRSV)

Peace is with you. Always has been and always will be because he is with you and he will never leave you or abandon you. Because of the cross, you are safe. You are loved.

Shalom.

Feel The Burn

Luke 24: 13-18 and 25-28
On the road to Emmaus.

Let's zero in on a scene for a minute. Visualize yourself walking along with these two men, listening in as they seriously discuss this whole Jesus situation, both of them struggling with huge disappointment that he wasn't the Messiah after all. It had all seemed so hopeful, so promising and exciting but now...what a gong show! The whole city was in a state of shock. Everybody was in a flap and all were talking about it, not just his followers.

Nobody could believe the priests had actually gone ahead and had him crucified. So many were appalled at how awful Jesus had looked as he carried his cross up to Golgotha, not like a Messiah at all. Most were sharing about where they were when the earth started quaking and how frightening it was. Everyone had heard about the body being missing and there were speculations about where the Romans might have moved it. Hypotheses were made, opinions were firmly stated, gossip was rampant and rumors were flying. The two men were talking about it all because there was nothing else to talk about.

"Mary said she saw him."

"Nah, she never saw him. I heard she just saw a gardener and thought it was him. Mary's a nice woman but not too reliable."

"Well, the tomb was definitely empty anyway. Some of the women plus Peter and John saw that."

"That doesn't mean anything. Lucas said the Romans came back a couple of hours after they sealed the tomb with a stone and moved him."

"How does Lucas know that?"

"I heard he was talking to some Pharisees and they told him that's what the High Priest had asked the Romans to do. Lucas thinks they took his body right out of Jerusalem so there's no chance of it being found."

"Well, no matter where he is now, he's dead. I guess we have to face up to the fact that he wasn't the Messiah after all. The Messiah would never have allowed himself to be nailed to a cross like a common criminal. So...what he was really all about we'll never know."
" All I know is I'm not hanging around Jerusalem waiting for the Romans to pick me up. Those women are crazy, going around saying they've seen angels and that he's alive. That's all the priests are waiting for – an excuse to round us all up."

Then this total stranger catches up to them. Doesn't know a thing. Never heard of Jesus, the Nazarene. What's with this guy? Everybody has heard of the Nazarene. He asks them to fill him in and so they do. They talk and talk about the Jesus they saw and heard. They talk about the miracles they witnessed and the ones they only heard about. They tell him about the impact Jesus had on everyone. They talk about what everybody thought he was and what everybody said about him. They tell him about the rumors they've heard. They talk about how everyone's excitement has been extinguished and their dreams shattered. Hope is gone and everything is as dreary and miserable as it was before he came. They talk until there's no more to say.

Then this strange guy has the gall to say, 'Oh, how foolish you are, and how slow of heart to believe all that the prophets have declared!"

It's interesting that when we read that line where Jesus says, 'Oh, how foolish you are," most of us assume that his tone of voice is one of derision, a tone where we could easily replace the word 'foolish' with 'idiotic' or 'stupid'. But in this instance, what Jesus was saying was not that they were stupid; he was saying they were being heedless of *all* the facts. They weren't considering the whole picture. They weren't looking for the divine design or seeking God's light to illuminate his patterns. They weren't paying attention.

We're not like that...right?

Oh, how foolish they were; they needed to pay attention. They had witnessed the wondrous culmination of God's complete plan of salvation and all they could see was the failure, the loss, the grief and the confusion. All they listened for were words that confirmed their worst suspicions and fears. All they wanted to talk about was why he failed, how he failed and perhaps even that they knew all along he would fail. As long as they could talk, analyze and critique, they felt a little more in control, a little less vulnerable.

But in order to see the larger picture, they needed to lose the thoughts, lose the fear, lose the opinions, lose the limited focus, lose the chaos of words, words, words and...

Pay attention! They needed to pay attention.

Pay attention to what? Perhaps to a single bird singing at dusk, alone but triumphant and strong. Words can't do it anymore. Words skim the surface and twist it. We line them up in our heads, dig them out, push them around, shape and reshape them, lay them out and then walk away still carrying them. And the birdsong is drowned out.

Pay attention.

Observe the sky between the notes of the one bird song. Watch for an unusually calm ocean, so still it reflects the deepening burnished sky. Bird song. Still ocean. A sky smeared with the silver of soft but amazing beginnings.

Pay attention. Not to the chaos but to the still patterns of God's incredible design.

In the beginning was the Word. The Word became seed, became lamb, became carved stone, became bread, became flesh, became Word, became lamb, became bread, became full circle...

Pay attention.

The Eyes Of The Shepherd

John 10: 1-10

Jesus says he is the gate for the sheep. The sheep don't follow strangers because they know the voice of the Shepherd.

Over the years there have been three well-known songs (that I'm aware of) that emphasize the phrase, "I can't keep my eyes off of you." A couple of the songs written more recently are quite haunting and beautiful and whenever I hear them something pulls at me deep within. The songs themselves are simply love songs but what always gets me is that one phrase, "I can't keep my eyes off of you." Whenever I hear that phrase, I see and feel the eyes of the True Shepherd.

Shepherds, the true shepherds Jesus was talking about, could not keep their eyes off their flocks. This wasn't just a matter of keeping a watch on valuable goods simply because it was their job; this was real love. True shepherds were intimately connected with every individual sheep in the flock and true shepherds were always watching to make sure each sheep was well fed, safe and comfortable.

Comfortable? Yes...comfortable.

- *He makes us lie down in green pastures.* A shepherd goes ahead of the flock to find good pastures for grazing and to make sure there are no predators and no poisonous plants. If a sheep is lying down it means the sheep feels absolutely secure.

- *He leads us beside still waters.* Sheep will not drink from rushing, turbulent water. It frightens them. The shepherd will find clean, still pools for his flock.

- *His rod and staff comfort us.* The rod and staff aren't just symbols of protection and discipline. In Christ's time, when the sheep went into the enclosure at night, the shepherd would 'lay down the rod'. Only one sheep could enter the narrow gate at a time and every sheep was examined and its fleece combed through with the rod as the shepherd looked for ticks, burrs and other irritants that might keep the sheep from resting comfortably.

- *He anoints our heads with oil.* Flies are a terrible bother to sheep and if flies irritate them, they are restless and upset and won't eat or rest. The shepherd would pour oil on the sheep's head to keep the flies away.

- *He is the gate. Whoever enters by him will be saved, and will come in and go out and find pasture.* At night, after the sheep were examined individually and were at rest in the enclosure, the shepherd would lie across the narrow gate. Nothing could get in and nothing could get out without the shepherd being aware of it. Jesus is the gate and no one gets in or out except through him.

It is no wonder the Pharisees in this week's Gospel had no idea what Jesus was talking about. They had never been true shepherds, not literally or figuratively. He was implying that they were the thieves and bandits who came before him. They were thieves and bandits because they did not love the sheep nor did they care much for the flock's comfort and safety. They did not minister lovingly to the flock but ruled with arrogance and selfishness, robbing the flock of its basic needs while attending only to their own love of status, power and authority.

Jesus was having none of that. He could not abide false shepherds who did not love his people the way he did. The way he still does. His heart raged at those who called themselves shepherds but had no concern for the lost, the 'cast down' (sheep that had somehow gotten onto their backs and were unable to get back on their feet), the lame, the harried, the anxious, the hungry and the thirsty. The rules were more important than mercy and compassion.

"... I can't keep my eyes off of you."

I was looking at a magazine recently and there was a heart-rending photo of a shepherd boy weeping in utter devastation and grief because a vehicle had run into and killed six of his sheep. The photo was called "Inconsolable".

"... I can't keep my eyes off of you."

If a sheep was prone to wandering off on its own, the shepherd would use the rod to break its leg – and then the shepherd would carry it everywhere until its leg was healed. By the time the leg healed, the sheep was deeply attached to the shepherd and no longer desired to wander. I don't know about you but I've had my spiritual legs broken a few times. I didn't want to be carried. I wanted to run, be free, do my own thing and fix my own problems. It didn't feel right to be incapable and it was uncomfortable to be carried. But now...

"... I can't keep my eyes off of you."

Thieves only steal and kill and destroy. Christ came that we may have life, and have it abundantly. He came to take back his flock, to lead his sheep through the Cross – through the mountain valleys up to green pastures of abundant food in the high plateaus, places that could only be safely reached by moving through the shadowed valley. He came to rescue his people from the cruelty of the ones who had left the flock to wander alone in the dry wilderness. He came to rescue his own from the ones who had taken their eyes off the flock and no longer cared for the wellbeing and comfort of the sheep.

He can't keep his eyes off of *you*.

Home Is Wherever I'm With You

John 14: 1-12

Jesus says not to be troubled and speaks of going to prepare a place for us. He declares that he is the way, the truth and the life and that he is in the Father and the Father is in him. He says that those who believe in him will do the same works as he and, in fact, will do greater works.

Whenever I read this Gospel passage, I feel like I'm looking at an intricately woven tapestry, a tapestry where the threads are the Father, Jesus and us. To find the Father thread, you have to find the Jesus thread. Follow the Jesus thread and there is the Father. Follow the Father thread and there is Jesus. And then there are all the other threads weaving in, through and around the main threads. These threads are us and we are woven deeply into this tapestry called Kingdom Life.

What a nice picture. The only thing is, Jesus never tried to simply paint pretty pictures for us. Whatever he said and taught was the blood and guts of real life so when we come across a passage like this week's gospel, we need to stop and ask, "Do I really understand what Jesus is saying here or am I as confused as Philip about what it all means?" No doubt, you accept what is said in this Gospel but accepting is not the same as walking moment by moment trying to grasp the dynamic meaning of the fact that we are in Christ, he is in the Father, the Father is in him and they are both within us.

Each one of us is someone who, through baptism, has a share in the 'pleroma' of Christ. The 'pleroma' is the fullness of the Godhead that dwells within Christ. In other words, we share in the fullness of the Godhead. Listen again. *We have a share in the fullness of the Godhead.* That's difficult to take in and comprehend but in the second reading, Peter gives us a picture of what it looks like to share in the pleroma of Jesus. Instead of the picture of a tapestry, he gets down to earth and speaks of stones and a structure.

"Like living stones, let yourselves be built into a spiritual house, to be a holy priesthood, to offer spiritual sacrifices acceptable to God through Jesus Christ." Then he goes on to talk about the cornerstone, which is Christ. A cornerstone isn't much good unless it is the foundation for an actual building. We are that building. *"But you are a chosen race, a royal priesthood, a holy nation, God's own people, in order that you may proclaim the mighty acts of him who called you out of darkness into his marvelous light." (NRSV)*

Every single one of us was created in order to be a vibrant home for God. The question is, can we be dwelling places by default without really grasping what it means? Of course we can because God is gracious even when we don't think we are big enough, smart enough, worthy enough or important enough to be a dwelling place for the most high God. But when we do grasp it, when we allow ourselves to believe that we have been incorporated into the pleroma of Christ and when we begin to walk in the grace and dignity of our calling, that's when we become dynamic instead of static dwelling places for the Father and Jesus. That's when we *"in fact, will do greater works than these..."* because Jesus went back to the Father in order that we could enter into the mind boggling mystery of living in God and having him live within us at the same time.

He asks, if all this weren't true, would he have said he was going to go to prepare a place for us. I don't believe Jesus was only speaking of a nice place we can go when we die, although that's part of it. Jesus was saying he was going home to the Father in order to establish a place for each of us within his pleroma – within his Godhead – right now. Through Christ's death and resurrection, we who are baptized are given the right to live within the fullness of God as well as become dwelling places for the Father and Jesus just as he and the Father dwell in each other. He indicates this in other places in scripture:

John 6:56. Whoever eats his flesh and drinks his blood abides in him and he in them.

John 14:20. We will know that we are in the Father and we in him and he in us.

1 John 2:24. If we let what we have heard from Christ abide in us then we will abide in the Son and in the Father.

Colossians 2: 9,10. The whole fullness of deity lives in Christ and we have come to fullness in him.

Scripture is clear about who we are. If this is all true, then what are you doing about it? No, no, I don't mean how you serve the church. That's certainly part of the picture but it's a part that becomes much more effective *after* you have come to grips with your identity in the Kingdom. What I'm asking you in particular is what do you believe about who you really are and about your relationship to and with Jesus and the Father? It is so easy to lapse into seeing yourself simply as a scruffy child, a cynical onlooker, a befuddled disciple, a wandering sheep, a loose thread in the tapestry or a pebble stuck into a tiny chink of a grand building: not terribly important nor truly necessary to the complete structure and probably not someone God would be contented to dwell within.

It doesn't please the Father's heart when we see ourselves that way. I'm not suggesting it's an offense to him but it must be hard on his heart when he creates a phenomenal work of art and the art refuses to believe in its own beauty or when he creates a dwelling place for himself but the door keeps being shut in his face.

Jesus died and rose again and now, not only does he dwell in the Father and the Father in him but both of them dwell in you. This is astounding. This is utterly amazing. This is the Good News of the Kingdom. It's kind of like the Gospel of both "Being at Home" and "Being a Home".

In him the whole structure is joined together and grows into a holy temple in the Lord in whom you also are built together spiritually into a dwelling-place for God. (Ephesians 2:22 NRSV)

We need to understand that each one of us was created to be a dynamic, effective, living spiritual structure, not a poor cold empty building but a rich family home full of life and ministry.

For this reason I bow my knees before the Father, from whom every family in heaven and on earth derives its name, that He would grant you, according to the riches of His glory, to be strengthened with power through His Spirit in the inner man, so that Christ may dwell in your hearts through faith; and that you, being rooted and grounded in love, may be able to comprehend with all the saints what is the breadth and length and height and depth, and to know the love of Christ which surpasses knowledge, that you may be filled up to all the fullness of God. (Ephesians 3: 14-19 NASB)

It's time to throw open our doors.

Back To The Circle of Love

John 14: 15-21
Jesus tells his disciples that the Father will love those who love him, and Jesus will also love them and will reveal himself to them.

Before they filed out for Children's Liturgy, our priest asked a group of children why they come to Mass. There was silence. No one raised a hand. He asked them again and still no response. After a long silence, one child finally piped up, "Because we have to."

What about you? Do you love Christ? Why? Do you go to Mass and do all that you do because you have experienced his love and have fallen in love with him – or because you feel you have to? Is your connection to Christ an ideology or a theology or simply an acceptable way to conduct one's life, or is it a relationship, a continually intimate encounter with a real person?

John, the beloved disciple, loved Jesus. He wasn't simply attracted to him because Jesus was so different or excited by him because of the miracles he witnessed. He didn't just follow Jesus because he was looking for an ideology that would create a new political order of freedom and justice. Obviously, he didn't follow Jesus just because his parents did nor because he thought that if he didn't, God would be angry with him. He simply loved Jesus. Peter and the other disciples loved Jesus as well but John was the one who intuitively picked up on who Jesus really was and what he was all about. Of all the male disciples, John was the only one who stood by the cross and watched Jesus die. His love for Jesus took him beyond the fear of repercussions; he just had to be there. Jesus loved John, too, and because of John's great love for him, he revealed himself to John. John was given a gift of seeing beyond the surface of Jesus' words. He saw the heart of Jesus and understood the Spirit of his words.

In John chapter 13, Jesus finished washing the disciple's feet and then gave them the commandment to love one another just as he had loved them. Again, in chapter 15 he said, *"Just as the Father has loved Me, I have also loved you; abide in my love. If you keep my commandments, you will abide in my love; just as I have kept My Father's commandments and abide in His love. These things I have spoken to you so that my joy may be in you, and that your joy may be made full.* (NASB)

Of the four Gospel writers, John, alone, recorded these particular words of Jesus.

John understood that love formed the pivotal part not only of Jesus' message but also of Jesus' complete nature. John understood that without the holy circle of love relationship, all the words Jesus ever spoke would dwindle into another set of laws. Dead laws. John knew that love within relationship holds the key to kingdom life. It is said that at the end of John's life all he would say to people was, "Little children, love one another."

You, as a Christian, understand that loving others is important. That's something all of us have been taught from when we were little. However, you cannot effectively love unless you have experienced love. You need to have personal encounters with the love of Christ. You need to fall in love with him so that he can reveal himself to you and show you that he is in you, you are in him and you are loved deeply by both him and the Father. How else can you love others? How can you give something if you haven't received it?

It's wonderful if you did have a deep encounter with Jesus at some point in your life. This kind of experience can totally change anyone's life - but once is not enough. You need to continue to seek him, watch for him and listen to him. You need to yearn to spend time with him the way a lover yearns to spend time with the beloved. Because it's so easy to be caught up in the demands of everyday life, long stretches of time can slip by and the desire to spend time with him slips by with it. Gradually, the knowledge of his personality can become hazy and the sense of how loved you are also becomes indistinct. He starts to look more like a taskmaster and a stern judge or you start to feel like he's a distant and disconnected God. He becomes simply an image, someone 'out there somewhere' rather than a real person closely connected with your every thought and movement.

If the understanding of how loved you are has slipped away, the one word that will jump out at you in this week's gospel is 'commandments'. That's because when you lose the love relationship, everything in your head gets distilled into law and punishment. You hear what you 'should' be doing, you see all that you're not doing and guilt sets in making you determined to try harder and get your act together or else freezing you in regret. There's certainly nothing wrong with endeavoring to do what you should be doing but Jesus wants so much more for you. St. Paul writes in 1 Corinthians 13 that unless you have love, nothing you do will have any meaning anyway; you'll be like a noisy gong and a clanging cymbal. Jesus is love, so really what St. Paul is saying is that unless you are in Jesus and unless you have a love relationship with the author of all love, your love lacks the power and effectiveness Christ promised to his followers.

If you are walking in relationship with Jesus, however, what will jump out in this week's gospel is how much love there is in those verses. Jesus instructs his disciples but he also reassures them and gives them great reason to hope. They don't understand that in a very short while he will die a horrible death by crucifixion but Jesus speaks words of consolation to them anyway. He says he will never leave them. They will not be abandoned or orphaned. He says he will send an Advocate, a helper, someone who will teach them everything they need to know and support them in everything they do. He speaks again of their connection to the Father because of their love for him. Even though they are confused and ignorant of what's coming and even though he knows they will fall, fail and betray him, Jesus loves them and completely accepts the love they have for him, imperfect as it is. This scripture passage brims over with immense love and promise.

In case it's been a while since you have spent time in the company of Jesus, have forgotten what he's really like and are feeling a certain stern distance separating you from him, I'm going to remind you of the nature of his voice. Go back to 1 Corinthians 13 and Paul's description of love. Jesus is not only the source of love – he *is* love. So, from this scripture, you know that Jesus is patient and kind. He is not envious, boastful or arrogant and rude. Jesus does not react out of the wounded ego like we do. He does not insist on his own way; he will not coerce you or brow beat you into doing his will and he shows you the difference between conviction and condemnation. He is not irritable or resentful. He does not rejoice in wrongdoing, but delights in the truth. Have you ever experienced Jesus' delight in you? After all, you are a baptized child of God and there is a great deal of truth within you. Jesus bears all things, believes all things (he believes in you!), hopes all things and endures all things. His love for you never ends.

The description of the fruit of the Spirit in Galatians also has some great definitions of Jesus' nature. He is loving, joyful, peaceful, generous, good, faithful and gentle. These things are not laws. They are the natural characteristics of Christ and he desires to make them your natural characteristics so that you no longer act lovingly because you should but because it's your desire to share all that you have received.

Do you love Jesus? Do you know why? Have you been with him lately accepting the love he has for you?

Perhaps it's time.

Home Is Where The Heart Is

Matthew 28: 16-20
The Ascension of Christ into heaven

In the Sunday gospels of the past two weeks, Jesus was emphasizing our oneness with him. He is in the Father, the Father is in him, he is in us and he will never leave us. Therefore, the feast of the Ascension is not just the celebration of Jesus ascending to heaven; it is also the celebration of our ascendance into heaven with him. This is the anniversary of us becoming Kingdom citizens. If the kingdom of God is within you, then you are in heaven with Christ.

I can just hear your brains turning over: "This sure doesn't feel like heaven to me."

One of the most significant turning points in my spiritual life was when I understood that I was not made for this world. Scripture says that we all are "aliens and exiles" or "visitors and pilgrims". (1 Peter 2: 11, 12) If you accept this as truth, it can make a difference to how you relate to this crazy world. You are in it but not of it, you are a nomad traversing a desert region, you are a stranger in a strange land. You are a landed immigrant, familiar with all the attitudes and customs of the world but not completely at home within it.

The other day I was talking to a fellow with a lovely British accent and he was reminiscing about "the Old Country." It had been quite a while since I had last heard England referred to as the Old Country and when he said it, it struck me somewhere deep inside. What it stirred up in me was a sense of the Kingdom of God. I have roots in God's country or 'the Old Country' and sometimes it almost feels like I have deep-seated subconscious memories of a home I once knew. There are moments when something catches my eye or I read a few lines or hear some song lyrics and suddenly I feel like I've caught an ephemeral glimpse of my real home. And I get homesick.

What do I see? What do I feel? What do I hear? It's hard to describe. I see the colors of desire. I feel a stir of excitement. I hear a voice that's nothing like a voice saying words that are nothing like words. All I know is that it's as if a window was very briefly opened and I was graced with a whiff of a fragrant, light filled breeze from 'the Old Country'. I'm always waiting and watching for these glimpses, these whiffs that often come from unexpected sources. I can't make them happen. The Spirit's breeze blows in his own good time.

What do these glimpses do for me besides give me a moment of sheer pleasure? They offer me tangible reminders that if I belong to a place so graciously beautiful and so familiar it hurts, it must mean that I am more than what this world would have me believe I am. In this world, I am faced constantly with irrational, unhealthy and distorted goals, goals that are almost impossible to attain. Even if I were to achieve one small goal such as, say, a perfect body, I would immediately be faced with a mountain of ideals I have not attained. In themselves, many of these ideals would seem to be admirable but living in a broken world causes a subtle perversion of these desires. This perversion skews our perceptions and contaminates the purity of the goals. When we think we are simply reaching for a good and worthy ideal, most often what we are trying to attain is acceptance. We desperately want to be accepted and, even more ideally, admired and respected. Much of what we do is to gain approval, rise above the 'norm' and show that we are worthwhile. We ache to be considered valuable.

There is a place where we have immense intrinsic value. The 'Old Country'. Home. This is a place where we have (not just 'will have' but have now) great beauty and dignity. This is where Christ went to prepare a dwelling place for each of us. If it were not so would he have told us? His ascension in his glorified body was the grand finale of his saving act – he became the indestructible bridge back to our original home, the place where we truly belong, where we are higher than the angels and a place where we are infinitely full of worth, dignity and grace.

Don't get me wrong. Being in touch with our kingdom value doesn't mean we can't fail, do the wrong thing, say things we shouldn't, harbor anger or resentment and generally get on the wrong track. But I've personally noticed that I am most susceptible to sin when I am focusing on the values of this world and wasting energy on actions designed to gain control and elicit approval, acceptance or admiration. When I am mindful of who I really am, where I came from and where I'm going, I am less susceptible to being stuck in the heart-numbing mud of this earth's 'approval mill'. It's amazing, really, how many of our negative or sinful actions stem from a deep inner need to simply be recognized and loved, which is what we're really wanting when we seek approval. We just want to know we're wholly loved, accepted and admired for who we really are – not for what we suspect everybody thinks we should be. Actually, we'd like to know we are more than loved. We understand that God loves us. What we really want to know is that God is wholly contented with who we are.

An anonymous person once wrote that we were put here on earth to help each other get home. Before Jesus ascended to heaven, he commissioned the disciples to Go and make disciples of all nations and teach them the precepts of Christ. In other words, he commissioned the disciples – and us – to help the world come home.

Next Sunday, June 12th, is the feast of Pentecost. Why not spend the time from now until that wonderful feast day praying that the Holy Spirit will awaken within you a deep abiding sense of where you really belong...

...and who you are when you're at home.

Making Room For The Creator

John 20: 19-23

Jesus appears to the disciples in a locked room, greets them with, "Peace be with you," and says that as the Father sent him, he is sending them. Then he breathes on them and says, "Receive the Holy Spirit."

Pentecost: a time of renewal and change. Before Pentecost Sunday comes around, we spend time praying that the Holy Spirit will descend upon us in a fresh way to open our hearts and create growth and expansion. On Pentecost Sunday, we sing to the Spirit and ask him to come to fill our hearts and enkindle in us the fire of his love. At the end of Mass, we receive the blessings of Pentecost and we are sent out just as Jesus sent the disciples.

Then on Monday, life returns to normal and nothing feels new or changed at all.

All of us would love to sense the power of the Spirit working in our lives and experience a lively awareness of dynamic changes taking place in our hearts. We yearn to feel the breath of God blowing over us, healing, creating and recreating us. We thirst for the Spirit to move within us and fill us with joy. We are all very open to that, so why does Pentecost often come and go leaving us feeling like nothing much has changed at all?

Perhaps it has to do with our mental rooms – our thought habits and the kinds of perceptions we are locked into. When Jesus appeared to the disciples in today's gospel, they were locked fearfully in a room. Their hearts, minds and spirits were in disarray and the future, from their perspective, was depressing and distressing. Within that locked room, Jesus entered, breathed on them and said, 'Receive the Holy Spirit,' but it was not at that point that the Spirit began to energize them with power and enthusiasm from on high. A few things had to happen first.

We know that Jesus' words about forgiving and retaining sins foreshadowed the sacrament of reconciliation, but let me just put another little twist on them. Perhaps Jesus was also letting them know that before anything could happen, they had to forgive themselves and each other for their failures during his arrest and crucifixion. They had to get past laying the blame for their own defeat and each other's inadequacies before they would be ready to receive the power of the Spirit.

Between the time he breathed on them in the locked room and the time when the Spirit filled them with power in the upper room, Jesus was at work healing their self-inflicted wounds and inner self-loathing. He filled them with peace and hope. He served them. He told them he loved them and would never abandon them. He told them the Father loved them and would always be with them. We are privy to a beautiful moment of healing and reconciliation between Jesus and Peter when Jesus asked him three times, "Peter, do you love me?" Before the Spirit could fill these men with power, they needed to have their attitudes of self-blame, their fears of rejection, their expectations of condemnation and their pessimistic outlooks healed and changed. It is very possible that there were unnamed disciples who refused to believe in the love of Jesus and refused to trust in his love in spite of Jesus' appearances and reassurances. Scripture mentions that at the Ascension there were disciples present who still had lots of doubts. It is quite possible that a number of these disciples could not or would not allow themselves to be healed of their cynicism and simply went their own gloomy way, missing the visitation of the Spirit on Pentecost.

Reconciliation is one way we can prepare our hearts for the coming of the Spirit. However, reconciliation, as effective and beautiful as it is, cannot prepare our hearts for the bubbling over of the Spirit within if there is no determination in us to put into practice the hope of the forgiveness received. If we leave the sacrament and immediately allow our regular thought habits to fill us again, we are blocking the flow and movement of the Spirit in our hearts. Note that I didn't say we are blocking the Spirit from being with us. He is always with us. The question is not whether he is present; it's whether we can be alive to his presence in order to fully experience and participate in his action in our lives.

What are these thought habits that can block the flow of the Spirit in our lives? Here are a few of the more common ones: self-denigration, blaming others, inner complaining, constant criticism of self, other people and situations, resentment, self-pity, cynicism... There are lots more but you get the idea. These thought patterns and reactions to daily life become normal and habitual – so habitual that often we aren't even aware that we are engaging in unhealthy negative behavior. These thought patterns are addictive. In the short term, they give us a kind of satisfaction when we engage in them but in the long term, they form us. The longer we think in the negative, the more negative our lives become. These thought habits become our creators instead of the Holy Spirit.

There's a prayer we often pray, "Come Holy Spirit, fill the hearts of your faithful and kindle in them the fire of your love. Send forth your Spirit and *they shall be created...*" If we are serious about allowing the creativity of the Holy Spirit to form and shape our lives and have full reign in our spirits, then we must be open to building new and different habits of thinking and reacting. We must be willing to replace old negative thought habits with new life giving ones. We must be willing to prepare our hearts so that the Spirit will find within us an environment that is compatible with his holy and exceedingly positive nature.

St Paul says in Philippians 4.8: *"Finally, brothers and sisters, fill your minds with everything that is true, everything that is noble, everything that is good and pure, everything that we love and honor, and everything that can be thought virtuous or worthy of praise. Keep doing all the things you have learnt from me and have been taught by me and have heard or seen that I do. Then the God of peace will be with you."* (Jerusalem Bible Version) Paul knew the power of thoughts and attitudes. He knew how negative thoughts could not only tear apart individual hearts but whole families and communities as well. It's easy to find what's wrong with ourselves, with other people and with situations around us and focus on those things but we are called to discover what's right about ourselves and everything around us and to keep our hearts and minds focused on these things. That's what the Holy Spirit does. The Spirit is not a dark faultfinder. He is the High Celebrant of all that is good and beautiful.

An old Cherokee chief was teaching his grandson about life. "A fight is going on inside me," he said to the boy. "It is a terrible fight and it is between two wolves. One is evil - he is anger, envy, sorrow, regret, greed, arrogance, self-pity, guilt, resentment, inferiority, lies, false pride, superiority, self-doubt and ego. The other is good - he is joy, peace, love, hope, serenity, humility, kindness, benevolence, empathy, generosity, truth, compassion and faith. This same fight is going on inside you - and inside every other person, too."

The grandson thought about it for a minute and then asked his grandfather,
"Which wolf will win?"

The old chief simply replied,

"The one you feed."

The Divine Proportions of the Trinity

Exodus 34: 6 (from the first reading)
The Lord passes before Moses and proclaims that he merciful and gracious, slow to become angry, loving and faithful.
John 3: 16 (from the Gospel)
The well-known verse about God loving the world so much that he sent Christ so that that all who believe in him will be saved.
Blessing from the Liturgy of the Mass
May almighty God bless you, the Father and the Son and the Holy Spirit. Amen.

I've been thinking about visual weight today.

Anyone who has composed a photograph or a piece of art, laid out a page, framed a painting, planned some interior decoration, arranged some flowers or done anything that has elements of composition to it has dealt with visual weight. A large bold painting with a dark heavy frame on a wall has a lot of visual weight while a same sized delicate painting with a narrow light colored frame has much less visual weight. If you have the two situated on either side of a wall, it will feel like the room has the potential of tipping over on the side of the heavy item. It feels uncomfortable and out of balance.

As I was assessing how to balance out the visual weight of an item on my wall, I thought briefly about Trinity Sunday. As I thought about it, I recalled old images that in my younger days always came to mind whenever I thought about the Trinity.

First, there was God, the Father, the Almighty, and the spiritual heavyweight of the Three in One. My personal image of him probably came from the Old Testament. Yes, he was merciful and loved me but he was also omnipotent, powerful and a little irritable, a God who filled the heavens with his heavy awesome presence and was definitely not someone to take lightly. His expression was stern. The God of Tough Love.

Next came Jesus, his Son. He loomed large in the line up but his presence was more light-filled than his Father's presence. Whereas the Father was surrounded by thunderclouds, the clouds Jesus stood on were fluffy and benign. His expression was one of forgiveness but it was always tinged with an ever-present disappointment. "How could you do that to me?"

Then came the Holy Spirit. I think. It was pretty hard to see him. He didn't seem to have much form or shape at all, let alone a facial expression. He was white bird, a shimmering feathery wind with little bits of flame here and there. He didn't seem to have a real personality or will of his own but was there to benignly carry out the wishes of the Father and the Son. If the word 'issue' could be painted, I guess that's what the Holy Spirit looked like to me. Maybe. Hard to tell. If only he could have stayed still for a minute I might have been able to make out more detail. He was definitely the visual lightweight of the three.

Of course, these images flashed through my mind in the space of a couple of seconds but what struck me was the visual imbalance of what I used to imagine the Trinity to look like. I don't think I'm alone in having these subconscious images, mostly because these images reflect how a lot of artists have portrayed one or the other of the Trinity down through the ages. They are common images.

And very misleading.

It's misleading to have any images of any one of the Trinity at all just because of our limited capacity to understand and define

God. St. Augustine said something to the effect that anything we say about God or anything we envision him to be will be more wrong than it is right. Thomas Aquinas, after contributing so much to Catholic theology as well as composing amazing hymns, had a mystical experience of God near the end of his life that caused him to write, "All that I have written appears to be as much straw after the things that have been revealed to me."

When we envision the Trinity and see three different manifestations of God's nature, we are unwittingly dividing him into separate entities and putting each of these individual sets of characteristics into little boxes. And what are we supposed to do with these interesting boxed frozen images? Put them up high on a shelf somewhere outside of us? Go and look at them when we want to pray while keeping a respectful distance between them and ourselves? Without thinking about it, we create static images with imbalanced weights. Often, we choose a favorite image, one that we feel most at ease with, one that doesn't make us feel insecure, uncomfortable or out of balance.

It's not easy to grasp the reality of the Trinity but the importance of that reality is one of the reasons why we celebrate the mystery of the Trinity. There are no different visual weights within the Trinity. Each person of the Trinity is fully and completely God. To put it in very human terms, every quark, lepton and boson of God is present in all three persons of the Trinity. Every thought, every shape of wisdom, every powerful movement and every atom of sacrificial love and unbounded creativity is fully present and active in God the Father, in God the Son and in God the Holy Spirit.

It would seem harmless but by divvying them up in our heads, we dilute our own grasp of the full power and love of God. By making the Father symbolic of one certain aspect of God and Jesus symbolic of another aspect while the Holy Spirit comes and goes hither and yon, we subtract elements of God from each one of the three, making each of them, in our minds, much less than they really are.

To show you what I mean, the next time you read something from the Gospels, substitute 'the Father' or 'the Holy Spirit' for the name of Jesus. I wrote a Good Friday reflection last year and I said that the Father did not abandon Jesus on the cross to suffer alone. The Father was on the cross with him suffering exactly the same things Jesus was suffering. Where was the Holy Spirit in all this? On the cross, dying horribly. We cannot put the Trinity in different places feeling and doing divergent things like random characters in a story.

We read in this week's gospel the famous passage from John 3: "For God so loved the world..." You might as well read that as, *"For God so loved the world that he gave himself..."* or *"For the Holy Spirit so loved the World that he gave himself..."*

What difference will all this make to your spiritual life? Does it seem like what I've been writing is all a matter of semantics, something for theologians to quibble about but has little to do with the day-to-day struggles you have? Is there something in all of this that could transform your prayer life and your relationship with God?

It could, if you take the time to contemplate your own strong but very limited images of the Trinity in order to see that the little boxes are too tight, too small and too static. It could, if you begin to feel like you never really knew God at all and that every picture you've ever had of him was more wrong than right. It could, if you are suddenly set adrift in a mystery so profound that all you can do is begin to blindly trust in an eternal kindness and steadfast love so immense that there is no way you can ever hope to capture, visualize, or define them adequately. It could, if you begin to realize that prayer should be less 'to' someone and should be more 'in and with' someone, an entwined intimacy so complex that words become like straw when it comes to precisely describing who you are with – or who you are when you're with him.

The Trinity is the deepest, heaviest ocean of lightness and balance you could ever find. You cannot judge each of them visually or describe each one adequately. Staying outside of them will keep you uncomfortable and a little out of balance. You can only take a deep breath, plunge into their midst and trust that what you are unable to define is what is able to save you.

May almighty God bless you - the Father *and* the Son *and* the Holy Spirit. May you fall into fullness of all three and become one with the divine proportion.

Storage Facilities Not Included

John 6: 51-59
Jesus shocks his audience by proclaiming that whoever eats his Body and drinks his Blood will live forever. Many stop following him.

We humans are by nature collectors and hoarders.

As you read that, some of you thought of basements, closets and drawers crammed with junk that might possibly be useful someday and mumbled, "Guilty as charged." Others of you were a bit indignant because you are more likely to jettison or give an item away than shove it in a drawer. A lot of you were somewhere in between those two reactions.

However, it's not just material possessions we are prone to collecting and hoarding. There are so many other things we collect and hang onto without realizing that our mental closets and inner drawers are overflowing with useless items that 'might come in handy someday.' A lot of people love to gather spiritual knowledge and others stockpile definitive opinions. Some have secret stashes of status and power. In many people's drawers are tucked away all the major and minor sacrifices made in the past, kept handy so they can be taken out and pointed at when they feel God's not being fair. Some people collect approval and admiration while others hang on to the various ways they have been disappointed, disapproved of or rejected through the years. Every one of us, if we looked closely at the basements of our hearts, would find immense collections of something down there. We are by nature collectors and hoarders.

God knew this. Indeed, he actually created us that way and in times past and in other civilizations, the same inclinations would be called 'hunting and gathering'. But even though he created us with these inclinations, he knew that when it came to his circle of life, these God-given abilities would become disabilities.

When God provided manna for his people in the desert, he stipulated that they were only allowed to gather as much as each person could use in one day except on the day before the Sabbath when they could collect enough for two days. Anything over and above what they needed for the day would rot, stink and become infested by maggots. Naturally, some of them didn't listen. They gathered more than they needed and then found out that God wasn't joking and that there definitely was no point in stockpiling the manna. Nobody got to have more than they needed. No one could feel smug or smart for having more than others. No one could secretly compare their own pile of manna to a neighbor's and make judgments. No one could say, "My manna is much better or purer than your manna."

In the first reading, Moses says to the Israelites that God humbled them by letting them hunger and then by feeding them with the manna. We are indeed humbled when we are completely dependent on someone else to provide all that we need to live. It is hard on our pride when we cannot 'own' the provision we receive, cannot reproduce it, accumulate it, control it, make it into a power base or use it to increase our status. It stings the pride to receive and not even be able to control how much we receive.

When Jesus came as Manna incarnate, the rules stayed the same. We still can't own it, control it and stockpile it as if we created it. We could try to impress others with our collection of intellectual knowledge about it but in the end, knowledge doesn't make much difference to anyone at all. A child, the Pope, an illiterate peasant, a saint, a layperson, a priest or a bishop are completely equal and equally in need at the table of the Lord. All must come humbly and empty to receive the food needed for the journey. All are welcome and no one is more welcome than anyone else. A prostitute will receive the same amount as a Pope. Positions, qualities, quantities, definitions, value systems, knowledge – all the things we love to collect and store away – none of these things are important. The important thing is to come empty and receive.

God knew that if we were allowed to collect and hoard the Bread of Life, we would start to feel like we are the ones in control and that we are the ones who are responsible for satiating our own hunger. We would make sure we had more than enough for our own needs and then we would stop coming to the table. We would stop being humble and needy. Worst of all, we would begin to lose the understanding that in order to have life and have it to the full we need to constantly return to the Lord to receive his food. And with Jesus as Manna, a new dimension was added to God's provision for us. We still receive only what we need – and then we have to give it away!

If we receive the Body and Blood and then go away to live our own life without making our Bread of Life available to others, without ever being sensitive to the needs of those around us and without seeking to freely share all that we have received, then we have gone once again into collect and hoard mode. And we all know what happened to the manna that was hoarded. It rotted, developed maggots and stank. It definitely was not filled with Bonus Odor Christi: the Good Fragrance of Christ. This is not a pleasant picture but truly, the table of the Lord cannot be just a personal fast food stop. We are receiving the very nature of the Christ-Manna and the nature of Christ is to freely give himself away. When he was on earth, he hoarded nothing. He gave it all so that we could have it all and when we have it all, we have to give it all. It doesn't work any other way.

The Feast of the Body and Blood of Christ is the Celebration of the Circle of Generous Life: you come empty; you receive the finest wheat, not because you deserve it but because you are loved. Then you give it all away, especially to those whom you think don't deserve it and you come back empty to receive again. Somewhere along the way you should joyfully discover that, "a good measure, pressed down, shaken together and running over has been poured into your lap." (Luke 6.38. Jerusalem Bible.)

Empty the storehouse. Abide in the Circle.

The Yoke of Grace

Matthew 11: 25-30 (Jerusalem Bible Translation used in reflection text.)
Jesus invites all who are weary and carrying heavy loads to come to him because his yoke is easy and his burden is light.

It's hard to pinpoint the most beautiful words Jesus ever spoke because many of his words were words of extravagant love and mercy. We're so used to hearing all his words that we often don't stop to really allow these words of soft Kingdom rain to soak into our dry cracked hearts and give them the chance to soften the soil and make us ready to receive the seeds of his life and love.

"Come to me…" I am often struck by the fact that we have a God who says, "Come to me." It's easy to become confused and think we have a God who shouts, "Get over here right now! What do you think you're doing?"

One evening a friend and I were out for a walk when a dog went ripping past us, its leash trailing behind it. The owner came running after it in a panic because it was a busy street and the dog was obviously frightened, running as fast as it could without being aware of its surroundings. The owner, in his own panic, was yelling the dog's name and shouting for it to "…stop and get over here NOW!!" This just frightened the dog even more. Suddenly the owner came to his senses, stopped, knelt down on the grass and completely changed his tone of voice. He kept all panic and anger out of it, became comforting and friendly and called the dog's name. The dog immediately stopped its frightened frantic racing, turned around and ran to its master. You could sense the dog's relief in finding the calm security of its owner. If we could stop and really listen we would realize God's not yelling at us. He is on his knees inviting us to come back to his safe arms.

"...all you that are worn out and are overburdened." Let's see, who does that leave out? Who is excluded from this invitation? I actually sat for a few minutes and thought about all the people I know and I couldn't think of one person who is completely outside the category of 'All Who are Weary and Burdened'. It's a human condition. Sometimes the weariness and burdens are deeper and heavier than at other times but Jesus knew all the difficulties of walking in this world. He knew weariness and the feeling of being overwhelmed. He was accustomed to the burden of being human and understood what a challenge it is to figure out relationships, to juggle complicated situations, to bear the brunt of injustice, to lose a loved one to death or to watch a child make terrible choices. He walked our lives and faced our fears.

Therefore, the words, ***"I will give you rest,"*** were spoken and continue to be spoken with huge compassion. "I *will* give you rest." Not, "I *might* give you rest if you are good and you deserve it." 'Will' is a strong word. When someone says, "Yes, I will..." to us, we take that as a promise and believe it but only if we discern that the person is capable of delivering what is promised. When we hear Jesus say, " I will," our initial reaction is to think, "Of course he will." But, if we examine our hearts, we often find traces of doubt there. We try to have faith that he will do what he said he would do but it's so easy to find just a smidgen of skepticism arising from times when it seemed like he didn't do what we thought he would or should do. Does that means he can't be relied upon? No, what it means is that we have definite ideas of what he should do in any given situation. It means we have interpretations as to what his promise keeping should look like. It means we want things to go a certain way and we're not always open to his wisdom. When Jesus says, "I will" he also says, "*My* will." We need to understand that he did not ever promise to conform to our wills or to our ideas of how things should go. And thank God for that because our ideas and visions are so shortsighted and limited. We really have no clue yet we still try to be God's executive directors.

"Shoulder my yoke and learn from me, for I am gentle and humble in heart, and you will find rest for your souls." This is the key. When Jesus invites us to put his yoke on, he is saying, "Take this yoke. It's exactly the same as the one I am under. It's the yoke of a heart that is trusting, gentle and humble; it's not the yoke of a heart that is fearful, controlling and demanding." It's in gentleness and humility that the heart finds rest. I definitely believe there are times when we do need to wrestle with the Lord but if we are always in a fearful demanding mode with the Lord and if our attitude is always, "Of course I know what's needed in this situation, Lord. Any smart person would agree with me," then we need to step back and ponder on what it means to be gentle with God. Jesus, in his gentleness and humility, trusted God moment by moment to supply his needs. He also trusted that God knew exactly what he needed and when he needed it. If he encourages us to wear the same yoke as he wore, there must be a beautiful and nourishing restfulness of soul within it.

"Yes, my yoke is easy, and my burden light." Jesus was mostly contrasting his yoke to the yoke and the burden of dead law but the yoke of the law is not much different from the yoke of the world. It's the yoke of shouldering all responsibility for one's broken human condition. It's the burden of having nowhere to turn and nowhere to run but to self. It's the load of feeling completely alone with no hope of being forgiven and loved no matter what. When we are weary of trying to be in control all the time and when we finally turn to Christ, gently and humbly saying, "I give up. I just can't do this anymore," we will indeed find that his burden is much lighter and that his yoke sits much more easily on the shoulders.

How can we turn to Christ with gentleness and humility? How can we unload the backbreaking yoke of sole responsibility? This is only possible when we stay in the present moment and deal only with what is in front of us in that moment while keeping our eyes on him just for that moment. If we refuse to allow our clamorous desires and fears to become chafing heavy yokes, we can become much more in tune with Christ's quiet gentleness. This in turn creates within us a gentleness and quietness of spirit.

We can maintain a humble spirit by remembering that we have no knowledge of what the future holds and by understanding that our perceptions of what could go wrong, what we need or what others need are terribly limited. When we assume we know what's best or what's wrong with everything or when we allow fear to settle on our shoulders, it creates within us frantic and aggressive prayer that brings no rest for our souls. Without realizing it, we often pray as if God won't know what is necessary unless we tell him.

Remember, the easy yoke and the light-filled burden is completely available to us in the present moment. He has never asked us or wanted us to carry the burden of the future or of the past. His yoke of grace is now. His burden of light is here. Go to him and receive.

He is on his knees; his arms are wide open.

Grounds For Joy

Matthew 13: 1-23
The parable of the Sower and the Seed.

After hearing this gospel, my natural inclination is to examine myself and try to determine: what kind of soil am I? Am I the infertile pathway, trampled and worn with too much traffic running over me? Am I the rocky ground planted with grand plans, exciting ideas and inspirations that never seem to go anywhere and which die quickly when things get difficult? Am I thorny, proud and cynical, never able to really commit myself to really believing in anything? Or am I good fertile soil where the planted seed becomes a dependable source of good fruit or healthy grain?

We all hope we're in the good rich soil category; that would be our desire and our intention. However, it's not that simple, is it? If I were honest with myself, I would see that I carry within myself patches of all soil types. I am a microcosm, one that isn't always being sustained in a healthy way. Our inner beings are reflections of the world at large so if we have a tendency to point fingers at the more obvious rocks and thorns we see 'out there', we need to stop and realize that whatever is 'out there' is also 'in here'. When we look closely at the various soil types described in the gospel, we can easily identify other people that we think fit into each category. That's easy. The difficult trick is to see how we maintain the same soil conditions in our own hearts.

Amazing, isn't it, how weeds can grow and flourish anywhere, even in the hard pavement of sidewalks and pathways? Do you find it easy to identify those weeds in your family or church community? Do you know of people who are martyrs, ones who do what they are asked but are always letting others know how busy they are, how much they are doing and how little thanks they get? These people aren't always easy to be around. Even though they are always in service mode, it just doesn't seem like their service is life giving. They bring to mind the old adage: the only person who can live with a martyr is a saint.

Now look within yourself. Do you allow yourself to be trampled upon and then lay little guilt trips on those around you? Are you passive aggressive? Do you say yes to every request until you are worn out, worn down and have little or no time to allow God's water of life to soak into you? Do you feel like the seeds that do come your way get pecked away before there's time for them to take root? Are the seeds that are able to take root actually weeds of resentment and self-pity poking up through the hard-pack surface of your heart?

We all have unproductive pathways running through us that are hardened from constant traffic and busyness. Often, along the side of the path are little signs that say things like, "Jesus is coming. Look busy," or "Everything that you are asked to do is a direct request from God. If you do it all, maybe God won't blame you for your failures." The trouble with that last one is that we can never do enough. We're way too busy to spend time with a loving God and we always feel guilt and pressure to do more and more. Meanwhile the seeds we receive wither away from lack of care and we blame others for our weary dryness.

Have you observed spiritual trends and ideas that have come along and have grabbed the attention of groups of people causing a great stir of exciting inspiration? Have you then watched these promising movements eventually die out, leaving people seeking the next latest and greatest idea or theology to fill the empty gaps? Did you notice that though these movements seemed promising, they didn't always inspire people to go deeper or further than the next spiritual high? You may also have perceived that some people find it very difficult to adjust to a life where there isn't always something exciting and inspiring on the horizon.

Now look within yourself. How many spiritual books have you read or speakers have you listened to that you just had to share with other people because the ideas that were expressed were so amazing and inspiring. How much of any of those inspirations can you actually remember? How successful were you at taking any of those spiritual precepts and making them a deep integrated part of your spiritual life? How often did a fantastic inspiration get completely lost in the grinding heat of everyday life?

We all have patches where the soil is shallow and where inspiration springs up with great promise but just cannot be maintained. There is always the hope that the next book or the next homily will hold the magic key to an amazing spiritual life. We forget that there are no magic keys; there is only relationship with the Lord. This relationship requires us to dig deep, plant deep and water often or else our spirituality remains on the surface, vulnerable to the hot sun and drying winds.

Do you know of people in your community who always seem to be angry and opposed? It doesn't matter what the church is endeavoring to undertake or how it's trying to encourage growth, these people have seen it all, seen it fail and know it's going to fail again. They might be disillusioned with the system – it's become too conservative or too liberal. Things aren't like the good old days or the church is too slow to change. There's always something wrong and always something to criticize.

Now look within yourself. Are there pockets of disillusionment? Were there times in your life when things didn't turn out the way you wanted or expected? Did someone in authority ever hurt you? Did this cause you to put up walls of cynicism and criticism in order to protect yourself from further wounds? How often do you find yourself criticizing and tearing down rather than commending and building up? Is your inclination to look for the best in people and situations or to expect the worst? We all have walls of thorny bushes that have been cultivated in order to protect ourselves from disappointment and wounds but the problem is they also inhibit the implantation of good seed.

We all have these patches of unproductive, infertile soil. It's called being human. We also have areas that are made of rich loam full of nutrients and life giving minerals. We have soil that is dry and shallow and soil that produces good abundant spiritual crops, enough to feed others and ourselves. We have barren stretches of arid desert and inviting groves of lush fruitful beauty. The point is not to get stuck in the mud of guilt over the parts of our innermost beings that have resisted the planting of the seed. The point is to be aware that this journey we are on is the great Soil Reclamation Project. Bit by bit, little by little, God's goal is to reclaim the stony hardness of our hearts and expand our arable and fruitful land.

May your inner soil be brought back to the fertility of the First Garden where *the earth brought forth vegetation: plants yielding seed of every kind, and trees of every kind bearing fruit with the seed in it. (Genesis 1.12)*

And may *God see that it is good.*

Yours Is The Kingdom, Part I

Matthew 13: 24-43
The Kingdom of Heaven is like:

- **the field sowed with good seed but had weeds sown in it by an enemy.**
- **a mustard seed.**
- **yeast that a woman mixed with flour**

Whenever we hear the "Kingdom of heaven" parables, there is a tendency to turn them back on ourselves. We imagine the Kingdom as a static place in which we are called to be and do certain things like sow good seed, grow like mustard trees and be like yeast. We turn the precept of the Kingdom into a place where the price of admission is a list of our spiritual accomplishments. With this kind of imagery in mind, along with the knowledge of how we struggle to make ourselves become tiny seeds or grains of yeast, the Kingdom is reduced to a place full of dry expectations that we aren't able to adequately live up to. It feels like a classroom where the subject taught is often difficult and hard to grasp and where we fear a failing grade rather than anticipate joyful success.

This kind of imagery is the Gospel turned inside out, backward and upside down. It reduces God to an exacting schoolmaster and makes the Kingdom life feel like a series of dreaded lessons in vaguely understood subjects we never graduate from and are doomed to repeat over and over. This imagery is so far from the radiant truth that it sometimes makes me think, "An enemy has done this." Jesus began the parables this week with the image of God sowing healthy seeds only to find that weeds had sprung up as well. In the fertile field of the nature of God, subtle weeds of lies about who he is and who we are have been deviously planted alongside the wheat of truth. However, God in his wisdom and goodness doesn't just rush in and violently pull up the weeds because he knows that the roots of these misperceptions are so entwined with our hearts and souls that to just yank out the mistaken ideas all at once would do more damage than good to our fragile psyches and would leave us vacant and vulnerable. He will patiently wait until the truth is deeply rooted, healthy, strong and flourishing before he attacks the weeds of deceit.

Then Jesus moves on to parables of the mustard seed and the yeast to show who he really is and how, in the end, these weeds of deception cannot overcome the Kingdom. We are not the mustard seeds nor are we the yeast. The Kingdom of heaven is the mustard seed and the Kingdom of Heaven is the yeast. This changes everything. This turns the Kingdom into a dynamic, vital, growing and spreading life force that has no concern for borders or boundaries. The Kingdom is not a place at all; it's the complete and full nature of Christ. The earth is so full of it that nothing can escape it. It's his personality, his energy, his desire, his blessing and his love, and he is nothing but lavish in pouring it out for us and on us.

In the parable of the mustard seed, it's noteworthy that Jesus didn't liken the Kingdom to just any big tree; he chose a tree that starts out incredibly small and insignificant (perhaps like the son of a poor carpenter from Nazareth?) and has the characteristic of totally taking over the area in which it grows.

"Mustard... is extremely beneficial for the health. It grows entirely wild, though it is improved by being transplanted: but on the other hand when it has once been sown it is scarcely possible to get the place free of it, as the seed when it falls germinates at once." (Pliny the Elder, in his Natural History, written approx. AD 78)

This is the Kingdom. It immediately germinates, takes root, takes over and spreads in an almost profligate way. The mustard tree, in reality, doesn't attract birds to rest in its branches but Jesus, the Kingdom Mustard Tree, magnanimously offers his plentiful branches and invites all who need rest, healing and protection to rest in him. Our God is full of unexpected and surprising lavishness.

The woman adding yeast to the flour was not making one little loaf of bread. Three measures of flour are equivalent to eight and a half gallons or thirty-eight liters of flour. Jesus is likening himself to a woman mixing in enough yeast to make at least a hundred loaves of bread. In scripture, the number three is used to signify God's purpose or his will and the number 100 signifies completeness or fullness. Jesus became our Bread of Life according to God's will and he became the complete fullness of God abundantly available to us in the Eucharist. Our God is not stingy or miserly with his love. He is bountiful and extravagant.

A few years ago, Fr. William Hann gave a homily on the nature of God in relation to the parable of the sower and the seed and something he said made my spirit leap within me at the time. I know the things he said came straight from his heart and are precepts he utterly and intimately knows to be true. They aren't just interesting ideas he read somewhere; they are bedrock in his life. Listen to these words that truly reflect the Kingdom of heaven:

*"... today's parable of the sower invites us not to discount the fact that a gracious God is also part of our world scene; not as a threatening, punishing or destructive God but as **a God who is generous to the point of being prodigal in the way he brings forth new life in our world. It is my firm belief that God is too much for us--too generous, too imaginative and too down to earth ... too close.** Like the seed bursting open, God will change us-*

-if we allow it. We long to be changed, and we fear it. This parable is of great comfort to us--all of us to whom the gospel has been entrusted. The seed of God is potent and sometimes the harvest is rich. What takes root in our lives bears fruit and can yield even a hundredfold. That's great news and, as someone said, "it's like a refreshing shower" that brings our drooping spirits back to life." (Quoted with permission.)

The Kingdom of heaven *is* Christ. He was planted and he immediately germinated to become the bountiful tree of life that cannot be eradicated. Jesus is the powerful yeast mixed in with the flour of God's will to provide the nourishing risen Bread of Life – enough for all and enough for all time. If we insist on thinking of the Kingdom as something apart from us or as something that's withheld from us unless we get our act together, we will find our ability to be open to change sporadic and often ineffective. As Fr. William said, *'we long to be changed – and we fear it.'* We fear it because we don't understand that God is the yeast that causes the rising action within us. He does the planting. He is the creative seed and the harvest he brings forth is joyously and riotously abundant. We look at our own meager resources and of course we fear change. We fear it because we are incapable of making it happen. We have too little to work with and we know it. We need to turn around and run to a God who is *'too generous, too imaginative, too down to earth ... too close'*. If you pondered just those words for the rest of your life, you would find yourself being changed without fear or strained effort and you would know that it was the Kingdom of heaven who laughed you into freedom and loved you into life.

Let anyone with ears to hear please listen. For the love of God...listen!

Yours Is The Kingdom, Part II

Matthew 13: 44-52

The kingdom of heaven is like:

- treasure hidden in a field,
- a merchant looking for fine pearls; when he finds one he sells everything he has to purchase it.

There are a lot popular songs today that are encouraging people to believe in their intrinsic worth and value. The message is, "You're great, you're valuable as a person, don't put yourself down and believe in yourself." It certainly is a timely message because the world is filled with people who feel like they are worthless. The sad thing is, a song on the radio won't help much. That kind of inner brokenness is not healed by a positive message with a catchy tune.

Something that is even sadder is that the Church is filled with people who are convinced of their innate worthlessness. It is heartrending that so many people, who follow a loving and beautiful God, have as much trouble believing that they are worthwhile and valuable as do people without any faith at all. Something is wrong with this picture.

We always think that Jesus is the 'Pearl of Great Price' who is worth the selling of all that we own in order to have him in our life. But have you ever considered that Christ was talking about you as the Pearl of Great Price and that God gave all that he had in order to re-possess the treasure that is *you*? You, indeed, are a Pearl of Great Price paid for in blood.

There is a tendency to accept the basic fact that God loved the world so much that he gave his only Son but then to feel as though each of us is just one of a billion Christian people who make up this vast world. It's similar to you loving and appreciating a tree or a huge mountain but rarely stopping to consider, let alone love, each molecule that is part of that tree or mountain. It's easy to feel that you are an insignificant molecule within the whole mass called 'the world' and to feel that God takes the most notice of the 'you molecule' only when you are out of line or when you fail to do what you should be doing. Do you not get more of a sense of God gazing directly at you when you've done something wrong than when you do what you know is right?

Think for a minute. How easy is it for you to allow yourself to come before the Lord to see complete love and delight in his eyes? How willing are you to open the ears of your heart to hear, "You are my Pearl of Great price. I gave everything I had for you even though you're broken and soiled from being hidden in the earth. I created you and I only create wonder and beauty and *...you are precious in my sight; you are honored, and I love you.* (Isaiah 43.4 Jerusalem Bible)

Is this comfortable for you? Do you have an underlying feeling that you're not good enough to see delight in his eyes or to listen to how much he loves you without also hearing the caveat that you should clean up, shape up and stop being so disappointing? Are you able to spend time with the Lord and simply enjoy being loved by him with no strings attached? Is this allowed?

It's not only allowed, it's also crucial to becoming a whole and holy child of God. Being immersed in his love is what creates the changes in us that we yearn for and that we mistakenly think are our responsibility. Our responsibility is to show up, be there, stay there and yearn. Experiencing the fire of his immense love is what does the work of transformation (pearl cleaning) that we strive to do on our own – and at which we fail miserably.

Listen to what St. Catherine of Siena, a Doctor of the Church, says as she prays to the Lord:

"Eternal Trinity, Godhead, mystery deep as the sea, you could give me no greater gift than the gift of yourself. For you are a fire ever burning and never consumed, which itself consumes all the selfish love that fills my being. Yes, you are a fire that takes away the coldness, illuminates the mind with its light and causes me to know your truth. And I know that you are beauty and wisdom itself. The food of angels, you gave yourself to people in the fire of your love."

Do you hear how the action is all God's? It is God's fire of love that consumes the selfishness, takes away the coldness, illuminates the mind and causes inner recognition of truth. And what does Catherine do? She comes to him. She simply recognizes with utter gratitude that he is beauty and wisdom. She glories in that. She revels in the 'food of angels'. That kind of experience of God was not given to her because she was so good and finally deserved it. She became the saint she was because she *allowed* herself to sit before the fire and *allowed* herself to receive the gift of fierce love. She *allowed* herself to be treated by God as a pearl of great price and a wonderful treasure.

She allowed herself to find her own reflection in the burning eyes of the Kingdom of Heaven.

When you sit before the Lord and simply recognize and receive his love, you will become like a scribe who has been trained for the kingdom of heaven. Then, like the master of a household who brings out of his treasure what is new and what is old, you will begin to recognize and rejoice in the beauty of everything you have always been (what is old) because he created you, and you will anticipate with joy all that you will be (what is new) because he is the one who will love it into being in his own good time.

The Kingdom of God is within you. Look within and look into his eyes. Behold the Kingdom. Behold the love. Behold the real truth of your value and worth in the eyes of the Master.

Consumed In Grace *(by St. Catherine of Siena)*

I first saw God when I was a child, six years of age.
The cheeks of the sun were pale before Him
And the earth acted as a shy girl
Like me.

Divine light entered my heart from His love
That did never fully wane.

Though indeed, dear, I can understand how a person's faith
Can at times flicker.

For what is the mind to do
With something that becomes the mind's ruin:
A God that consumes us
In His grace.

I have seen what you want;
It is there.
A Beloved of infinite tenderness.

I Won't Take No For An Answer *(by St. Catherine of Siena)*

"I won't take no for answer,"
God began to say
To me
When he opened His arms each night
Wanting us to
Dance.

The Letter

Matthew 14: 13-21.
The Feeding of the Five Thousand.

To my honored friend, Nicodemus,
Peace be with you.

I have often missed you since you moved from this region; our debates and discussions on the law and the scripture were stimulating and deeply satisfying and I have not found another friend with such keen insight or depth of knowledge as you. I have often wished we could sit once again in the quiet shade of your olive tree to deliberate over the greatness of G_D's laws but lately I have also desperately wanted to put before your shrewd mind an experience that has disturbed me deeply.

You must have heard of Jesus of Nazareth by now. The chief priest has denounced him as a troublemaker and I had no desire whatsoever to seek him out in order to listen to him or witness one of his miracle tricks. I felt that my duties left me no time to listen to madmen and itinerant preachers. However, his name was on everyone's lips and I couldn't go anywhere without hearing questions, whispers and speculations about this Jesus. I became concerned about his influence over people, especially over those who are ignorant of the law and who depend on people like us to guide them in righteousness. The last thing I thought they needed was to be completely misdirected by some lunatic who claims that G_D is his Father.

Two weeks ago, there was great excitement in our region. The rumor was that this Jesus was on his way to the other side of the lake where there is that hillside that has a natural amphitheater.

People were closing up their market stalls, downing tools and gathering their families as fast as possible in order to go see him and soon the whole region was almost empty. The only ones left in the village were a few of the lame and sick sitting in the streets grieving about being left behind. I exhorted them to cease their whining and told them they were better off staying in town begging G_D to forgive their obvious sinfulness. I was about to return to my duties when I thought, "Perhaps I should go. People will come back full of this braggart's words. They'll be confused and pestering me to explain things. I'd better know exactly what it is he is teaching these people so I will know what we're fighting against."

When I arrived at the spot where his arrival was rumored to be, I was dumbfounded. I had expected several hundred people to be there but there were several thousand! I was filled with alarm for it was obvious that his influence was more widespread than I thought. I knew it would be difficult to hear him from the edge of the crowd (where I very much preferred to stay) because no man can make himself heard by four or five thousand people, natural amphitheater or not. Crowds are always unruly and noisy. So, I shouldered my way as close to the front as possible until I could go no further because there were too many people. I resigned myself to being a short distance away and sat down to wait. I looked to my left and found I was very close to a woman whom I had no doubt was a prostitute. She gave me a very disrespectful look and turned her face away quickly. I was going to get up and find some place better to sit but the crowds were too dense. I had no choice but to stay where I was. I glanced behind me and who do you think was sitting right there, his knee almost touching my back? Ezra, the tax collector. Could I have found a worse place to situate myself? You have no idea how uncomfortable it was to be sitting with such sinners in order to listen to a self-proclaimed prophet as if I, too, was seeking something. I felt quite humiliated.

Suddenly the noise of the crowd died away completely. People who had been standing and milling around in the front sat down quickly and children who had been yelling and chasing one another immediately sat quietly on the grass. It was as if a wave of stillness washed over the whole crowd. Even I, who am not easily influenced by crowd-induced emotions, felt a kind of peace moving through me as if everything was all right. That's the only way I could describe that stillness, Nicodemus. Everything was all right. I had never had that sense in my life before.

Then a fishing boat filled with several men came close to the shore. The men, upon viewing the crowds, turned to one man sitting wearily in the stern and they were obviously discussing the crowds and pointing back to where they had come from, perhaps indicating that maybe they should go elsewhere. The man they were talking to stood up and gazed at the crowds. The people were still silent but you could feel their hope and yearning palpably reaching out to him. He finally stepped out of the boat, waded to shore and began making his way through the crowd. As he walked, he reached out and touched those he passed by. That's all he did. A light touch, sometimes a caress on the head...he was especially gentle with the sick and more than once I saw a great stir of joy and excitement after he had passed by and touched someone. The amazing thing was that the crowd remained quiet, respectful and orderly even though all desired to be touched by him.

When he reached the top of the hill, he climbed onto a large boulder and began to speak. What did he say? For the most part, I have no idea. He must have spoken for three hours or more and I only remember him saying a couple of things. At one point, he looked directly at me, right into my eyes, and asked with great love, "Why do you spend your money on that which is not bread, and your labor on that which does not satisfy?"

Nicodemus, would you think me a complete fool if I told you that at that moment I felt terribly ashamed? I was ashamed of my gold rings and my fine linen robes, which only a few moments before had been proper symbols of my status and of G_D's blessing. I felt ashamed of...of everything, Nicodemus. I thought of the sick and lame I had left behind in the town, people who had simply wanted to see this man. I felt as though everything I had ever deemed terribly important and valuable and all the judgments I had ever made were like dust and ashes as his eyes penetrated my heart. But the wonderful thing was that even though I felt ashamed, I didn't feel condemned. I felt so free as though all the 'important stuff' I had been carrying around in my head and heart didn't matter anymore. I didn't *have* to carry it. I had no idea how much of a burden it had been until it was gone.

Before I could think much more about it, I noticed there was something going on up at the front. His followers were talking to him, pointing at the crowd then pointing at the sun in the sky and they were urging him to move back to the boat. He just smiled at them, indicated the crowds and said something. They were at a complete loss. You could tell how confused they were even from where I was sitting. Then a young boy came up to one disciple and handed him a basket that the disciple took to Jesus, perhaps thinking that at least Jesus could eat even if no one else could. Some of the people in the crowd, sensing that he had finished teaching, were standing up and getting ready to go even though it was a long journey to where they could get food or lodging. Jesus told everyone to sit again, held the basket high so all could see it, asked for the blessing of G_D upon it and began to break the bread and hand it to the disciples. He indicated that they were to hand it out to the people.

Things became very confused then and I couldn't quite see what was happening as the disciples asked more men to help them distribute the bread. Obviously, the bread and fish weren't being depleted but I couldn't quite see where it was coming from. It just seemed to keep coming. In fact, it seemed like they were having trouble distributing the food quickly enough before their baskets were filled again to overflowing.

I was just about to jump up and try to see what exactly was the source of all this food when I felt someone tug my sleeve. I turned and there was the prostitute holding out two big pieces of bread and a large fish to me. She looked like a totally different woman. Her face, instead of being hard and resentful, was glowing, warm and soft. Normally I would never have taken food from such a woman but I received it with a sense that I was being given an incredibly valuable and beautiful gift. I looked into her eyes and said, "Why don't you keep it? You need it far more than I do." Do you know what she said? She said, "He looked directly at me and he spoke to me. He said, 'The eyes of all look to you and you give them food in due season." I don't know exactly what that means but my heart yearns to share the abundance with you and everyone around me."

All I could do was accept it with great thanks. Then there was a voice in my head that said, 'Ezra hungers'. I immediately turned around and said, "Ezra, this food is for you. Eat well and may the blessings of the Lord be on you." As he received the food, he had tears rolling down his cheeks. I had to turn away because I felt I wanted to weep as well knowing it was not physical food Ezra hungered for but for the bread of acceptance and respect. When I looked into my lap, there were two pieces of bread and a fish where nothing had been a moment ago. Again, I heard Jesus' voice resonating inside of me saying, "You open your hand, satisfying the desire of every living thing." I looked up and again he was looking directly at me. Did he say the words out loud? I somehow don't think so. It just felt like I was a deep part of him and of his ministry to the people - and I felt like I had come home.

From that moment until the time I arrived back home, everything was a peaceful blur but since then I have been vacillating between feeling like my whole life has somehow been made right and feeling a kind of terror of not knowing who I am anymore or what I should be doing, as if everything I ever knew and thought has been turned upside down and inside out.

I started out this letter to you, Nicodemus, hoping that perhaps you would write back with words that would pull me out of my chaos and set me back firmly on the solid, secure ground of law and reason but now, after writing out my experiences, I know that it is not possible. I must accept that the old wineskin has burst and is not reparable. I must be open to the new wine that has penetrated the deepest parts of my soul. I keep remembering the psalm, "The Lord is good to all and his compassion is over all that he has made." Funny how often I have read that line and never heard it.

It's no use, my good friend. I have been completely undone by the Nazarene. I know now that he is not a madman or simply another wandering teacher. He is the Son of God and he is everything I have been looking for, even though I didn't know I was looking for anything. I pray that you will soon have an opportunity to see this Jesus of Nazareth – or better yet, to speak with him. You will never be the same.

May the grace and peace of the beautiful Holy One of Israel be with you and your house.
Your humble servant,
Joseph of Arimathea

Peter's Perspective

Matthew 14: 22-33.
Peter walks on water.

Peter:
Look at me. My hands and legs are shaking. After it was all over my legs were so weak that I could barely get out of the boat when we reached shore. I wish they would stop asking me if I'm all right and if I need anything. I know they're just concerned, but right now the last thing I want to do is talk about it. I know they're dying to ask me what it felt like to walk on water. How can I tell them that it felt like hell?

I've always been a pretty brave man, one who has never been afraid of storms or taking risks so how can I explain a terror that was like icy fire running through my whole body? Before we saw Jesus walking toward us, I definitely was concerned about the storm but was too busy handling the boat to pay attention to my fear. If a fisherman is going to be paralyzed with anxiety every time a storm springs up, he might as well pack it in and take up weaving. This is our life. This is what we do. What we don't do is face spirits walking on water. I wasn't the only one who was terrified either. All of them were yelling, "It's a ghost!" and they were crowding over to one side of the boat so much that we were in danger of capsizing. They all know better than to do that in a boat but that's how frightened they were.

Then came the voice. "Take heart, it is I; do not be afraid." The voice was definitely his but, idiot that I am, I yelled back, "Lord, if it is you, command me to come to you on the water." What made me say that? What was I thinking? Nothing. I can recall no cohesive thoughts in my head, no logical or reasonable ideas about the whole situation. I just opened my mouth and out came, "Tell me to walk on the water." What did I think this was going to prove? If it wasn't Jesus coming toward us on the water, did I think that this ultimatum of mine would somehow protect us from an evil spirit? Was I thinking that even if it were Jesus, he would never take me up on my stupidity? I have no idea what I was thinking or why I said what I did but when he said, "Come," I looked into his eyes and I knew it was him and not a ghost. His eyes, so full of life, looked into mine and what I saw in those eyes filled me with a huge desire to go to him and be with him. I wasn't thinking about storms or waves or danger or risk. I didn't stop to think about what going to him actually meant. I just wanted to be with him. I couldn't take my eyes off of his eyes even when I was climbing over the side of the heaving boat. For all the notice I was taking of my surroundings, I could have been walking toward him on a village street on a sunny day instead of moving through deep troughs of violent waves.

And then *he* looked away – not me! He broke eye contact with me and I was immediately aware of where I was and the danger I was in but I was also aware of so much more than that. That's when I became filled with gut wrenching fear. It wasn't the thought of dying that filled me with dread and panic; it was the thought of living or dying without him that overwhelmed me with utter terror.

When I shouted, "Lord, save me!" I wasn't asking so much for protection from drowning as I was screaming for deliverance from an eternity without him. And he knew it. I immediately understood that he had broken eye contact with me on purpose in order to give me a glimpse of who he really is and of how bleak my life would be without him. He showed me a petrifying reality I never could have seen without him showing it to me.

See, up until that moment, in spite of his teachings and all the miracles I had witnessed, I still felt like I was weighing and judging his validity and his importance to me. I felt like he had made a mistake in choosing me and would reject me once he saw how much I still struggled with believing in him. I still felt like I could choose to turn away, go home and make it all simple. I thought that if I did leave him, there would be no major consequences, except life wouldn't be so exciting. In a flash, he showed me what life and death without him really meant and the vision of it was desolation and devastation. Then he reached out, caught my hand and lifted me above the waves, above my terror and above the prospect of an eternity without him.

Everyone in the boat heard what he said to me. 'You of little faith, why did you doubt?' They probably thought he was asking why I doubted that I could actually walk on water but I knew that he was asking me how I could doubt that he was the One who was to come, the Messiah, the Son of the Living God. He was asking how I could have thought that he would ever reject me. He was telling me that he would be with me through all eternity no matter what. He was saying that storms, persecution, distress, death – and, yes, even my doubts and failures – would never separate me from his love. How do I know this? It was in his eyes and in the grip of his hand. By that grip, he bound me to him for all eternity. By that grip, I knew I was saved from far more than drowning in the storm.

Yeah, they will all want to know what it was like to walk on water. They will want to know what made me get over the side of that boat in the first place. They will want to discuss it, probe me about being part of this outrageous miracle and perhaps a few of them will make some little digs at me about my failure to make it all the way without sinking. Let them make insinuations. How can I tell them that walking on water is *nothing* compared to knowing that he loves me and that he has promised to be there for me in all the coming storms? How can I explain that his words were not words of castigation but words of deep assurance? He was saying that he would be never ever let go of me even though I am weak and even though my faith may waver. To those watching from the boat, walking on water would be the most important and fascinating part of all that happened. I don't blame them; I would think the same if it had happened to someone else. I would be equally slow to grasp what else could be more important than human feet treading on top of water.

I have witnessed him feeding thousands of people, seen him walking on water, walked on water myself and saw the storm die down at his command but now I know that a miracle is not what rescues me and sets me on solid rock. What rescues me is the understanding that I can't do anything to save myself; the Lord is the one who reaches down to me to save me from drowning in my brokenness and fear.

My hands and legs are still shaking.

The Perfect Man created a perfect storm to show me, a perfect example of imperfection, what love really is.

The Higher Law

Matthew 15: 21-28

The Canaanite woman asks Jesus to heal her daughter and he replies that it is not fair to give the children's food to the dogs. She persists and he responds to her faith by healing her daughter.

This is certainly not an easy passage to deal with but, as in all scripture passages, reading it out of context with the rest of scripture as well as with the culture of the times can make it seem harsher than it really is. In our day and age of heightened awareness of the destructiveness of racism and religious elitism, it can read as though Jesus was being unnecessarily cruel by comparing the pagan woman to a dog, even if the dogs referred to were beloved house pets.

The more I pondered on this story, the more it seemed to me that it was really the disciples who were receiving an object lesson through Christ's interaction with the Canaanite woman and that Matthew included it in his gospel because he was passing along the same lesson to the Jews to whom his Gospel was directed. Of course, we all need to pay attention to this lesson because it's too easy to fall into a distorted understanding of knowing when rules are good and when they need to give way to something higher.

Just prior to this story, Matthew wrote about a conflict Jesus had with some scribes and Pharisees who were challenging him about eating with unwashed hands. Jesus berated them for being so assiduous about rules but forgetting about love and mercy, saying that it's what comes out of the mouth that makes a person unclean, not what goes into the mouth and his statements deeply offended the Jewish authorities. After this incident Matthew goes on to write about the Canaanite woman, which at first glance would seem to have nothing to do with the previous scripture. However, what we actually see here, when the two passages are juxtaposed, is that the 'clean' Jewish community that Jesus was sent to was more likely to reject him than the 'unclean' pagans and Gentiles were.

The Canaanite people were polytheists and when the woman came to find Jesus, he was in her eyes perhaps just one more prophet of the strange Jewish God, someone who might have some sway with his God. In a society where multiple gods were worshiped and many of those gods were so capriciously cruel and demanding that the offering of children as a sacrifice to appease them had been common in their history, she obviously did not feel castigated or belittled by his words referring to dogs. His words were probably pretty mild to her. Coming from the society she did, she surely would have reckoned that the Jewish God would frown upon her religious allegiances, yet she had the courage to hope that Jesus would be open to healing her daughter even though she wasn't a converted follower. She wasn't ignorant of barriers on both sides between the Canaanites and the Israelites but all she wanted to ask for were crumbs of compassion for her beloved daughter. Since she was devoted to her own gods she wouldn't have been seeking the whole meal of Christ's friendship or even have suspected it could be hers for the asking. She simply came. She somehow intuited that Christ's quality of mercy would not be constrained by human constructed boundaries. Jesus could not resist that kind of faith.

Her faith in what mercy should look like contrasts sharply with the scribes and Pharisees who could not and would not look beyond the rules even when mercy and compassion cried out that they do so. Christ is filled with joy when he comes face to face with people who ask for the sake of merciful love and don't think they deserve to be blessed simply because they are affiliated with the right group and have always followed all the prescribed rules to the nth degree.

There is another aspect to this story that echoes the story of the wedding in Cana (no connection to Canaan) where the host runs out of wine and Mary asked Jesus to do something about it. Here, as with the Canaanite woman, Jesus stated what might be called a Prophetic Law. To Mary, he said that the prophetic time to begin his ministry had not yet come. To the Canaanite woman he proclaimed the prophetic law that he was sent to redeem the lost sheep of Israel. In both cases he stated the circumscribed expectation arising out of prophetic law but when both women argue for the sake of compassion and mercy, he deferred to a higher and holier law: the all encompassing Law of Love.

Notice that he didn't lay down any conditions on the Canaanite woman. He didn't say that he'd heal her daughter if she would give up her pagan beliefs and convert to the Jewish religion or agree to follow him. Jesus knew that she had to make the journey to him of her own volition and not because she was held hostage to her fears for her daughter. When she left Jesus her heart was doubtlessly overflowing with the image of a prophet who could have made harsh demands, but didn't; instead he responded in compassion to knees bent in humility and a courageous heart motivated by love. Her encounter with Jesus as God was not only the beginning of her own spiritual journey but also of a life story which would have a powerful ripple effect, alluring and changing many of the Canaanites she would have contact with over the years, beginning with her own daughter.

Meanwhile, if all the disciples were paying as much attention as Matthew was, Jesus had once again made the powerful statement that if laws, boundaries, taboos, prophecies and common expectations ever dictate that we need not or should not engage in compassion and mercy *for everyone and anyone,* there is some other agenda being played out.

And it's not his.

The Naming

Matthew 16: 13-20
Jesus asks his disciples who people say that he is and then asks them who they say he is. When Peter answers that Jesus is the Messiah, Jesus proclaims Peter to be the Rock on which Christ will build his church.

There's something a little strange about this gospel.

When Jesus told Peter he was the rock on which Christ would build his church, Peter said nothing.

This is motor mouth Peter we're talking about. This is the Peter of the gospels who was the perfect example of someone who starts to talk before his brain gets into gear. If you glance through all the gospels you will often see the phrase, "Peter said..." He is the only one of all the disciples whose words are recorded so often and, frequently, what he blurted out revealed his proclivity for speaking first and thinking later.

"Go away from me Lord. I am bad man." (What if Jesus had taken him up on that?)

"God forbid, Lord. This must never happen to you!" (When Jesus spoke of his coming Passion.)

"Let's make three tents up here on the mountain, one for each of you." (Let's keep you all up here on the mountain forever.)

"Lord, how often do I have to forgive?" (Once was probably difficult enough for Peter, let alone seven times seven. Seventy times seven must have shaken him up a bit.)

"We have left everything to follow you. What do we get out of it?" (Of course, *we* never say things like that...)

"I will never desert you or leave you..." (No comment necessary.)

"Why can't I go with you now? I will lay down my life for you..."

"You will never wash my feet...well, OK then, if you insist, but wash everything not just my feet." (I wonder if he started stripping.)

However, when Jesus named Peter the Rock on which he would build the church, Peter was uncharacteristically silent. He didn't start protesting that he was a sinful man or that he had no skills to build a church – whatever a church was. He didn't suggest to Jesus that it would be much better if Jesus was the Rock and he, Peter, would tag along and be a pebble in Jesus' shoe. He didn't get all excited and start making plans to start the next week by drawing up committees and getting volunteers. He didn't ask, "Why? We have a perfectly good temple right now."

Peter said nothing.

I believe Peter was silent because he had heard his True Name and there's not much you can say when you first hear your True Name. It is a moment of joyful clarity, a moment of realizing you were moving toward this point your whole life. It is full of the sense that you finally know who you are and who you were always meant to be. It feels like coming home. You fully believe it but you can hardly believe it. It's a moment where language fails you.

It is significant that Jesus begins this dialogue with the disciples, especially with Peter, by asking, "Who do people say that I am?" and then going on to ask, "Who do *you* say that I am?" We need to take notice of this and seriously question ourselves as to whether our understanding of who Jesus is comes from what we have heard others say or from personal encounters with him, face to face, not just once but many times. He is always asking you, "Who do you say that I am?" You need to look him in the eye and, from your own deep inner conviction and heart knowledge, be able to answer, "You are the Messiah, the Son of the living God." And once having said that to him, you need to allow yourself to hear him say back to you, "Blessed are you! For flesh and blood has not revealed this to you, but my Father in heaven. And I tell you, you are_____."

Most people don't stop to listen to him say, "You are_____," because they are too busy paying attention to who other people say that they are or who they think they should be. Some people are totally connected to the negative voices of the past and of the world, which say to them, "You are unworthy, selfish, inadequate, a failure and a hopeless sinner. Your body is all wrong, you don't have the possessions you should possess at your age, you lack so many skills and you make poor choices." Other people listen to voices that define them according to what those other voices think they *should* be doing. Most people think they should be able to find their identity in their vocations and then muddle around in guilt or frustration when they find after a while that a life of marriage, parenthood, the priesthood or the religious life doesn't necessarily fulfill the deepest desire all humans have: to be unique, effective and wholly loved.

God has a name for you. Whatever that moniker is that everyone calls you by right now is more like a nickname, really. Like Peter's true name, 'Rock', God's name for you holds everything you were created to be. God's name for you is a journey of discovery and it will grow as you grow. God's name for you may look nothing like who or what you are right now, so don't assume anything. Jesus called Peter, "Rock On Which I Will Build My Church," but consider who Peter was in the Gospels. Did he look like a solid and wise foundational rock type person to you? He was an impulsive, rough and poor fisherman with no education to speak of. He was a man those other voices would have sneered at and condemned as a sinner. God does not name us according to how we see ourselves, according to what education we have or haven't had or according to how others see us or judge us to be. He names us according to what he created us to be. He names us and when we open our ears to hear him calling us by name, we begin to grow into the fullness of who we were created to be, just as Peter grew into becoming Rock, Healer and Shepherd or the way the stern, legalistic and self referential Saul became Paul (which means small or humble), a man who grew into finally beholding the mystical Christ and learned that wisdom resides in the spaces in between black and white.

Hearing one's name does not lead to instant spiritual success. Both Peter and Paul had to fail, fall, fumble and betray Jesus. Both of them had to go through desolation and desperation, otherwise they would have tried to form themselves into being whatever they first thought their names meant. Both, in different ways, had to come to a point of realizing that their egos, their Wounded Warriors of false self, had no place in their journeys of becoming who God meant them to be and they had to understand that their visions of what the future *should* look like were completely erroneous. No one could have envisioned all that happened in the Acts of the Apostles. No one could have foreseen the high numbers of people who came to believe in the name of Jesus. Even if it had been predicted, no one would have believed the advent of explosive truth that went so far beyond the parameters of acceptable Jewish theology. No one, not Peter or Paul or any of the other disciples, could have anticipated or envisioned what God's names for them would bring about in their lives or in the lives of the people around them.

Who do people say that you are?

Who do you say that you are?

Now...who does God say that you are?

Listen to him...it will be *nothing* like what you expected.

Living In Denial

Matthew 16: 21-27

Jesus begins to let his disciples know that he has to go to Jerusalem to die. Peter forbids him to do this. Jesus rebukes Peter and lets everyone know that whoever wants to follow him must deny themselves and take up their cross.

The following is an email I received from a good friend and I am quoting her with permission. She was just emerging, full of grace, from an extremely difficult time in her life. She discovered the *true* meaning of taking up her cross and practicing self-denial:

I've been thinking a lot about what we discussed during our visit and I am feeling freer and freer all the time. I think that is essential to living in the moment. When you are at the beginning of the journey, trying to balance and understand the church's role in our salvation, 'how to be good' and then wrestling with all that as you develop your own conscience and beliefs - living in the moment is so hard! It's got so much more fear and uncertainty at those stages. You want to 'cover your butt' - make sure you are 'building up enough 'points', even if not with full awareness. But once you trust that you are truly loved, once you can abandon your future and your salvation to that God who loves you, THEN you can be in the moment. I am feeling freer not to focus on keeping the law. Not to say that his directives aren't important, but they flow naturally out of loving relationship. If you keep trying to follow the directives without the loving relationship, it sort of becomes bean counting, and a 'you owe me based on my faithful obedience' exchange. I want more freedom that that. I want to live NOW, not wait for heaven. I want joy! I want self-sacrifice too, but to have it flow out of joy, not fear, not a bartering tactic. (Michelle Holmes)

These words are a perfect illustration of how we should listen to this week's gospel. It would be easy to interpret Jesus' words as a hard and inflexible perspective about the rigors of following him. In the first stage of the spiritual life, when we hear the words "deny yourself", we endeavor to accept all our sufferings willingly and perhaps try to add to the pile, not just because Jesus suffered and carried his own cross willingly but also because we fear that if we don't pick up our crosses, there'll be payback time later on. There's a subtle hope that if we carry all the crosses that come our way, the reward will be a pat on the back and free entrance into heaven. That's how the first stage goes. It's a stage of learning the rules and growing up straight and strong. It's in this stage that we learn the parameters of the law and develop our inner moral compass. We focus on what's expected of us. We could say that the first stage is about learning self-control.

The next stage is discovering how to be out of control.

Last week, Jesus told Peter his name was, "Rock On Which I Will Build My Church". This week, Jesus speaks about his coming Passion and Peter gets right back into gear. His statements would have been shocking anyway but Jesus talking about going to his death did not fit in at all with the visions and expectations that were swirling around in Peter's head. "Jesus can't talk about dying! We're going to build a church together!" Peter immediately rebuked Jesus because what Jesus said didn't fit in with Peter's idea of how things should be. It didn't fit in with his desire to keep Jesus in his pocket as a talisman to keep around, someone who would bring good luck and keep everything on track and everyone happy. To Peter, Jesus was still the 'Magic Messiah': if you rubbed him just the right way, amazing things might take place. Peter was willing to let Jesus be in control as long as what Jesus did fit into Peter's idea of what Jesus should do. As soon as Jesus indicated that life might not fit into Peter's perceptions of what was right and good, Peter's false self kicked in and tried to gain control. *'God forbid it, Lord! This must never happen to you.'*

'If any want to become my followers, let them deny themselves and take up their cross and follow me.' The ultimate denial of self is to say to the false self, "You have no idea of what should be happening and you have no capacity to understand what is truly needed in any situation." What false self wants to do is to get control, make judgments, put everything into categories, decide what is right and what is wrong and then strive like crazy to make everything happen according to those judgments and categories. The second stage of the spiritual life is where we discover that the perceptions of the false self can be very faulty and that we have absolutely no capacity to really know how our judgments and actions will affect the lives of those around us or affect us personally. The false self would view "letting go" as being flung precariously into the winds of circumstance but when we finally trust in God's immense love and say, "Your will, not mine," we start to discover immense freedom. As my friend put it, *"...once you trust that you are truly loved, once you can abandon your future and your salvation to that God that loves you, THEN you can be in the moment."* It is false self that takes us out of the present moment where God dwells, shoves us into the chaos of our own limited visions and fears and makes us fight hard to make sure our spiritual life is under control. We pray but we pray with certain outcomes firmly in mind and do everything we can, to make sure those outcomes are realized.

When Jesus invites us to deny ourselves and take up our cross, he is inviting us to be out of control. It is indeed a cross for all of us to step down off the platform of false self. The circumstances that lead us to allow God to be in full control are often situations of great inner crucifixion and pain. These crosses present us with cross roads or crisis points where we can either decide to continue to fight and struggle to keep everything in line with our set in stone perceptions of what's spiritually right and necessary or we can decide to step down, let go of the awful responsibility of being 'right' and walk into the resurrection power of a life that flows out of the freedom and joy of being loved by the God of the present moment.

'For what will it profit them if they gain the whole world but forfeit their life?' When our false selves are in control of our spiritual life and are struggling mightily to stay in control, we are forfeiting real life. We can make everything happen that we think should happen, we can line everything and everyone up according to the pictures in our heads and we can be totally right - but the real life of knowing our true names and knowing how beloved and cared for we are is forfeit.

In this week's gospel, Jesus is inviting Peter - and us - to discover greater freedom and peace by taking our minds off of human perspectives and moving our hearts into divine truth. Remember, in John 6:63, Jesus said, *"It is the spirit that gives life; the flesh* (false self) *is useless. The words that I have spoken to you are spirit and life."*

The false self is utterly useless. Can you deny it?

Transitions

Matthew 18.15-20

Jesus is teaching his disciples about how to resolve problems and disputes within the Christian community.

After reading this week's gospel, I wondered how Jews in the time of Christ would normally resolve disputes. I discovered that the Jews would ask the "bait din" (house of justice) to meet. Highly educated rabbis who were supposedly completely impartial would listen to both parties and award a judgment based on the Jewish law, not the Roman law.

Jesus knew that this Jewish system of justice and dispute resolution would not work out well for his community of followers after his death so he had to set up a new way for them to resolve problems and disputes. The 'bait din' or the Sanhedrin was supposed to be impartial and disinterested but Jesus knew that it was rife with corruption. At that time it was an old boys' club where appointments were given to close friends and relatives or to those who had enough money to buy a position. Jesus certainly was not going to get a fair trial at their hands and his followers would stand no chance of being treated fairly by the traditional Jewish court. Besides, the Sanhedrin operated on the Old Covenant and Jesus was establishing the New Covenant, a covenant in which mercy, love and forgiveness would be substituted for 'an eye for an eye'. If you read the verses leading up to and following this week's reading, you will get the whole context. Jesus speaks in-depth about not hanging a millstone around the necks of his beloved, about leaving the ninety-nine and going out and finding the one lost sheep, about forgiving each other seventy times seven, about receiving God's mercy and passing that mercy on to our neighbors. Jesus was establishing a completely new order of justice.

All this made me think about those good Jewish men and women listening to Jesus and hearing him speak about this new order for the first time. To us, his words are so familiar because we've heard these gospel passages over and over. We're so accustomed to phrases like, 'love your neighbor' and 'forgive as you have been forgiven' that we almost have to struggle to pay attention. Christ's words are standard operating procedure – in theory if not in practice. But to Christ's disciples, it was radical and really shocking theology. The more they listened to Jesus the more they were thrust into a time of immense transition, a time where their lives were rapidly shifting and where they had no maps to guide them. They only had Jesus.

What kind of shock waves did they experience as they went through this time of shifting from one spiritual foundation to another? Were there moments when they were filled with homesickness for the simplicity of the old ways? Was it tempting for them to go back to a spirituality where they knew the routines, were familiar with the traditions and understood what was expected of them from day-to-day?

Transition from the known to the unknown is terribly difficult. It's even more difficult if the shift was not planned and if the unknown is laced with difficulty. Transition can feel desolate and lonely. There's no easy way through transition. It has to be walked moment-by-moment, step-by-step with the eyes focused firmly on God as one navigates the unfamiliar and sometimes terrifying terrain.

Very often, transition brings with it an inability to pray in ways that were once comforting and God can seem confusingly distant, as if he's just an idea with no real meaning. The spirit can feel dry and irritated by spiritual precepts, precepts that were once comforting but now seem more like sharp brittle twigs, not supportive, life-giving branches. The disciples must have struggled terrifically with what was now expected of them. How should they pray and act within Jesus' unfolding, completely new theology? There must have been times when the temptation to run back to the familiarity of the old law was overwhelming. Some followers succumbed to the desire for comfort and safety and left when Jesus' words were just too radical. "Will you also go away?" he asked the twelve. "Lord, where would we go? You have the words of eternal life." What a brave and faith-filled admission that was. "We don't really understand what you're talking about or where we're all going to end up but we have to trust that you're taking us where we should go."

There are times in our spiritual journeys when our hearts are so dry and confused that all we can say to the Lord is, "Where else can I go? You have the words of eternal life," and our words are a cry from a wasteland where nothing inspires, nothing nourishes and where moving forward seems impossible. If we experience this inner barrenness and are lost in the desert with no inner clarity or direction, it's easy to feel guilty and to treat it as a personal failure.

There is no failure here. There is only the hand of God shepherding us across the wasteland toward fresh water and abundant food. How else can God move us on into the wide and beautiful unknown if there is not first an inability to find sustenance in the known?

At any given point, every one of the disciples had a choice. They could move forward with Jesus into the confusing and sometimes terrifying landscape of new ways, new thoughts, new procedures, new perspectives, new relationships and new dangers, or they could run back to what was safely familiar: the old law and the comfortable old ways. What seems safe because of its familiarity can honestly feel like the best place simply because it is known and understood. However, when God is moving us through transition, running back to what is familiar and safe will stifle inner growth and prevent deeper insights into the wonder of life with a loving God who won't allow us to stay in our comfort zones if we are slowly atrophying and aren't even aware of it.

Being willing to move forward is not a rejection of the past; it is a recognition of the maturing process we should all be embracing. As we grow and develop, our needs change. It's as simple as that. Are you still praying the same prayers as you were ten years ago? Has your image of God or Jesus changed over the years? Has your image of yourself changed? Are you growing more compassionate and less judgmental? Have your spiritual desires become deeper? Do you pay attention to your spiritual desires or know what they are? Has there been an increase in the number of times you communicate with the Lord throughout the day? Are you growing more grateful and graceful? Are you afraid of God or are you discovering the supreme joy of his companionship?

The spiritual life is a *whole* life. This is the concept that Jesus presented to his disciples every day. He brought them out of an existence of simply attending to the law and into a life permeated with challenges but rich with growth and amazing revelations. Challenge, growth and revelation continued until death for all those disciples who did not turn back. There was no point where any one of them could say, "O.K. I'm all done. I've got the basics and I'll just coast from here."

Often we don't seek opportunities to move forward and grow because we can't fathom what we could be doing differently or how we could be thinking in a different light or from a different angle. We need to reflect on the fact that from one day to the next, the disciples had no idea what Jesus was going to put on their plates next. There was no way they could have anticipated his next step or his next teaching. They must have woken up every day anticipating what was in store for them and wondering how Jesus was going to stretch them once again beyond the boundaries of what they thought they knew. We have to consider how crucial it was for them - and ultimately for us - that they struggled through their confusion, that they accepted the risks and that they didn't run back to old familiarities. They were called to transformation and so are we.

Just because we are familiar with most of the words in the Gospels doesn't mean any of us have gone the distance to where we are called to go on this amazing journey. Here is a good way to measure your spiritual life:

If you're comfortable where you are, you need to move on.

The Power of Conversion Part I

Matthew 18:21-35

Peter asks how often he should forgive and Jesus tells him seventy-seven times. Then Jesus tells the parable of the king forgiving a slave all his debts but then the slave went out and demanded payment from those who owed him money and would not let them off the hook. When the king found out he handed the slave over to be tortured until he could pay his whole debt.

"Wicked slave!"
"...in his anger..."
"...over to be tortured..."
"So my heavenly Father will also do to every one of you..."

Tell the truth, now. Aren't those the words that rattle around uncomfortably in your head after you read this Gospel? These are the kinds of words that, taken alone, can form an unwholesome image of the Father in our hearts and create in us an unhealthy fear of God and of our own humanity. We are negativity magnets. No matter what we read or listen to, what stick with us are the negative, the scary, the wounding and the hurtful. Why don't phrases like, "out of pity for him..." or "...released him and forgave him the debt..." become the words that inform our hearts and our images of God? They don't because we are afraid of ourselves.

When we retain words like "slave, anger and torture", we are reacting in fear because we know we're guilty without even needing to do an examination of conscience. However, the knee jerk reactions we get into, such as kicking ourselves, struggling to forgive someone when we haven't been successful so far or becoming mired in a self-induced puddle of guilt, are reactions that will get us nowhere fast. We become like Sisyphus, the king who was condemned to rolling a boulder up a hill, watching it roll back down and then repeating the process forever.

It never enters our consciousness that *before* the angry king berated the slave so strongly, he had forgiven the slave a huge debt. The slave had personally experienced unconditional mercy and extravagant forgiveness. The king had given him an outrageous gift of freedom, joy and relief. The king could have said, "O.K. You don't have to pay your whole debt now. Let's draw up a payment plan that you can handle." That would have been generous enough but the king, in pure mercy, forgave him his whole debt. Everything. He had to pay nothing, ever. He walked away a free man.

The king gifted the slave with an open door into a new way of living in freedom. Remember, Jesus was introducing New Covenant justice to his disciples, a justice based on unconditional love and mercy. In Jesus' parable, it was the king who opened a new door to a higher law and a higher spirituality. The slave virtually slammed that door in the king's face and immediately returned to the old system of justice, which was "an eye for an eye and a tooth for a tooth." The slave went back to the law. He not only took advantage of the king's mercy but he also showed utter contempt for the New Covenant of love. His sin was not so much in turning around and demanding another slave to pay up, as much as it was in showing clearly that he had rejected the king's covenant of mercy and was determined to live by the old law. Therefore, the king handed him over to the old law. And if you want to live a tortured existence, live according to the law and not according to love and mercy.

The slave would not have been culpable if he had not personally experienced the complete forgiveness of his debt. If he had simply heard about another slave being forgiven a great debt or if he had heard some people in the market place debating the idea of forgiveness, he would have had just a sketchy intellectual knowledge of this new order of justice. It wouldn't have made much of an impact on him and if he had come across someone who owed him money, the ideological idea of mercy and love would simply have remained just that - an ideological idea without power or known consequences. His whole point of reference would still have been the Law.

But the slave in Jesus' parable had an eye-opening, intimate encounter with mercy and had known what kind of consequences mercy has: peace, freedom from fear, a clean slate and room to breathe and praise. The slave, in other words, had a life changing conversion experience. He knew the power of that kind of justice but still he turned away and rejected the power of love - and therefore rejected Love himself.

Have you had a conversion experience? Or have you just heard about love and mercy? Have you come face to face with the King in fear only to have him tell you that you are completely free and that there is no debt to pay? No. Debt. To. Pay. You owed him more than you could ever have repaid, you were in crushing debt for life and he said, "No, there's no debt. It's been completely cleared by...let's see who paid your debt...oh yes! Christ paid your debt. You're free and clear. Remember to thank him on your way out." Have you had your whole world shifted by his immense gift – or have you just heard about it? Did you grow up hearing about it and always assumed that you knew the meaning of 'forgive as you have been forgiven'? Do you personally know the consequences of forgiveness or does forgiving those who have hurt you feel like a boulder God requires you to push up a mountainside all on your own?

The problem with endeavoring to live any part of the new spiritual order without first experiencing the King's gift of life-shifting love, is that you actually are trying to move boulders and the only tools with which you have to move them are intellectual ideas and tenets. Loving without knowing God's love, being merciful without having experienced God's mercy and forgiving without truly knowing God's forgiveness are hard, hard, hard things to do. Especially forgiving. It's so difficult because without conversion we try to be our own sources of power. We feel like it's our responsibility to be good and do well at being a Christian. We are fearful and tight about our limited inner resources and then, when someone else depletes us even more by not respecting our dignity or undermining our authority or by saying something about us that's critical or wounding, we deeply feel a jagged hole within. It's as if they snatched something away from us without permission. They stole something from us and they owe us. Whatever they took feels vital to us; otherwise we wouldn't be so wounded and concerned about getting it back.

In the King's kingdom, as a converted soul you not only receive forgiveness of debt but also the gift of yourself. As a converted soul you see yourself reflected like gold in the King's eyes. As a converted soul you know that you are a wondrous creation and you rejoice in that creation. The more you experience conversion, the more you know how beloved you are. The more you know this, the less likely you are to experience inner loss at the hands of another because your value and self-worth do not depend on how other people perceive you or treat you. The more you know the King's love, the less you will feel that everyone who has hurt you owes you because they stole something from you.

When you experience conversion and know what it is to have all your debts forgiven, the only thing you can say to people who have hurt you is, "You owe me nothing. The Lord paid for both our debts and he paid abundantly." You can say this in truth, honesty and with great love because you know it's true. You've seen it in the King's eyes and there's nothing else to say. There's nothing else you want to say.

Anyone who experiences such a gift would be crazy to go back to the law. As I said before, the law is where the torture is. The law is where God is an 'eye for an eye' deity. The law is where we see how guilty we are and how we have no ability to do anything about it. The law is a room devoid of love, a city with no mercy and a kingdom without Christ. Don't believe me? Read Romans.

Forgiveness without conversion is a cart without a horse. Sure, you can move it a bit by yourself with a lot of struggling but you'll get exhausted and the smallest of obstacles will confound you. And if there's a hill? Forget it.

Conversion is a Kingdom Clydesdale. You don't push it – it pulls you.

The Power of Conversion Part II

Isaiah 55: 8, 9
God says through Isaiah that his thoughts are different than ours and his ways are higher than ours.

Matthew 20: 14-16
Parable of the landowner, who hires laborers throughout the day and then at the end of the day, pays everyone the same wage.

The first reading and the Gospel this week are passages of scripture that are difficult to put into context. We accept the Gospel because it is the word of God but it is a contradiction to our natural way of perceiving justice. This week's parable is one that's on par with the Prodigal Son. Who wouldn't commiserate with the laborers' shock that the last would be paid the same wages or empathize with the resentment of the faithful, obedient older brother who had to stand by and watch his completely irresponsible sibling get a party? How can we view these scriptures in a way that makes us leap with joy rather than grumble in frustration?

Conversion. We need conversion to come close to the heart of this week's scriptures as well as to other scriptures that seem to place God way out in left field playing his own mysterious game while we all huddle around home plate struggling to learn the moves and play within the rules of what sometimes seems like a completely different game.

Conversion. Normally we think of conversion as the one time act of turning from one thing to another. I was a convert to the Catholic Church. Unless I decide to leave the church and convert to Buddhism, I won't seek conversion in that way again. As it is,

I'm here and I'm Catholic. Done. However, within the spiritual life, conversion is a journey that's never done and unless there is awareness that conversion is a constant need, the journey will stagnate. We will stop growing. It's like brushing our teeth – it's a good healthy discipline but it won't produce new teeth. We're just maintaining what we've already got.

Conversion: causing something to change in form, character or function. Con means 'altogether' and vertere means 'turn'. As soon as anyone says, "I don't need conversion. I was converted a long time ago," that person has shut down and has gone into basic maintenance mode. The openness to conversion means openness to being *altogether turned around*. If you look again at the scripture passages above, you will gather that to move closer to the mind of God we not only need God to turn us around altogether, we also need him to lift us up to the point where we know that *all* our thoughts and *all* our ways are limited and inadequate when it comes to knowing him. Without conversion, we can understand this but it becomes a heavy burden as we try to shoulder the responsibility for all our inadequacies and limitations. After conversion, knowing how limited we are is a precept of utter joy for it means that we can let God be God and we can let our false selves – those selves that have such a poor handle on everything – die and fade away.

We know that dying is part of the spiritual life but what is harder to grasp is that just because we need to die to something, that thing is not necessarily bad or sinful. Listen: *Unless a grain of wheat falls to the ground and dies*...there will be no conversion. The grain of wheat cannot develop in its present form but its present form is not a mistake or a failure - it's just not enough. The simple fact is, death must occur before a grain can develop into a new and different form of life. We all need to die to the false self because it retains images and pictures of God that may not be bad but are as incomplete as grains of wheat are incomplete before they die and begin to grow into stalks and leaves. The false self resists changes to its treasured images of God. If the images can change, it means that lots of other things may change too and that is a very insecure feeling. The false self hangs on desperately to what it thinks it knows. The incomplete images are part of false self's sense of identity. Loss of those cherished images could mean a loss of self.

As soon as we capture some images of God and try to make life work according to images we possess, we slowly lose sight of God. That doesn't mean he leaves us or loves us any less. It just means we've stopped looking at *him* and have made our image of who he is and what he expects of us into a substitute for his real presence. Every image we have of him is two-dimensional, inaccurate and lacking in depth and power. I can take a photo of a sunset and hang it in my living room but that doesn't mean the sun is actually rising and setting beside the fireplace. The photo is simply a reminder of something that happened in the past and has no dynamic life of its own.

We have no power to change our images into present creative life. A conversion moment is a moment when we are given the grace and power to behold a portion of God's reality and realize that all the perceptions we had of him until that moment are like faded and torn photographs. We no longer desire to hang onto those old images because they cannot even begin to compare to the beauty of God's present moment reality. Conversion is a series of turnings: turning away, turning to, turning from and turning into and there comes a turning point where it becomes quite clear that we cannot capture and own God. Conversion introduces us to a life that dances on the pinhead of the present moment. We can't 'make it work'; we can only be there in gratitude.

Conversion is a gift from God. That means that you cannot

convert yourself. You cannot do anything that will make you more or less worthy of conversion. You cannot demand it; you can only desire it and be open to it. And, yes, you have to turn up at the vineyard. You might be first or you might be last, you might be faithful or profligate, you may be a cloistered contemplative or one who is trying to keep up with the frantic pace of secular life but God's gift of conversion is for all who turn up. Extensive religious knowledge is most unnecessary. Previous experience will not prepare you. You will never be able to imagine where conversion will take you until God converts you and takes you there. The mind and heart of God cannot be comprehended in the way we like to comprehend things. The authentic spiritual life is not a possession we can 'own'.

Conversion often occurs during or after times of great crisis or stress. Sometimes God has to take us through crisis to strip us of all the captured images of him that we've got buried within us. He needs to disable the sources of inspiration that were right for a time but now are not. He wants to replace the garments that we have outgrown. If we always have to have a handle on everything, always have to be in control, always insist that everything fits fine and never allow ourselves to experience doubt we can miss that conversion opportunity. The period leading up to a conversion experience can feel painfully stormy and uncertain but it is the living breath of God blowing our boat to shores we never knew existed.

Paul says in 1 Corinthians 2:7-11, *"No, the wisdom we speak of is the mystery of God—his plan that was previously hidden, even though he made it for our ultimate glory before the world began. But the rulers of this world have not understood it; if they had, they would not have crucified our glorious Lord. That is what the Scriptures mean when they say,*
"No eye has seen, no ear has heard,
 and no mind has imagined

**what God has prepared
for those who love him.**"
But it was to us that God revealed these things by his Spirit. For his Spirit searches out everything and shows us God's deep secrets. No one can know a person's thoughts except that person's own spirit, and no one can know God's thoughts except God's own Spirit."
(New Living Translation)

We can never plumb the depths of what God has prepared for us. No matter where we are in our spiritual journeys, we can never assume that what we know about God or how we have experienced him so far is pretty much all there is. There will always be hidden treasure waiting for us. There will always be something more prepared for us if we are willing to let him take us there. There is no saint or mystic who deserved or deserves conversion more than any one of us. Saints and mystics are the kinds of people we think God chooses to receive the blessings of conversion; however, God has a vastly different take on these things. The first shall be the same as the last and the last shall be the same as the first – and all are welcome to the feast.

The only thing *we* can do is turn, yearn, seek, be open to the risk - and wait.

...but those who wait for the Lord shall renew their strength, they shall mount up with wings like eagles, they shall run and not be weary, they shall walk and not faint. (Isaiah 40:31, NRSV)

The Power of Conversion Pt. III

Matthew 21: 28-32

Jesus tells the Pharisees the parable of the father who asked his sons to go and work in the vineyard. The first refused but later decided to go. The second agreed but did not go. Who did the will of the father? The Pharisees agree that it was the first son. Then Jesus tells them that tax collectors and prostitutes will enter the Kingdom before they will.

Jesus' parable of the two sons seems self-evident. Of course it was the son who actually made it out to the vineyard who did his Father's will. That seems so obvious. Jesus compares tax collectors and prostitutes to the son who changed his mind and went to the vineyard after all, which leaves the scribes and Pharisees being uncomfortably represented by the son who confessed willingness but didn't carry through on his commitment. I'm not sure Jesus' audience of religious authorities even understood what he was getting at. As busy leaders, they would have seen themselves as very task oriented for God, laboring daily in his vineyard. They would not have found it easy to grasp that Jesus wasn't really talking about working for God. He was talking about having enough humility to know they were as much in need of conversion as the tax collectors and prostitutes.

In other words, they needed to realize that religious busyness does not necessarily mean that one has experienced conversion. John preached repentance as the crucial starting point of the Kingdom journey and when anyone asked him about the practicalities of repentance he was simple and to the point. Scribes and Pharisees listened to John's exhortations but felt no need to change how they were doing anything or be 'altogether turned around'. That was for other people.

That got me thinking. How easy is it to miss our own need for conversion? What kind of mindset did the second son have that made him think it was all right to say yes in principle but not carry through in action? Was he lazy, devious and dishonest – or did he simply hear the request and decide that he was too busy with all the other things he was doing on behalf of his Father?

What about the first son? Was he uncaring and irresponsible? Did he resent his Father's request but eventually give in to it out of guilt? Or was he, too, very busy doing what he thought the Father required? Did he immediately refuse to go to the vineyard because he was already up to his ears in taking care of what he thought was his Father's business? He may have been heavily involved in tasks he *assumed* were important to his Father and those tasks had become his kingdom of operation, a kingdom where he was the boss and much depended on him being on top of things and remaining in control. How could Dad ask him to work in the vineyard like a common laborer when he had all these other important tasks to do?

Perhaps what the first son became aware of was that his Father had never actually asked him to take care of all the stuff that he felt was requiring his immediate attention. Perhaps he suddenly realized that going to work in the vineyard was actually the only thing his Father had directly asked him to do in quite awhile. Maybe he intuited that it was not so much a request as an invitation and began to grasp something that turned his whole attitude around: being busy on behalf of his Father was not the same as being in relationship with his Father and learning first hand what was really important to his Father's heart.

The only thing that could have changed the son's mind and heart and given him clear insight was a conversion experience. He needed a revelation to make him understand that it was time to find out what his father thought was important and stop being so sure that his agenda was his father's agenda.

That was the attitude Jesus was railing against. The scribes and Pharisees were so certain that they knew God's agenda. They were very busy important men and they had their little kingdoms to look after. John preached a very simple message: "Be honest. Act with integrity toward your neighbor. Be lovingly generous with what you have. Don't bully people." This message was far too simple for these very busy and self-important people. They probably listened and thought, "Yeah, yeah, yeah...whatever. That's a message for a sinner, not for a good religious person like me. I know all that."

"I know all that." Dangerous words. They're dangerous because they block us from what we *don't* know. At any point in our Christian journey, admitting that we know very little is a freeing truth. It is a very humble but awesome prayer to say, "Lord, I know so little. Teach me what I don't know." It helps the heart recall that the adventure of this life is not to know it all but to learn and that no matter what we have learned or how much we have perceived, there is always far more to discover.

I want to impress upon you that I am not advocating that everyone should up and quit their parish ministries and stop serving in order to navel-gaze and meditate on "What don't I know?" What I am saying is we must not assume that we don't need conversion simply *because* we're busy. Sometimes busyness masks the deeper needs of our hearts and sometime busyness distracts us from really listening to what we are actually being called to do.

The vineyard in Jesus' parable didn't just represent the world our priest sends us out to at the end of Mass. The vineyard is also the heart of the Father and, like the 'Back to the Land' movement of the 60's and 70's, heading into God's vineyard is often accompanied by a great desire for a return to simplicity. When he asks us to open ourselves to conversion, he is saying, "Come home to the vineyard of my heart. Come and see where I live. Discover your daily tasks in the center of my creative love. See with my eyes, hear with my ears, let my hands guide yours as you work with me in the soil I have prepared for *you*. Don't make your home within your assumptions of who I am and what I want because your assumptions limit your understanding and are misleading. They can never encompass the glorious universe of my ways and my thoughts. In my vineyard, the small becomes large, the first becomes the last, the least becomes the most and every day I set up a feasting table under the Tree of Life. Come back to my heart. Come back to simplicity of a natural spiritual life. Come home."

Conversion: the act of turning around and going back to the land, back to the vineyard of the Father's heart.

They Shoot the Messenger...Don't They?

Matthew 21.33-46

The parable of the landowner who built a vineyard and leased it to tenants. The tenants keep killing the slaves who come to collect the produce and finally the landowner sends his son, whom they also kill. Jesus tells the Pharisees that God will take the Kingdom away from them and give it to a people who will produce the fruit of the Kingdom.

There is a hard question facing us in this week's Gospel: Are we a people who are producing the fruits of the Kingdom?

There are two ways to look at this question. We could ponder on it from a personal point of view, examining ourselves to see if our lives are producing good fruit, which is an exercise we should all engage in regularly. The other more difficult approach to this question is discerning whether our own faith community is producing the fruits of the Kingdom. Is there any danger of God taking our vineyard away and giving it to those who will produce those fruits?

Nah. God doesn't do that anymore. Does he?

He may not confiscate vineyards anymore but there's no doubt that innumerable vineyards have experienced the pain of seeing their vines wither and die. Many of us have belonged to or heard of parishes that were blooming with good fruitful life but then ran into conflicts, challenges and problems with the leadership or with groups of people within the community. Different factions drew their lines and established their territories. Anger spread like wildfire. There were hurtful divisions and wounds that festered. There were those who walked out in despair and those who grimly stayed to fight on. Once this happens to a community, it takes years to heal and once again become healthy and fruit bearing. No matter where you live, it's not difficult to find a faith community that has gone through the wars. These communities need God to send them a prophet to lead them to conversion and healing - and the people will only experience conversion if they are ready to listen. It's not easy to hear a prophet point out that your vineyard is no longer productive.

An anointed prophet does not come to just point out all the wrong attitudes, all the hypocrisies and all the traps people have fallen into; the anointed prophet will also re-awaken people to the amazing love of God. The prophet points to the withered vines and asks the people, "Will you not put down your swords and pick up the tools of your calling so that once again you will be fruit bearing people?" The prophet reminds the hearts of the people of what it felt like when they were tenants in a loving and healthy relationship with the landowner. The prophet will also recognize the smallest glimmer of life still within the vines and, with God, nurture this fragile life back to full health.

If the people don't want to hear and be healed or nurtured then prophets are usually killed. Sometimes they are killed by indifference and sometimes by the swords of angry confrontation and defensive criticism. In that case, even the Son's presence does little to soften the soil of the hardened hearts so that the vineyard can become a land of abundant harvests where the tenants actively seek the landowner, are able to recognize him and will openly welcome him. God no longer angrily abandons his people but he won't force his way into a vineyard that has stopped seeking him.

In Jesus' parable, the tenants kill the landowner's son, reasoning that maybe they will inherit the land. What? How can they think that they will inherit the land from the landowner after killing the landowner's prophets and his son? At that time, it was Jewish law that after someone had settled and worked a piece of land for three years, they owned the land. Kind of like squatter's rights. Perhaps when the landowner was an absentee landlord, the tenants were tempted to feel it wasn't fair for the landowner to claim a share of the produce when they were doing all the work, dealing with all the problems and making all the decisions. If they could just thwart the landowner's attempts to collect his due for three years, they could claim the land as their own.

It is a subtle but common situation within faith communities for the people to become possessive of their vineyard. It's an easy slide from an attitude of healthy responsibility, working the land and producing good fruit for the Landowner, to an unhealthy attitude of personal possession: "This is *our* community, *our* group, *our* program, *our* fruit..." The longer one has worked in the faith community, the more tempting it is to feel that one has earned the rights of ownership. Within the healthy attitude, there is simply gratitude for good provision received: safe shelter, abundant food and the warmth of communal life. There is always an awareness that the land is not their own and that they must always consult with the landowner and his Son before they make decisions. In the unhealthy attitude, the understanding that the land does not belong to the community is completely lost or ignored. They feel that it is theirs, that they are the ones who have built it up into a productive vineyard and that they have a right to form it into their own image. This possessiveness creates defensive stances and tendencies to attack anything or anyone who seems to threaten their right of possession or threaten the communal identity. Sometimes this leads to a community that is spending far more time in defensive positioning than in tending the land and producing a good crop.

Every faith community, whether it's a parish, a religious order, a diocese or a smaller group within any of those larger communities, needs to be aware of the trap of pride of ownership and of the desire to defend their prized possession. If they don't watch out, they will discover that the barriers they build to protect themselves are not only keeping out threats against their established ways of doing things but are also keeping out the Landowner, his prophets and his Son. If that is the case, God will hand over the privilege of producing his fruit to other communities, ones that have not been destructively divided against themselves and have not taken prideful possession of the Landowner's property while building walls and arming themselves against the prophets God sends.

A prophet is not just one who has strong opinions about all that is wrong and no qualms about expressing these opinions to anyone who'll stop for minute to listen. Opinions are not prophecy. A Prophet is one who, like Isaiah and Christ, experiences a powerful conviction that floods up from the innermost being and one who says, along with Isaiah and Christ,

"The spirit of the Lord is upon me;
the Spirit of the Lord has anointed me."
"He has sent me to bring good news to the poor,
to bind up the broken-hearted,
to proclaim liberty to the captives,
and release to the prisoners;
to proclaim the year of the Lord's favour,
and the day of vengeance of our God;
to comfort all who mourn;
to provide for those who mourn in Zion—
to give them a garland instead of ashes,
the oil of gladness instead of mourning,
the mantle of praise instead of a faint spirit.

Then they (the prophets and the people) will be called oaks of righteousness,

the planting of the Lord, to display his glory.
They shall build up the ancient ruins,
they shall raise up the former devastations;
they shall repair the ruined cities,
the devastations of many generations. (NRSV)

May the Lord raise up many prophets for our wounded communities.

May they not be killed.

Robes Required

Excerpt from Matthew 22: 1-14

The parable about the king at the wedding feast, who saw a guest with no wedding garment. The king tells his servants to bind the man hand and foot and throw him into the outer darkness.

Jesus certainly had no trouble letting let the Jewish leadership know that they were on rocky ground if they persisted in resting on their assumptions that they were the chosen, the elite, the blessed ones of God just because they were born to the Jewish race and faith. The parables of the wedding feast, plus others of the same ilk, were exceedingly dangerous ones for Jesus to put before the Jewish elders. I have this amusing image in my head of the disciples standing behind the crowd and facing Jesus, using mime to indicate that Jesus should re-think what he was saying. Fingers slashing across throats. Exaggerated pantomiming of zipped lips. Heads deliberately shaking while silently mouthing, "Stop NOW!" But Jesus knew that there was already a cross with his name on it; holding back would not gain him any points. Matthew wrote his Gospel for the Jewish people and Matthew related parables that pointed out that Jesus was serious about the fact that entrance into the Kingdom was not guaranteed just because someone was born Jewish and had all the right paraphernalia or even performed all the right actions. God looks at the heart not the outward show and it's still the same today.

What Jesus was saying to the Jews was, "Going to the synagogue doesn't make you a good Jew anymore than standing in a barn makes you a donkey." The modern translation of that is: Going to church doesn't make you a Christian any more than standing in a garage makes you a car. No wonder those leaders were out to get him.

Then Jesus finished off the parable with a somewhat obscure and alarming addition where the king orders his servants to bind up a guest and throw him into the darkness just because the guest had no wedding robe. Just before that, scripture said the king sent his servants to round up anyone they could find, good or bad. If the king was so anxious to find guests to come to the wedding banquet, why would he pick on one poor soul who wasn't dressed properly? Maybe the fellow was one of the poor and didn't own a wedding garment. Where was the sin?

In the time of Christ, it was the host who provided all male wedding guests with a white garment called a 'Kittel' to wear into the banquet hall. It looked a little like a bathrobe and it had no pockets. The robe was white to signify unity with the bride. It had no pockets to symbolize the act of marrying for love, not for what material possessions could be gained by marrying the bridegroom. For a guest to enter into the banquet hall with no robe on was completely inexcusable and utterly rude. The guest in Christ's parable had been caught out and he had no defense. He was not there in unity with the bride but was there for whatever he could gain.

So, now another hard question faces us: how often do we go to Mass, the great celebration-wedding feast, without our wedding garment? What would that look like in our attitudes and our expectations?

- The wedding garment that the host provided for the guests was white so that they could show their unity with the bride who also wore white. She wore white to signify purity. Our wedding garment was given to us at baptism where Christ clothed us in himself and in dignity but it is completely possible for any one of us to show up at the feast with that wedding garment hidden away.

- If there is no inner intention of or desire for unity with the bride of Christ, which the people of God represent, the wedding garment has been left in a closet somewhere.

- When we instigate or take part in any talk or actions that could bring wounds or division to the community, the bride of Christ – or even hurt to just one member of the body – we are refusing to wear our robes. Disagreement within the body doesn't necessarily mean disunity. It's how we work it out with each other in respect and love that shows unity with the bride's garment. We should be wearing the full robes of integrity, peace, mercy, wisdom, understanding, humility, gentleness, patience, faith ... wait, I'm describing the fruit of the Kingdom that Jesus alluded to in last week's Gospel. Interesting how all these things are woven together, isn't it?

- When we come to get, not give, we are coming to the feast with deep pockets. In last week's blog I spoke of the trap of wanting to possess the vineyard instead of simply being servants within it, dependent on the landowner's generosity. It is so easy for us to begin valuing and guarding our placement and position rather than simply appreciating the goodness of the host. We start making sure that we're getting what we feel is owed to us and that no one else is getting more than they deserve.

- We all have times when we go to Mass for our own spiritual benefit. If we are not open to interacting much with those around us or we go just to 'fulfill an obligation' and to receive our weekly merit badge for Mass attendance instead of being there because we are a royal priesthood called to serve God and one another, we have misplaced our pocketless robes. Remember, the lack of pockets symbolizes a relationship built on love and on what one can give not on what one can get.

A white robe is a great equalizer. When we recognize that everyone is wearing exactly the same garment as ourselves, it's not as easy to categorize and dismiss others. Nobody is too young, too old, too new, too poor, too rich, too ignorant, too knowledgeable, too insignificant or too important; everyone is simply a cherished invited guest at the feast, participating in a celebration of joy and being united with the bride and with one another.

White is not only a symbol of purity; in some cultures, white signifies death. At the wedding banquet, donning our white robes is a kind of death to self-importance. It says, "I am no more important or powerful or needed than you. We are both here for no other reason than that the King and his Son invited us to come. They opened their doors and their storehouse and sought us out of the highways and by-ways to come and be a part of the celebration. We are here because the King wants us, not because we have a right."

A wedding feast is the celebration of a love relationship. By feasting with the bride, the groom, the king and all the other invited guests, we affirm that love is the foundation of a holy union and of holy unity. We see the bride and the bridegroom gaze into each other's eyes and behold the joy lighting up their faces. We know that in the married life there will be challenges, struggles, wounds and hardship and that these messy times are going to affect all of us because of our unity with them. But we all need to keep returning to the feast, keep returning to the love exchange and keep remembering that it is love that keeps us all afloat. You can have good rules, great programs, strong disciplines and cherished traditions and many children but if love has been forgotten or lost, it is a cold and empty house.

The banquet is ready, the guests are arriving, the music is playing, the bread is broken and the wine is flowing. Let's get our robes and go to the feast.

Go And Do Likewise

Matthew 22: 15-21

The Pharisees, wanting to trap Jesus, send their own followers to ask him if it is lawful to pay taxes to the emperor. He answers that they should give to the emperor the things that are the emperor's and to God the things that are God's.

This is a Gospel passage in which Jesus is not just smart; he is brilliant. His brilliance has to do with the complex trap the Pharisees planned and sent their disciples to execute, and with how Jesus immediately saw the layers within the trap and neatly sidestepped all of them.

Jesus' immediate response to the ones who were challenging him is very interesting. The Pharisees had sent their disciples because they figured that if they came and put the question to Jesus, he would recognize who they were and be alerted to their scheming. They wanted Jesus to relax and say what he really thought, but Jesus knew exactly what was going on. He could read minds and hearts like they were open books. He could see through flattery and pretenses of innocence. He knew when antagonistic people were in his presence.

Did Jesus love the scribes and Pharisees who were challenging him and trying to trap him? Did he love the ones he knew were just waiting for him to make a mistake so they could crucify him? Answer: Of course he did. He died on that cross for them as well. He loved them deeply and yearned that they would allow him to soften their hearts. He wished fervently that they could know his Father's love and be freed from their greed and malicious behavior. But he also had an inner awareness of who could and who could not receive him.

Jesus had the gift of knowledge and insight that came from a relationship with the Father. He could read people and he immediately knew their inner thoughts, intentions and motivations. He could tell if someone had even the tiniest spark of spiritual desire within him or her. Isaiah said, *"He will not crush the weakest reed or put out a flickering candle,"* (Isaiah 42:3, NLT) but Jesus was also given the knowledge of when the light had gone out completely and when the love of power, status and riches had eradicated all love for God. He knew when it wasn't time to fan the embers. When he discerned a heart that had locked itself tight against his love, he did not waste time being accommodating or trying to reason with the person.

Jesus could have engaged any one of those Pharisees in a full on Talmudic debate and he could have won with no difficulty. They would have just hated him even more. He could have treated them with kindness and mercy. They would have despised him and crucified him anyway. He could have taken each one aside and pointed out every wound and every desire they had ever had that led them to a place of such hardness of heart. Their pride would have denied it all and they would have looked even harder for evidence against him.

Jesus didn't seek them out. They came to him. They sought him out to lay their traps and try to find fault but Jesus knew their hearts and he didn't spend time trying to bring them around. There were too many other people who needed him, wanted him and were ripe for the Kingdom. There were so many others who thirsted for his teachings and who desperately needed his healing touch and his love. When the Pharisees or the elders came around to question him, he answered their questions but he always got straight to the heart of the matter, exposed their hidden intentions, said what he had to say and walked away.

I wonder what Jesus would have thought of the question, "What's the Christian thing to do?" There seem to be two main common assumptions when it comes to that question. The first one is the assumption that the Christian thing to do is to always put up with the garbage, always give in and always try to do the most loving thing – and there are plenty of scriptures to support this assumption. The second assumption is based on the belief that the scriptures justify natural negative impulses and strong reactions. There are plenty of passages where Jesus showed anger or Jesus got upset with injustice or where Jesus put the Pharisees in their place.

I think Jesus would shake his head sadly at both assumptions. If we studied what Jesus constantly did so that we could define 'the Christian thing to do', we would discover that Jesus didn't have an agenda or a set policy. He simply listened to his Father. He was so in tune with his God and had such an intimate relationship with his Father that his understanding of what God required of him in any situation was instantaneous. Jesus didn't act out of impulsive emotional responses nor was he saddled by a simplistic generalized ethos of what it means to 'be a Christian'. He wasn't just making it up as he went along but he and the Father were definitely creatively responding very appropriately and powerfully to challenges, conflicts and needs as they presented themselves.

In John 5: 19 and 30 (NRSV), Jesus says *'Very truly, I tell you, the Son can do nothing on his own, but only what he sees the Father doing; for whatever the Father does, the Son does likewise. The Father loves the Son and shows him all that he himself is doing."* and *"I can do nothing on my own."* He did not heal unless he saw the Father healing. He did not teach unless he saw the Father teaching. No knowledge or miracle came from him alone and there was nothing he said to the antagonistic Pharisees that did not first come from the Father. His Father's voice was his delight, his shield, his fortress and his only guidance – and it should be ours as well.

When in doubt, the safest thing to do is love. You can't go too far wrong even though you may find yourself in a time-consuming, heart-rending, no-win situation with someone who is more likely to grind you down than change their ways. However, what you really need to do is get close to the Lord. Develop an intimate relationship with him. Fall in love with your Father and become familiar with his voice so that when it comes time to discern how to respond to the people in your life who are anything from challenging to downright abusive, your whole desire is to know what God sees is appropriate to the situation and for the person you're dealing with. God may call you to selfless love or call you to walk away. He may call you to be completely honest and to set firm boundaries or he may call you to tolerance. He might call you to strongly point out an injustice or he might tell you to walk softly for a time.

Ask for the gift of insight into the hearts you're dealing with and an understanding of the Lord's heart. Whatever he calls you to do, he will provide the grace to do it. Understand that you will never be called to resentment or revenge and be very wary if you think he is calling you to angry confrontation. I would check that one out with a spiritual mentor - several times! So much destruction can – and has – come out of unleashed rage erroneously labeled 'righteous anger'. Respectful confrontation is one thing but angry confrontation can cause wounds that are terribly difficult to heal – not only in the one you confront but in yourself as well. It's a two edged sword.

The main thing is not to assume that God always expects you to act in one certain way. He will appreciate your efforts to act in love but he will appreciate it even more if you go to him and ask for his perspective and his direction. Pray and listen – and then pray and listen some more. Seek him without assuming you know the answer. It's difficult to become familiar with the voice of the Lord if all you can hear is your own mind telling you, "If you were a *real* Christian, you would..." It takes time to be able to let go of preconceived ideas so that you can differentiate between your voice and God's voice. No, it's not easy. But guess what? It took Jesus 30 years.

Grow into a relationship with the Father. It's the 'Christian thing to do'.

The Third Element

Matthew 22: 34-40

A Pharisee, a lawyer, asks Jesus what the greatest commandment is. Jesus answers that we should love the Lord our God with all our hearts, all our souls and with all our minds. He says that the second greatest commandment is like the first; we should love our neighbors as we love ourselves. The law and the prophets hang on these two commandments.

In the time of Christ, all Jews agreed that the greatest commandment was the Shema: *"Hear, O Israel: The Lord is our God, the Lord alone. You shall love the Lord your God with all your heart, and with all your soul, and with all your might."* In Deuteronomy, God commanded the Israelites to memorize these words, teach them to their children and bind the words on their hands, foreheads and doorposts. However, there was disagreement about what the second greatest commandment was. Ultra conservative Jews, led by a scholar named Shammai, believed it was "Keep the Sabbath." The Jews who were less strict about the letter of the law and more in tune with the spirit of the law, would have answered as Jesus did: *"Love your neighbor as you love yourself."* The lawyer questioning Jesus was, among other things, probably trying to discover which school of thought or what yoke Jesus ascribed to.

Hillel the Elder was a famous Jewish scholar in the time of Jesus and when someone asked him for a concise summary of Judaism, he reputedly replied, "What you hate for yourself, do not do to your neighbor. This is the whole law; the rest is commentary." Jesus was obviously familiar with Hillel.

We are all good with the command to love God with everything we've got and we all agree that the Golden Rule is an excellent rule to live by. But our thinking gets a little cloudy when we get to "as you love yourself." If you pressed most people to define that part of the commandment, they would admit that they never assumed it meant that God was commanding us to love ourselves. They would most likely say that it meant that we tend to be self-serving and that God wants us to put that self-serving energy into serving others. Fair enough. There certainly are people who could use a little redistribution of their 'service energy'. But, you know, most people I talk to and listen to don't have that problem. They love God and try to show that love through service to others. Their problem really is that they don't love themselves at all.

If Jesus immediately knew what he considered the greatest and the second greatest commandments, we have to assume that he lived those words. We know he loved his Father with all his heart, soul and mind and we know the dramatic and far-reaching consequences of his love for others but here is a question that is never discussed much. Did he love himself?

Somehow, I just can't see Jesus going to prayer and belittling himself before his Abba. We know Jesus was without sin, but according to the Jewish leaders and according to common interpretations of the law, he was a major sinner. As he was growing up, how much did he have to struggle with accepted definitions of the law as opposed to his inner understanding of the heart of the law and the heart of his God? What finally led him to know that who he was, what he did and what he taught was not sinful? Was it intellectual knowledge of all 623 of God's laws or was it the intimate knowledge of how much he was loved by his Father? When he began his public ministry, was he able to teach, heal, set free, create something out of nothing and raise the dead just because he intellectually knew the greatest commandment was to love his God or was it because he had experienced firsthand the incredible love his Abba had for him and saw himself through the Father's eyes?

Jesus loved himself completely. That's not very comfortable for us. Many sources have taught us that self-love is selfish love. It's true that very often self-love actually is selfish love when it is not grounded in the kind of love relationship with God that draws one to seek him with heart, soul and mind. Many people can't conceive of a self-love of the kind that flows from deep relationship because they have not been told it is possible to completely love themselves without falling into the sins of selfishness and egotism. There is a common feeling that it's much safer to show God how aware you are of all your failings and inadequacies than it is to thank him joyfully "that I am fearfully and wonderfully made." (Psalm 139:14)

Jesus' teachings are whole teachings that lead us to the best possible way to live the spiritual life. If egocentricity has us wrapped up in self-love and then we try to love others the way we love ourselves, our love will not be healthy or very effective. Our love for God would also be limited because our thoughts would always keep coming back to how God is responding or not responding to our wants and needs while we try to figure out if we have done enough to earn God's approval. Egocentric self-love sees a relationship in terms of "Quid Pro Quo" or "This for That" – an equal exchange of goods or services. There is a tendency for the false self to say to God, "I did that for you so you should do this for me. That's not the kind of self-love Jesus meant.

When Jesus said to love others as you love yourself, he was speaking of the kind of love he had for himself: a respectful love, a love that acknowledged the wonder of God's creation and intention, a love that allowed him to be fully in the presence of his Father without fear or condemnation. He loved his God with abandon and he intimately knew the love God had for him. Not only did he know it but he also accepted it and reveled in it so much that he just had to share it. He loved each person he met because, through his experience of God's love for him, he knew the value and beauty of each one. In loving others and beholding them as marvels of God's creation, children who were loved unconditionally by his Father, he would fall in love even more with his God. He dwelled within a dynamic circle of eternal delight and from that ever flowing delight came a river of powerful compassion toward all of God's creatures.

The circle of God's love is a creative powerhouse. God calls us to that circle and calls us to participate in the power of his creative love. Jesus said, "Love each other as I love you." Jesus doesn't call us to hazy reflections or cheap imitations of him; he calls us to become the real thing. He calls us to fall in love with him, with the Father, with one another and with ourselves.

If two parts of the circle are present but the third is not, it's a lopsided circle and it's more difficult to experience full joy. Sadly, many people's circles are missing that vital third element of knowing that God is in love with them. This is a knowledge that goes beyond catechism lessons and beyond the theology books. It's heart knowledge. If the Father is perfect love and he loves you, how can you *not* love what the Father loves?

When you know that God is in love with you,

- you love being with him, walking with him and listening to him. Who doesn't enjoy being in the company of their Beloved?

- you don't consider yourself perfect or sinless. You know you need healing for many sins and failures but joy accompanies this knowledge because you also know God desires to heal you and that he *will* heal you. Instead of shouldering the unbearable burden of your inadequacies and struggling to change yourself, you walk with freedom and joy in the light of your God who will love you into change and growth. There's a reason Reconciliation is called a celebration.

- you love others in a different way. Your love is not patronizing or forced or given because it's expected. You are able to see the immense beauty, value and worth of others and you treat them with respect and even amazement because you know that God delights in you. Because you know God's compassion in your life, you are able to bring forgiveness and true compassion to others as well as receive the forgiveness and compassion of others.

Love of God, love of others, love of self: the full circle of Beloved Life. But it's hard to feel 'beloved' if you don't let yourself 'be loved'.

Try it and see.

31st Sunday Ordinary A

Rekindling The Flickering Flame

Matthew 23: 1-12

Jesus speaks to the crowds and his disciples and warns against the Pharisees. He encourages them to do as the Pharisees teach but not to do as the Pharisees do. They lay heavy burdens on the shoulders of others, they covet status and recognition, and they covet the places of honor. He says that all who humble themselves will be exalted and those who exalt themselves will be humbled.

Years ago, I attended a conference in Banff Alberta, which was also attended by all the Liturgical experts of the Canadian Catholic Church. Because the term 'good liturgy' was a common buzz phrase at the time and there was lots of disagreement as to what it meant, I decided I was going to approach each one of these well-known leaders and ask them to describe, in 25 words or less, what good liturgy was.

It turned out that asking them was not an easy task because none of them seemed too keen on hobnobbing with the common folk. At the breaks they would huddle together in small groups and engage in earnest discussion. I would stand there at the edge of a group until they noticed me and then I asked my question. They kind of looked at me and then looked at each other in discomfort. One fellow finally said, "Well...uh...it's all in the books. Read our books."

At one point I noticed this nondescript little man watching me. He was present each time I approached a group. Finally he came up to me and said, "I overheard you asking about good liturgy. It's a good question. Let me introduce myself..." His name was Frank Henderson and most people who had anything to do with liturgy at that time or in some years to come would have heard his name. He was the editor of, and a major contributor to, The National Bulletin on Liturgy, a publication most churches subscribed to and one that all the Liturgy experts would have contributed to regularly. In other words, he was the foremost liturgist in Canada. Frank adopted me for the weekend and sat with me at every liturgical celebration as we discussed liturgy, what it was, what its purpose was and where the challenges were. We continued our discussion by correspondence after the weekend was over. Frank was not just the editor of that publication; he was also an oncologist with a busy practice. He was a humble man.

Frank taught me a lot about liturgy. However, what had the most impact on me was that he was a man who didn't consider himself too important or too busy to make himself available to someone with an interest in learning. He gave me face and affirmed my worth. It was a gracious gift from a kind man who had no need to advertise and protect his status to define his own value.

Status. Jesus was castigating the scribes and Pharisees for their desire for status. He wasn't so much saying that titles like 'rabbi', 'teacher' or 'father' were bad in themselves; he was saying that seeking these titles for the status they conferred was terribly wrong. Status seeking is born of egotistical self-love and the consequences are often heavy. Usually the ones who suffer these consequences are those who have no status at all, for as Jesus said, one of the habits of status seekers is to "tie up heavy burdens, hard to bear, and lay them on the shoulders of others." At the very least, as in the case of the liturgists, they subdivide people into categories: worthy of notice and unworthy of notice.

Status. It's a subtle temptation and sometimes it pulls us in ever so deceptively. What can start out with a good motivation to do something worthwhile for others can end up as a personal exercise in just maintaining the position. Status feels good. It feels excellent when others depend on us, admire us and respect our skills. It's satisfying...for a while. And then it's not. Then we need to find something else to give us more status. Admiration and approval is addictive. Power is habit-forming. We all need to constantly be on guard against the subtle lure of status.

What Jesus said in this week's Gospel would have shocked all the people who were listening, not just the scribes and Pharisees. To all of them, 'long tassels and broad phylacteries' were signs of God's blessing and approval. Jesus was confronting hundreds of years of an ingrained spiritual culture as he tried to convey the truth that the values of God's Kingdom were completely different from the ones the people had grown up believing in. And you know what? He still hasn't totally succeeded in convincing us, his people, that the Kingdom does not thrive on the same values and principles as those of the world. I almost didn't approach those groups of liturgical experts because I felt they were in a higher echelon and were too prestigious to have someone like me bother them. I was applying worldly standards to judge who was important and who wasn't. The sad thing was that they seemed to agree with me.

God bases his whole Kingdom value system on love. That means that unless love is the foundation, we are building on sand. God does not call us, or the church, to be effective like a big business corporation. Really, in terms of worldly standards, love is the most inefficient way of doing anything. It's not logical, it's not quantifiable, it doesn't make money and it can feel like a waste of time. If you advertise it, it loses its power. You can't wear it to make yourself part of an identifiable group. You can't legislate it or charge for it. You can't put it in a box and label it or copyright it. It's often not a winning proposition. You can't analyze its trends or make an app for it. You can't download it and so far, it hasn't gone viral. Pity.

The standard of love means that the heart of the person right in front of you is more important than the mission statement. It means that accepting a brother or sister unconditionally has more value than making sure people see you stringently applying the law – or see you doing anything that gives you status. It means being totally fine if someone else gets the respect and recognition for something you did. We all talk about how love is so important but we've lost the urgency and the understanding of why Jesus castigated the scribes and Pharisees the way he did. They had traded knowledge of love for the love of knowledge as well as ostentatious almsgiving, long blue tassels and showy prayer habits. While they inscribed the greatest commandment on a piece of parchment and bound it conspicuously to their heads and arms, they had lost the inscription on their hearts. Their hearts had turned to stone and their spirituality had turned into form and show.

If we all wake up and actively turn back to love, if we recognize love as a real power and embrace it as more than an ideal, if we let go of our pride, our personal goals and opinions, if we try to root out all that is within us that strives for recognition, approval and status, if we realize that love is what it all hangs on and if we start practicing the law of love with one person at a time, we will be astounded at the life and growth that will flourish around us.

Teilhard de Chardin said it wonderfully:

"Someday, after we have mastered the winds, the waves, the tides and gravity, we shall harness for God the energies of love. Then, for the second time in the history of the world, man will have discovered fire."

In the Kingdom of God, playing with fire is not only allowed, it's mandatory.

On Wisdom

Matthew 25: 1-13

The parable of the ten bridesmaids waiting for the bridegroom. Five were prepared with enough oil for their lamps and five were not.

The Gospel message this week is clear: stay awake, pay attention and be spiritually prepared. However, underscoring the whole message is the Wisdom Edge. There is more to this scripture than just being ready for any spiritual eventuality, be it the end times or otherwise. There is a call for wisdom. Not knowledge – wisdom.

Wisdom is the oil for the flame that lights our way, but very often people get confused between knowledge and wisdom. It's all right to strive after knowledge because some knowledge is valuable and very helpful. It's a great beginning. All the bridesmaids in the Gospel had knowledge, even the ones who ran out of oil. They knew that some night the bridegroom was going to come and 'steal' the bride to take her to the house that he was preparing for her. They knew that he was coming - they just had no idea *when* he was coming, because it could take as long as two years for the groom to build a home for his bride. The bride and her attendants had to always be ready to leave suddenly.

This accurate knowledge of the rituals, traditions and the special event the night might bring was what brought all the bridesmaids to the right place at the right time, engaged in all the right motions. But five waited with knowledge and wisdom while five waited with just knowledge. The ones who operated just on knowledge of the tradition had no real inner attachment to the possibilities of what the night could bring, so they didn't bother to have more than barely enough provisions. They were waiting because that's what you do when you're a bridesmaid. It was the rule. It was the ritual. It was the way it was always done.

Wisdom goes beyond the way things have always been done; it looks for the spirit behind them, seeks the depths, senses the promises, envisions the unforeseeable and listens for the unheard. Then wisdom waits patiently and hopefully for the consummation of the promise. Wisdom dwells in the spaces between the black and white of knowledge. It's in those spaces that the mystery of God moves and one of the most potent parts of the mystery of God is wisdom. Wisdom is a gift, one that we should all ache to have and seek constantly because it is a light that will keep us ready for the moment the bridegroom comes to sweep us all away to the celebration. We can only receive it if we ask for it.

In the first reading from Wisdom it says: *"Wisdom is radiant and unfading, and she is easily discerned by those who love her, and is found by those who seek her. She hastens to make herself known to those who desire her. One who rises early to seek her will have no difficulty, for she will be found sitting at the gate."* (NRSV)

Anyone can seek wisdom and what is so wonderful is that the most illiterate peasant can be full of amazing spiritual wisdom. Conversely, the most knowledgeable person can be very much lacking in spiritual wisdom. Spiritual wisdom is not the same as the natural wisdom that comes with life's experiences. Life experience can contribute to spiritual wisdom but there's a point where experience just can't prepare us to recognize or touch the heart of God and it can't build up the grace to wait in patient hope. This is where we discover that wisdom is sheer gift and grace. Past experience teaches us to wait for something already known so if we experienced Christ in a certain way at one time, natural wisdom leads us to expect him in exactly the same way again. Through spiritual wisdom, the Spirit soaks us in the understanding that God comes in his own timing, sometimes unexpectedly and often in a form we won't recognize if we're depending on what we experienced in the past or on what others have experienced. Wisdom gives us eyes that are open, ready and waiting to see the fresh unknown.

Wisdom expects the unexpected. Wisdom delights in the fact that God is always the same but always new, always coming, always here, always a surprise and always more than what we thought or imagined. Wisdom teaches us to wait for the only thing worth waiting for: Christ's coming. Whether it's for his coming at the end of the world or for his coming into our present moment, wisdom teaches us how to wait: with the oil of patience, full expectation and joyful hope. Wisdom reminds us of our baptism and whispers, "You are an anointed one waiting for your Beloved. Watch out...he's coming soon. Keep your eyes open."

Wisdom is also what teaches us how to appropriately apply any knowledge we have gained through experience. It isn't always what we think and it isn't always what knowledge suggests would be reasonable. I love this definition of the difference between knowledge and wisdom:

Knowledge is knowing a tomato is a fruit; wisdom is not putting it in a fruit salad.

If wisdom's ways were always based on what is reasonable, we would not know the shocking unreasonableness of God's love for all of us. Wisdom goes beyond the rational and the logical into territories we are not always familiar with. Just because we know in our heads that Christ died for us doesn't mean we have explored where this astounding love came from. We can only reach that region with wisdom as our guide.

I am going to end this reflection with one of my favorite scriptures. It's from the book of Wisdom, written by Solomon who cherished wisdom above all else and was greatly blessed by God because of it. I'm including it here because not everyone has a bible that includes the book of Wisdom.

Read this description of Wisdom and then ponder on the precious mystery that you are called to walk all your days in companionship with her.

The Nature of Wisdom (Wisdom 7: 22-30, New Jerusalem Bible Version)

There is in her (wisdom) a spirit that is intelligent, holy,
unique, manifold, subtle,
mobile, clear, unpolluted,
distinct, invulnerable, loving the good, keen,
irresistible, beneficent, humane,
steadfast, sure, free from anxiety,
all-powerful, overseeing all,
and penetrating through all spirits
that are intelligent, pure, and altogether subtle.
For wisdom is more mobile than any motion;
because of her pureness she pervades and penetrates all things.
For she is a breath of the power of God,
and a pure emanation of the glory of the Almighty;
Although she is but one, she can do all things,
and while remaining in herself, she renews all things;
in every generation she passes into holy souls
and makes them friends of God, and prophets;
for God loves nothing so much as the person who lives with wisdom.
She is more beautiful than the sun,
and excels every constellation of the stars.
Compared with the light she is found to be superior,

for it is succeeded by the night,
but against wisdom evil does not prevail.

The Word of the Lord.
Thanks be to God.

Buried Treasure

Matthew 25: 14-30
The parable of the man who, before going on a journey, entrusts three of his slaves with his money. To one he gives five talents, to the next he gives 2 talents and to the third he gives one talent. The third one buries his talent because he is afraid of his master.

The above is the shortened version of the parable where the master returns to find that all his slaves except one had done well with his entrusted property. The one slave who did not do well was scared of his master. Instead of wisely investing the money he had been given, he buried it for safekeeping. It's good background knowledge to know that one talent was worth 15 years wages for a laborer in those days so even the one talent the master had entrusted to his slave was not negligible. That was a lot of money. The master had a right to expect at least an effort to use it judiciously and he was justified in being upset with the slave for burying his talent in the ground thereby relieving himself of all exertion and all responsibility of discovering his unique capabilities.

The phrase we need to pay attention to in this parable is *"to each according to his ability"*. The master was shrewd and attentive to the skill levels of his slaves. He understood the abilities of the slave who only received one talent. He did not overwhelm this man with responsibility he couldn't handle and in the same way, the master understood the abilities of the ones to whom he entrusted larger amounts. He knew what he was doing. In that way, he was not only a fair and merciful master but also a master who observed his servants and knew what he could realistically expect of each one. Perhaps the problem of the servant who buried his talent wasn't just that he knew his master was a hard master; perhaps his problem was that he compared himself to the ones who were given more and upon observing their skills, became discouraged, gave up and said, "I'm no good. I'll never be able to make 5 talents like him. I don't know how to wheel and deal in the marketplace like he can. I'm not aggressive or knowledgeable and all I've learned to do is grow crops. I'm sunk. I'll just bury the talent in the garden where I can keep an eye on it."

He never thought that with his one talent, which was an enormous amount of seed money, he could have used his skills and started up a business of growing food for others. It would have been totally within his capacities and it would have made some profit for his master. However, if his idea was that he had to look just like the other slaves and operate exactly the way they did with the skills they had, it was game over for him. He was definitely going to fail or at least struggle mightily to hang on to that one talent.

Who has not gone through that agony of comparing oneself to someone else and feeling like an inadequate loser? There is a kind of backward spirituality in comparing self negatively to others. It's easy to feel that if we tell God that we know we're inadequate, we're failures and not as good as someone else, it will forestall him from making that judgment on us himself. Maybe he won't point his finger at us if we're already pointing our fingers at ourselves. Self-examination is a healthy thing but it can also become an unhealthy negative habit where we recognize what's bad about ourselves but are totally afraid to recognize what's good. We end up 'burying our talents' because we have this image of God as a hard master. Surely he will be happier with us if we bury our one talent because at least he'll know we aren't arrogant and cocky.

The master in the parable was, indeed, angry with the servant but not because he didn't make the same amount of money as the other servants. The master was angry because he did not give the servant more than what the servant could handle and he did not expect the same from that servant as he expected from the ones who received more talents. The problem was that the servant got all caught up in his negative self-analysis and in his fear of the master and didn't even try. He didn't even try to evaluate the positive aspects of himself and come to an understanding that the master only wanted him do what he was trained to do and use his gifts in the best way he knew how.

That kind of fearful lack of effort on the master's behalf is called going underground as a gifted creation of God. We are afraid of crossing a line and going to the other extreme. "Oh God, I thank you that I am not like other people. I tithe, I go to Mass on Sunday, I am busy in my parish..." We are honestly afraid of arrogance – and we should be. But if you have a fear of becoming arrogant, then recognizing and being grateful for your gifts and abilities will not lead to arrogance; it will cut arrogance off at the root. The trick is retaining and actively maintaining humble gratitude to God for *everything* that you are.

I don't blame the master of Jesus' parable for being angry, knowing that the master symbolizes God. I can understand that the Father would be disheartened if he created something uniquely beautiful, loved it, shaped it to have a specific reason for existence that no other created being had, and then that creature started looking at everything it was not created to be and decided it was no good. God might want to say to that creature, "Who do you think you are? Who gave you the wisdom to decide that you are not beautiful and not uniquely formed for a work made just for you? What gives you the right to second-guess my intentions and my decisions? Do you think you are greater than me that you can decide that you aren't good enough, strong enough, intelligent enough or gifted enough? Have you even thought about how I define success and value? Do you stop to think about what's valuable to me? Or are you always looking at someone else and deciding they epitomize what I want in everybody? Are you basing your judgments on the world's definition of success? Look at me. Look into my eyes. See what's there? It's called love. It's called delight and desire. *You* are what I desire – the you I created you to be. Keep your eyes on my eyes and don't ever look away because if you do, you'll start to fall into the bottomless dark pit of everything you are not."

What Jesus is telling us is that God would like us to go further than "do no harm". It's not enough to just maintain the essentials and keep ourselves out of trouble. It's not enough for him and it's not enough for us. It's not enough for him because he has given each of us a unique character, unique gifts and a unique role to play for the building of the kingdom and it's not our responsibility to decide that, compared to somebody else, we don't have much value or importance. And it's not enough for us because as long as we are judging our own capabilities and our value as insignificant or trivial we stay in a mode of fearing God as a harsh master and we lose out on the joy of being a true gift.

A friend emailed me recently. Because of an accident, she has struggled for years with her self-worth because she can't physically and mentally take on what she was once capable of doing. In her email, she said that she had decided to appreciate people more and to make sure she expresses that appreciation to them instead of just thinking it. I don't know if she realizes what an astounding journey she could be embarking upon and what that kind of ministry can do for the building up of the kingdom. If I had to choose between someone who speaks to thousands at conferences and someone who commits to saying to someone else, "Thank you for what you did and for who you are," I would choose the Ministry of Appreciation as the action that would have the most long-lasting impact on people and the capacity to actually change a community - especially if she expresses that appreciation to those who are usually in the background and who wouldn't often receive appreciation. I hope she does not compare her ministry to a ministry that has higher visibility and feel that hers is lacking or insignificant. The Church desperately needs her and many more people like her.

Unearth the buried treasure that is you. Dust it off and shine it up. It's priceless. It cannot be found anywhere else.

"Oh God, help me to believe the truth about myself, no matter how beautiful it may be."(Macrina Wiederkehr)

"Do not forget that the value and interest of life is not so much to do conspicuous things...as to do ordinary things with the perception of their enormous value." (*Teilhard de Chardin* SJ)

The Sparrow King

Matthew 25:31-46

Jesus says that whatever we do to one of his small ones, we do it to him and whatever we neglect to do for the least of his people, we neglect to do it for him.

I'm going to look at an aspect of this Gospel that isn't normally emphasized. The Gospel itself definitely a warning message to all of us about how critical it is to consider each person we encounter as a manifestation of Christ himself, but the message this Sunday is not only about caring for the unfortunate. This is the feast of Christ the King and in the first reading and the psalm we receive the understanding that he is not just a distant and removed king waiting for judgment day. He is a shepherd king, a king who walks with his flock and shepherds them. He is a parent, a father, an older brother and one who suffers with his people.

Whether or not you are a parent, you have or had parents and I would hope that when you were a child you experienced the secure feeling that came from knowing that if things got really rough, one of your parents would always go to bat for you. Wise parents allow their children to fight most of their own battles but they also discern when a child is in a situation where he or she is just not capable of dealing with the problem and needs a parent to step in and take control. Those of you who are parents can no doubt think back to many situations where your child was bullied or was ill or was struggling with a situation where you recognized that adult intervention was definitely needed. The point here is that a good parent doesn't just objectively recognize situations where a child needs help; a good parent acutely feels the child's pain. Even when parents judge that it's all right to allow the child to try to deal with the challenge, parents die a thousand deaths if they think their child is scared, hungry, alone or physically threatened. The feeling is, "When you do it to my child, you do it to me."

When you read or listen to the Gospel where Jesus says, "Truly I tell you, just as you did it (or did not do it) to one of the least of these who are members of my family, you did it (or did not do it) to me," think about a king who, like every good parent, is sliced to the core when one of his little ones is hurt, scared, lonely, excluded, sick, hungry or in an emotional, mental or physical prison.

Certainly we should always be aware of easing the suffering of his people, and that doesn't just mean other Christians. It means everyone. Still, to be able to effectively see Christ in the suffering ones, the small ones, the Anawim, we need to back up a bit and embrace the fact that we, too, are small ones. We all suffer. We all experience loneliness, fright, depression, spiritual or physical hunger, and all the traumas that go with being a broken human in a broken world. We all need to spend time pondering the fact that our king is not a king in absentia. He is not an unapproachable autocratic type king who sits on a throne of distance or disapproval. He is present with each one of us and when we are hurt, he dies a thousand deaths. Every good parent knows the truth of that.

When the Israelites of the Old Testament demanded to have a king over them rather than a judge, they said, "Give us a king to judge us like all the other nations have." They wanted their nation to look like the other nations of the world and God warned them that the kingdoms of the world they were wanting to emulate had rulers who took from the people. *"This is how a king will reign over you,"* Samuel said. *"The king will draft your sons and assign them to his chariots and his charioteers, making them run before his chariots. Some will be generals and captains in his army, some will be forced to plow in his fields and harvest his crops, and some will make his weapons and chariot equipment. The king will take your daughters from you and force them to cook and bake and make perfumes for him. He will take away the best of your fields and vineyards and olive groves and give them to his own officials. He will take a tenth of your grain and your grape harvest and distribute it among his officers and attendants. He will take your male and female slaves and demand the finest of your cattle and donkeys for his own use. He will demand a tenth of your flocks, and you will be his slaves. When that day comes, you will beg for relief from this king you are demanding, but then the LORD will not help you."* (1st Samuel 8: 11-18, NLT)

Still the Israelites insisted on a king and, except for the reign of a few good kings, kingship became equated with dictatorial inaccessibility, cruelty and bondage. Jesus came to turn the entire worldly image of a king completely upside down. He came to release his people from bondage. He came poor and whatever he possessed was freely given away. Instead of cruelty he dispensed healing and love. Instead of arrogance he displayed humility. Instead of intricate political maneuverings he walked in glowing transparency with no hidden agendas. Instead of building up armies and power, he built a group of twelve weak men. And instead of maintaining a cold, regal and demanding headship he became our Shepherd, our Father, our Brother, our Offering, our Healing, our Safety and our Beloved.

He became the Shepherd King, the Parent King who knows when it's healthy for us to struggle through and when it's time for him to step in and take over – if we will let him. He knows when we don't want him and he knows when we're longing for him like a deer thirsts for a running stream. But no matter what his wisdom knows is right and appropriate and no matter if he knows we will reject his hand or gratefully cling to it, his heart always acutely

---

feels our pain. It is imperative that we experience the truth that we are small and lost and that we have a King who comes to us daily with compassion, understanding and an open hand, not the clenched fist of enforced subjugation. If we do not first experience our own beautiful smallness and the astonishing healing humility of our king, our efforts to reach out to others in need will be sporadic, mechanical and often patronizing. We will find ways to give so we don't have to become involved.

I've said it before: you cannot give what you haven't got. You cannot share a compassion that truly heals if you have never experienced seeing your king coming to you in your own pain, coming in the rags of a shepherd to show that his authority does not reside in regalia but in the love he wears.

When you have experienced your king in this way, then when you go to others in need you will go to them with the full authority of the king, which is the authority of love. You will go to them as Jesus the King came to you saying, "You are my brother. You are my sister. Because of this I have suffered with you and whatever has been done to you has been done to me." We cannot go to the poor and suffering as if we are separate from them in any way because Jesus does not come to any of us separated from our pain.

I love the story of the man who looked out his window on a bitterly cold winter day and saw a flock of sparrows huddled in the snow, perishing from the freezing winds. There was a barn there and the door was open but the sparrows didn't understand that there was shelter, safety and warmth in there. The man went out and tried to shoo them toward the barn door but the sparrows would just take fright and fly in all directions before settling back on the frozen ground. The man sadly realized that the only way he could get the sparrows into the barn was if he became a sparrow. Only then would he be able to speak their language and lead them to shelter.

This is what our King did for us. He became what we are because he felt our pain. When we know that the king himself wants to lead us to healing warmth and shelter, how could we not do the same for others? When we do so, we are at one with the nature of the divine King – the King who does not separate himself from his people.

"May we come to share in the divinity of Christ, who humbled himself to share in our humanity." (Liturgy of the Mass)

YEAR B

And When He Comes Again...

Mark 13: 33-37

Jesus exhorts us to keep awake in case the Master of the house returns and finds you asleep.

Welcome to Advent. Welcome to the time of Arrival. Pay attention. Be aware. Keep alert. Keep awake. In the Gospel, Jesus' words have a sense of urgency and maybe even of danger. If we're not paying attention, the time of arrival could come suddenly and we could miss it. That would be a tragedy! Yes it would be a tragedy and it *is* a tragedy – because we miss him all the time.

The celebration of Advent in the church year has a three-fold purpose. The first two purposes are easy to identify: to focus our attention on the first coming of Christ and to reawaken our anticipation of the second coming of Christ at the end of the world. It's the third purpose that gets lost, not only during these next four weeks of chaotic Christmas preparation but also in the busyness of our whole lives. And what Jesus said in the Gospel holds true for every single day of our lives, not just for Advent. We don't know when the Master will come and he may find us asleep when he comes suddenly. The church graciously offers us this season of remembrance – a time to remember that not only did our Lord come and will come again but also that he is always coming, sometimes at dawn, sometimes during the day, sometimes in the evening and sometimes in the dark of night. Pressures and obligations distract us; we struggle with daily life or we are spiritually asleep and we miss him. It's true. All of us continually miss important Advents every day of our lives.

So, the Church offers us a season to renew our spiritual

attentiveness, but how? How can we sharpen up our awareness so that when the gifts have been opened, the food consumed and the lights and decorations are packed away for another year, we still have a spiritual alertness within? How can we develop a habit of anticipation and longing for his coming and his arrival? Prayer is the answer but often prayer is dry and uninviting or it has become a dull routine that we tend to hurry through – if we get to it at all with all the demands life dumps on us. The Christmas season is an especially difficult time to renew our sense of prayerful waiting simply because of all the added pressures and demands on our time. How, then, can we reconnect with prayer to make this period of waiting a time of true anticipation?

What would you like for Christmas from God? If you could ask for any spiritual gift, a gift that was for you and you alone, what would you ask for? Take some time to think about that and don't just give an answer that you think is the right one or an answer that you think would please your priest, your spiritual mentor or your friends. Somewhere deep inside of you is a spiritual yearning and it could be so deep that you haven't paid a lot of attention to it. What do you really want from God? The reason it's so important to name your deepest spiritual desires is because God put them there. Once you recognize and name a spiritual desire, go to God and tell him that this is what you want for Christmas. But don't leave it there. As often as you can remember, pray and ask God for the gift of your heart's desire.

This prayer shouldn't be a long one. The shorter the prayer, the better, so that you can pray it at any time no matter what is happening. I call it "Pocket Prayer". It's a prayer small enough to pull out of your heart any time of the day. When we were discussing such a prayer in a small group, one woman brilliantly termed it, "Tweeting God". Think in terms of a prayer of 140 characters or less. Less is better because in this prayer, wordiness doesn't count for anything, but continually turning to the Lord is critical.

Recognizing one or more of your inner desires is important for this Advent prayer because you will then pray from your heart with a yearning that underscores your waiting. Listen to what St. Augustine said about desire: *"The desire is thy prayer; and if thy desire is without ceasing, thy prayer will also be without ceasing. The continuance of your longing is the continuance of your prayer."*

What could be simpler? What could be more in tune with Advent, the season of waiting daily for the arrival of Jesus? You don't even really need words at all. All you need to do is turn to God, open your heart and show him your desire.

Something happens when you pray often like this. You start to develop a prayer life, not just a prayer time. Because your prayer is simple, short and frequent, you begin to "tweet God' about more than your inner desires; you begin to speak to him about everything. He becomes the receptor of all your thoughts. You develop a deeper sense of the God in whom you live, move and have your being. You awaken your awareness and you become more alert to the times when Jesus comes to you unannounced. You suddenly catch glimpses of him watching you in the eyes of another person. You will see him and welcome him in the middle of a busy mall, while you're at work, when you're walking down the street, when you look at the starry universe or when you're gazing at some magical Christmas lights. And then you will tweet him. "Thank you. The world doesn't know you but you are here. I can feel it."

Naturally, I can't guarantee that God will give you the specific spiritual desire of your heart right on Christmas day. God has his own calendar and his own perfect timing. Both Simeon and Anna in the temple waited patiently on God's timing for years and God blessed them with their own personal and perfect Christmases: *"Master, now you are dismissing your servant in peace, according to your word; for my eyes have seen your salvation..."* and *"...[she] began to praise God and to speak about the child to all who were looking for the redemption of Jerusalem."* (NRSV) If Simeon and Anna had not been prayerful people and had not been awake and fully aware of what the subtle manifestations of God felt like in their lives, they would have completely missed the Christ child. Really...he was just another baby in the arms of his mother. No one else in the crowd sensed anything special or wonderful about this particular child. But the hearts of both Simeon and Anna were so immersed in prayer that they immediately sensed they were in the presence of everything they had ever hoped for, desired and waited for all their lives. This was not a thunder and lightening-bolt revelation. This was a penetrating but subtle shift in the spiritual atmosphere. All the other weary, busy and distracted people in the temple missed it but Simeon and Anna knew without any doubt that the veil between heaven and earth had been dislocated just enough for the son of God to slip through into the world. They recognized him because they knew him. They were so familiar with him that even clothed in the humanity of an infant, they knew exactly who he was.

It was enough for them. It was more than enough for them.

Pray. Pray short but pray often and lace your prayers with thanks. Eventually, your prayer will become more than you talking at God. It will create within you a vibrant and aware heart that is awake and able to recognize the Lord when he comes.

And he *will* come.

Kingdom Storytellers

Mark 1: 1-8
John the Baptist appears in the wilderness to proclaim a water baptism for the forgiveness of sins. He prophesies that Christ is coming to baptize with the Holy Spirit.

As it is written in the prophet Isaiah, 'See, I am sending my messenger ahead of you, who will prepare your way; the voice of one crying out in the wilderness: "Prepare the way of the Lord, make his paths straight" ', John the baptizer appeared in the wilderness, proclaiming a baptism of repentance for the forgiveness of sins. And people from the whole Judean countryside and all the people of Jerusalem were going out to him, and were baptized by him in the river Jordan, confessing their sins. Now John was clothed with camel's hair, with a leather belt around his waist, and he ate locusts and wild honey. He proclaimed, 'The one who is more powerful than I is coming after me; I am not worthy to stoop down and untie the thong of his sandals. I have baptized you with water; but he will baptize you with the Holy Spirit.'

"History repeats itself." Usually when we hear that, someone is expressing something negative about the world and how, as a human race, we never seem to learn from our mistakes. However, we need to ponder on it in a more positive light when it comes to our spiritual life. When we listen to the Gospel at Mass, we are hearing the Church's story – its history. As familiar as it is, it remains somewhat removed from us unless the story we are listening to becomes the personal story of each one of us and becomes a deep part of our own spiritual history. If our own stories don't correlate to and exemplify the Church's story, we may need to examine our spiritual life to make sure it's a life and not just a dogma.

Have you ever had a John the Baptist in your life? Was there ever a time when you were longing for something more, wanting an upheaval that would break open a stream of life in the dreary dryness of your spiritual landscape? Did God send someone who spoke words that drew you to a river of inner change or who pointed out the One you were waiting for? The person may have been a friend, a teacher, a priest, an author or a speaker. Whoever it was, and whatever it was they said, those mountains that were overwhelming you seemed far less threatening. Either that or you just felt stronger and more able to move ahead and climb those mountains with excited determination instead of fear. Perhaps this person opened the Word in a way you had never heard before. Maybe they spoke of the love of God rather than the condemnation of God and inspired you to be gentle with yourself and eager to open your heart to the Lord.

If you can think of someone like this then God sent John to you. He sent you a voice that cried out to your wilderness, one that made your paths straighter and prepared your heart to hear the voice of the Lord. This voice turned you toward the Messiah and said, "There. There is the Lamb of God. There is the one you seek. Go, follow him." The reason you were able to take the first step toward the Lamb was because you heard the love in John's voice and you knew that this Lord who inspired such love was the Lord you wanted to follow too.

God sent you a John. God made the history of the Church part of your personal story and now the story of John the Baptist appearing in the wilderness, heralding the coming of the Messiah, is the story of you.

Perhaps you have been a John the Baptist to someone else. Have you ever gone through your own wilderness and come out stronger and more sure of who you are and who your God is? Have you ever found yourself at just the right time in the life of someone who desperately needed the comfort of a smoothed path? In the first reading, God said, *"Comfort, oh comfort my people. Speak tenderly to them. Tell them everything is all right."* (NRSV) Have you ever heard those words of Isaiah and felt a stirring within your soul? Then you are a John. What you have heard and learned in the wilderness is for the speaking of to the people. The history of the Church is your story.

Maybe you need a John the Baptist in your life right now. Are there crooked paths and rocky mountains blocking you? Have you been living on the edge of a wilderness longing for the Messiah to come to you? You can ask God for a John the Baptist to come to you but remember that in scripture, John cried out to many and not all responded to his words. The ones who came away unchanged and unmoved were those who thought they knew exactly what the Messiah should look like when he came. They had fixed preconceived ideas about God and who he was. They were unwilling or scared to change their ideas and perceptions and when John said, "Behold the Lamb," they could not see Jesus for who he was. Do you have set boundaries in how God can speak to you or touch you? Are you waiting for a God of the Old Testament, a God of condemnation, fire, thunder and upheaval? Are you open to a Messiah who may come quietly through surprisingly ordinary events? Are you willing to experience God's love and comfort? There are many who are not. They don't think it's allowed or they don't think they deserve it. Some don't think they need it and some are afraid of change even though their present spiritual lives are anything but satisfying. That, too, is part of the history of the Church and is being relived in the personal stories of many.

Advent is a good time for seeing our stories in Scripture and realizing that it is not just history we are listening to; it is the present moment Advent of our lives. We have voices in the wilderness among us and Jesus continues to come to us all. The wilderness is within us and the Jordan is available. We have yearned for our Messiah and we have fallen asleep waiting for him. We have pointed him out in love and we have been lukewarm and careless about his presence. We have accepted him and we have made judgments and turned away in self-righteousness. We are living out the story over and over. We write our stories daily and each day we have a choice as to who we want to be. We can be a John in the wilderness, a broken one being submerged in the river or Christ holding out a hand to someone in pain. We are free to choose if we are going to be open or closed. We are free to say yes or no to moving forward and to change. We just don't have the freedom to *not* be part of the story. Even those who think they have absolutely nothing to do with the story are a major part of it.

There is one other thing that is necessary: sharing our stories with one another. If we never communicate with others the flow and rhythm, the valleys and mountains, the rough spots and leveled paths of our own personal stories, the Liturgical community will never become fully what it is meant to be: all of us working together to integrate The Big Story into the world through the medium of our own stories. The Mass cannot remain to us an individual private time of worship because this is not part of the real story and it is not what leads to full Advent. When Jesus comes, he comes to create one unified story by inserting himself into each of our histories. If we never share, we never really understand what the coming of Jesus means in totality. If we are all strangers to one another, Mass almost becomes like spiritual technology – we push the right buttons and click on the right links and we follow the instruction manual – but we remain isolated from one another, never quite experiencing the fullness of the story come to life.

The readings during Advent and Christmas are beautiful and true but they aren't just 'once upon a time' stories. They are the narrative of our lives, stories we listen to and should resonate with deeply because:

We are the story. We are the Word made flesh.

We are Advent.

The Gaudete Three

In this reflection I will be looking at the first reading, the psalm and the Gospel.

Isaiah 61: 1-2, 10-11
(The spirit of the Lord is upon me. I will exult in my God and the desert will bloom.)

 Luke 1
(The Magnificat)

John 1: 6-8, 19-28
(John is a voice that cries out in the wilderness.)

In this week's readings we hear the words of Isaiah, Mary and John: the Gaudete Three. Each one was anointed by God to be Christ bearers and each one experienced a different essence of rejoicing so it is good to spend some time reflecting on the quality of the rejoicing each one experienced. None of them entered into rejoicing because life was easy and uncomplicated or because everything was going their way. From these three we learn that their spiritual rejoicing emerged not out of pleasant experiences but out of a full relationship with God, out of the anointing that was upon them, and out of their deep desire to be all that God called them to be. If we are to be a rejoicing people, we have to know where true rejoicing comes from.

Isaiah
"The Spirit of the Lord is upon me," Isaiah wrote. As God anointed him to bring his living word to a wayward people, he was given a glimpse of the coming Christ and was filled with the knowledge that there was more to come than an eternity of God angrily

chiding his people into obedience. Listen to what he says in the first reading: *"I will greatly rejoice in the Lord, my whole being shall exult in my God; for he has clothed me with the garments of salvation, he has covered me with the robe of righteousness."* (NRSV) Then he speaks of the bride and bridegroom and his joy is the joy of knowing that the Beloved is coming and he is coming with gifts. He will bring beauty for ashes, the oil of joy for mourning and the garment of praise for a spirit of heaviness. Isaiah saw the face of Jesus, the bridegroom who was coming to give himself completely for his loved one, to bind up her wounds and heal her shame. He foretold the virgin birth and he gave us images of the suffering Christ seven hundred years before the advent of Jesus. Isaiah's rejoicing came from being privileged to understand that God had a plan that was beyond anything anyone could imagine. Isaiah didn't know if the Messiah would come in one year or several hundred years but he still rejoiced because he had seen the perfection of completion and knew that the Messiah was coming to save not only the future people of God but also all people in all of history, Isaiah included. Isaiah was caught up in the timeless compassion and goodness of his God.

Mary

Mary! Mary possessed Pondering Joy. God anointed her to bring the Joy Of All Joy to birth but in the beginning of her pregnancy she had no idea what this would eventually look like. Everything about her pregnancy was completely out of line with the common perception of the promise and it was all so much bigger than what her mind could grasp. So she became a child and a woman of contemplative joy. Contemplative joy comes from complete abandonment to God. It does not demand immediate answers to immediate problems nor does it require God to conform to any presupposed ideas. As soon as Mary said, "Let it be done to me according to your word," she lost herself and gained insight into the quiet but explosive creativity of God. She was a vessel of his creative love. Pain and difficulty were already her companions but instead of being foes that she had to conquer, they were her friends to attend her on her way because she trusted so completely in the love of her God. *"My soul magnifies the Lord and my spirit rejoices in God my Savior..."* Her rejoicing ran deep and flowed straight to the heart of God – a river of connectedness, a current of immense trust that caused her to exclaim, *"Surely from now on all generations will call me blessed."* She felt so blessed and her joy overflowed.

John

"The rejoicing of John." That sounds like an oxymoron. In scripture he seems like a terribly serious figure, so sure of himself that it didn't bother him in the least to publicly and loudly point out hypocrisy and sin where he saw it - and he saw it everywhere. He knew his anointing was to prepare the way for the appearance of the Christ and no one was going to deter him. Because we tend to think of rejoicing as a happy emotion, it's a bit difficult to envision John rejoicing. But sometimes rejoicing has very different overtones from those of exultant happiness.

I would guess that John rejoiced with an awesomely serious joy, a joy that was born in and shaped by an unforgiving wilderness. That kind of joy would be a joy with no excess baggage and very few expectations created out of self-oriented desires. It would be a stark joy of simple purpose and few distractions and anyone who saw joy as a lovely feeling might not have looked at what John carried in his heart and called it 'joy' or labeled his responses as 'rejoicing'. It may have looked more like grief to them and they would have been partly right. What they couldn't have seen was the understanding that this terrible need to cry out to a deaf and blind people was balanced by a knowledge of momentous promise. Perhaps he was given a grave and solemn vision of all the stars and planets in the universe lining up in honor of the One who was about to begin everything the earth and heavens had been waiting for. I believe that out in the wilderness, John knew that all creation was waking up to the realization that the Christ had come and that the Christ was ready. It was time. The joy he felt made him want to roar, "People... WAKE UP!"

In the reflection for the first Sunday of Advent, I asked you think about what you wanted from God for Christmas. At Mass that same week, our priest asked the people of the parish a wonderful question: "What do you want to give birth to this Christmas?" Within the answer to either of these questions is your anointing and your path of rejoicing. Will you be like Isaiah, a man or woman of far-reaching vision, speaking of the promise of the coming Christ? Will you be like Mary, a quietly surrendered but strong vessel of the beauty of Jesus – someone who is pregnant with hope? Will you be like John, determined to clear a way for the one who will save, heal and baptize with the fire of the Spirit?

It is your anointing, your Name, that will fill you with a kind of rejoicing that cannot come from anything in this world and depends on nothing the world has to offer. The anointing of the Gaudete Three is your anointing. The same Spirit of the Lord is upon you and he has sent you to bring good news to the poor. He has clothed you with the same garment of salvation as Isaiah. He has looked with favor on you and has done great things for you like he did for Mary. And God has anointed you to bring the same knowledge of salvation to the people as John did.

He is coming. He is here. He is ready. Oh people! Find your path of rejoicing!

The Great Disturbance

Luke 1: 26-38
The angel appears to Mary to tell her that the power of the Most High will overshadow her and she will bear a son. She was very perplexed by these words.

There was a humorous story with variations that made the rounds on the Internet about a woman wondering why her husband was being quiet and withdrawn. In her head, she explored myriads of possible reasons, all having to do with the history of their relationship, their current problems and what she may have done to upset him. Her reasoning was complex and her conclusions were multiple. Then we get an insight into what the guy was thinking: "My truck won't start."

The Gospel this week says that Mary was much perplexed. In the Jerusalem bible it says that she was deeply disturbed. I'm thinking that Luke at some point asked Mary about that moment of annunciation and Mary tried very hard to explain what it was like to have an angel speaking those particular words to her. Luke probably listened patiently for a long time and then wrote down, "She was disturbed."

Fair enough. The Gospels were not written as mini-novellas with all the characters' thoughts and feelings opened up to us. They are records of specific events and the teachings of Jesus. Still, there are times when I'm reading the Gospels and I wish the writer could have written a little more than the bare facts. On the other hand, Luke probably could have written a whole book about Mary being deeply disturbed. I prefer 'deeply disturbed' to 'much perplexed' because I think she experienced something infinitely more profound than simple confusion or puzzlement over the words the angel said to her. When I read that Mary was deeply disturbed, it makes me think of a body of still water over which a strong wind begins gusting, sweeping and swirling. A Ruah (Spirit) wind. This wind of the Spirit was rushing over her and through her, moving her and evoking senses within her that were completely foreign yet strangely familiar - like echoes of a home known long ago, in a place somewhere far beyond memory.

The Spirit was roiling the waters in Mary's being. The moment the angel spoke, she was no longer just 'Mary'. She was 'Full of Grace' or 'Favored One'. She was "Blessed Among Women". She had heard her True Names and knew that nothing would ever be the same again. The dictionary meaning of the verb 'disturb' is: "interfere with the normal arrangement or functioning of". It wasn't just Mary's surface emotions that were disturbed so deeply by God; God was in the process of disturbing her whole inner and outer life.

Our God is a disturbing God. But you shouldn't take that statement and think it simply means that the struggles and challenges we all deal with every day are what disturb us. It's not just another way of saying that life is messy. God seeks to disturb you in the same way he disturbed Mary. He calls you by the Name he has chosen for you and if you listen for that name, hear it in your innermost being and, like Mary, respond with, *"Here am I, your servant; let it be done unto me,"* you will know a disturbance like no other. Like Mary, you will hear echoes of home. You will never be the same and your life will never be the same. And you wouldn't want it any other way.

The Advent time of conception, waiting, and bringing to birth can be a beautifully disturbing time if you allow it to go deep. It is the Name that God calls you by that beckons you, and it is the 'Yes!' of your heart that opens you. One of the reasons the Magnificat is so wonderful is because Mary was reveling in her name. She knew she was a simple servant but at the same time she also knew and fully accepted with joy that she was 'Blessed Among Women' and that all generations would call her 'Blessed'. She knew she was a vessel being used to bring forth the Son of God but she also knew how immensely and intimately loved she was. Her vocational Name and call was to bring forth the Son and, in giving her assent, she found her true self. God called Mary to a role in salvation history that none of us will ever experience but that doesn't mean we aren't called, like Mary, to listen, hear, respond and find our true selves in the eyes of the Father. She was the first mystic of the New Testament and she opened the way for us all. She didn't live in a monastery or have a lifestyle we normally associate with contemplatives. Anyone who looked at her without knowing the details of what was happening would have said she was an ordinary woman living an ordinary life.

This period leading up to Christmas is often hard on us. It's a time of inconveniences, weariness, pressure and often pain and loneliness, but this is where God meets us and where he calls our names. Mary's Advent was also full of these things. Life was also disturbing on the surface for Mary and it is disturbing for us. However, this is the chosen birthplace of the Son of God: in the midst of chaos, struggle, wounds and uncertainty.

Nothing became easier for Mary because she said yes to her Name and to her God. She wasn't exempt from the challenges of life. In fact, life became infinitely more challenging and complex for her. But Mary had been given a profound knowledge of something we all have access to within our own Names: a deep-seated knowledge that God is. That's it. God is. It's hard to finish that sentence with one adjective. We can say he is mighty but within that mightiness is a helpless infant. We can say he is terrible and awesome but within that awesomeness is a God who overshadows us in intimacy. We can say he is holy but within that holiness is complete accessibility, a God who humbly waits for us to crawl into his arms. The knowledge that 'God is' sets us free to be wide open to infinite possibility.

We can resist the challenges we face or we can open our hearts to allow the disturbance to go deep. We can allow ourselves to crash up against our solid God and suddenly discover, as Mary did, that God's solidity is like liquid gold that pours into our hearts and stirs up sudden remembrances of who we really are: Advent people, Christmas people, people who belong to another world altogether, people who are strangers in a strange land and are on a pilgrimage home. But before that we must learn how to allow ourselves to be disturbed, how to allow the Ruah wind to drive us deep into the Shekina overshadowing, a shadow made of fiery light. We need to learn how to be open to bringing the Child of the Light to birth in the small part of the world where God has placed us.

During this last week of Advent, try praying as often as you can, "Let it be done to me according to your word."

And then wait to be disturbed.

Upsizing For Light

Matthew 2: 1-12
The story of the Magi.

Wise men. Magi. Magicians. Astrologers. If these wise men were alive today they would most likely be called New Age practitioners and be looked upon with suspicion and perhaps even fear by Christians. At the very least they would be dismissed. It is interesting to note that at the time of Christ's birth, the people who should have been aware of the significant signs accompanying the coming of the Messiah, people like the scribes and Pharisees who studied the prophetic writings endlessly, had no idea that the Light had come. They were completely in the dark, blinded by their preconceptions of what the 'brightness of the dawn' would look like. Thick darkness had covered the people. God manifested his signs to all, but the ones who saw and responded to these signs were either social outcasts or strangers with strange practices who, according to the Jewish belief, should have been the last ones to be led to the light.

This should make us sit up and take notice. It should make us examine our expectations of what we think it will look like when Christ manifests his light in our lives. If we have set ideas about what is light and what is not or where the light will come from or how it will reveal itself, we may find ourselves groping in the darkness of skewed preconceived ideas. We all search for the light every day of our lives. We all hope, like the Israelites, that Christ will manifest himself in the midst of our sufferings and challenges to lead us to freedom. When he doesn't come the way we think he should we become terribly discouraged and end up blaming ourselves for lack of faith or blaming God for not paying attention to our needs. In the meantime, he is very present, attentive and active but he is unrecognized because we are looking for something entirely different.

Everything about the birth of Christ was an antithesis of all the common expectations of the Jewish people. Because they thought they knew exactly how the story would play out, they could not see the unfolding of an astounding Kingdom narrative in which God planted the Light deep within the ordinary night. The glory of the Lord rose upon them but their eyes could not see it. *"Then you will look and be radiant, your heart will throb and swell with joy,"* (NIV) wrote Isaiah. But it wasn't the Israelites who noted the star, followed it over a huge distance, saw where it stopped and were filled with joy. It was magi from a foreign nation. They were open to mystery however it manifested itself. *"When they saw that the star had stopped, they were overwhelmed with joy."* (NRSV) Overwhelmed with joy. That's a strong phrase. It's a little disconcerting to realize that in all the gospels, a respectable Israelite being absolutely overwhelmed with joy because of Jesus was relatively rare. Samaritans, Roman soldiers, lepers, prostitutes and those on the outer edge of acceptability were the ones likely to be overwhelmed by joy. For those who were educated about the Messianic prophecies, his presence was more likely to cause consternation, confusion, resentment, anger, fear and indignation. Joy seemed to come most easily to those who didn't really know who or what Jesus was *supposed* to be.

The first Epiphany – the manifestation of the Light to the Gentiles – was not an event designed to fire the intellect or affirm traditional expectations. This Light that reached out beyond the prescribed and acceptable borders was a visceral light, a light that moved those magi in their guts. Something far beyond them called to them and whispered of ancient yearnings fulfilled. It spoke to them about kingship, priesthood and death. The voice was irresistible. The voice of light was so magnetic and so consistent that even being led to a poor child with poor parents in a poor shelter didn't quench their joy; they understood that their minds could not define all the mysteries of heaven and earth and they knew they had no right to create definitions of the Light and keep those definitions in a well guarded box. All they could do was offer their gifts and weep for a people who could not see the glory that was right in front of them. Gold for kingship and Frankincense for priesthood were the gifts that Isaiah spoke of but perhaps those magi had an intuition that the darkness over Christ's people had only one possible outcome. Myrrh for death. Myrrh for burial. Myrrh for the journey beyond the grave.

We live in a dark world where it isn't always easy to discern the light but it does us no good to cling to our black and white talismans against the night. Like the magi, we need to be able to recognize God's pinpoints of light in the dark universe and be willing to strike out across a wilderness terrain without all our theological comforts around us. We need to be fully aware that the light can be a star, a child, a dream, a long arduous journey, a dangerous proposition, a diligent search, an overwhelming joy or a flight back into the wilderness. It is rarely what we expect.

We need to allow the Spirit to expand and open our hearts so that we, like the magi, can perceive and recognize the light. We often keep our expectations too small, too enclosed, too safe and too rigid to play host to a light that knows no boundaries and is always on the move, changing everything in its path. Isaiah said that we should enlarge the sites of our tents and let the curtain of our habitations be stretched out. (Isaiah 54.2-17) He was telling the Israelites that the Light was on its way and the light was bigger than anyone could conceive.

The light has come. The light is coming. The light will always be coming. It's still on its way.

Enlarge your expectations. Widen up.

Have You Found What You're Looking For?

John 1: 35-42

John the Baptist points out Jesus to two of his disciples who immediately follow Jesus. Jesus asks them what they are looking for and they ask him where he lives. They stay with him for the day then Andrew goes to get his brother, Peter, saying that they have found the Messiah.

What are you looking for? If you sat down quietly for fifteen minutes and visualized Jesus asking you that question, would you find yourself answering with generalizations – answers that you think are what every Christian should be looking for? Would you immediately think of all the spiritual gifts and solutions that you think you *should* have in your life? Or would you discover that you're not sure what it is you're looking for? Would you discover that it's hard to pinpoint what you are really looking for?

Don't feel bad if a clear and definite answer doesn't come immediately to mind. The disciples who followed Jesus didn't have an answer to the question either. They didn't immediately say, "We're looking for the hole in our hearts to be filled. We're looking for a faith that's filled with life and light. We're looking for peace and inner happiness. We're looking to find out who we really are. We're looking for the Messiah. Are you the one who can give us these things?" They didn't even get close to being able to answer with what their hearts were really searching for. They asked Jesus where he was staying because they had no idea what else to ask. They didn't realize it but asking him where he was staying was a beautifully right response. It was a Spirit-led response.

We always feel like we have to know the answers. We feel like we should know what we need in our spiritual journeys and we think we should be able to find the key to all the answers we need or want in our lives. When our definition of how our spiritual life should be manifesting itself doesn't match up to what it really looks like, it is hard on us. We allow the 'failure hat' to sit on our heads and we assume that we're not doing everything that is required and it's entirely our fault. We get discouraged or we hide behind overt busyness, hoping that others won't guess how close to empty our tank is. When we pray we think we hear Jesus asking us to do more, be more, give more, pray more, love more, suffer more and relinquish more until we are in danger of being completely 'more-tified'.

When we come to this point, we very much need to hear Jesus ask, "What are you looking for?" When we hear him ask that we should honestly respond, "Lord, I don't know. I have no idea what I need. I don't know who I am and I've forgotten who you are. I need to stop demanding that you come to where I live because I think I'm doing all the 'right' things. I need to leave myself behind and go to where *you* stay."

The disciples went to where Jesus was staying. What happened then? They listened to him and came away with a deep sure knowledge that he was the Messiah. What kinds of things did he say to them? In my experience, there is always one thing that will connect us immediately and deeply to the reality of who Jesus is and that is hearing him tell us who we really are – hearing him call us by our spiritual Names. You'll notice that in this week's readings there are several references to names:

John points out Jesus and says, "Look, there is the <u>Lamb of God</u>." The disciples ask Jesus, "<u>Rabbi</u> (which means teacher), where are you staying?"

Andrew says to Simon, "We have found the <u>Messiah</u>."

Jesus says to Simon, "...you are to be called <u>Cephas</u> (which means Peter)"
And in the First Reading, Samuel hears God calling his name in the night.

I fully believe that Jesus was not only teaching those disciples about his identity and mission, he was also showing them their true selves. He was revealing to each of them on a very personal level who each had been created to be. They knew then that they were in the presence of someone they would follow to the ends of the earth. When Jesus says your True Name, you know you have found what you were always looking for.

When Jesus saw Peter, he immediately called Peter by his true name: "Cephas" or Rock. Did Peter or the other disciples know where their names would take them or what they would have to do to get there? Absolutely not. The only thing they could do was follow Jesus and stay with him wherever he was day-by-day and moment-by-moment. They could say, "Here I am," but they could not make their own decisions as to what Jesus would require of them. They couldn't create themselves. They just had to stay with Jesus where he was in the moment and hear him speak their names – names that not only defined who they really were but also were names that reflected an aspect of the nature of Jesus, the one who is the Name Above all Names.

In order to stay with Jesus and hear their names, the disciples had to leave behind much. Most significantly, they had to leave behind their own self-conceptions. They had to leave behind their half-baked dreams, visions, expectations and ambitions especially spiritual ones – because none of their ideas of themselves, their dreams, their longings or their theologies were big enough to hold Christ. And neither are ours. As long as we cling to what we think we *should* be or how our spiritual life *should* be, we won't be able to go stay with Jesus. Whatever we think we know is too small for the reality of Christ or the reality of our names. Peter could not form himself into The Rock. Andrew could not turn himself into a Fisher of People, Preacher and Evangelist. Only Christ could. But Peter and Andrew had to take the journey of leaving behind their set in stone ideas of *everything* and be with Jesus wherever he was. Peter had to lose himself to the point where he couldn't even be true to his professed convictions, and he betrayed his Lord. In that terrible act he lost the last vestiges of all those self-oriented perceptions that kept him from really knowing Jesus and knowing himself. Only then was he free to finally move into the amazing existence of who he really was: The Rock, named so by the Rock of Ages.

Every time you hear Christ speak your name you will grow a little more into the reality of that name. Your Name will form you little by little, root by root, branch by branch, leaf by leaf. It will slowly draw you away from everything that is not life giving to your real identity. It will form you in a way 'more-tification' never can. This requires you to take the time to listen to Jesus asking you, "What are you looking for?" It requires you to be brave enough to answer, "I don't know. I have no idea. All I want is to be where you are and nowhere else. All I want is to be with you and hear you calling me by my true Name. I want to know where you are staying, Lord." And he will say, "Come and see..."

Go. See. Stay. Listen. And find what you've always been looking for.

The Voice

Mark 1: 14-20

Jesus sees Peter and Andrew casting a net into the Sea of Galilee and tells them to follow him because he will make them fishers of people. They leave their net and follow him.

Is there anyone else out there who secretly thinks the disciples had it easy when it came to hearing the call and following immediately? They heard a voice, looked up and Jesus was right there, in the flesh. There was no mistaking who he was and what he was asking them. There have been a few times in my life where I knew without a doubt that God was calling me to do something and that it was his voice I was hearing but, for the most part, I'm not having "leave your net" experiences every day.

The disciples heard Jesus' voice calling to them, "Leave your net. I have another kind of fishing for you to do," and they immediately dropped their net and followed him. What else were they going to do? They had distinctly heard Christ's call and they knew who he was. Of all the sincere Christian people I know, I can't think of one who wouldn't drop what they were doing and immediately follow Jesus if they had no doubt it was his voice they were hearing. The problem is, we don't always hear God's voice in a way that leaves us with absolutely no questions or fears in our hearts. It's actually a rare and beautiful thing to hear God's voice in the same way Samuel heard the Lord's voice calling his name. Rare and beautiful.

Why does it have to be so rare? Why is it so difficult for us to discern God's call for our lives sometimes? I said at the beginning that there have been a *few* times in my life where the call was distinct and unmistakable. And the rest of the time? Hard discernment. "Is this God's voice leading me or not? Am I supposed to do this or not do it? If I'm not supposed to do this, I'm sure God will close the door...oh please God, close that friggin' door!" Meanwhile, I'm being pushed through the door as I grab onto anything I can to keep myself from going through. "Quick! Shut the door, Lord! Shut the door!"

Then there are the things I would really like to do but I can't get a handle on whether they're things God wants me to do. "Is God leading me or not? If I'm not supposed to do this, God will close the door." However, if he actually does shut the door, I'm ready to find a window and if he shuts the window, I have this fire axe...

Why is it so hard to hear God? From my experience, I know that when God really wants me to hear his voice, I'll hear it. I know this because the few times I did hear him clearly it wasn't because I was engaged in any deep spiritual prayer and it wasn't because I was actually trying to hear his voice in that moment. It was simply his time for me to hear him clearly and that was that. So, what about the rest of the time when nothing is clear and the struggle to discern is heavy and painful? Is it our fault when God's voice is indistinct? Is it because we don't spend enough time in prayer or in the right kind of prayer? Does God get frustrated with us because we're so deaf?

I don't believe that. I believe that he allows us to struggle in order to discover that his voice comes in many different forms. He allows us to pray, ask, seek and search some more. If he speaks clearly in one situation, he may completely change his voice in another because if he always made it easy for us to hear, we wouldn't seek him anymore and we wouldn't discover how immense and all encompassing he is. We would be so busy listening for a single note that we would be missing the whole symphony that is God. We would wait for a singular voice to tell us what to do and where to go and we would respond like good little robots. We would be 'push button Christians'. We need to understand that it's not always about *what* God calls us to do; it's often more about our relationship with him as we struggle to discern his will and move into new situations. Sometimes his will is simply, "Stay close to me and dance. Don't try to figure out the moves or the end results. Just find my rhythm and I'll take care of the rest."

We tend to focus strongly on end results and accomplishments. God is not all about end results and accomplishments. He is about being known. If we seek to know him intimately, try to become less hung up on what to do and more keen on who he is, we will start to recognize his voice in places we never thought we would hear it. He will become the Lord of everything we encounter and we will hear his voice everywhere: in silence, chaos, a sentence, a homeless person, an enemy, a rock, a hard place, a fear or a wound. If all we listen for is "Yes, go," and "No, stop," what kind of a relationship is that?

At Mass I sat behind a couple that I hardly knew. The communion hymn was, "Here I Am, Lord." I just happened to glance at the man in front of me and I saw him wiping his eye. Dust? An eyelash? I watched him. There it was...a single tear quietly coursing down his cheek. He had heard the voice of God in the song. And I had *seen* the voice of God in his tear. We were both blessed and probably changed without a word being spoken or an action made. I saw the voice of my Lord and it was sweet. He heard the voice of his Lord and was moved. Dare we question what was accomplished?

In John 20:29, Jesus said to Thomas, *"Have you believed because you have seen me? Blessed are those who have not seen and yet have come to believe."* (NRSV) He could well have said to any of his disciples, *"Have you *followed* because you heard me? Blessed are those who do not hear and yet follow."* Blessed are the confused, the afraid, the ones straining to hear, and the ones who would willingly stay or go if they only knew what God was asking of them. Blessed are you, for when you do finally hear his voice, your joy will be like an ocean. You will know that he was speaking the whole time. You will realize that you didn't hear his voice distinctly because it wasn't time for you to hear it distinctly. He reveals his voice when it's time. What will amaze you is how his voice gently guided you and led you even while you were achingly praying for clarity and his voice was the last thing you thought you could hear.

The Lord is calling you right now. If he wasn't, you would have absolutely no desire to know his will or to follow after him.

Your desire is the sound of his voice.

As One Having Authority

Mark 1:21-28

Jesus goes into the synagogue to teach and all the people were amazed because he taught them with authority and not like the scribes. They are astonished that even the unclean spirits obey him.

When I was younger, I began to realize that I always seemed to be in a self-judgment mode. I scrutinized myself to see if all my thoughts, actions and responses measured up to the accepted spiritual standards and ideals. Somehow, inspiration would rapidly dwindle into law, leaving me trying desperately to make it all work. I would try to grab onto what I thought was my spiritual authority and use it to bring shape and meaning to my inner life but it was exhausting. I had not yet learned that the Authority of God is not something that can be apprehended by a force of the intellect or will. We can only be absorbed into it by knowing the Author.

Scribes had a huge amount of authority in the Jewish culture. The scribes copied Scripture and taught the Law. Their roles were to copy, read, amend, explain, and protect the law. They were extremely learned in the law and lectured on it in synagogues and in schools, debated it and used it to make judgments in conflicts brought before them.

Jesus was also very familiar with God's law. He, too, was able to quote scripture, apply it and debate it. But when Jesus taught the people, they were amazed at his authority, which was nothing like the authority they were used to. Jesus' authority brought change and healing. It brought light where there was no light and freedom where none existed. Jesus 'knew' the scripture in the same way the scribes did but his knowledge went deeper and was more intimate. His knowledge of all things to do with God wasn't based on principles and laws or a myriad of interpretations of that law; his knowledge was based on relationship. When he taught the people, he wasn't simply quoting something he had learned by rote; he was talking about someone he knew intimately. When he spoke of God the Father, he spoke from experience and from his constant connection with the Father. He spoke only about what God had spoken to him. He could teach love with authority because he knew the Author of Love. He could heal with authority because he was one with the Author of Healing. He could bring deliverance with authority because he lived within the heart of the Author of freedom.

Christ's authority naturally flowed out of his heart knowledge of the Father. The scribes knew everything there was to know about the law but, as St. Paul was fond of pointing out, the written word is dead and cannot bring life, only awareness of sin and failure and condemnation. Jesus' intimate knowledge of the Father astounded and amazed the people because he spoke of things he really knew, not just things he had read about, heard about or was taught in school.

It is interesting to note that the unclean spirits were completely freaked out by Jesus' authority but those same spirits couldn't have cared less about the scribes' authority. The spirits knew that dead knowledge (law) regulates and controls people only on an insignificant surface level but living knowledge goes deep into the inner heart and sets people free. While the scribes were no threat, they wanted nothing to do with Jesus.

The lovely thing about Jesus is he not only was able to share his knowledge of the Father with the people, but he also wanted everyone to have the same experience of the Father as he did. In fact, that was the reason Jesus came – to show what it is really like to walk intimately with God. He came to share the good news that God is indeed a Father and that God wants a close relationship with each one of us.

We are all called to share in Christ's authority. But what does that mean? What did it mean when I finally realized that I was trying to manufacture and use authority to shape my life without having any idea what it meant to have authority? How does one get to a place of true authority? For me it meant letting go of all the ideals, goals, precepts and standards that I thought I had to make operative in my life and be totally poor before God. I had to admit that in spite of all the spiritual knowledge I had built up in myself over the years, I knew nothing, could do nothing and had no idea where to go. Furthermore, I told God I was not going to do anything about it. I was going to wait on him. I wasn't going to seek him in more books or more speakers, continuing to add to the useless and weighty type of knowledge authority I thought was necessary. I was going to wait for him to speak the living word to my heart.

What a relief that was to my whole being. It was like I had been carrying a mountain of useless and heavy knowledge, knowledge I didn't even know how to use or apply properly let alone gain authority from. All it did was sit on my shoulders and condemn me for never quite getting it right. When I said, "I'm not carrying this anymore," it was as if God answered, "Yes!! I've just been waiting for you to say that and to drop that load. My burden - my authority – is the yoke of lightness. Just walk with me and stop worrying about 'application' and 'succeeding' and 'doing it right'. Take a break from having to find the right spiritual tool for every situation. Just walk with me."

It is always good to regularly review one's spiritual life and ask the question: Do I have a primary relationship with words, principles, ideas, precepts and rules, or do I have a primary relationship with the living God? A relationship with rules and principles is a complex and heavy burden, one that always seems to point out one's failures. It often involves lots of guilt and self-criticism. It seems that when we start trying to wield what we think of as authority, all we do is become heavy authoritarians, constantly banishing others and ourselves to the dunce's corner.

The Latin for 'be still' is vacate, the root word for vacation. A relationship with the living God is a vacation. And, is not ' holy day' the origin of the word 'holiday'? Go on a holiday with God. Chill out, relax and let him take care of the details.

Being loved, not being in control, is the root of kingdom authority.

Moving On.

Mark 1: 29-39

Jesus heals Peter's mother-in-law of a fever, then spends the evening healing people and casting out demons. In the morning he goes off by himself to pray. When the disciples find him, they say everyone is looking for him but he says they need keep moving on to other towns to proclaim his message.

At one time I was involved in music ministry. The small group I belonged to led the music every Saturday evening and we did it for years. We started to get a little burned out but, because there was no other group to take over, we kept going. When we finally got more than a little burned out we decided we just had to let it go and trust God to provide music for the Saturday evening Mass. The thought that kept coming to me was that if we just kept going, no one would realize there was a need for another group and we could very well be blocking a new ministry. But it was still very difficult to tell people we were stepping down. It felt like we were quitters, even though we had been doing it for so many years.

Within a very short period of time after our resignation, several musical families started a family choir. Parents and children played instruments and led the singing and they were fabulous. They probably would never have started if our group hadn't let go and made way for something new to spring up.

In this week's Gospel, Jesus listened for more than *what* he was supposed to do. He also listened for *when* and *where* he should be doing it. He came to Peter's home, healed Peter's mother-in-law and then spent his evening ministering to the people. Word spreads quickly when people are being loved, healed, delivered and forgiven, and soon the whole city was gathered in front of Peter's home. The need was huge and he probably ministered to the people until late into the night. There was no one else who could do what he was doing.

Early the next morning, Jesus slipped away to pray. He spoke to Abba and listened to what Abba wanted him to do. He spent time soaking in the beautiful nature of God and listening to his father's heart. When the disciples finally found Jesus, they assumed he would continue to do what he had been doing the night before. In fact, everyone assumed that's what he would do. They were all searching for him and waiting for him to get on with the program. But Jesus did not give in to what everyone thought he would do or should do. The night before was the time to heal in that city and now it was time to move on. There must have been more than a few unhappy people when they heard he was not going to stay. For those who hadn't had the chance to be touched by him it would have been especially disappointing.

That seems kind of hard hearted of God. Surely he could have allowed Jesus to stay a while longer. Or Jesus could have anointed someone else to stay with the people and continue to heal and deliver. Why didn't he do that?

How do we know he didn't? My mind keeps popping back to Peter's mother-in-law. Why mention her in particular when there were so many people who were healed that night? Could it be that besides healing her of a fever, Jesus also placed within her a gracious and yearning heart for others who were suffering? Perhaps she not only served Jesus by preparing a meal for him and the disciples but maybe she also spent the evening at his side, tending not only to his needs, but also comforting those who were waiting anxiously or were in pain or grieving or depleted of hope. In receiving Christ's healing touch, perhaps she also received an infusion of his compassion and mercy. As she worked by his side and watched him touching and loving the people, she probably began to understand where his authority came from and was deeply stirred by the concept of a God who loved people to wholeness and didn't condemn them to misery.

And maybe, just maybe, the next day before he left, Jesus anointed her and said, "Feed my sheep. Tend my flock. I place them in your hands. If you need anything, ask my Father and he will give it to you." And then he left to bring the good news to other people and to find others who could receive a portion of his authority so they could continue his ministry of love and hope. Maybe they wouldn't be amazing healers like him but they could keep hope alive and point people toward a loving Father which is the best miracle of all.

It wouldn't have been easy for Jesus to leave when he knew that the hopes of many were pinned on him staying and continuing his healing. He was not a hard man – he was a man who deeply felt the burdens of the people. But over and above the cries of the poor, he always heard the voice of his Father and trusted him completely. As the old spiritual song says, "You gotta move when the Spirit says move."

I would bet that there's not one person reading this reflection who hasn't been caught in the thorny trap of sensing it's time to move along, time to change direction or time to let go of a ministry in the church but has felt bound by the expectations and needs of the community or individual people. It's a very tough place to be. If committed Catholics are anything, they are faithful to what they are committed to. It's terribly difficult when it seems obvious there's no one else to take over or it feels like you're quitting instead of carrying your cross to the end. Even Pope Benedict was heavily criticized for abdicating and not carrying on to the end. But he had heard his God. It was time to do what he did and it was a brave act.

If you are in the position of feeling it's time to move on but are constricted by outward pressure, remember Jesus rising early, prayerfully listening and hearing his Father telling him to move on. Maybe he, too, wrestled with the feeling that he was leaving a work unfinished and leaving a people disappointed. But maybe, in his struggle, he heard the Father speak these words of scripture into his heart:

To everything, my son, there is a season,
a time for every purpose under the sun.
A time to be born and a time to die;
a time to plant and a time to pluck up that which is planted;
a time to kill and a time to heal ...
a time to weep and a time to laugh;
a time to mourn and a time to dance ...
a time to embrace and a time to refrain from embracing;
a time to lose and a time to seek;
a time to rend and a time to sew;
a time to keep silent and a time to speak;
a time to love and a time to hate;
a time for war and a time for peace.
(Ecclesiastes 3: 1-8. KJV)

Do *you* know what time it is?

The Great Family Physician

Mark 1:40-45

A leper asks Jesus to heal him, saying that if Jesus chose to he could make the leper clean. Jesus answers that he does choose to do so and heals him.

Good parents are amazing, really. From the time the first child is born until the last child is able to utilize a toilet and navigate to it in the middle of the night on her own without calling for help, parents are called on countless times to deal with body issues (pun intended) that would turn the stomach of a childless person. Besides dealing with mind boggling numbers of dirty diapers, I cannot tell you how many times I was up in the middle of the night with a sick child cleaning the results of stomach flu or diarrhea off of them, off the bedding and off the floor. Yet I also cannot remember one time when, faced with a smelly gross mess, I had any desire to turn away from my child and let him or her wallow in the sickness and the muck. I might not have enjoyed the smelly mess but it in no way affected my love and concern for my child or my desire to be with the child. In fact, my concern and desire to comfort and be present to that child was heightened by their illness. There is nothing more heart wrenching to a parent than a sick child.

Those of you who have no children may remember times as a child when you were ill and your mother or father sat with you, cleaned up your messes, spoke gently to you and brought you little treats to make you feel better.

Quite often we are encouraged to relate to ourselves as the leper in this Gospel passage and to see ourselves as the untouchable one whom Jesus saves. But, just for a moment, instead of putting yourself in the lowest place, put yourself in Jesus' sandals.

A leper was repulsive, unclean and dangerous to be around. Open sores and missing body parts made a leper a horror to look at. No one was allowed to go near a leper and they especially were not allowed to touch him or her. Most people would have found the idea of touching a leper repugnant anyway. But Jesus chose to touch the leper – because he wanted to.

"Such a kind man." We might think. Well, it wasn't just an act of detached pity that made Jesus reach out and touch the leprous man. To Jesus, this leper was not a repulsive, filthy, distorted person; this leper was his beloved sick child. Jesus loved this man and he could no more turn away from him than good parents can turn away from their sick and helpless children. Can you understand the love now?

There are times when you feel leprous inside, as if all your faults and failings and disabilities have caused open sores on your spirit. There are times of great discouragement in your life because it seems like the more you try to control your failures the more they get away from you. Like the person with leprosy, the sores of your inadequacies just keep appearing and eating away at you. It just doesn't feel like Jesus would be particularly happy to keep company with someone who has such a diseased and disabled spirit. Yes, you know that he loves you and forgives you but does he really want to be with you? Does he *like* to be with you?

Tell me who made the hearts of parents? We need not be overly sentimental here. A parent's heart isn't always the epitome of patience, mercy and love. Parents get tired and worn out and snap when they're pushed too far and have moments of resentment and even desperation, but when they have a sick little baby in their arms, a baby or a toddler who's burning up with fever and can't keep food down, the kind of patience and deep concern that fills their hearts comes straight from the heart of God. They don't blame the child for being sick. They are just so sorry for the child for being the victim of whatever virus or disease she is fighting. They do not walk away from the child saying, "When you get over this illness and when you've cleaned up your messes, come and see me."

Sin is an illness. When the scribes of the Pharisees saw that Jesus was eating with sinners and tax collectors, they asked his disciples, 'Why does he eat with tax collectors and sinners?' When Jesus heard this, he said to them, *'Those who are well have no need of a physician, but those who are sick; I have come to call not the ones who think they are righteous but sinners.'* He doesn't hold himself back from us when we are ill of spirit, mind and heart. He comes *because* we are sick. He is burning the midnight oil at our sides, cooling the fever, cleaning up the messes. He stays with us until we are better even if that takes until the breaking of the dawn. He will never leave us or get upset if we don't seem to be getting better. Because he is a physician, he knows so much better than we do that we are on the mend. Jesus can see what we can't.

He did not come to earth to condemn it; he came with mercy - and did you know that the Hebrew word for mercy actually means the quality of love felt by a mother nursing her child? That's powerful love. If you're feeling sick inside, let him nurse you back to health. Your sickness is not what breaks his heart; it's when you don't let him in to take care of you because you're ashamed of being sick.

Can you imagine how heartbreaking it would be to go into the room of a sick child only to see the child frantically trying to clean up the vomit on the floor because he's afraid his parents will be angry and disappointed with him for being sick or that they won't want to be with him because he's so sick. God sees this in us all the time. When this actually happens in a natural family, we say that the parents are dysfunctional for creating that kind of fear and anxiety in a child. Yet, when we fear God will be angry or disappointed with us over our inner illnesses, we don't stop to think that we are attributing to him the characteristics of a dysfunctional parent.

Perhaps the problem is that you just don't want to be his sick child. You want to be whole, healthy and saintly – one who has got all your inner illnesses well under control. Well, good luck with that. If you are a human being, you are ill. You are broken and you need mending. Don't you see? That's the beauty of it. Christ comes joyfully to you in your brokenness and illness. He doesn't come to you out of reluctant obligation; he chooses eagerly to dine with you, to sit with you and to touch the most leprous parts of your spirit just as he chose to touch the leper and to eat with publicans, prostitutes and sinners.

If you're unwilling to fit in with the sick, the addicted, the sinful and the marginalized then you'll miss out on the wondrous company of the compassionate Christ.

Because that's where he is. Because that's where he *chooses* to be.

The Redemptive Power of Love

Mark 2:1-12

Jesus heals and forgives the sins of the paralytic who is lowered down through the roof by his friends.

For some reason, whenever I envision those men lowering the paralytic through the roof, I see them as young men. From my days as a chaplain at the University of Victoria, I can think of several young guys who would have enthusiastically done what the men in the Gospel did for their paralytic friend. Their friend was in need; there was a problem in getting through the crowd so they got creative and improvised. Obviously they had heard about Jesus' healing powers and in their minds it was totally worth it to do whatever it would take to get their friend into Jesus' presence. Older and 'wiser' minds would have probably just accepted that the paralyzed man wouldn't be seeing Jesus that night and maybe never. But these young guys decided they weren't going to miss this once in a lifetime opportunity, even if it meant tearing up their neighbor's roof.

I believe that Jesus loved it. I think he was completely delighted. I can just visualize him watching this jerry-rigged bed descending to the floor and then peering up at the hole in the roof and seeing four grinning faces looking down at him. What's not to love about these guys?

The other thing I think Jesus loved about these young men was that they "got it". Up until that moment when ceiling dust started sifting down onto his head, Jesus had been preaching his message to a room crowded with people and there were a lot of scribes and teachers of the law in that room. They weren't there to learn or receive anything from Jesus. They were there to check him out. They were most likely listening with skeptical minds and cynical hearts and a number of people would have been waiting to see what the spiritual leaders' judgments of Jesus were before they committed themselves to his teaching. There were most likely many individuals there who weren't listening very closely to much of what Jesus said because they were just hanging out in case a miracle happened. So, there was Jesus sharing his precious message with a crowd, a high percentage of which were arrogantly cynical or were waiting to see what everybody else might think or were just inquisitive looky-loos. Jesus was probably heaving the odd sigh inside himself but, still, the Father wanted him there at that moment so he would wait to see what would happen.

No wonder he immediately responded to these four faith-filled men who found a way to get their friend to Jesus. These young men weren't judging Jesus, they weren't just there to catch something sensational and they weren't hanging back to see what everybody else thought. They were taking Jesus at his word and their friend was in need of Jesus' Word.

Jesus responded to that fresh and alive faith by forgiving the fellow his sins - no questions asked. The paralytic didn't even have a chance to say, "Lord, I am not worthy to enter under this roof where you are but only say the word..." It wasn't necessary because 'Jesus saw their faith'.

Have you ever heard that love covers a multitude of sins? This is something to think about in relation to the people you love and are concerned about. It wasn't repentance on the part of the paralytic that caused Jesus to pronounce forgiveness. It was the fresh love, faith and hope of the friends – love that hoped for great things to happen and faith that refused to accept limitations based on how things have always been. *"Now faith is the substance of things hoped for, the evidence of things not seen."* (Hebrews 11:1 KJV)

According to the law, the paralytic was a condemned sinner. If he weren't a sinner, he wouldn't be paralyzed. According to the law, his suffering was the result of sin and he deserved to be paralyzed but his friends did not abandon him to the definitions of the law. How many family members and friends do you worry about because, according to the definitions of the law, they are outside the pale of acceptability? It may be because of anything from refusing to go to Mass anymore and denying the existence of God to being caught up in destructive and ugly behavior. You can't wrestle them into repentance. You can't berate them into belief. What hope is there for them?

Your love is their hope. Your faith that Christ can heal them in a blink of an eye whenever he chooses is their hope. Your willingness to walk with them in love and acceptance, no matter what, is their bridge to Christ and his forgiveness. If Christ doesn't forgive them for your sake, he will forgive them for his own sake. In the first reading, God said through Isaiah, *"I, I am He who blots out your transgressions for my own sake, and I will not remember your sins."* (Isaiah 43:25. NRSV)

We forget the utter redemptive power of love even though Christ came to show us what redemptive love looks like. He showed us so that we could follow him and participate in redeeming the world by allowing the power of his unconditional love to shine through our love. With the love of Christ we can walk with those paralyzed by disbelief and wounded by weakness.

Our love can break through the hardened ceilings of many hearts and open the way to the healing and forgiving power of God.

He drew a circle that shut me out —
Heretic, rebel, a thing to flout.
But Love and I had the wit to win:
We drew a circle that took him in.
(Edward Markham, 1913)

Stop worrying. Start loving.

1st Sunday of Lent B

On Dwelling in the Desert

Mark 1:12-15

After Jesus' baptism, he goes into the wilderness where he is tempted. After this he goes into Galilee and proclaims that the time is fulfilled and the Kingdom of God is near. He calls people to repent and believe the Good News.

If there's one thing any serious Christian is familiar with it's the spiritual desert and the last thing we think about when we're in a spiritual desert is that it's a good thing. It doesn't seem good at all. What usually comes to mind is, "This must be my fault. I must have screwed up somewhere." When one is in a vast wilderness where God seems so far away that it's hard to recall when he ever felt near, it's natural to blame oneself.

"Perhaps if I prayed harder or more often...maybe if I wasn't so selfish...maybe if I was able to get to Mass during the week. I should be reading more scripture. It must be something I'm doing or not doing," and the real killer: "God must be teaching me a lesson, but I have no idea what it is!"

In the desert your heart is cracked and dry, scripture is lifeless and boring and prayer feels like you've been chewing gum for too long. All your prayers seem to be a variation on a theme of "Please help me...please give me..." and it feels like your petitions hit a brick wall and fall to the ground as lifeless words. But you hide these thoughts away because you are absolutely sure you are the only one who feels so isolated from the fruitful abundance of being a child of God. Everybody else seems all right so you act as if you're all right too.

The great tragedy of a lot of spiritual teaching is that we are not trained to understand the immense value of the desert and so when it comes, it is a shock to the spiritual system. And, it needs to be said, those who have discerned their spiritual vocations and have entered into them, whether it's marriage, priesthood, the religious life or dedicated single, are the ones most vulnerable to the shock of finding themselves in the middle of a howling wilderness.

We are all taught the importance and beauty of our vocations. It is impressed upon us that within our vocation is great spiritual and emotional fulfillment. Therefore, it can be a little terrifying to discover that rather than leading you to a mountain top of spiritual gratification, your vocation may actually lead you into a spiritual desert like you've never experienced before. Guilt ensues. "I must be incredibly deficient if I'm not finding all of my fulfillment, spiritually, intellectually and emotionally, in my role as a spouse, a parent or a member of a religious community. What's making me feel so empty and dissatisfied? What is stopping me from feeling any kind of connection with God?"

The Father is.

What a surprise, huh? Why would the Father keep you from experiencing great spiritual satisfaction when you have answered his call and entered into such a wonderful vocation, no matter what that vocation might be?

It's because before you were called to be married, be a parent or become a Religious etc., you were called to be a child of God, a being he created to be in relationship with him. Of course it blesses him tremendously when you answer his call to enter into a special vocation but your vocation and the people you serve within your vocation aren't meant to fill up the last aching abyss of your heart. Only God can fill that spot. There's a place within you that is big enough for only two: you and the Lord. It's a place that's meant for you as *you*, not for you as wife, husband, parent, priest, Brother or Sister or you as whatever you are in your calling or ministry. These areas of calling are illuminated and blessed by your intimate relationship with the Lord but they are not your total fulfillment. Certainly, there will be fulfilling times within your vocation but it is impossible for the role to which you have been called to fill you up inside or nurture you the way your innermost being needs nurturing.

And so, the Father calls you to the desert where nothing fills, nothing comforts and nothing edifies. It is a place of simplification. It is a place of stripping – because none of us know how much we have come to depend on roles, ministries, friendships, rituals and head knowledge to define our relationship with the Lord. The desert is not a place of punishment; it is a place of great grace because the Lord knows how easy it is for roles, actions, ideas and perceptions to subtly take the place of a real intimacy with him. He just wants us to get back to the beginning of everything, a place that may be relatively unfamiliar to us. It's a place where we're not following our parents' faith or our friends' faith or the faith of our favorite spiritual teachers. It's a place where all promises fall flat because we had the wrong idea of what was being promised.

Take heart! All is well. You are the beloved of God, his daughter or son in whom he is well pleased. The very first place the Father wants you to find fulfillment is in him before everything else. In the desert it is just you ... and the Lord. Not you and your spouse. Not you and your children. Not you and your vocation or ministry. Just you and the Lord.

Just like it was with Jesus. It was just he and his Father in the wilderness.

Consider this: Jesus was called, baptized and heard his Father speak excruciatingly beautiful words of love and approval to him. Then, instead of being pushed into the deep end of a fulfilling ministry, he was *driven* into the desert! The desert was as necessary for him as it is for us. When he came out he clearly knew his vocation but more importantly, he knew his Father more intimately than he ever had before. In Jesus' vocation and ministry, his relationship with God came first. It came first. It came first. It came first. It was just he and the Father out there in that wilderness. No crowds, no people to serve or minister to, no people to teach, no people to feed and no people to love him, follow him, challenge him or despise him. His one on one relationship with God came before everything else. It was foundational to everything that came after.

This is the first Sunday of Lent, a time of meditating on our spiritual life and a time when most people choose some sort of act of self-denial or spiritual discipline to reconnect themselves with the Lord. If you are presently experiencing a spiritual desert in your life, I suggest that your focus of spiritual discipline be one of complete acceptance and one of meditating on what it would have been like to walk with Jesus, day by day, in the wilderness. Allow yourself to accept that the desert is an important, valid and valuable place to be. Pray for the grace to recognize and be able to let go of everything that you have been mistaking for the face of God. Pray to be healed of false expectation.

Jesus walked into that desert and committed himself to it fully. Therefore, you are also called to accept the desert and to be fully committed to it, and then to be open to the particular kind of healing it can bring you.

It can happen nowhere else.

Transfiguration Conversation

Mark 9:2-10
The Transfiguration on the Mount.

Have you ever wondered what Jesus, Moses and Elijah talked about? It's a fascinating question to which there is no answer since scripture does not enlighten us as to what their conversation was about. However, a priest I once knew said, "The most important faculty is not intellect or emotion; it is imagination." So, let's allow our imaginations free reign for a bit and listen in on a possible conversation between the three of them…

Jesus: "Moses! Elijah! You have no idea how good it is to see you, brothers! Just last night I was speaking with the Father and telling him how isolated and lonely I've been feeling."

Moses: "It's glorious to see you, too, Lord. We were deeply honored when the Father said we could come to you."

Elijah: "We asked him why he chose us and he said we would be able to understand your challenges better than anyone else because of our earthly experiences. Tell us your sorrows, Master."

Jesus: Right now I'm carrying the Prophet's wound, the one that every prophet has had to bear. It's the wound that comes from the incomprehension of the people. Not too many are able to hear what I have to tell them and even the ones who are willing to listen are having a very tough time comprehending my message. Look at those three men over there – they're terrified. They've heard my message, seen my miracles and I've told them I am the Son of God but it hasn't penetrated. Every time something out of the ordinary occurs they can't believe what's happening and they either misinterpret it or they panic."

Moses: "You don't have to say anymore! I can't count how many times God did amazing miracles of deliverance for his people in the wilderness and all it did was frighten them into temporary obedience rather than create a loving trust in their God. Then before long they would forget all about God's merciful provision and begin to complain angrily again."

Elijah: "It is tremendously discouraging when people just cannot grasp who our God really is. Miracles excite them and create awe in them but it doesn't take long before they forget his power and start trying to do everything themselves again. Trying to teach them the truth about God was very difficult for me as well. They wanted to believe and understand but they just wouldn't listen well enough to grasp it all. I have to say, though, after spending the time I did on earth and now having experienced the lightness of the kingdom, I realize that there is something about the world that fogs the truth. The Fallen One has done such a good job of creating a miasma of half lies and confusion. The truth is difficult to see and hard to hold onto. God's people really do have a challenge to hear, believe and grasp the Light."

Jesus: "That's true, Elijah. Sometimes it feels like even I am moving through muddy clouds even though I know exactly who I am and why I'm here. The spiritual atmosphere in the world is immensely dense and heavy. I get frustrated sometimes with my followers but I love them so much for how hard they try under very difficult circumstances to grasp who I really am and what I'm teaching them. They *try* to comprehend it all. They *try* to understand what the Father is asking of me and of them. They know the light is there and I can see the great desire in them to reach out and hold on to it. They may be confused, anxious and terrified but they have given themselves to me and I'll do whatever it takes to bring them all safely home."

Moses: "I felt the same, Lord. My mission wasn't anything like yours but I loved my people with a passion that came from beyond me. Even though I often felt inadequate and frustrated, I would *never* have abandoned them in the wilderness. I, too, just wanted to 'bring them home'."

Elijah: "I agree. Even when God was teaching the people to turn away from false gods by stopping the rain from falling for three years or sending fire down from the heavens to consume animals and stone altars, the strongest emotion in me was not so much anger at their stubbornness but compassion and longing. I knew that what I was feeling came straight from God's heart. I was not big enough myself to be able to have that kind of passion for the people. It had to come from our God!"

Jesus: "Still, I wish that even for a few minutes they could stop listening to their own fearful confusion and really hear what I'm saying to them, absorb my words of love and know that the time has come and the Kingdom is really here! When I was telling the Father how homesick I was, I thought of all these people following me, trying so hard to love me in spite of their bewilderment. Suddenly I saw streams and rivers turning into torrents and floods of people throughout the ages, people trying to love God and people aching for their true Home. I was overwhelmed with the deluge of their desire. I told the Father that no matter how discouraged or lonely I feel I want to do whatever it takes to bring them all home to him. All of them. I will bring home the ones who have gone before me, the ones who tried to follow the two of you, the ones who only suspect there is something more, the ones throughout the ages who hear my Name and even the many who can't hear it. I want to bring them all home no matter what the cost. But I admit, my heart cried out in agony, "Father, please let them listen to me!"

Moses: "Yes, Lord, we know. We heard you. All of heaven heard that cry and we have come to tell you that you were heard in the Heart of all hearts. We want you to know that the Father and all of heaven are with you in full sustaining love. You are not alone. Ever. Remember us and know that you have our utter gratitude for what you are doing.

Elijah: "My Lord, we have to go now but the Father said to tell you that when we've gone and the light fades, there will be a Word for you and your disciples from him."

Jesus: "Ah...I long to hear my Father's voice once more! But it's still hard to let you go. You have no idea what it has meant to me to see my brothers from home. I feel much stronger now and not so all alone. Thank you."

At that point, the three of them looked over at Peter, James and John. Peter was scared and very uncomfortable. He didn't know what to say, but he felt like he should say something. He said, "Rabbi, it is good for us to be here; let us make three dwellings, one for you, one for Moses, and one for Elijah." Jesus, Moses and Elijah looked each other and then looked back at Peter with great delight and amusement. Elijah whispered to Jesus, "Does he think we would actually choose to *live* here again?"

Then a cloud overshadowed them all and from the cloud there came a voice so filled with love it was hard to bear. "This is my Son, the Beloved; listen to him!" The cloud dissipated, the light faded and when the disciples looked around, they saw only Jesus.

And Jesus was laughing.

"Come on, my good brothers, let's go back down the mountain. There's much that needs to be done. Oh...don't try to tell anyone about what you saw, all right? They wouldn't be able to hear you anyway."

Lenten question: Are you listening to Jesus or are other fears and voices drowning him out?

Now Enter In

John 2:13-25
Jesus clears the temple of all the moneychangers and those selling sacrificial animals.

As a spiritual director, I listen to the wounds and struggles of people. Mothers, fathers, elders, young adults, and single adults – all struggle with the chaos of life and especially with finding their center in God in the midst of the chaos. Between careers and vocations, raising children, dealing with health issues, fears, interpersonal relationships and all that goes with just living life, people are often stretched beyond capacity. They find themselves running on empty and achingly poor in spirit. They need the Lord to pour himself into them because they don't have what it takes to climb over obstacles, pull themselves free of encumbrances and clear away the inner debris in order to find him. They write spiritual checks and get N.S.F. notices from their hearts.

When Jesus walked into the outer courts of the temple, what he saw made his heart ache for his people. Before they could even enter the temple they had to deal with a chaotic cacophony of demanding noise of greed and extortion. Foreigners had to exchange their money for the Jewish currency so they could pay the temple tax – at an inflated exchange rate of course. People couldn't just bring their own animals or doves for sacrifice because their animals would be judged as blemished and unacceptable so they would end up having to buy their sacrificial animals from the "Purveyors of Fine Cattle and Sheep – Guaranteed to be Without Blemish" (and guaranteed to line the pockets of the temple coffers). Naturally, the animals being sold were quite expensive. The law made it so that no one was exempt from having to make a sacrifice of some sort. The people were being ripped off and they were helpless to do anything about it. If this was allowed in the courts of the Temple of God, what did that say to the people about their worthiness to freely come to God in their need?

When I read the Gospel, I imagined some of the people I know feeling empty, poor and so needy of spiritual sustenance. I saw them going to the house of the Lord to place themselves before God to ask for his blessing and grace. And I imagined them in the temple court being faced with chaos and noise and grasping hands reaching out to strip them of the little they had. I saw them crushed in spirit before they even had a chance to be in God's presence.

Jesus saw this too. When he saw the vendors and moneychangers gouging the people, people who had so little to begin with, materially and spiritually, I believe Jesus looked down through the ages and saw his Anawim, "the poor ones of the Lord", stumbling to God to ask for his help, graces and blessings but finding themselves faced with hurdles and hoops to jump through before they could approach the throne. "My Father's house is a house of prayer!" he said. Prayer: conversation and intimate relationship with his Abba. How can people pray to a loving Father if they're hungry or scared of the authorities' displeasure or unsure of whether there will be enough money left over to feed a family? How can they seek love and healing if they don't know they are worth being loved and healed, if they feel they are only worth being taken advantage of and then ignored in their neediness?

When Jesus said, *"Destroy this temple, and in three days I will raise it up,"* he was referring to the temple of his body, of course, but he was also saying his temple would be a temple where the poor could come without money and without feeling like there was a price of any kind to pay before they could enter into the presence of his Father. In his temple there would be a standing invitation: *"Oh, come to the water all you who are thirsty; though you have no money, come, buy corn without money and eat, and at no cost buy wine and milk."* (Isaiah 55:1 Jerusalem Bible) No hoops. No distortion or extortion. No abuse. No class distinction. It was his intention that all would be priests, no one would be higher or lower than anyone else and all would be welcome.

One of the reasons Jesus came was to let us know that God is our Abba...our loving Father or Papa. There is no good father who doesn't want his little ones to run into his arms freely, especially if they are ill, scared or uncertain, don't know how to handle things or just need arms of reassurance. This is Father Love. Jesus said, "Let the little children come. Don't turn them away. Don't make it hard for them to find my arms." He also said, *'If any of you put a stumbling-block before one of these little ones who believe in me, it would be better for you if a great millstone were fastened around your neck and you were drowned in the depth of the sea.'* (Matthew 18:6 NRSV)

We often think of the poor in spirit as someone other than ourselves because, no doubt, there is always someone worse off than we are. But, you know, you are allowed to be a poor one. You are allowed to say, "I have nothing. I can't pay the price I've been told it costs to come to my Father and climb into his arms."

And Jesus answers, "It's all right, Small One. I paid the price."

This is the third week of Lent. If you have a moment in your poverty, think of Jesus stopping on his journey to the Cross to clear the temple *for you*. Think of him driving out the noise, chaos, unfair demands and grasping hands reaching out to rob you of your dignity and ability to freely enter the Holy of Holies. See him turn to you to say, "There. It's done. They're all gone. Now you can enter and be with my Father."

<u>Lenten question</u>: Has anyone ever made you feel inadequate, unworthy of God's love or anything less than a dignified and beloved child of God? Remember, *absolutely no one or anything has the authority to do that to you*. By the same token, we all need to remember that we have no authority to do this to anyone else.

The Reply

John 3: 14-21
Jesus speaks with Nicodemus in the night.

In Year A, I posted a reflection titled "The Letter" which was a fictional letter from Joseph of Arimathea to Nicodemus. This is Nicodemus' reply:

Dear Joseph,

I have to admit that when you wrote exhorting me to go see Jesus of Nazareth, everything inside me rebelled at the thought. I was deeply concerned for you and for your standing within the temple if it ever became known that you had been won over by the Nazarene. I was also angry that you would encourage me to follow the same path of utter folly.

You have heard by now that this Jesus came to the temple and drove the moneychangers and the sellers of sacrificial animals out of the temple courts. The people were terrified because he was acting like a madman. When Annas, Caiaphas and the rest of us who were in the temple, came running out to see what the commotion was, we saw Jesus, whip in hand, in the center of great confusion. When he saw us, he cried out,

"My Father's house is a house of prayer!"

Then he looked directly at me, Joseph, and it was as if my heart was cut open and he could see everything within it. Everything. I looked around at the dust, the milling animals and the chaos of scattered coins and overturned booths and my eyes suddenly saw the jagged ugliness of something we have taken for granted for years. I looked at Annas and Caiaphas and was shocked at what I could see in their eyes. It wasn't just anger, Joseph, it was hideous, frustrated lust. Suddenly I knew, just from the look in their eyes, that the profits of the moneychangers and sacrificial animals weren't going for the upkeep of the temple. Caiaphas and Annas were lining their pockets with the money of the poor. Money that was meant for G_d was being used to keep them in luxury. Why I never knew this before, I don't know but it was as clear to me in that moment as the phylacteries they were wearing. My disgust was overwhelming.

It came to me then that I had to see this Jesus. I *had* to talk to him, Joseph. I had no idea what I would say or what I would ask. I just had a burning desire to speak with him one on one.

I'm not a courageous man. I found out where he was staying and I went in the dead of night, the hood of my cloak over my head so no one would recognize me. If Annas, especially, knew what was in my mind I shudder to think what he would do. He is a hard man but I didn't know how evil he is until that moment on the temple steps.

When I got to the place where Jesus was staying, it was dark and quiet within and I didn't know what to do. Had I thought about the lateness of the hour? No, I hadn't. All I had thought about was seeing him without being seen. I stood on the street thinking I should just head back home but my heart was pounding and the desire to see him was too much to ignore. What to do? Wake him up? Wake them all up?

Then I heard a quiet voice coming from above me, "Peace be with you, Nicodemus. I've been waiting for you."

I looked up and there he was, relaxed and leaning over the parapet of the roof. "The family has gone to sleep," he said. "Come up the outer steps and join me, brother. You'd better hurry before someone sees you." I couldn't clearly see his face but his voice told me he was smiling at my furtiveness.

I quickly went up to the roof and when I got there he was sitting at a small wooden table. On the table were a loaf of bread, a jar of wine and two cups. He really was expecting me, Joseph! He indicated the other chair and invited me to sit with him.

"Eat and drink, Nicodemus. I know you are hungry and your thirst is great," he said softly as he broke the bread and poured the wine. "Ask what you have come to ask."

We talked for hours, Joseph. Too much was said to write in one letter. The words that confused me the most were 'born again'. I had no idea what he meant so I challenged him but he said, "'Honestly, Nicodemus, I tell you that we speak what we know and testify to what we have seen; yet you don't receive our testimony. If I have told you about things of the earth and you don't believe, how can you believe if I tell you about heavenly things?"

When he said that, I wondered whom he was talking about. He said *we* speak and *we* testify. Who did he mean by 'we'? I was about to ask him when the light changed. I know it was night, Joseph, but I swear, the light changed. Or it appeared. Or it was always there but I never noticed it until then. At that moment light was all around us, and standing just behind Jesus were two Beings. If I had to describe them, I'd say one was like Wind and one was like Fire but they were much more than that and words are inadequate to describe them. I had to drop to my knees from the force of the overpowering love that was surrounding the three of them. I began to weep. I wept with tearing grief, absolute joy and for the sheer beauty and authority of that love. I knew never wanted to be without it again.

Then Jesus stood and the two Beings stood beside him, one on either side. I still don't know if Jesus could see them but his own face was like lightening and his eyes were like fire as he delved deep into my heart again. It was as if he was purging it with that fire. It hurt so bad but felt so right. He didn't seem to be speaking aloud but his voice filled my spirit, "For God loved the world so much, Nicodemus, that he sent his Son so that everyone who believes in him will not perish but will have eternal life." When he said that, the love flowing between the three became so intense I could hardly bear it.

"Lord! You are my Lord!" I cried through my tears. "I will openly follow you wherever you go. Everyone can know that you are my master. Let me never hide from the truth again! Let me be with you always, Jesus."

He pulled me to my feet and when I wiped my eyes on my sleeve, the light was gone. It was just an ordinary rooftop in the middle of the night. He put his hand on my shoulder and said, "No, Nicodemus, now is not the time to come with me. Go back to the temple. I know that isn't where you want to be now because you have seen that some people have loved darkness rather than light because their deeds are evil. Those who do evil can't stand me, brother. They hate my light and are deeply afraid their deeds will be exposed and the people will see them for who they really are.

"Go back to the temple, Nicodemus. It is still the house of my Father even though there are some who have perverted his truth and live to serve themselves. Serve me there. Let the people see there is goodness in the midst of evil. Be a servant of the light you have seen here and a voice of righteousness in the darkness. There will come a time when I will have great need of you – both you and Joseph of Arimathea. Tell Joseph you have spoken to me and that I said a time will come when both of you will give me shelter and a place to rest my weary head.

"The sun will be rising soon. You'd better go quickly, brother." As I turned reluctantly to go, he stopped me, laid his hands on my head and said, "My courage and grace goes with you. I will always be with you. *We* will always be with you."

And now, Joseph, it is without any qualms, with great humility and utter joy that I say to you: you were right. The Sun has risen in our midst. The Light has come and we knew it not. You and I are blessed beyond all telling. I look forward to the time when you and I will be able to give him shelter. I wonder when that will be?

Peace be to you and your house, my good brother. May his light continue to fill you and illuminate your path. I greatly look forward to our next meeting as brothers of the Son of G_d.

Your servant in him, (or in *them*!)
Nicodemus

P.S. I feel like I've been born again...

Take A Good Look At Yourself.

John 12: 20-33

Jesus speaks about a grain of wheat needing to die before it bears fruit. He also says that those who love their life will lose it and those who hate their life in this world will keep it for eternity.

Whenever we read Jesus proclaiming that those who love their life lose it, and those who hate their life will gain eternal life, it's always a shock to the spiritual system to hear Jesus using the word 'hate' as he does a few times in the gospels. I wanted to know what he really meant by 'hate' so I looked up the Aramaic word for it. Turns out that there are several and the one that makes the most sense in the context of Jesus' teachings is the word "sna". You can pronounce that however you want as, funnily enough, I don't speak Aramaic. Sna means, "To put to one side or set aside."

"Those who hold on to their life lose it and those who *set their own life to one side* will gain eternal life." Now that sounds more like the Jesus I know.

Lent is a good time to assess the state of your spiritual life but very often there is a common assumption that this kind of assessment means that what you'll find are a lot of areas where you've fallen down on the job and maybe have become a bit lax. I contend that many people fail to appreciate where they have succeeded beautifully and they fail to discover the things they do that epitomize holiness. This kind of discovery and appreciation should not lead a person to say, "I'm fine. I don't need to grow anymore." It should lead a person to understand that there is much in their life that is worthy of being offered to the Father as gift and as holy sacrifice.

Few people see the holiness of what they do and go through on a daily basis. Perhaps this is because all good people do what they do. But why would that diminish recognition of the holiness of their actions? Perhaps it's a misconception of what holiness means. Holiness means, "Set aside for God – consecrated to God." (Sna'd for God?) For example, most Catholic parents are serious about their faith and about raising their children to know and love God. How much more consecrated can one be? Holiness, as it pertains to us, doesn't mean perfect. Think of a chipped and blemished clay cup. If a priest takes that cup and blesses it and sets it aside to hold the blood of Christ at the Eucharist, that cup becomes holy – intended for a special purpose. It is its special purpose that makes it holy, not its state of perfection. So parents following their vocation have a consecrated purpose. In order to fulfill that purpose, they sna, or set to one side, many things that might lead to self-fulfillment and self-satisfaction.

If you spent years at university studying for a career, you gave up numerous pleasures and desires to do so. If you go to work daily in order to house, feed and clothe a family, that means other personal desires and dreams have been set aside. If you and your spouse have brought children into the world, you made a commitment to set aside your life for sake of your children. Those are just a very few examples among many.

It is hard to ascribe holiness to a life that's full of pressure, schedules and deadlines or to a life that's immersed in dirty diapers and mounds of laundry, endless meals and chaotic noise. There is a romantic idea of a holy life, a term that brings to mind glowing saints praying and contemplating in lonely cells. Yes, Religious give up much to answer the call to their vocation - but so do you. It is time we all started seeing marriage and raising a family as a holy vocation equal to that of the Religious vocation. It is time we began to respect deeply the single working mother or father. It is time we stood in awe of those who have never married and have led a life dedicated to the Lord while living in the world and supporting themselves. We need to honor the couples with no children who often seem to end up in nurturing roles, welcoming various lost souls into theirs hearts and homes. There is no hierarchy of holiness in the Kingdom. Every person who sacrifices, every person who sets to one side self satisfaction and every person who struggles with growth, prayer and following the will of God is one who is enveloped in a holy life. The life of a Religious has different struggles, but certainly not better ones or harder ones.

I have to tell you that I am often overcome by a sense of immense awe and holy respect when I hear of a mother working through a round of sickness in her children while being sick herself or when I see a busy student refusing to miss Mass and offering time to something like St. Vincent de Paul in spite of deadlines and looming exams. When I observe someone who has worked at a job for years and would love to retire but still needs to bring in money to provide for the family, I see a saint in the making. I see retired people giving of their time and resources to work in the church or volunteering to help those less able. I see grains of wheat falling to the ground and dying. I see lives and personal desires being set aside. I see it all the time – and so does the Lord.

Holiness abounds in the people of God and I am blessed to witness it. It makes me want to weep with gratitude sometimes for what people will set aside in order to bring life to others and in order to make sure the Lord is a part of their lives. When I witness this holiness I turn to the Father and I say, "Look at that, Father. Isn't that beautiful?" and he says to me, "It fills my heart. I know what they have given up for me and I cherish them for it."

The two Greeks said to Philip, "Sir, we wish to see Jesus." If those two men came to me today and said the same thing, I would reply, "Look at the ones who follow him without having seen him.

Look for the sacrificing mothers and fathers who die daily for their families. Look for the committed ones without partners, young and old, who follow with the single purpose of knowing his will. Look for the busy ones, the weary ones and the pressured ones who still take time to worship and have set aside their own dreams in order to follow God's dream. Look for these people and you will find holiness. You *will* find Jesus."

"And when I am lifted up from the earth, I will draw everyone to myself." This week, ponder on what you have set aside in your dreams and desires in order to follow Christ and your vocation. Bring these things to the Cross and know that he has drawn you to himself.

Blessed are you. Holy are you.

The Love Up There And The Love Down Here

The Gospel this week is the very long passion narrative with which everyone is familiar.

Perhaps too familiar?

Sometimes it's difficult to pay close attention to this Gospel as it's being read on Passion Sunday and again when it's read on Good Friday; it's so long and it really is very familiar. It's so easy for the mind to wander off in spite of all good intentions.

There are two short things I would like to draw your attention to and perhaps in lodging them in your mind, you will hear whatever you hear at Mass with a different frame of heart.

The first is something Jesus said to his disciples after the Last Supper when they had gone up to the Mount of Olives. It wasn't very flattering. He said, *"You will all become deserters."* This was said to the ones who would carry on his mission and especially to Peter, the one who would be the Rock on which he would build his Church. In other words, he was telling them that they would let him down, betray him, fail him, be inadequate for the job, and make the decision to be absent when he was most desperately in need of their presence, their support and their love.

He knew all this in his heart; he knew it without a shadow of a doubt. In all of history, before and after the crucifixion, there has never been such betrayal as when Jesus' friends and brothers ran away and left him all alone to die. They abandoned him to face the terror and pain on his own.

Do you think that when Jesus was on the cross and he gasped out in pain, "Father, forgive them, they don't know what they are doing," that he wasn't just praying for forgiveness for the Roman soldiers who were taunting him and causing him such excruciating agony? Could he not have also been praying for the disciples who were not there, who were hiding in terror? He was suffering on that cross for the ones who had ultimately betrayed his love and he had never loved those disciples as much as he loved them while he was on that cross.

The disciples' weakness, fear and poorness of heart, which resulted in terrible failure, was not the end of the story. *Not* the end of the story. NOT THE END OF THE STORY.

How often do you stop at your failures, weaknesses and inadequacies and write the end of your story right there? If that was where Jesus had stopped in his love there would be no cross and no salvation. But he says, "That's the end of the story only *you* can write but I'm the one who picks up the pen and keeps on writing in blood right through to the resurrection. I have won! I am now the True Author of your story."

The second incident I want to draw your attention to is nearer to the end of the reading: *"There were some women watching from a distance; among them were Mary Magdalene, and Mary the mother of James the younger and Joses, and Salome. These used to follow him and looked after him when he was in Galilee; and there were many other women who had come up to Jerusalem with him."* (Mark 15: 40, 41, Jerusalem Bible) In John's gospel we read that Jesus' mother, Mary, was there, as was John himself.

The women did not desert Jesus nor did John, who was the disciple closest to the heart of Jesus. I truly believe this is because the women and John understood Jesus' teachings better and in more depth. They were not receiving his message with just the

303

intellect; they understood the heart language of his message. When we believe in the Lord with just our intellect we understand and agree to the rules. When we believe with the heart we become submerged in the rivers of his compassion, forgiveness and mercy. Our intellect is needed for assent, but it's our heart that leads us to fall deeply in love with Jesus.

John and the women who stayed at the cross didn't just intellectually agree with Jesus' message; they had fallen completely in love with him. They loved him like a son, a brother, a best friend, a teacher and a savior before they even knew what salvation was. He was their Beloved Lord before the other disciples understood what a fullness of relationship with Jesus meant. John and the women were probably terribly afraid as they stayed near the cross, but their love and their grief were stronger – stronger even than death. To know how they felt, put your child, your husband, your best friend, your mother or father or your favorite brother or sister up on that cross and imagine if you could see yourself running away, even if you were afraid.

Don't think that Jesus did not catch the significance of the presence of those who stayed with him. The Father had brought True Love to stay with him in his hardest hours. Perhaps the presence of his mother and John as well as the other women was what gave him the grace to say, "Father forgive them, they know not what they do. Forgive the ones who ran away and left me. They don't know me yet so they don't know whom it is they have betrayed. Blessed are the ones who are with me. Thank you for their love and their presence. Thank you…"

As Jesus gave up his life, John and the women were beautiful signs to him that he was cherished and not alone. He had not been completely abandoned. They were the ones who intuitively understood how far Love would go to rescue the lost. It is said that at the end of John's life the only thing he could say to the people was, "Little children, love one another." He knew that love, not intellect or even a harsh death, was the saving power of Jesus. It all came down to love. It all comes down to love.

During the readings of the Passion this Sunday and on Good Friday, even if you lose concentration at times, be there as one of the women who stayed with him in his final hours or be there as John. Grieve with them. Weep with them. Ache with them.

Be there...and be blessed by his gratitude.

I Will See You There

The women and the disciples go to the tomb, find it empty and are told that Christ has risen, just like he said he would.

Alleluia!!

In one gospel the angel tells the women, *"But go, tell his disciples and Peter that he is going ahead of you to Galilee; there you will see him just as he told you."* (Mark 16:7 NRSV)

In the Greek, there are two words for "seeing". The first one is "blepo": to physically see with your eyes. When the women first came to the tomb they could see (blepo) that the stone had been rolled away.

The second word for 'see' is "orao". It, too, means seeing with your eyes but it can mean much more than that. It encompasses experience, inner knowledge, perception and understanding. *"...there you will see* (orao) *him just as he told you."* Jesus, through the angel, left an invitation for his followers to come to Galilee to not only behold him with their physical eyes but also to experience him with their hearts and minds.

But, for us, over 2000 years later, there can be a stumbling block when we're told we can see Jesus or experience him. Think of a tree. You can see (blepo) the tree with your eyes and have a tactile experience of it. You can touch its bark and leaves and you can enjoy its beauty as the wind blows through the leaves or the frost turns the leaves gold and orange. You can write poems praising the tree and you can long to sit in the shade of the tree. But always, you know that no matter how much you love and enjoy the tree, it is not aware of you. It doesn't know you are touching it, appreciating it or sitting in its shelter. It just does what a tree does: be a tree.

Or you can see (blepo) famous spiritual leaders at a conference and you can experience those leaders to some degree by what you hear them saying. Their teachings and experiences can influence you but one thing is lacking. They don't know you. They are aware that there are many individuals listening to them and they are giving themselves the best they can to this amorphous crowd of which you are just one small part. You are experiencing them but they are not experiencing you except as a tiny anonymous contributor to the group dynamics of the crowd.

For many people, the concept of "seeing Jesus" holds all the intimacy of beholding a beautiful tree or seeing a spiritual leader up on a stage from afar. Reading about Jesus' followers discovering that he is indeed alive and wants to see them in Galilee is a story that can feel far removed from our every day lives here and now.

It's all very well for the followers of Jesus to go to Galilee to see him, experience him and receive his love and forgiveness but what about us? Do we expect to have a one on one encounter with the risen Lord - or do we approach the story of the disciples' reunion with Jesus as a memorial story, something that happened then but not so much now. If we really explored the desires of our hearts, we would discover that what each one of us yearns to know is, "Can I see (orao) Jesus?" And, even more, each of us also wants to know, "Does Jesus 'orao' *me*? Does Jesus *see* me? Does Jesus experience me? Does he want to?"

It's one thing to want to have an experience of Jesus but it's quite another thing to understand that Jesus absolutely wants to experience you. He is not a tree. He is not this spiritual leader looking benignly down on an adoring crowd of billions. His saving act didn't just save you because you are a member of the club and all club members are saved. He knows you. He sees *you*. He suffered, died and rose again with *you* in his heart's eye.

But then you may start to think, "Yeah, and what he sees is how I am not a very great person. He sees how I lack discipline in prayer and how I forget to trust him and how I keep doing all these shameful things I know very well are wrong and unhealthy for me. He sees my negative reactions and my impulsive mistakes. He sees me and is sad and disappointed because I don't try harder to be worthy of his love."

You might not believe me if I told you how theologically incorrect this idea of Jesus is, but perhaps you will listen to a doctor of the church, St. Catherine of Siena:

"...We should not act as unwise worldly folk act who transgress the precept of holy Church when they say, "I'm not worthy!".... Oh, stupid humility! Who can't see that you aren't worthy! How long are you going to wait to be worthy? Don't wait; you'll be as worthy in the end as at the start, for even with all our uprightness we will never be worthy. God is the one who is worthy, and *with his worth he makes us worthy*."

Our resurrected Lord is not as interested in critiquing our unworthiness as we think he might be. If that were so, he would have left this message for his followers with the angel in the tomb: "Tell my disciples and Peter that they really screwed up and I am so disappointed in them and wounded by how they treated me. I will be in Galilee but I would prefer that they first spend time contemplating what they did to me and only come to Galilee when they've realized their inadequacies and have done something about them. And they'd better be really sorry when they come!"

Jesus, in fact, said nothing about the disciples' wounding actions. He just desired that they all come to see him, to 'orao' him. Jesus knew that if the disciples, especially Peter, sought him out and just looked into his eyes they would experience the healing power of being seen, individually, by a risen king who loved each one stronger, better and deeper than anyone had ever loved them before.

No doubt, before they encountered Jesus in Galilee, the disciples, especially Peter, had to struggle terribly with crippling shame and even struggle with whether they actually wanted to face Jesus after what they did to him. They didn't know he would be receiving them with pure love. They didn't know yet that what he did on the cross was to break the power of guilt and shame – not just all guilt and shame but also *their* guilt and shame.

They did not yet know the Alleluia Joy of Easter, which is the joy of seeing and being seen by the risen Lord, the joy of knowing that the slate has been wiped clean and a new invitation sent out:

"Come home. Let me see your face. Let me love you to wholeness. Come home."

2nd Sunday of Easter B

The Gift Of Doubt

John 20: 19-31
The Story of Thomas refusing to believe in the risen Christ unless he touches Christ's wounds.

When I met my husband, he wasn't just a mere doubting Thomas; after having drifted away from the Catholic faith, he had become a committed agnostic verging on atheism. He certainly was not looking for proof that Christ was raised from the dead. He was simply looking for female companionship and thought the best way to open doors to my heart was through expounding on all he knew about religion. In the middle of all this, I felt a strong leading to wash his feet, a suggestion to which he acquiesced in an attitude of patronizing amusement. Meanwhile, I was desperately hoping that it actually was God who had urged me to do this. I had no idea what I should say or do after I finished.

But as soon as I began to wash his feet, he fell completely apart. It was as if Jesus appeared to him in mercy and love and it was impossible for him not to believe. All his unbelief was washed away with his past sins and transgressions. Christ became his Lord and God in a matter of seconds. In that moment he had received a gift of faith. He had seen Jesus. Even though he tried to question it later, the gift proved too strong for him.

When Thomas saw (orao) Jesus, he had a full experience of Jesus. He didn't just see with his eyes, he saw with his heart. His exclamation of "My Lord and my God!" was not just an exclamation of recognizing the Jesus he knew before the crucifixion; it was an exclamation of recognizing the total reality of the risen Christ, *spoken in terms that had not been spoken by anyone before that.*

He fully recognized that Jesus was "Ho Theos" or *The* God. His statement explicitly said that he recognized Jesus as God, and Jesus did not deny it. Let me repeat: no one else had addressed Jesus as "Ho Theos" before Thomas did. Thomas didn't just recognize him as the Messiah, the Son of Man, the Master or the Supreme Teacher; he recognized that Jesus was God. Boom! This kind of recognition is not possible for a human unless the Lord reveals it. Jesus filled our "Doubting Thomas" with an inner revelation he hadn't even given to the other disciples yet.

We always seem to interpret this Gospel as a put down for Thomas and it really does sound like Jesus is gently rebuking him for not believing. But why would he rebuke Thomas? The other disciples had been allowed to see Jesus and it says that after Jesus greeted them, he showed them his wounds. It's not as if they had amazing belief based on nothing other pure faith and their belief in Jesus is never pointed out as less valid just because at first it was based on visual proof. The visual proof Jesus gave to all his followers in the days following the resurrection was actually crucial for the future of the church. Believers could safely believe because there were actual eyewitnesses to the fact that not only had Jesus truly been raised from the dead but he also had a body, a real body that could be touched and one that could consume food.

Have you ever had doubts about your faith? If you answered "No!" to that, I don't think I would believe you. They may not have been long lasting doubts leading to total unbelief but everyone has moments of doubt, especially in times of dryness or difficulties. You may have been simply going through a period where life was a grind and nothing was on the horizon to bring inspiration or relief or joy. Everyone has times like that. Maybe work is unchanging day after day and the same irritating people are always there. Or you've been very ill for a long time and nothing helps or brings relief. Or you've been in a period of stress and busyness where it feels like everyone always wants you to cater to their needs and desires but no one notices that you, too, have needs and desires. In times like these it's very easy to suddenly feel like the existence of a loving and nurturing God is a bit of a fairy tale, relevant to nothing. It makes you want to yell out, "Is anybody home out there??"

But, being a good Christian, you quickly tuck these doubts away and you certainly don't express them to anyone, especially not the Lord! Many people interpret these doubts as proof that they are lacking spiritually. It can be a bit of shock to see how easily these doubts can pop to the surface even if one has always been a strong, faithful Catholic.

Thomas did not hide his doubts and even if he had, Jesus would have known he had them. But perhaps it was Thomas' honesty with himself that laid the groundwork for a deep encounter with the risen Lord. Thomas didn't just want to believe because others had told him it was true; he wanted to believe because he had experienced Jesus for himself. This is a desire that Jesus can't resist. And he didn't resist. He came to Thomas and Thomas didn't even need to touch the wounds because Jesus revealed himself in a way that created a deep and true faith in Thomas' heart, one that physical evidence alone could never produce.

Every once in a while we all need to examine our faith and ask ourselves, "Do I believe because I have had an encounter with the risen Lord, or do I believe because someone has told me I should believe and I'm afraid not to?" Jesus certainly does not despise belief based on the testimony of others; in fact, he says, "Blessed are those who believe with no physical evidence to support that belief." But he definitely was not offended by Thomas' desire to see him face to face. If he had been offended by it, he would not have given Thomas the amazing gift of insight into the true nature of his Godhead.

Notice, though, that he didn't appear immediately to Thomas; there was a space of time between Thomas expressing his need to see and touch Jesus and the moment when Jesus actually appeared. In this period of time, Thomas had much opportunity for his desire to see Jesus to become stronger and stronger and for him to struggle with what he was prepared to believe about Jesus if Jesus *didn't* appear to him. What went through his mind during this period? He had no idea how long it would be until Jesus made an appearance or even if Jesus would appear. Everyone else was probably floating in their joy of knowing Jesus was alive while Thomas probably felt he was on the perimeter looking in, an outsider to faith and excluded from the joy of the rest of the disciples. What a tough time for him.

What a tough time for you.

But, if you are honest with your desire to see Jesus face to face, Jesus will come. I can't tell you when he will come and I can't tell you what kinds of emotions and inner struggles you might need to go through until he does come but do not ever believe that he is offended by your struggles to believe or your desire to experience his presence in your life.

How could he be offended? How could he not want to gift you like he gifted Thomas – or my husband, the resolute atheist – with a deep sense of being face to face with a Lord who loves you wildly, completely and with so much mercy that all you could possibly say is,

"Ho Theos! My Lord and my God!"

****

Did you know that the Greek phrase "Kyrie, Eleison" (Lord, have mercy) has the fuller meaning of, "Lord, soothe me, comfort me, take away my pain, and show me your steadfast love"? Mercy in scriptural terms is not the same as our modern meaning of justice. So next time you pray "Lord have mercy" at Mass, think of the above meaning and pray with all your heart, "Lord, have mercy. I want to see Jesus. Come, Lord Jesus."

"...A bruised reed he will not break, and a smoldering wick he will not snuff out." (Isaiah 42:3 NIV)

Momentous Peace

Luke 24: 35-48

The two men, who encountered Jesus on the road to Emmaus, are telling the other disciples about it when Jesus appears to them and greets them with, "Peace be with you." They are all terrified but he asks for food and eats it in front of them. Then once again, he opens their minds to the scriptures that prophesy his coming.

In both last week's and this week's Gospels, Jesus greets his disciples with, "Peace be with you." That was a common greeting in those days but we know now that Jesus did not and does not speak idle words. He knows that we all long for peace, a deep, continuous inner peace that will protect us from the raging storms and give us confidence that we will make it to a safe place. If that inner peace and confidence is missing, just like the followers of Jesus after the crucifixion we can feel like we are drowning in our anguish, our fears, our loneliness or in our spiritual destitution, and it's not long before we are chastising ourselves for a total lack of faith or wondering if God is displeased with us or if he really cares about our struggles.

Reading further in the Gospel it says, *"Then he opened their minds to understand the scriptures."* Remember, last week I pointed out that Thomas received a gift of knowledge as to who Jesus really was. What we are discovering here is that the faith and understanding that result in inner peace is a gift. We humans are not capable of manufacturing that kind of faith. It has to be given to us.

I can hear your minds churning with questions. "Why do some people seem to have so much more faith and inner peace than I have? Did they receive more than I did? Are they more deserving of the gift than I am? It doesn't seem fair, especially with something so basic and necessary to living the Christian life. If I have been given faith why do I often feel so bereft of this gift and so helpless to access it?"

If you have ever really listened to anyone who has gone through great grief and anguish or someone suffering with a long term physical painful illness or anyone who has had immense stress and struggle thrown at them for an extended period, what you will often hear them say is, "I have to take it one day at a time." Indeed, in times of great suffering and struggle it often comes down to one moment at a time or one second at a time. If those who struggle with grief and anxiety are also struggling with their faith, what they will eventually discover (whether they can express it this way or not) is that God dwells in the present moment and faith is given *for the moment, in the moment.* It is not given for tomorrow or for any time in the future. Faith is a gift for the holy Now. It cannot be stored up or collected. It is like the manna in the wilderness that was given daily and could not be hoarded or stockpiled because God wants his people to look to him every moment of every day. Our inclination is to get what we need and then forget that God wants a relationship with us. He doesn't just want to be 'the God of handouts', someone we run to in times of trouble but sort of forget about the rest of the time.

Alcoholics Anonymous has always recognized and captured the healing power of the principle of walking in the present moment. For Catholics, it is a beautiful mystery that invites us to enter into God's indwelling presence in our lives. We must pay more attention to it. It isn't a principle just for those who are struggling and in pain; it is the key to always living in fullness with Christ and it is for everyone who longs for a deeper connection with God in their spiritual walk.

It is not easy to stay in the present moment. It actually seems to be against our broken human nature to do that. We are all given a full portion of faith but we rarely live in the place where our faith is dwelling. Our minds are continually in the past with wounds we have endured and resentments we still carry, or else in the future dealing with fearful imaginings or desires for situations and things we think we want and need. Even the followers of Jesus who had seen Jesus and had received gifts of understanding and deeper perception, still had to grasp that they had to stay with Jesus in the present moment and not allow their fears and imaginings to dictate what the future might hold. Staying in the present moment is a spiritual skill and often it's a skill learned in the furnace of pain and struggle, where thinking ahead or remembering the past can cause emotions to spin completely out of control.

Jesus instructed his followers to wait in Jerusalem for the infilling of the Holy Spirit. They waited for fifty days, fifty long, tense and arduous days of having no idea of what Jesus said they should wait for. Each one of them had been given the gift of faith to believe that Jesus was indeed alive. However, that time of waiting was not filled with deep inner peace. They had to learn to be in the present, to wait day-by-day, moment-by-moment, second by second for the promise of Jesus to be fulfilled while being acutely aware that they could be hauled off to prison or crucifixion at anytime. And I have no doubt as to who was with them, teaching them the fine spiritual art of waiting, believing and walking with the Father in the present moment and of seeking grace just for that moment without looking one second ahead to an uncertain and perhaps terrifying future.

Mary.

Yes, Mary was with them nurturing them in the clarifying truth that God's power is mighty and that God's power dwells in the present moment. Whenever they began to run away with visions of a future they couldn't control or when they started castigating themselves and each other for their past mistakes, I'm sure Mary was there gently calling them back. "Stay here. Don't go running off like that. He's not in your past failures and mistakes nor is he in your limited imaginings of what the future might hold. He's here. Be here. Speak to him. Be with him. Stay here." If her words didn't reach them, her inner peace did. Mary knew what she was talking about. She had the authority of experience - about 34 years of it.

Does God send painful circumstances into our lives to "teach us a lesson" about living in the present moment or about trust? I don't believe that. Life is just hard and it is often very painful simply because we live in a broken world with broken bodies and broken relationships, and Jesus never said he came to make everything really easy for those who had enough faith. He came, died and rose again in order to be with us (Emmanuel: God with us) on this difficult journey so that instead of becoming even more broken we can walk moment by moment with him and find in him the wholeness, life, peace, healing and daily provision we all yearn for.

He is in the present. He is with you. Your faith is full and intact waiting for you to dwell within it so that you can learn to hear, just as Mary learned to hear, the Master's gentle voice whispering in the midst of the chaos,

"Peace be with you."

Don't Leave Your Staff At The Door

John 10:11-18

Jesus says that he is the Good Shepherd who lays down his life for his sheep. He says the hired hands run away at any sign of danger but the Shepherd protects the sheep. He knows his sheep and they know him.

I have a confession to make: There are many times when I go to Mass and behave like a hired hand rather than a shepherd. I don't think I'm alone in this. In fact, I know I'm not alone in this.

The whole image of the Good Shepherd is very comforting but in this scripture Jesus wasn't actually speaking to his followers. He was speaking to the priests, scribes and Pharisees who were challenging him about healing a blind man. Yes, he was saying that he is the shepherd of his people but he was also identifying himself as the God of Israel who, in Ezekiel 34, spoke of himself as the True Shepherd of his people. In Ezekiel, God was immensely angry with the leaders who were leading his people astray, abusing them, being careless of their wellbeing and abandoning them to great dangers. Jesus, in portraying himself as the Good Shepherd, was making a statement to those listening that he was God and he was very clear that he was not happy with the spiritual leadership of the day. Compassion, mercy and caring for the people was not the first priority of many of those entrusted with the welfare of God's people. Power, riches, political advantage, image protection and the letter of the law were of far more concern to many of the leaders than the spiritual well being of the people.

In Jesus' time, a shepherd was with his sheep 24/7. He looked after the wounded and searched for the lost. He would never let a sheep wander off on its own to fend for itself. If a small lamb couldn't keep up he would carry it on his shoulders. He led his flock to pastures that he had already scoped out to make sure it was safe and there were no noxious plants or dangerous predators. He led the sheep to pools of still water because sheep will not drink from running water. He was intimately aware of every sheep in his flock and knew the needs of each one.

When the Holy Spirit anointed the disciples on Pentecost, there was a huge shift in the common perception of a spiritual community. There were no longer a few designated shepherds controlling a large flock of hapless sheep. In the new Church, all were sheep – and *all were shepherds*. Yes, the early church had appointed leaders but those leaders were no longer the priestly elite with everyone else falling into the category of sheep just waiting to be told what to do. People were joyfully alive to their own anointing. People cared for one another spiritually, physically, emotionally and materially. This was a church where everyone was called to be priestly shepherds and those early Christians took their new role very seriously.

To say that modern churches do not fulfill a mandate to shepherd the poor of this world would be completely untrue. There are so many amazing organizations and initiatives that seek to shepherd those who are suffering or needy or hungry as well as wonderful people who have hearts for the sick, the lonely, the homeless and all sorts of others in need. But there is one place where we all tend to abandon our shepherding roles: the Mass.

Vatican II called the Eucharist "the source and summit of the Christian life and the center of the Christian community." Yet, how often do you go to Mass and leave as soon as possible? How often do you go up to someone you have never talked to before and initiate a conversation? How often do you immediately seek out the people you know and are familiar with and chat only with them? Are you aware of the people who arrive alone and leave alone with no one ever greeting them and conversing with them? Do you ever offer to pray with or for someone you don't know well who is struggling with loss or illness? How many times do you express gratitude or appreciation to a reader, a musician, a Eucharistic minister, an usher or an altar server? When you give the sign of peace, do you look people in the eye or are your eyes searching for the next person you have to shake hands with?

If we can't be true shepherds to one another at Mass there is a huge chunk missing in our priestly ministry. Mass is not a time for all the sheep to be herded into a walled enclosure so they can each spend private, one on one time with the Shepherd. It is the source, summit and center of the Christian life and of community. A Christian's vocation is one of being a priest and a shepherd – it doesn't matter if this plays out in marriage, the ministerial priesthood, the single life or in the Religious life. Our call is to shepherd one another. We are all pastors and the Mass is where all our priestly activities should culminate in a community gathered *with* each other in mutual love and awareness at the table of the Lord. If we go to Mass with the intention of just minding our own business, attending to our own spiritual communications with Jesus, saying hello to a few people we know and then heading home, we have abdicated from our royal priesthood and our community is much poorer for it.

If Mass is the summit of Christian life then that means it should be an inspiring epitome – a shining example – of the Christian life. Of all the things we do as Christians in our daily lives, the Mass should be the one place where we consistently go to act with the full intention of being True Shepherds. That's what Liturgy means: "The work of the people" or "The work of the Shepherds."

Jean Allen

The next time you go to Mass, take a look around. Look at all the people: the young, the old, the irritating, the good friends and the relative strangers. Look at the faces: the stony, the prayerful, the sad, the contented and the distracted. Look at them and think, "These are my people. These are my flock. This whole church is my pastoral field." If everyone approached the Mass this way, the life of our Masses would cease to hinge on the ministerial priest up front and on whether he is a dynamic, wonderful priest who gives great homilies or is a cantankerous old soul just putting in time. The life of our Masses would hinge on what they were meant to hinge on: the people of God coming together as anointed shepherds to be united with the Good Shepherd, loving him and one another.

Once again, I admit it. I sometimes go to Mass and abdicate my vocation as a priestly shepherd. I go as a hired hand. It's a choice I make. The church suffers because of it…

…and so do I.

Branching In

John 15: 1 – 8

Jesus speaks about being the True Vine. Unless you abide in him, you cannot bear fruit.

Two reflections ago, I spoke of the importance of staying in the present moment and not allowing ourselves to constantly dwell in future desires, wishes, dreads and possibilities, or in past resentments and regrets or even in the memories of happier and more pleasant times.

It is difficult to find the words to impress upon everyone how important this is for the spiritual life. Oh. Wait a minute...Jesus already said those words: "Those who abide in me and I in them will bear much fruit, because outside of me you can do nothing."

Definition of Abide: stay with, remain, continue without fading or being lost.

It's that last phrase that caught my attention: "continue without fading or being lost." It creates a pretty accurate picture of what happens to us all the time; we fade away into the past or the future, into our desires, anxieties and guilt. We fade away and get lost.

Jesus tells us in this week's gospel that if we want to bear fruit we need to abide in him. It follows that in order to abide in him we have to stay with him where he is, which is in the present moment. Jesus is here now. Because we live in a world of illusion, it will often seem like the past and future are terribly real and relevant especially when one is dealing with broken relationships, sick bodies and other difficult circumstances.

These things will seem to be the reality we need to deal with, the situations in which we want the Lord to meet us. But, as one very astute person put it, the Kingdom is now or never.

If any of you have been trying to stay in the present with the Lord, you'll know it's not easy. The complaint that is often expressed to me is, "But most of the time I don't like the present moment! There's hard stuff happening in the present moment and when I try to be there I can't immediately find God and so I slip off into the future or the past." I had to find an analogy that would give a clear understanding of why we should stay as much as possible in the present even if it's not pleasant and even if we cannot immediately perceive the Lord's presence.

In this day and age it is difficult not to be aware of healthy nutrition. An occasional treat is fine but most of us understand that a constant diet of fatty and sugary foods is unhealthy. If we feel like eating piece of cake 10 minutes before supper we know it's better to resist because the cake will take away our appetite for the good healthy food that is being prepared. And as for the idea of constantly feeding ourselves fast food and allowing ourselves to snack all day on momentarily satisfactory but unhealthy foods, we know that eventually good food will become more and more unpalatable and we will lose the desire and will to eat healthy food. Good food will seem unexciting, bland and unsatisfying.

When we spend an inordinate amount of time in the future or in the past, eventually our appetite for and ability to stay in the present moment is diminished. Present moment becomes more and more unpalatable. The truth is that the present moment can be painful or at least boring or unpleasant and not easy to deal with. There's often a burden there we have to carry. But by heading off into the past or the future we usually pick up more burdens and pain and add them to the load we are already carrying. Then we complain that we can't find the grace to carry the load. I do that. You do that. It is human nature to do that.

The grace is there. The grace is provided but the grace is for the load of the moment, not for all the extra illusory loads we pull onto our shoulders indiscriminately.

Not only is there grace available for the given load of the moment but also when we stay in that moment and abide with Jesus, fruit eventually starts to grow and flourish. When we are not with him in the present we can do nothing; we cannot produce fruit and we cannot solve our problems. Our spiritual life becomes like dry dead branches.

"Whoever doesn't stay with me is thrown away like a branch and withers; these branches are gathered and burned." This sounds like a harsh condemnation but I don't believe Jesus meant it that way. It's just that the consequence of not abiding in him is that we become dry, brittle unfruitful and very easily burned up by the fire of life.

Burned up and burnt out.

How familiar does that sound? So many people I have talked to lately are burned up and burnt out. They feel consumed by the heat of their struggles, challenges and busyness. Jesus hasn't condemned them, gathered them up and burned them; it's just what happens when we forget about abiding in him – forget or never knew how to abide in the first place. We shouldn't immediately condemn ourselves for not abiding in Jesus because so many of us have not been taught how and have not been made aware that this is where we should be.

I have been sharing with some people my personal prayer for staying in the moment. I don't regard this prayer as one that makes things happen immediately or one that guarantees that what I want and desire will come to be. It's not the key or The Mythical Secret Prayer That Makes Everything Great. It is simply a prayer of placement. It is a short prayer that brings me back to where I should be.

The prayer is: "I am here. You are here."

The prayer is uncomplicated and I don't add to it. It is a prayer to bring me back to the moment and to remind me that God is in the moment and nowhere else. When I pray it I am saying, "I have come back to this present moment. I have come back to you. I am consciously placing myself here." When I pray, "You are here," I am reminding myself that he is indeed present. He is Lord of the moment and Lord of all that is occurring in that moment. It is saying that the moment is his; he owns it and I trust him to do with that moment whatever he wills even if it means the moment stays unpalatable or difficult or boring. I am also proclaiming that the future and the past are also his, not mine, and I am going to allow him to be responsible for all the past and future moments of my life. It is a prayer to help me detach from my expectations of what I think he *should* be doing for me. He is always there for me but if I am always focused on my expectations and interpretations I miss him 99% of the time.

God's presence, help and inspiration often go completely unrecognized because we are looking for and waiting for fire and wind that look like the images in our minds. Our understanding of the Lord's power has been distorted. We usually only think of one kind of power - the kind that moves the mountains *we* think should be moved. When we become more and more aware of the consistent and always present power of God, a power that is quiet and non-intrusive but entirely awesome, we begin to get addicted to running back to that present moment and waiting and watching for him. The more we stay there, the more observant we become and the more adept we become staying in the present, the more we catch delightful glimpses of him and his actions.

The deep joy that grows from encountering the power of the Lord in innumerable small but distinct ways is infinitely superior to encountering that odd display of power that cannot be missed because it's so obvious. As one stays present in the moment and stays attached to the vine watching for the stillness of his power, one's connection to God grows less and less dependent on how situations are developing or on how one is feeling and begins to be based on a sense that God can do anything, anywhere and at anytime. And will! "I am here. You are here," is an official prayer of abdication. "You are the Lord, not me. I'm stepping down now. You take over."

Jesus made this promise: "If you abide in me, and my words abide in you, ask for whatever you wish, and it will be done for you."

I have to laugh about that promise. The thing is, when we are truly abiding in him the only thing we really want to ask him for is to be able to stay there with him – while he takes care of everything else.

Sweet.

Chara

John 15: 9-17

Jesus explains that as the father has loved him, he loves us. He says he has spoken about abiding in him in the same way he abides in the Father so that his joy will be in us and our joy will be complete. He does not call us servants anymore but friends and we don't choose him; he chooses us. He calls us to love one another.

"Even after all this time the sun never says to the earth, "you owe me." Look what happens with a love like that. It lights the whole sky."
[Hafiz of Shiraz]

"I pray that you will understand the words of Jesus, "Love one another as I have loved you." Ask yourself, "How has he loved me? Do I really love others in the same way?" Unless this love is among us, we can kill ourselves with work and it will only be work, not love. Work without love is slavery." (Mother Theresa)

"How has he loved me?" What an astounding question Mother Theresa proposes. We could think on that one long and hard and come up with numerous answers but the trick is to come up with an answer born of personal intimate experience, an answer no one else could give because no one else has been loved by Christ the way you have been loved by Christ.

Has Jesus' love for you lit up your whole sky? Have you been loved in a way that has completely obliterated the concepts of 'obligation' and 'owe'? We have made the grave mistake of reducing the love of Jesus into an obligation and have been made to feel we owe Christ something. On some vague intellectual level I suppose one could say we should love Christ because we owe him one. But that's not how he wants us to love him or experience his love. He desires that kind of love about as much as we desire to be loved by someone just because they feel they owe us something or because they feel obligated to love us.

That's the love of keeping accounts. Ledger love. The biggest problem with have a ledger love relationship with God is that we eventually start to feel like he owes us as well. Little resentments subconsciously prick our hearts. "I did this for you so how come you didn't do that for me, God?" Ledger love is a basic and broken human way of experiencing love. It's a love based on 'what I have done for you and what you should do for me' and it's so pandemic that we have huge difficulty relating to Jesus' love for us on any other level.

Jesus talks about abiding in his love – staying in it, resting in it and not fading away from it. He doesn't just say to his disciples and to us, "Love one another." He says we must love one another *as he loves us* – in the same way but also at the same time. An ongoing intimate experience of his love is implied. His commandment is that we must first experience and abide in that intimate love and then share it. If the first two parts of the equation are missing (experiencing and abiding) then, as Mother Theresa said, we aren't journeying as his friends but rather as his slaves.

It's easy to read Jesus' words about loving one another as he loves us as if we're reading an instruction manual. Here's how you do it: step 1, step 2, step 3.... end result: Christian life. But Jesus slips something in there that indicates something far more profound than that. He says, *"I have said these things to you because I want my joy to be in you, and so that your joy may be complete."* The Greek word for joy is 'chara', a word that means "a great calm delight that comes from deep within". What is striking about Jesus speaking about 'chara' in this passage is that he will soon face death by crucifixion, yet because he abides in the Father's love and stays in the present moment with that love, he can speak of his joy, his chara. The joy that has its source in present moment abiding is the joy he wants to share with his disciples and with us.

The chara joy that Jesus is speaking of is not the emotion we tend to think about when we hear the word 'joy'. We think of happy, happy, happy. We think of good feelings bubbling up over wonderful circumstances. But the great calm delight Jesus wants us to experience has nothing to do with circumstances. It has nothing to do with balanced accounts or obligations fulfilled. It is far removed from striving and reward. It is simply the deeply soul-satisfying experience of being gazed upon in absolute love by God. It is the profound revelation that there is nothing one can do to earn or create that gaze of love; it is simply there, full, abundant and ready, just waiting for us to come and abide. All he asks is that we come, receive, stay and not fade away.

You cannot love completely unless you know you are completely loved. Jesus wants you to know how loved you are so that your joy will be complete. The word complete is like the word 'unique'. It is an absolute concept. Something can't be more complete than something else. So, if Christ loves you completely, there is nothing else to be done that can make it 'more complete'. You can do nothing to earn it or perfect it. You are completely loved. What is left is to experience his love, experience joy and then love others in the way he loves you: with spiritual eyes that see that you and everyone else have been "fearfully and wonderfully made and marvelous are his works". (Psalm 139: 14)

"How has he loved me?" This question is crucial. The answer is, "With joy." Believe in that answer. Abide in it. Dwell on it. Contemplate it. Soak it in. Begin to sense chara, that great, calm delight within your innermost being and begin to realize that that amazing sense of chara is what he is feeling about you.

This is not the time to start thinking, "Oh, but I'm not worthy. I have this failing and that obstinate sin. I'm so inadequate here and feel like such a loser there." Do you know what that's called? That's called fading away. That's called moving away from him and just spending time with your self-perceptions. There's no joy there.

Abide, be loved, then go love. It's complete joy.

Gifted And Sent

Mark 16: 15-20

Jesus tells his disciples to go out to the whole world, proclaim the Good News and baptize them. He tells them that marvelous signs will accompany them. Then he was taken up to heaven.

There's always a tendency in people to be attracted to – or repelled by – the sensational. In reading the gospel this week, the phrases about picking up snakes and drinking poison are sure to raise even fleeting questions about one's own faith levels given that most of us wouldn't be too enthusiastic about putting our faith to the test by going out and finding a snake or looking under the sink for a poisonous substance.

As always, scripture must be read in context. This week there is a choice of two passages for the second reading and in one of the passages (Ephesians 4: 1-13 NRSV) we are told *"When he ascended on high he made captivity itself a captive; he gave gifts to his people."* And further on it says, *"The gifts he gave were that some would be apostles, some prophets, some evangelists, some pastors some pastors and teachers to equip the saints for the work of ministry..."* In the total context of all the readings, what is being said is that there are many signs that will accompany all believers, but not necessarily will *all* the signs accompany every believer. Not all of us will be evangelists, not all will be teachers and not all will pick up actual snakes or consume poison – unless it is the handling of someone who has fangs of negativity and is ready to sink those fangs in us in an attempt to poison our self love and God confidence. There are lots of snakes and poison of that sort that every believer must handle.

According to scripture, each one of us has been Gifted and we are all required to open ourselves to the Spirit so that our Gift can be used for the formation of our own spirits, the building up of the body and for the good of the whole world. It is not up to us as individuals to decide arbitrarily that we should be teachers or healers or that we should go snake hunting in order to prove that our faith is alive and well.

Jesus ascended into heaven after he completed his mission, but before doing so he indicated, "I have done all that I was called to do and now it's your turn." What we need to do is ask him, "What do you want from me, Lord? What is my Gift? Who have you called me to be? What is my mission?"

At this point most people would look at either their talents and skills or their vocation to determine what Gift God has given them for the building up of themselves, the body and the world. Some would say, "I am a parent or I am single or I am a Religious. That's my Gift for the building up of the body." Others might look at a talent they have, a talent such singing or leadership or administration. Someone else might ponder the skills they have learned in school or elsewhere, ones they are good at, and see how those skills could benefit the body of Christ. For instance a doctor might donate her skills to helping the poor or a good cook might bring people together around the table for communion and fellowship, thereby building up community.

All these skills, talents and vocations are absolutely critical to the body of Christ and are used by the Lord for building up his people. But we all need to go one step further. Talents, skills and vocations can be lost due to circumstances of life or they can change or they can fade away eventually. Parents will not always be involved in the intensive giving called for when children are young and living at home. Spouses can die suddenly. A singer can lose his or her voice due to old age or illness; a good reader can go blind. A carpenter can get arthritis. The Gift God gives for the building of the body will never die and never fade, though it is possible for it to be forgotten. A talent, skill or vocation is the medium through which the Lord may administer the Gift. The Gift is the electrical current; the talent, skill or vocation is simply the wire. I will go even one step further and state that those who are in the process of discovering their Gift are hearts that are discovering who they are in God's eyes and have begun to understand their full personal value to him, to the body and to the world. The Gift is not only powerful, it is immensely attractive and has the capacity to inspire others to thirst for God himself as well as bring the bearer of the gift to spiritual fullness.

I have mentioned before that there can be a great deal of agony when we discover that we can be fully engaged in the vocation we were called to and not feel entirely fulfilled by that vocation. Certainly there are times of great joy in our vocations but there are far more times of weariness, frustration, anger, resentment and boredom. It doesn't matter what your calling or vocation is, this will be true.

The vocation is not the Gift. It is simply the vehicle God has chosen for you. Once committed to one's vocation, one still needs to recognize and allow the Lord to develop the Gift.

By now you will have noticed that I have been capitalizing the word "Gift". That's because the Gift is a person. The Gift is a manifestation of Jesus himself and that is why The Gift of God is so attractive, so beautiful, so healing and so powerful. It's also the reason why the Gift cannot fade, wither or die. Jesus is alive! He ascended to heaven so that we could become vessels of the Gift for the world, so that we can all become Christophers, or "Christ Bearers".

Listen to me! I did not say that you should simply act like Jesus. You are to become conduits of Christ himself so that in offering your Gift, what you are offering is an aspect of himself that he has anointed you (you!) to carry and give. What a Gift! If each of you were to freely offer to your family, to the Body and to the world the unique part of Jesus he has anointed you to offer, the church would be turned upside down and the world would be astounded. And you would experience a deeper spiritual fulfillment than you could imagine.

A prayer that you may hear at Mass this weekend is written by St. Paul and is the beginning of one of the alternative scriptures for the second reading (Ephesians 1: 17-23 NRSV). Please read this slowly and know that you are under this powerful prayer. Pray it for yourself; pray it for your family and all your brothers and sisters in Christ.

"Brothers and sisters, I pray that the God of our Lord Jesus Christ, the Father of glory, may give you a spirit of revelation and wisdom as you come to know him, so that, with the eyes of your heart enlightened, you may know what is the hope to which he has called you, what are the riches of his glorious inheritance among the saints, and what is the immeasurable greatness of his power for us who believe, according to the working of his great power."

Amen and amen.

After note: When I was typing out "...with the eyes of your heart enlightened", I accidentally typed, "...with the **yes** of your heart enlightened". I thought it was equally appropriate. Sometimes our "Yes" to God needs to be enlightened and filled with a deeper revelation of Him.

More Beautiful Than The Sun

John 15: 26-27, 16:12-15
Jesus tells his disciples that when the Advocate (Holy Spirit) comes he will testify on Jesus' behalf. He says that when the Spirit of Truth comes he will guide them into all truth. He will take what is Christ's and declare it to them.

You are a good Christian. You attend Mass on Sundays and perhaps other days of the week, you yearn for God's presence in your life, you pray in times of trouble and give thanks to the Lord in good times and you are concerned about being who the Lord has called you to be.

Have you ever stopped to think that on your own steam you have absolutely no capacity to be the spiritual person you are and that the only reason you can desire God and make efforts to include him in your life is because the Holy Spirit is blessing you moment by moment with vision, desire and capacity? It is the Holy Spirit who prepared your spirit for creation and continues to do so in the same way he hovered over the chaos of the world and prepared it to hear the Word. "Send forth your Spirit and we *shall be* created." His action is constant and never ending if we allow it. The Holy Spirit's presence in our lives is a gift beyond comprehension.

Yet, the Holy Spirit has been called The Forgotten Paraclete. Why? Perhaps it's because we remember to ask Jesus or the Father or Mary or our favorite saints for help and guidance but we often forget to direct our attention to the Holy Spirit. This may be because Jesus, Mary and the Saints had human bodies with human natures and the word 'Father' is basically a human concept that embodies in our minds a certain set of familiar characteristics. But the Holy Spirit in scripture was never presented to us in a human form and has not been portrayed as a being with a human face or human characteristics. He is usually symbolized by flames of fire, a mighty wind or by a dove and that makes him a little more difficult to comprehend or apprehend with our minds. It's challenging to have a close relationship with fire, wind or a bird.

Which is a pity. Just think of a few of his alternative names: Comforter, Counselor, Advocate and Paraclete. The word Advocate comes from the Latin Advocare - "to call to one's aid." The word Paraclete comes from the Greek words para, "alongside", and kletos, "to call". The Holy Spirit is on call 24/7 and he walks alongside of us completely available to comfort, counsel, teach, change and give aid to us.

Still, who is this Holy Spirit, really? What can we say about him that would fix in our minds and hearts the reality of the person that he is?

I've got a little list. I have referred before to this list from the book of Wisdom, (chapter 7: 22-30 and 8:1, Jerusalem Bible) but it is one of my all time favorite scripture passages and worth including again. It is said to be a description of Wisdom (personified in the old testament as a 'she') but in reading this descriptive list of the characteristics of wisdom, it is obviously a description of the Holy Spirit. Read this list and you will have a much clearer idea of the amazing and awesome nature of the Holy Spirit who was sent to be our constant companion when we were baptized and who has remained with each one of us ever since.

"There is in her (wisdom) a spirit that is intelligent, holy, unique, manifold, subtle, mobile, clear, unpolluted,

distinct, invulnerable, loving the good, keen,
irresistible, beneficent, humane,
steadfast, sure, free from anxiety,
all-powerful, overseeing all,
and penetrating through all spirits
that are intelligent, pure, and altogether subtle.
For wisdom is more mobile than any motion;
because of her pureness she pervades and penetrates all things.
For she is a breath of the power of God,
and a pure emanation of the glory of the Almighty;
therefore nothing defiled gains entrance into her.
For she is a reflection of eternal light,
a spotless mirror of the working of God,
and an image of his goodness.
Although she is but one, she can do all things,
and while remaining in herself, she renews all things;
in every generation she passes into holy souls
and makes them friends of God, and prophets;
for God loves nothing so much as the person who lives with wisdom.
She is more beautiful than the sun,
and excels every constellation of the stars.
Compared with the light she is found to be superior,
for light is succeeded by the night,
but against wisdom darkness does not prevail.
She reaches mightily from one end of the earth to the other,
and she orders <u>all things well</u>.

Whenever I read that, I am comforted and excited. This is the One whom Jesus sent to be with us forever to guide, console, help, counsel and make us more aware of who Jesus and the Father are.

There is one word in that description I love the best: "subtle". The Holy Spirit is so subtle that he penetrates all other subtleties.

What this means is that if we are not experiencing blatant displays of God's power in our lives in ways we would like to see, it does not mean we are forgotten or that nothing is being accomplished. The Holy Spirit is subtle and his power is more likely to subtly penetrate the deepest areas of our lives causing slow but deep-rooted change rather than wowing us with lightshows of his power which can thrill us in the moment but leave us unchanged in the roots of our beings. That doesn't mean we can't witness the beautiful movement of the Spirit. It just means we need to pay way more attention than we normally do. He is always there, always working and always creating, but we usually miss his presence and workings unless he graces us with a really obvious display of power. Again, living in the present moment is how and where we will gain a huge appreciation for how the Spirit moves. It rarely will be the way we think he should move or the way we want him to move but the wisdom of the Spirit permeates our lives. The Spirit "orders all things well."

In his famous prayer, St. Patrick wrote, "I arise today through a mighty power..." Try making this your morning prayer: "I arise today through a mighty power. Today, by the power of the Holy Spirit I shall be created."

Then step back and let him do it.

The Fourth Person

Matthew 28: 16-20

The disciples go to the mountain where Jesus directed them to go before his ascension. He directs them to make disciples of all nations, baptizing them in the name of the Father and of the Son and of the Holy Spirit. He tells them that he will be with them to the end of time.

Most small children go through a stage where they prefer their mother to their father. Mom hands the child to Dad to hold while she completes a task and the child starts screaming and reaching for Mom. It's disconcerting for Dad and for Mom it's flattering but annoying. She also feels a bit embarrassed for her husband who is feeling a little excluded. Yesterday his child adored him; today she will have nothing to do with him. It's just a stage but an uncomfortable one.

As we get older, we discover we prefer to share our thoughts and feelings with one parent over the other. Some of us relate very well to our fathers and some of us find our mothers more in tune with who we are. It mostly has to do with the meshing of personalities, but these preferences can still create within us mild to strong feelings of guilt that we feel so much more comfortable with one parent rather than the other.

Parent/child relationships are immensely complex with innumerable issues influencing the dynamics of those relationships. It's no wonder that when we go to relate to God all the familial wounds we carry from our own past and present relationships with our parents are projected onto our relationship with him.

It's also very common and natural to feel a little guilty about the fact that we have a strong preference as to which member of the Trinity we address when we pray. If one's natural father was distant or harsh and demanding when one was growing up, there is a tendency to shy away from God the Father. We expect him be the same kind of father with the same kinds of demands or judgments. That is a common projection in the spiritual life but definitely not the only one. There are as many projections about the Father, Son and Holy Spirit and as many comfort levels with each member of the Trinity as there are Christians. We each bring our own parental and sibling relationship baggage to our relationship with the Lord.

It is difficult to get away from projecting onto God all the minor and major complexities of human relationships and there is often a lingering sense of guilt for paying attention to one and ignoring the other two members of the Trinity as if the other two might be hurt by our preference for the one we feel most comfortable with.

The truth is there is no hurt or resentment within God when we pray and relate more to one person of the Trinity over another. Human relationships are made complex and difficult by one thing: broken egos. Ego (Latin for "I") is the inner sense of self-esteem and self-identity and our human egos are constantly searching for evidence that we are worthwhile and valuable in the eyes of others, especially if one or both of our natural parents withheld approval and acceptance. Another name for ego is 'false self'. When we suspect that another person prefers someone else's company or abilities to ours, it is extremely hard on our egos. There is very little that we do in this life that is not somehow influenced by the needs of our wounded and fragile false selves. Much of what we do is saying, "Please accept me. Please appreciate me. Please recognize my value."

It's almost impossible for us to understand that the Trinity does not possess a broken ego. God is completely at home with himself. He does not need our love, worship, adoration and obedience to complete or add to his self-image and sense of self worth. In fact, 'self-image" and "self-love" are relative terms totally inapplicable to the Trinity. The Trinity is the whole Image. They are complete Love. They need nothing because they are everything. We are so wrapped up in the needs of our own egos that we can hardly comprehend a God who does not operate out of ego.

God is pure Love, and pure Love's nature is self-giving, not self-serving. It is no wonder then, that out of pure Love's total nature of giving, sharing and creating, came the three persons of God: the Father, the Son and the Holy Spirit, a circle of creative joy and mutual service, each at one with the other in completely selfless openness to one another other - and to us. When one of them receives love from one of us, the whole Trinity joyfully shares that love in a flow of undiluted selfless giving and receiving. To be in relationship with any one of them is to be integrated into their unbroken circle of joy.

If God ever did say, "Please love me. Please appreciate me. Please realize my value," it would not be because he needs our recognition and appreciation; it would be because he wants us to become part of this circle of joy. His whole nature is to share with us the outrageous beauty of being in relationship with a Trinity of pure love. The Trinity is not a closed circle. The Circle of Three is eternally open to a fourth: you.

Don't attribute to the Lord of life, light and love the heavy, dark and broken nature of human ego, the false self that senses rejection, takes offense and builds resentment. It is only in the Trinity's complete freedom from ego that we can find deliverance from the prisons of our own egos. The Trinity calls out to you,

"Come and swim in our Circle of Life! Come and be part of the joy. Take off your ego clothes and jump into the waters of Love. Go to others and invite them to come with you. Bring them all to the waters of Baptism and immerse them in the awesome joy of the name of Father, the Son and the Holy Spirit. And remember: *We are with you 'til the end.*

Once in the Circle, always in the Circle! Yes, *you* may walk away but the Trinity never will.

From 1 Corinthians 13, here is an amazingly beautiful scriptural description of the nature of the Trinity for further contemplation:

The Trinity is patient; the Trinity is kind; the Trinity is not envious or boastful or arrogant or rude. It does not insist on its own way; it is not irritable or resentful; it does not rejoice in wrongdoing, but rejoices in the truth. It bears all things, believes all things, hopes all things, endures all things.

The love of the Trinity never ends.

Corpus Christi B

Circulation Theology

Mark 14: 12-16, 22-26
The institution of the Eucharist.

This Sunday we celebrate the Body and Blood of Jesus. The Real Presence of Christ in the consecrated bread and wine is a beautiful and wondrous tenet of our faith and is a powerful truth that is worthy of many books, reflections and homilies.

But this time, I am going to focus on an aspect of the Real Presence that only since Vatican II has been really emphasized and then not always emphasized well or consistently. The Church teaches that Christ is not only truly present in the consecrated bread and wine but he is also truly present in his Word and in his people. While we treat his Word with respect and honor I don't think we have come to a place of full respect and honor for the other aspect of the Body of Christ, for the Real Presence of Christ in those who come and worship along side of us or in people we come in daily contact with whether they are Christian or not.

It is actually easier to believe that Christ is present in the consecrated bread and wine than it is to believe he is present in that person across the aisle who wounded us so badly or disagreed openly with our opinions. It certainly takes real faith to believe in Christ's presence in a consecrated wafer but to believe in his presence in someone we can't stand or in someone who doesn't strike us as very spiritual or someone who makes us uncomfortable - wow! That takes immense faith.

When we are unaware of the Lord's Real Presence in his people or when we avoid that somewhat uncomfortable aspect of our faith, preferring instead to focus on the consecrated elements, our faith life suffers and the Body of Christ suffers. Unless we are serving one another and honoring and respecting each other as a true part of the whole Body and Blood of Christ, the flow of the Spirit through us gets plugged up. There may be a trickle of life coming through because most of us do try to give what we can, where we can, but we miss so many opportunities to have the river of Christ's blood, the blood of everlasting life, flow through us in a torrent of love.

Jesus gave of himself without measure in his life and on the cross and he did not limit who could receive his love. If we receive his Body and Blood in the Eucharist and simply make it a private devotion or if we place limitations on who is or isn't part of Christ's body, there is a serious blockage. Christ's body, in effect, suffers from a restricted flow of his blood.

It is against the nature of Christ to withhold his love from anyone. He shares with us his whole life energy in the consecrated bread and wine and if we come away from Mass sometimes and wonder why we don't feel more stimulated and spiritually empowered by our reception of his Body and Blood, it's most likely because we're receiving the gift but we're not allowing it to flow out again. It's stagnating inside. The whole point of the Christian life is to keep the river of the life-blood moving in fullness and that fullness is not possible if we have put conditions on who we love or if we do not view the people around us as equally worthy of our love, service, honor and respect as Christ is. We are especially called to allow the flow to cascade over those who, in our judgment, seem to deserve it the least. It is judgment, unforgiveness and an unwillingness to serve others that blocks the flow.

When we reflect on the Gospel passage this week where Jesus instituted the Eucharist, we should keep in mind that in John 13: 13-17, (NIV), Jesus immediately went on to wash the disciples' feet and after doing so, he said, *"Now that I, your Lord and Teacher, have washed your feet, you also should wash one another's feet. I have set you an example that you should do as I have done for you. Very truly I tell you, no servant is greater than his master, nor is a messenger greater than the one who sent him. Now that you know these things, <u>you will be blessed if you do them</u>."*

The washing of the feet of those around us must follow our reception of the Eucharist. In Jesus' mind, the one naturally follows the other. It was no accident that he washed the disciples' feet immediately after instituting the first Eucharist. These are not two separate and unlinked incidents. Jesus was teaching his followers that partaking of his body and blood is not the end of the story. He was saying, "Yes, partake of my body and blood - but then you must serve one another. You might not understand now but later on you will." Later on, the disciples understood very well that the vitality of their own inner lives and the life of the community didn't just depend on receiving the body and blood of Jesus; it completely depended on giving that life away. They may not have understood the circulation system of their own physical bodies but they certainly understood the circulation system of the body of Christ.

If Christ is the heart, then we are the veins. The blood we receive *must* continually pulse through us nourishing the rest of the body. It *must* flow freely in love or else the body will become cold, sluggish, prone to major internal problems and vulnerable to sudden death. The body might look all right on the outside but on the inside, everything suffers if the blood is not in full circulation. When we receive the Body and Blood in the Eucharist without the intention of washing the feet of those around us, we are like blockages of the arteries or blood clots. Both lead to death.

Without the body, blood has no function. Without blood coursing through it, the body dies. If we receive Christ's body and blood and keep it to ourselves, simply making it our own little private moment of connection with God, we have completely misunderstood the basic principle of being alive in Christ.

St. Augustine wrote, "At Communion, the priest says, 'The Body of Christ,' and you say, 'Amen.' When you say 'Amen', you are saying yes to what you are."

Say yes to what you are and then give yourself a cardio workout. Wash some feet.

11th Sunday Ordinary B

The Wild Kingdom

Mark 4: 26-34

Jesus teaches about the Kingdom of God, saying it is like seeds that grow even though the sower doesn't understand how. It is also like a tiny mustard seed that grows into a huge shrub.

. See this dot? The one right at the beginning of this paragraph? That's the approximate size of a mustard seed. Most of you know that the mustard seed is miniscule but if you're thinking that this tiny seed grows into a huge tree like a stately old oak with generous leafy branches spreading out to offer shelter to birds and animals, you may be in for a surprise. You'll note that Jesus didn't say that the mustard tree was the greatest of all trees; he said it was the greatest of all shrubs. It's a fairly large and tall shrub but not an impressive or valued tree. It was actually considered an invasive weed in Jesus' day.

So, what's Jesus' point here? If he was trying to paint a picture of the greatness and glory of the Kingdom of God, something that starts small and then spreads throughout the earth becoming great and mighty, he didn't choose a very good example. Perhaps for good reason.

In the first parable of the growing seed, Jesus said that the seed would sprout and flourish without the farmer knowing how and that the earth itself produces the stalk and then the head and then the full grain. Then Jesus goes on to liken the Kingdom of God to the mustard tree. Again, he speaks of mystery, of the wonder of how a seed so tiny can grow quickly into a large invasive shrub. 'Invasive' means it will reproduce without any input from human beings.

Whenever Jesus told a parable, he was shaking up common perceptions and trying to get people to go beyond what they thought they knew. He was moving the people towards repentance or metanoia: a complete change of mind and heart. The term 'metanoia' is derived from the Greek words 'meta' (meaning "beyond" or "after") and 'noeo' (meaning "perception" or "understanding" or "mind"). The mind change he was inviting people to was more than a surface shift from one familiar option or idea to another. He was inviting the people to go beyond what they commonly thought and, quite often, he challenged people to change their whole perception of what it meant to have faith and what it meant that the Kingdom of God was within them. Today he still challenges us to metanoia. No matter who we are and where we are on the faith journey, we are continually called to have our minds, hearts and assumptions radically changed. This isn't a one-shot deal.

The parables of the growing seed and the mustard tree were far more than simple little stories illustrating the need to plant our tiny seeds of faith and trust in God to provide for us, although that's a good beginning. They're more than snapshots of how a church grows and develops. What we tend to lose sight of is that neither the grain nor the mustard shrub were created by humans and both had the astounding capacity to develop and grow without human understanding and without human intervention and control. God can take something that to us seems insignificant, inadequate, unattractive or relatively useless and create whatever he wants out of it. Not only can he create whatever he wants but he can use it however he wants.

I've noted before that the natural historian, Pliny the Elder (AD 78), wrote that the mustard shrub, which was considered a malignant weed, *"is extremely beneficial for the health. It grows entirely wild, though it is improved by being transplanted: but on the other hand when it has once been sown it is scarcely possible to get the place free of it, as the seed when it falls germinates at once,"* and *"a real mustard plant is unlikely to attract nesting birds."* There are some contradictions here. It is considered a malignant weed but beneficial to health. It grows entirely wild but is easily transplantable. Once planted you can hardly get rid of it so it was never deliberately planted in proper Jewish gardens. It's not a plant that's easily controlled. And Jesus seemed out of touch with reality by indicating that birds of the air could make nests in its branches. Birds weren't naturally attracted to it. But in the Kingdom of God, what we often assume is right, natural and logical isn't always the supernatural reality.

How would I describe the Kingdom of God? It's a mass of contradictions. The Kingdom is a mystery that defies all our efforts to neatly define it. We cannot paint a tidy little picture of this Kingdom that is wholly contained within us yet is rampant and invasive, inherently unattractive yet entirely hospitable. It is a Kingdom of love peace and joy and at the same time it is one of tension, struggle and grief. It is a Kingdom where the balm of healing flows out of the agony of crucifixion. If we insist on orderly definitions, if we need precepts that stay in one place and if we expect garden friendly seeds of life that we can understand, put in order and completely control, we will constantly be foiled and frustrated. The Kingdom of God is within us...but it's not ours. It's not under our tight control and was never meant to be.

The Kingdom of God is like a trek into the vast unknown. We are not called to know; we are called to go. In one moment the Kingdom is a precious pearl. In another moment it's a wild weed. At other times it's a grain of wheat, a lost coin or a measure of yeast. One day it's a dying grain and the next it's an abundant harvest. The Kingdom is pristine symmetry encased in wild chaos. Faith, then, is not the possession of a precisely laid out map against which you can measure your progress and judge your journey; it is a leap into the unknown where what's around the next bend can never be predicted. It is a present moment walk with a present moment God. The walk must be with him because you will never figure out on your own where you are, let alone where you've been or where you're going.

Metanoia: to go beyond your present perceptions and assumptions. To strike out into the unknown, understanding that your small definitions, preconceived ideas and long held images most likely have nothing to do with the powerful reality of God's spiritual landscape.

The Kingdom is like that.

Now!

Luke 1: 57-80

Elizabeth gives birth to John. Neighbors are surprised that she chooses the name John because no one else in the family was named John. Zechariah's mute tongue is loosed after he confirms the child's name. All are amazed.

"What's in a name?" Shakespeare wrote. "That which we call a rose by any other name would smell as sweet." Why the big deal about naming the baby 'John'? Why did John have to be called 'John' and not given a family name as the neighbors and relatives assumed would happen? Why was the name so important that the moment Zechariah confirmed that they would name the baby 'John' as God had directed, his tongued was loosed and he was able to speak and prophesy?

A clue may be found in the reason why the people were surprised by this name choice. "None of your relatives has this name." Before Jesus was even born, God was challenging common assumptions and letting people know that he is not held captive by human traditions, normal expectations or by what people think should happen because "we've always done it this way." The name 'Zechariah' means, "God has remembered," a name that implies looking back at the past. The name 'John' means, "God is gracious," and simply by changing a name, God made the people sit up and ask, "What? This is something different...this is not what we were expecting!"

God is gracious. Is it possible that the graciousness of God is deeper, wider and more powerful than what we think? Could his graciousness mean that the reign of his Kingdom will turn our expectations upside down and make us look to him in the present moment, the now, rather than back at what has always been – because God *is* gracious? Not was gracious or will be gracious but *is* gracious. Might graciousness hold the gift of present moment new beginnings within a new covenant? Could graciousness lead us into a different way of perceiving the light or into new opportunities to repent and enter into metanoia (going beyond what is understood)?

After I posted the last reflection (The Wild Kingdom), I received this email from someone who has been going through an extremely difficult time – and when she wrote the email, she wasn't out of the difficulties yet. She wrote: "Just read your post on the Kingdom. I'm feeling like I'm living the Kingdom of God in its fullness right now. Humbled and friggin' rocked by it … in every which way!!" This woman is continuing to discover that God's graciousness exists powerfully in the present moment in the Kingdom. The present moment in her world at this point is by no means simple or comfortable but it is where she meets her God of graciousness. She will, no doubt, still have moments of feeling bereft and full of grief but she is learning deeply where the grace is and where new life resides.

In their astonishment that Zechariah and Elizabeth intended to name the baby, "John", it was as if God was saying to the people, "*Now* is my Kingdom. *Now* my Kingdom has come. My life now is not what was or what has always been. My Kingdom has come. My Kingdom is here. It is presently in a womb but it is here. Grace has come to live on earth and grace has come to stay. Grace may look like a barren desert or it might be manifested as a river of forgiveness. It may look like birth and it might feel like grief. Sorrow will hold my grace and joy will be grace's companion. My grace will fill empty casks and my grace will overshadow bread and wine. My grace is as heavy as a cross and as light as a new dawn. Now is when it begins."

What is in your life right now? What assumptions have you made about your life situations? Are there circumstances that grieve you but you feel like they are frozen into your existence because 'those things/those people have always been that way'? What are your fears, tensions, frustrations and anxieties about the future? How much of all that is based on experiences of the past that have formed your expectations or on strong ideas of how things should be – but rarely are? Do you have plans, desires or goals that aren't really yours but have been pushed on you by the expectations and wishes of others? Do you have plans, desires or goals that are yours but have been waylaid by unexpected circumstances or people's judgments of how they expect things should be?

We are rarely in complete control of external circumstances or of the people in our lives; we are only in control of where we choose to be and whom we choose to be there with. We always have the choice of being in the present moment with God – with the Grace of new life and new beginnings.

When Elizabeth and Zechariah said, "His name is John," they unwittingly turned away from all that was and all that always had been and opened the door to metanoia for themselves and for the world. They gave up control and they gave up assumptions of how the future would or should look. They simply trusted their gracious God. When they said, "His name is John," what they were really saying to themselves, to the people around them and to the world for all time was,

"Let it all begin...NOW!"

13th Sunday Ordinary B

Safety Warning

Mark 5: 21-43

Jesus is beseeched by Jairus to come and heal his daughter. When he arrives at the house, the people are mourning and weeping because the girl has died. But Jesus tells them that the child is not dead but sleeping. The people laugh at him but he goes in and says, "Talitha cum (Little girl, get up) to the girl. She gets up and starts walking around. All are amazed.

Sometimes the Gospels can be distressing when they tell of Jesus performing miracles such as healing the sick and raising the dead because too many of us have been in the position where we have prayed desperately for Christ to touch and heal us, or someone we love, and healing didn't come. If a child or a partner dies, we can't understand in our agony why death is allowed to take the ones we love. Is it Jesus' will that a child should die? Is it his will that a spouse should die? Is it his will that people endure long-term sickness and physical pain?

If we say, "No, it is not his will." then what happened? Is he in control of life and death or not? Was it our faith that was at fault? Was it too weak? Did we not believe hard enough, even though we know we desperately wanted to believe strongly enough to move God's hand?

If we say, "Yes, it is his will that a person should suffer or die," it makes him seem capricious, harsh, cruel and arbitrary, one who willfully sends suffering to his people, a God we could come to fear, avoid and perhaps reject.

I think the problem lies in our daring to say anything at all.

C.S. Lewis, one of the most respected theologians of modern times, expressed a very startling idea about God in one of his Narnia children's books. The children are being taken to see Aslan, who represents Christ in the Narnia series. Before setting out on the journey to find Aslan, they are trying to find out who he is, and because they have encountered many talking animals in their adventures, they ask if he's a man. When they discover that he is actually a lion the children feel somewhat nervous about coming face to face with a lion. Mrs. Beaver says that they are right to feel nervous – anyone who wasn't nervous would be incredibly brave or else just silly.

Then they ask if he is safe. Mr. Beaver says that of course he isn't safe. But he's good.

I read the Narnia series first as a child and many times since, and I am still astounded at how C.S. Lewis expressed deep theological and contemplative truths in these simple stories. Since my childhood I have had the words of the beaver impressed upon my mind that of course he isn't safe, but he's *good*. Real faith is a deep belief that God is good, not because he always does what we want or because he's a tame God but because he always does what is…good. No matter how much the brokenness and darkness of the world seem to be in control, the goodness of God is triumphant in the end.

We are human. We are limited. We live in an incomprehensible universe and we cannot see one day ahead. We cannot even see one minute ahead. It is so natural to want God to be a safe God, a God who follows our plans and who is predictable, one who will raise our dead when we want him to. We want to know there are set ways to pray and believe which will always procure our desired results and keep us from hurt and sorrow. We want to know these things because we are small and we are traveling in an alien land. Whether we admit it or not, we are often scared to death even when actual death is not staring us in the face.

Are we honestly open to the goodness of God? Can we believe that his goodness is not what brought death and suffering into the world? Are we able to believe so strongly in God's power and goodness that we are willing to risk abandoning our limited ideas of what we think should be happening and trust that what is happening is being soaked in his goodness? Yes, he has the power to heal, to raise the dead, to calm storms, part seas and move mountains and at times he inserts himself very obviously into our lives and shows us these wonders. And other times he does not. Why? Because he is Good. He cannot do anything else than what he does because he knows eternities and universes and eons of consequences, effects, repercussions and results. Whatever he chooses to do to overcome darkness and death, he does so because he is Good, because he can do nothing but good and because he loves us in a way we will never comprehend. "Bonum est difusivum sui," is a Latin tag meaning, "It is the nature of goodness to diffuse itself (spread over a large area)." Another translation is, "The good capable of spreading, spreads to those capable of receiving it." We will never fully understand unconditional love that is not a love that always gives in to what we want but a love that never fails to lead us to goodness if we're willing to be led.

For God, "good" is not a label or an adjective. It is who he is. And if what happens in our lives causes us pain and suffering, he does not abandon us or hide in the shadows. In his goodness he becomes one with our pain. The word 'compassion' means 'to suffer with' and he is always one with our suffering; we cannot separate him from it. There is absolutely no space between our pain and his – but still, he will only do what is good.

When we finally grasp that God's goodness is higher, deeper and more far reaching than any goodness we've ever known, we will begin to let go of our desire to make Christ into a kind of icon of power who heals when we want healing and who leaves us alone when we want to be left alone.

We will abandon ourselves to a God who is not safe – but is Good.

Soaked In Goodness

Mark 6: 1-6

Jesus teaches in a synagogue in his home town. Everyone is astounded but take offense at him because they know his family. Jesus states that prophets are never with honor except in their own home and he could do very few miracles there.

In my last reflection I talked about how belief, no matter how great it is, cannot dictate to God what he should specifically be doing in any situation. He will do what is good. But, are we able to block God's power and action in our lives through a lack of belief or a lack of willingness to accept his goodness? Certainly.

You may recall that I quoted the Latin tag, "Bonum est difusivum sui", of which one translation is, "The good capable of spreading, spreads to those capable of receiving it." If there is no openness to God moving and working in a person's life and no willingness to believe, God will not force that person to receive his gift of goodness which is the gift of himself. He will definitely present himself and his gifts to people and give them opportunities to accept his love but lots of people have seen the power of the Lord at work and have remained unmoved.

Think of a rock in water. Even though it is completely immersed in the water, the water does not soak into it and never softens it. When it comes out of the water, the water runs off of it and the rock is as hard and impenetrable as it was before. Now think of a sponge in water. The sponge may have been quite hard and brittle before it was plunged into the water but as the water soaks into it, it permeates the sponge, and makes it soft and pliable. It becomes like a vessel of that water, holding the water and dripping it everywhere. Belief, then, is a quality that transforms us from a hard, brittle mass into a soft, saturated bearer of God's goodness. We all know many people whom we would label as rocks, people who have hardened their hearts and refuse to allow God's goodness to penetrate and soften them – although we really don't have the insight to judge as to whether someone is actually a rock or if they are a brittle sponge that is being slowly saturated. God can and does work soft and long on rock hard hearts.

But, what about us? Can we not be dense rocks sometimes?

The moment we decide we know exactly what God should be doing in any situation is the moment we begin to form a crusty rock like shell around us. The moment our limited perceptions dictate our expectations, we restrict our ability to soak up goodness or even recognize it.

The people in Jesus' hometown thought they knew all about Jesus. They thought they knew who he was and what his real job was and how he should be conducting his life. They could not see beyond that. Even though they recognized that he was expressing great wisdom and that he was capable of performing deeds of power, they just couldn't get over their deeply ingrained ideas about what the Messiah should look like and Jesus, their next door neighbor, just wasn't fitting into the vision. To the people, two plus two should equal four and Jesus was a five. Jesus couldn't saturate them with his goodness because they were rock-hard and immoveable within their preconceived ideas.

A few years ago I had my two grandsons, who were cousins, visiting me. One was 14 months and the other was18 months. They were both at that stage where when their little minds decided they wanted something and if it didn't immediately happen in the way they expected it to happen, they would blow a fuse. They would plop down on their little bottoms, refuse to move and then wail. I especially remember one time when their respective mothers said to them, "Do you want to go outside?" and what was meant was that they were going to be dressed and taken in the car to go to a playground. Both of these little guys headed for the deck door, assuming that they were going to go outside on the deck, a favorite daily activity for them both. When their moms led them away from the deck door and began to put shoes on them, you should have heard the screaming.

Going out, getting in the car and heading off to a park where there are swings, a slide and all sorts of other amazing things to discover and experience had infinitely more potential for excitement and pleasure than going out on the deck. However, these little guys had a certain idea in their heads and this preconceived idea, this immediate perception, made them like little rocks. They weren't remotely interested in finding out what was really going to happen. What a struggle it was to get them into socks and shoes and out the particular door they weren't expecting to open up to them.

Do we ever get certain ideas about what should be happening and then have a melt down when it's all turned upside down? Usually we assume that things are going wrong. We get all rock hard and start to dig our heels in instead of saying, "Wait a minute. This isn't what I was expecting but the Lord must have something infinitely more beautiful in store." The moment we turn ourselves away from set preconceptions and open ourselves to God's plan, we become sponges. Even better than that, we become adventurers into the kingdom of God's present moment goodness. We learn how to move through unexpected doors, take risks, explore, discover and anticipate new and different horizons with him and in him.

Like my grandsons, we need to learn to see that there are now, and will always be, many new doors through which we are called to venture. We need to take the risk of believing that God's power and goodness is vaster and deeper than what we see in front of us. We need to let go of everything we think is the best plan and let go of what we think God will look like when he manifests himself in the midst of our ordinary lives. Very often he looks so ordinary that instead of rejoicing in his presence, we become offended or miss him completely.

Belief, then, could be described in this way: it is a willingness and openness to look for and see God in everything. It is being very attentive to the present moment and to all God's infinite possibilities in *everything and everyone* we see, touch, hear, experience and think about. Belief is a softness of spirit and a wideness of heart. Belief makes us realize that the whole world and everything that's happening is God's powerful venue, a place where he can be encountered anywhere and at anytime.

Belief softens our innate crustiness, our rigid expectations and our resistance to metanoia. Belief is the water of new life and new beginnings.

Soak it in.

Traveling Light

Mark 6: 7-13

Jesus sends the twelve out two by two and gives them authority to heal and cast out unclean spirits. He instructs them not to take anything for the journey.

There's a familiar saying that goes, "God does not call the equipped; he equips the called."

The first reading this Sunday is from Amos who was a shepherd and a farmer. God called him to prophesy to Israel but he didn't consider himself a prophet. *"I am no prophet or a prophet's son; but I am a herdsman and a dresser of sycamore trees and the Lord took me from following the flock, and the Lord said to me, "Go, prophesy to my people Israel."* (NRSV) Then, in the Gospel, Jesus sent out his disciples in pairs and directed them to take very few possessions with them. Amos in no way felt equipped to speak the word of God and I doubt that any of the disciples felt like they were ready to go out to preach, heal, cast out devils and speak the word of God. Jesus knew this. He wasn't being overly optimistic about their capabilities, nor was he being obtuse. He was teaching them all, and us as well, something extremely important. God doesn't use you and send you because you're highly trained or full of self-confidence or because it's right down your alley in terms of the talents you possess. It's not because you're rich in capability or rich in resources. He actually prefers to send the ones who have very little, the ones who are poor.

When we feel completely confident that we know what we're doing, the job may end up to be efficiently done, all loose ends tidied up and all goals successfully attained but often there are some things missing. Life. Power. Joy. Creative growth. Peace and reconciliation within the community. A renewed vision of who the Lord is and who we are. When we feel the Lord calling us to do something, the very first thing we should do is reflect on this week's Gospel and begin to see what possessions we need to *lose* before we head out with the Lord to participate in his will.

When we hear the word 'possessions', what always springs to mind? Most people think of all the material goods they own. Some of us own a lot and some of us not as much but all of us feel a pang when we think the Lord might like us to lose some of these possessions in order to be good disciples. The idea of simplifying our material goods becomes overwhelming and complex. Yes, it's true that sometimes our possessions own us and take up more of our focus than is healthy or necessary but the material goods we own are not the only possessions we have. In fact, I would say that for most of us our material possessions are the least of our problems. It's those other possessions we have that block us from opening up to God's love and his will for our lives.

What possessions am I talking about? What are these other things that we lay claim to, hold tightly to and which end up restricting, owning and controlling us more than we own and control them?

How about opinions? Don't we all have a huge number of set in stone preferences and ideas that, when challenged, make us stubbornly and angrily dig in our heels and refuse to be moved?

What about past wounds? Certainly the Lord is compassionate toward his wounded people but there are times when we want to hold on to our wounds and allow them to dictate to us what we will or won't do.

What about control? We all have a need to be in control and have everything go according to what makes us comfortable or according to how we've always done things or how we perceive things should be done. Who doesn't have any areas where it's "my way or the highway"?

How about ambitions – all those wonderful goals we have to be the best, do the most and carry the biggest load? Lofty goals can start out pure but gradually they begin to direct and run us until the goals become more important than the people involved in our lives.

And what about those teachings we have received which somehow got twisted around to become rigid stances that keep us from the softness of acceptance, love and compassion?

I'll never forget running into an older woman whom I had not seen for several years. When I had known her previously, she was Lioness for God. She was a deeply spiritual woman and a very good woman but if anyone did anything that contradicted one of her spiritual or moral principles, she could be quite harsh. When I saw her again, I asked what she had been up to in the last while. She told me that against her natural inclinations she had become involved in Hospice. The one thing she had never been able to handle was interacting with dying people but after her husband's death her doctor heavily pressured her to become involved in the Hospice Association. The thing about Hospice is that you are not allowed to proselytize. If the person you are ministering to wants to talk about God that's fine, but otherwise you may not bring up religion at all. This forced her to love without boundaries, accept without limitations and listen without offering judgment or advice. She said to me, "It took me 64 years to find out that love is more important than doctrine." Her face was shining and softer than I had ever seen it. She looked like Jesus.

Yes, we can be pretty possessive with our doctrines and our theologies.

Indeed, whenever God sends us out to share his good news or to offer healing and love to one or more of his people, we often head out loaded to the max with such heavy restrictive possessions that it's a wonder we can move at all. They're awkward, heavy, burdensome and bothersome and they deplete all our energies. No wonder Jesus sent out the disciples equipped with so little. He was freeing them to move. He was gifting them with the joy of being able to immediately respond to the leading of the Father. He was showing them the "Light Way". They had nothing to depend on except the Lord. Don't forget that those disciples came back from that journey flying high; they couldn't believe all the wonderful things God did and how he allowed them the honor of participating in his power and grace.

They had been freed of their possessions so they could dance with God.

May we all be so blessed.

Rise Up, Shepherds!

Mark 6: 30-34

Jesus tries to take the apostles away to a quiet place to rest and eat but the crowds follow them. Jesus has compassion on the people and begins to teach them many things.

The disciples had just come back from ministering to God's people and they were drained. While on their mission, they were totally dependent on the Father for everything – not only for their own needs but also for the needs of everyone around them. It was the first time they really had to accept the fact that Jesus not only chose them but he chose them *in order to send them.* They discovered that Jesus called them not only to follow him but also to act and speak the way he did. It was the first time they had to absolutely trust that God could and would work through them in the same way he worked through Jesus.

You know what? Believing in your call and putting your complete trust in God can be exhausting. Jesus knew how tired his disciples were. He knew they weren't only suffering from physical exhaustion but also from mental, emotional and spiritual exhaustion and he wanted to give them time to recharge. The demands of the people were so strong that they didn't even have time to eat and it's not God's will that anyone become burnt out in his service. But when they arrived at the place Jesus had chosen for them to take some time off, more crowds met them. At least the disciples just saw crowds. What Jesus saw were individuals; he saw people in pain, people grieving, people hungry for the kind of truth that didn't burden them with impossible demands, people struggling to be good, people who were confused, people who wanted nothing more than to be told, "You are the Father's Beloved." He was filled with compassion.

Jesus was unable to turn away from the poor, the lost or the wounded and he was drawing his disciples to have the same heart as he did.

This was not easy on the disciples. Their hearts must have sunk within them. They may have asked themselves and each other, "Haven't we done what we were called to do? We gave all we had to give. Isn't that enough?" It doesn't say so in scripture but I think the disciples had to learn one more lesson. I believe that the disciples, as they moved among the crowds of people, discovered that they did have more to give. It didn't come from themselves or from a belief in their own spiritual capabilities. It came out of witnessing the compassion of their Master and allowing that compassion to become their own.

It may have been their most powerful hour up to that point. Mind you, there was nothing about the disciples that outwardly differentiated them from the rest of the crowd. The disciples were exhausted and drained. They were hungry. They were poor. They were as needy as many people in that crowd. The difference was an inner one. They had experienced the distinction between being a sheep and being a shepherd. The difference came from listening, hearing, going out and discovering that they, too, were called to be Christ to the people. And they found out that being another Christ meant being open to the call every moment and everywhere.

As a lay person, no matter who you are and what your lifestyle is, it's hard to grasp that you are anointed to be pastors and shepherds as much as those who have been officially recognized as pastors and shepherds. It's difficult to keep in focus that sense of being chosen and sent when you feel no different from millions of others who walk the same earthly path as you do and outwardly look just like you. There are no visible and tangible reminders for us that each one of us is indeed sanctified, chosen, named, called and sent. We are not given robes or titles but our missions are as sacred and critical as the missions of those who are publicly recognized.

When the disciples were sent out, there was nothing to mark them as special people. There was nothing to distinguish them from anyone else traveling the same roads and walking through the same villages. Like us, they had to keep focused on one thing: "Jesus sent us." They had to summon up a belief within themselves that they had been chosen and sent for a purpose. But they most likely didn't know exactly what that purpose was at any given moment. They had to watch and pray. They had to remember who Jesus was and how Jesus acted – with the divine authority of love and compassion. Then they had to step out in faith. The more they moved in the belief that they were chosen and sent, the more they *knew* they were chosen and sent. The more they prayed and reached out with the heart of Christ, the more the power of God flowed through them.

It's the same with us. Exactly the same.

In the first reading this week, God said that he would raise up shepherds who would shepherd his people and the people would no longer fear or be dismayed, and none would go missing. God wants to raise us up if only we would listen. Every person we meet challenges us to make a choice – to act as one who has been sent by God or act like one who is just passing by with no responsibility, purpose or calling. Every person, moment and situation invites us to be like Jesus who was so connected to the Father that he knew whether to speak or not speak, to touch or not touch, to challenge or not challenge, to heal or not heal. There are no hard and fast rules about what we may be called to do as Christ's chosen and sent ones. Each of us is known, chosen and called individually and each one of us has a unique mission. Like Jesus and his disciples, we need to learn to be constantly connected to the Father, listening, paying attention, being in the moment, staying alert and always ready to step out. Hard? You bet it is.

No, it's not easy. I don't think there's anything you can do to make it really easy. It is a constant challenge in this world and I have no doubt that the best priests and Religious, if they were completely honest, would acknowledge that even they can find it difficult to stay focused every moment on their relationship with the Father and remain completely alive to what the Father has chosen as their mission in any given moment. The point is not to become perfect in mission. The point is to try and to keep trying until we begin to recognize the voice of the Father over all the other voices out there – especially our own inner voices that will try to convince us that we're not specially chosen and not particularly important.

We've believed this for too long. We've believed that we are common and ordinary and that as long as we faithfully follow Jesus, we're doing the best we can. However, just as it was for the disciples, following is simply the beginning. Jesus wants us to be more than followers; he wants us to learn to walk along side of him and be co-shepherds, participating fully in his mission. The Gospels show us exactly what that looks like. The Gospels are more than just faithful records of Jesus' words and actions showing us what a great Savior we have. They are the pattern for our lives and our missions. We should not be content to pattern our self-images after the blind, the sick, the lame and the hungry, waiting for Jesus to touch and heal us. That is simply the first step. The second step is to pattern ourselves after Jesus, always praying that we will come to believe like him, speak to the Father with the same faith as he did, listen to the Father's voice like he did, have the same desire, self-knowledge, compassion and wisdom as he did and touch people with the same authority of love as he did.

You have been chosen. You can stay safe and simply be a follower or you can take a risk and believe in who you have been called to be since before the beginning of time. That's a large and astounding concept to try to grasp but it's the truth. We were not called to be small, anonymous or inconsequential. That was never in God's plan.

God made his choice. Now it's your turn.

Open Table

John 6: 1-15
The feeding of the five thousand.

Have you ever read this Gospel and wondered why Jesus felt he *had* to feed this enormous crowd coming at him?

You have most likely assumed, as I always have, that Jesus just randomly chose to miraculously feed an enormous crowd in order to teach his disciples about God's abundant provision. If you're going to teach a lesson, do something big that will really make an impression. Providing enough bread and fish for five thousand people and ending up with leftovers obviously did make a big impression, not only on the disciples but also on the crowd itself.

But let's go back to the beginning of this 'lesson'. I don't think this was so random at all. Notice that the disciples didn't gasp and cry, "What?? You're planning to *feed* these people? That's not your responsibility! These people can feed themselves. They're the ones who decided to come to hear you teach and see if you will heal them. If they didn't bring food, that's their problem."

The immediate answer to Jesus' generous gesture to total strangers might be that he was simply being compassionate – and that's true. Compassion was part of his caring for the needs of the people. However, Jesus was also following a Mitzvah, one of the great commandments that came from the heart of his compassionate Abba and one that devout Jewish people had written on their own hearts: the great commandment of hospitality.

- *"Judaism defines hospitality as a sacred obligation; it is the mitzvah (commandment) called 'hachnasat orchim', literally, "the bringing in of guests." (Jewish Gateway, Internet.)*
- *"Hospitality is, according to Rabbi Johanan, even more important than prayer or, according to Rabbi Judah, than receiving the divine presence." (Jewish Virtual Library. Internet.)*
- *Biblical law specifically sanctified hospitality toward the ger ("stranger") who was to be made particularly welcome "for you were strangers in a strange land" (Lev. 19:34 and see Ex. 12:49)*
- *As soon as Abraham saw the three men of Mamre "from afar," he hurried to invite them into his house, ministered to their physical comfort, and served them lavishly. (Gen. 18 as quoted in the Jewish Virtual Library, Internet.)*

At this point it would be easy to jump into a little object lesson about how we are called to be a hospitable people but as important as that is, it isn't the heart of this week's Gospel. It's actually very difficult to practice hospitality in all its fullness unless one has personally experienced what this Gospel story is all about: that our God is a hospitable God. God welcomes his people with a heart of generous hospitality. Jesus looked at the crowds coming towards him and immediately placed himself in the position of a host welcoming strangers into his home. And what did devout Israelites do when strangers entered his or her home? Fed them. The disciples didn't question his intention to feed the people because they understood the seriousness of God's commandment even though they may not yet have understood that God gave that commandment because he is a hospitable God.

We don't know how far the people in that crowd had traveled in order to see Jesus. We do know that it was near the Passover festival so many in that crowd had probably already traveled quite a distance from their own villages toward Jerusalem. The Sea of Galilee is about 68 miles from Jerusalem so some of the crowd were probably on their way to Jerusalem and had made a detour when they heard Jesus was in the region of Galilee. The point is that a good portion of the crowd probably weren't just popping over from the nearest village. They were strangers in a strange land, on a long hard pilgrimage to the Holy City, and Jesus shared his Father's heart when it came to hospitality. He didn't just resign himself to dealing with yet another crowd and then decide he would do a cool miracle and feed the people to teach his disciples something. He saw the crowd and thought,

"These are my guests, my beloved people. They are weary and hungry and it is my joy to seat them at my Father's table and feed them."

We know that as Christians we are called to be hospitable but how often do we stop to understand that God is entirely hospitable towards us? How often have you turned to the Lord in your weariness and your poverty with the knowledge that his first action toward you is one of abundant hospitality? How often have you stopped to consider that your God wants nothing more than to welcome you and feed you just as you are? You are a stranger in a very strange land on a difficult and long journey. It is his desire to welcome you in, wash your dusty feet and feed you. Would he not be the first to enfold you into his own law of hospitality? Would he command his people to do something that was not a living characteristic of his own heart?

'Let your house be open wide for relief, and let the poor be members of your household.' (Pirkei Avos 1:5)

God's heart is open wide for relief and he has welcomed you as a member of his household. As Jesus demonstrated in this week's

Gospel, his provision is abundant – and it's all for you. God says, "Take...eat. There's more where that came from."

The table is ready, weary traveler.

18th Sunday Ordinary B

Created Desire

John 6: 24-35
The crowds go looking for Jesus and when they find him, he tells them they were seeking him because he gave them bread for their bellies, not because he gave them signs. They ask for a sign so they can believe in him. He tells them that it is God who gives the true bread from heaven and they ask him to give them this bread. He says that he is the bread of life and whoever comes to him will never be hungry and whoever believes in him will never thirst.

Have you ever noticed that children are never happy for very long with what they get? Even with something they have desired for a long time, they're happy for a while but it doesn't take long before they think something else will make them happier. This state of never being really satisfied begins before a child can even speak or reason well so we have to conclude something from it. It must be human nature to be dissatisfied. And if it's human nature, then we adults are prone to the very same kind of innate dissatisfaction where we're always looking for something better, something different, or something that will fill the hole inside.

The first reading this Sunday is the one where the Israelites complain to Moses because there was no food to eat. When they were in Egypt they longed to be a free people but when they were free, they wished they were back in Egypt. God sent them manna and quail but it wasn't long before the Israelites found more to complain about. They were more concerned about satisfying their physical desires and need for security than about having a relationship with God who provided miraculously for them time after time.

In the Gospel, the people follow Jesus and he tells them they are following only because he provided bread for them, not because they witnessed a sign that told them that a loving God was in their midst. They were seeking for more bread or more miracles, not for the truth of who Jesus was. They knew Jesus had something they were looking for but they weren't sure what it was. He had put bread in their hands so they looked for more bread because they didn't know what else they should be reaching out for.

Our response to this often is, "What obtuse, shallow and immature people," but the truth is, we all live in a state of restless dissatisfaction and we are always filled with a desire to reach out for something more than what we have. We know we want something so we look around and try to find what it is we're missing and what we seem to be missing is what we perceive other people have that we don't have and wish we did. We reach for more time, more money, more recreation, better relationships, a more satisfying job, nicer possessions or more choices. It's so hard to be completely satisfied and fulfilled by what we have right now. Why is this?

Because we were made that way. We were created to be unsatisfied.

St. Augustine wrote, "You have made us for yourself, O Lord, and our hearts are restless until they rest in you." We are not so much shallow and immature as much as we live in complete unawareness of what it is we really want. Even when we are told it is Jesus we want and that he is the bread of life which will satisfy all our longings, we don't know how to receive Jesus in such a way that we can easily let go of all the desires we have that we think might make us happier and more contented. The people who were following Jesus and asking for more bread or more signs were confused as to what they really wanted and really needed. They had Jesus right in front of them and they still could not grasp him in the way their hungry inner beings yearned to.

We can go to church at least once a week and receive Jesus in the Eucharist. We can have our daily prayer time. We can belong to a bible study or a prayer group. We can offer our gifts to the church. We can do all the things required of us as practicing and believing Catholics and still be enveloped in a restlessness and a longing that cracks our peace. How can we receive this Bread of Life so that our thirst is truly slated and our deep inner hunger is satisfied?

In the Gospel, the people are trying to discover how to find this deep satisfaction. Jesus told them not to work for things that perish but for that which brings everlasting life. Then the people asked him, "O.K., what work can we do to ensure that we get this bread of eternal life?" Please notice that Jesus does not give them a grocery list of things to do. He does not say, "Go to Mass, feed the poor, help the sick, pray daily, attend scripture study..." He refuses to bring it down to a formula, a series of works that can be accomplished with no real connection to him as a person. He simply says, "The work of God is to believe in me."

That's hard work! It is the hardest task you will ever undertake because it means opening up every pore of your life to the belief that Jesus is the Lord of you and of the universe in which you exist. It means opening up your spiritual pores every minute to the understanding that you exist because he loves you. It means recognizing that all your restlessness and all your desires come from one great desire: to know Jesus, to know his heart, his mind, his Spirit and his love and to know him intimately in the moment, every moment.

You may say, "I believe in Jesus" but here's the cruncher: do you allow him to believe in you? You profess to love him. Do you allow him to love you? You desire to serve the Lord. Do you believe that he also wants to serve you? If you are uncomfortable with the thought of Jesus serving you then you haven't quite grasped the true nature of Jesus. We all tend to make our spirituality a one-way street where we're the ones who make all the effort and make all the professions of belief and love but we don't stop to listen to him profess his belief in us. Jesus has already fallen in love with each one of us individually. He stands ready, waiting and aching to be able to fall into your heart and begin to fill it up with all that you truly want.

Growing in capacity to receive Jesus and be fed by him is a life long process. As soon as you experience him filling a little hole in your heart, the hole gets bigger! Little by little, he expands your longing and your capacity. Continually desiring and *believing* in him is the lifelong work of God.

Pay attention to your dissatisfaction. Do you know that the all the strong desires you have, the longings, the yearnings, the restlessness and aching for more, whether it's spiritual or otherwise, are echoes of his immense and intense desire for you?

Boggles the heart, doesn't it?

The Wholesome Tongue

John 6: 41-51

The Jews complain about Jesus stating that he is the bread that came down from heaven. Jesus emphasizes that he is indeed the bread of heaven sent by the Father and that whoever eats of this bread will live forever, and the bread that he will give for the world is his flesh.

When was the last time you complained about something? Yesterday? This morning? Two minutes ago? Maybe you were in the middle of a good solid complaint when you started reading this reflection. Complaining comes very easily and naturally to most of us and, the truth is, it feels very satisfying to get into a good complaining session.

Jesus is faced here with the complaints and negativity of the Jews who were questioning his credentials because they had known him as he was growing up and they knew his parents. The first thing he says to them in this Gospel is, "Stop complaining among yourselves." This is important. Jesus wasn't just reacting in irritation; he was setting a prerequisite for being able to receive his words and therefore receive him as the Bread of Life.

Jesus knew that negativity, cynicism and complaining can become more than just an expression of a momentary upset and he wanted them to know that it was, and still is, an addictive barrier to receiving spiritual truth and nourishment. When we continually speak out our negativity and irritation, our inner dissatisfaction is rarely resolved. It seems like all that happens is we become more and more aware of things that are all wrong and of people and situations that are dragging us down. In the moment, it feels good to complain or make cynical observations.

It feels like we are more in control because we are able to identify what's wrong in our lives or with the lives of people around us. We tell ourselves that we're being realistic and that our complaints are completely justified.

And watch out when a group begins to share complaints. Complaints that are agreed upon and shared by a community have the power to exponentially build and reinforce negativity and cynicism. There is a strength of energy in 'group negativity' that's pretty scary.

We may be totally right about what we see is wrong in a situation, a person or an institution but that does not justify patting ourselves on the back for maintaining 'healthy cynicism', 'righteous anger' or entering into a state of continuous complaining.

"Do not complain among yourselves."

Why would negativity hinder us from receiving the bread that is Jesus? Because our focus is on the power of something other than the power of God and the more we focus on something other than his life, the less we are able recognize that life when it comes to us and fully trust in it. The more adept we become at recognizing the bad, the ugly and the wrong in our lives and the lives of others, the less ability we have to see and appreciate the lovely, the beautiful, the gentle and the right. Complaining creates solid walls around us and solid walls do not allow the light through nor do they allow us to see further than our self-constructed densely righteous opinions. Then we wonder why we feel so dry, empty and forlorn.

"Do not complain among yourselves."

I need to be clear about something here. There are times when we very much need to vent about situations or people in our lives that are causing us wounds or making life hard. This reflection is not advocating that we deny our difficulties and stuff them away until we're ready to explode. For this purpose we need to connect with a trusted friend who could be our spouse, sibling or a parent, a priest we feel comfortable with or a spiritual director – someone we know will listen to us and will be balanced and wise and help us to sort through the struggles we are dealing with. This is healthy, good and wonderful for the spirit and soul.

But we desperately need to understand that acknowledgment of God's wondrous goodness in all things is like gentle rain for the spirit and soul. It softens the inner earth and prepares it to receive the nourishing grain that becomes the bread of life. It clears the air and leaves a fragrant freshness in our hearts. It acts as a prism separating the white light of God into a spectrum of colors, giving meaning and full purpose to our existence.

"Do not complain among yourselves."

Do not feed yourselves on empty soul-destroying words, words that harden the heart and promote hopelessness and disbelief. If the fact that Jesus said it doesn't convince you, take time to slowly do this scripture meditation. The following passages make it abundantly clear – our mouths have the creative ability to form who we are and how we open ourselves to the Lord. If goodness flows from our tongues, we slowly develop the capacity to see goodness everywhere. If negativity is always in our mouths, we cannot see God. We can only see darkness.

It's as simple as that.

Scripture Meditation on a Wholesome Tongue: (from NIV)

I will extol the LORD at all times;
his praise will always be on my lips.
I will glory in the LORD;
let the afflicted hear and rejoice.
Glorify the LORD with me;
let us exalt his name together.
Those who look to him are radiant;
their faces are never covered with shame.

Whoever of you loves life
and desires to see many good days,
keep your tongue from evil
and your lips from telling lies.
Turn from evil and do good;
seek peace and pursue it. (Psalm 34, psalm for this Sunday)

May my prayer be set before you like incense;
may the lifting up of my hands be like the evening sacrifice.
Set a guard over my mouth, LORD;
keep watch over the door of my lips. (Psalm 141: 2,3)

May these words of my mouth and this meditation of my heart
be pleasing in your sight,

LORD, my Rock and my Redeemer. (Psalm 19:14)

Rejoice always, pray continually, give thanks in all circumstances; for this is God's will for you in Christ Jesus. (I Thessalonians 5: 16-18)

Finally, brothers and sisters, whatever is true, whatever is noble, whatever is right, whatever is pure, whatever is lovely, whatever is admirable—if anything is excellent or praiseworthy—think about such things. (Philippians 4:8)

The soothing tongue is a tree of life,
but a perverse tongue crushes the spirit. (Proverbs 15: 4)

A happy heart makes the face cheerful, (Proverbs 15:13)

The LORD detests the thoughts of the wicked,
but gracious words are pure in his sight. (Proverbs 15:26)

The mouths of the righteous utter wisdom,
and their tongues speak what is just. (Psalm 37:30)

Open my lips, Lord,
and my mouth will declare your praise. (Psalm 51:15)

What goes into someone's mouth does not defile them, but what
comes out of their mouth, that is what defiles them." (Mt 15:11)

A good man brings good things out of the good stored up in his
heart, and an evil man brings evil things out of the evil stored up
in his heart. For the mouth speaks what the heart is full of. (Luke
6:45)

Out of the same mouth come praise and cursing. My brothers and
sisters, this should not be. (James 3:10)

For it is with your heart that you believe and are justified, and it
is with your mouth that you profess your faith and are saved.
(Rom. 10:10)

20th Sunday Ordinary B

Water And Bread For The Wilderness

John 6: 51-58

Jesus says that he is the living bread that came down from heaven and unless you eat his flesh and drink his blood, you will have no life within you.

When I was a child in Saskatchewan, every farm had a hand operated pump in the yard. In order to get the water flowing they had to prime the pump. They would pour water into the pump to improve the seal and then start pumping the handle. The part I remember best was waiting with thirsty impatience as someone vigorously moved the handle up and down, up and down. It seemed to take forever but suddenly the water would start gushing out. It was clear, cold, abundant and wonderful water on a hot dry Saskatchewan summer day.

In the last reflection, we looked at how crucial it is to keep a watch over our mouths and over the thoughts of our hearts and to build up habits of praise and gratitude rather than habits of judgment, grumbling and complaining. Speaking with gratitude and building up habits of positive trust in the Lord could be likened to spiritually "priming the pump". You receive the Bread of life in the Eucharist, in the Word and in community. Jesus the Bread, the Word and the water of life is deep within you just like the water was deep in the well on that hot dusty Saskatchewan farm. It was a fascinating mystery me that in order to get water to flow out of that pump, water had to be poured in first. In order for the water of the Spiritual life to begin to gush out of us, we need to pour water in. Practicing gratitude, hope and trust in the Lord is what primes our pumps. Eventually what will come out is a supernatural flow of grace. But you have to prime the pump. That's your job.

Jesus keeps referring to the Jewish ancestors who received natural food and drink in a supernatural manner. He was saying that God can provide for his people and he can do it in a way that creates awe and wonder...for the moment. Time after time in the wilderness, the Father provided for his people in miraculous ways. They had food, meat, drink and healing provided in ways that no one could deny was the hand of a mighty God. But manna, quail and waters gushing out of a rock did not fill these people with an attitude of lasting gratitude and grace. As soon as their physical and emotional needs seemed to be unmet again, they immediately lost heart, became resentful and started complaining. They kept drying up spiritually. The desert was as much in their hearts as it was in the land around them. Their souls were howling wildernesses. The most they could come up with was 'in the moment' gratitude, which faded away when the next set of difficult circumstances arose. Most of these people died in the wilderness without really understanding the true provision of God.

In the Gospel, Jesus said to the people, *"...whoever eats me will live because of me."* It seems so simple doesn't it? If we go to Mass and receive the Eucharist, we should be full of the dynamic life of God but it often doesn't feel much like it. Well, in fact, we are full of this life. The problem is getting it *out* of us. The life within us is like the water sitting deep in the well to which the pump is connected. It's there and it has the capacity to nurture life. But it has to be brought to the surface. We have to prime the pump.

Do you want the grace of the body and blood of Christ to flow through you and out of you? Then prime your pump. Prime it with the music you listen to. Prime it with the people you spend the most time with. Prime it with scripture and spiritual books. But most of all prime it with the words of your mouth and the attitudes of your heart.

Our environment, whether it's people or our physical environment, has a strong influence on how we feel and think but we also need to start seeing that our thoughts, attitudes, judgments and what comes out of our mouths are environments in themselves. We live within our thoughts and within what we speak. When we speak and think negativity we are creating a wilderness for ourselves to live in. There is no lush growth because there is no flowing water. There is no flowing water because the well is deep and the pump is rusty from disuse.

A friend's teen-aged daughter left a note asking her to buy her some nuts. Her little brother left an answering note: "You are what you eat..." I'd like to twist this around a little:

You eat what you are.

If negativity is what you constantly think and speak, this is the food you are feeding yourself, the food you are living on day by day. Then we can go back to the original maxim: you are what you eat. If you constantly feed yourself negative thoughts and self-judgments you will eventually become negativity personified. And so the circle goes. And so the wilderness grows.

You receive the bread of Christ but what kind of a constant diet are you feeding your inner self about your value and worth to the Lord? Do you say, "I am so bad. I am so stupid. I'm such a failure." Or do you say, "Thank you Father, for making me who I am. You are the magnificent Creator and you only create beauty. Help me to see myself as you see me and love myself the way you love me." Macrina Weiderkher, a Benedictine nun, once prayed "O God, help me to believe the truth about myself no matter how beautiful it is!" This, too, is bread that nourishes us for the journey.

*"Those who eat my flesh and drink my blood **abide in me, and I in***

them." Abiding is not meant to be a sporadic activity and if you confine 'eating and drinking of me' to just the reception of the wine and bread in the Eucharist, and feel as though you've done your bit while filling the rest of your time with self-condemnation and negative thoughts about everything else, you aren't really eating and drinking Christ. You are nibbling at him.

Prime the spiritual pump. Change your inner diet. It isn't complicated...just critical.

Quantum Leap

John 6:53, 60-69

Jesus continues to speak about eating his flesh and drinking his blood. Many think this is intolerable language and leave. When he asks his disciples if they also want to leave, they say, "Where would we go? You have the words of eternal life."

Definition of quantum leap: "an abrupt change or step, especially in method, information, or knowledge." A quantum leap is not a change that occurs gradually over a continuous period; it's sudden, like jumping off a cliff. In this Gospel, Jesus asked his followers to take a quantum leap and go beyond simply thinking and talking about what they believed in. He did not ask them to take their time and grow slowly into this knowledge; he challenged them to take a sudden a leap of faith into the unknown based on nothing - but him.

Thomas Merton says that communication and communion are two fundamentally different modes of knowing. Communication is a logical, linear and one-dimensional way of imparting information that leads up to a definite conclusion. Communion is a way of knowing that which can't necessarily be verified or quantified using visible proof or logical argument. The Gospel this week is one that is very close to the heart of Catholic theology but even if you are not Catholic, you can ponder on the principle I'm going to write about in relation to any words of Christ in the Gospels because Jesus continually pushes his followers to take quantum leaps of faith and to experience the difference between communication and communion.

I want to ask you something, whether you're Catholic or not: do you believe what you believe because it has always been part of your upbringing and your faith culture or do you believe it because at some point you had to take a quantum leap of faith? Did you ever look at the basic tenets of your faith and cry out, "Lord, I believe. Help my unbelief!" If you've never done that, I'm not sure if that's something to be proud of or not. Quite often our beliefs come from what has been communicated to us by our parents and teachers but we have never allowed ourselves to examine our beliefs to the point where we either have to walk away or we have to take a quantum leap into the arms of a God we actually know nothing about but cannot live without.

In this week's Gospel, the disciples are faced with a moment where they had to make a radical decision. Their options were:

(A) They could decide to walk away.

(B) They could decide to stay on the safe edge of a relationship with Christ, define that relationship by everything Jesus said and did but never seek for anything beyond what they heard and saw. They could create a safe world of rules and interpretations based on what they heard and saw and stay there indefinitely.

(C) They could decide to plunge themselves into the depths of mystery, a mystery that went far deeper than being aware of the outward actions of Jesus. This mystery required them to assent to go somewhere unknown - not a place that was familiar because they had always been there, not a place that was comfortable because a lot of people they knew were in that place, and not a place that made sense because they were totally familiar with the concepts within it. It certainly was not a logical place where everything had been discussed, clearly defined and written down. They were asked to take a step and make a commitment without knowing anything that could be verified or substantiated.

Jesus asked them, *'Do you also wish to go away?'* and at that precise moment they had to make a huge, life-altering decision. Peter's reply, "Lord, who would we go to? You have the words of life," was pure communion and it plunged Peter, as well as those who agreed with him, into the center of the mystery of relationship with Christ. In that one sentence, Peter identified Jesus as the heart of everything he desired and needed: the alpha and omega, the beginning and the end, the way, the truth and the life – the only way to go. In that one sentence, he said, "Yes," to everything he knew absolutely nothing about.

We can know in our heads all there is to know about our faith and we can consciously assent to all that knowledge. That's communication. But it's not communion. When Jesus asked his disciples if they too would leave, Peter had no doctrinal grounds for his reply. There was no theology of the Eucharist. There was no creed, no New Testament, no books filled with complex theology. Peter's statement of faith had nothing to do with what he knew in his head. It was all about his heart and his heart said, "I have nothing if I do not have you. I will go with you wherever you go."

The fact that Jesus lived on earth and died on a cross is a historically verifiable fact. All the factual information about his life has been communicated to us by scripture and by historical documents. But our hearts need more than that. His life and his death on the cross communicated his immense love for us but we need more than that knowledge. We need to be in communion with that love. We need to leap into it even though we have no idea where that leap will take us. The sad thing is that for many people, the Eucharist and other faith challenges Jesus presented have dwindled to being a linear communications. We can continue to receive and believe without challenging ourselves with the question Jesus posed to his disciples. We can live without ever fully jumping into the abyss, preferring to simply think about it.

What if we went up to receive the Eucharist and instead of saying, "The body of Christ", the priest said, "Will you also go away?"

What a jolt that would be. If we are always remaining on the edge, staying behind the safety of what our heads know and only participating in linear communication rather than plunging into communion with the unknowable, Jesus has the right to wonder how far we're willing to go. If we're not taking the quantum leap of pondering all we think we know and then coming to the essential conclusion that we could never leave simply because we have nowhere else to go and he has everything we need and want, then we may be unconsciously keeping open the option to stop at a certain point and go no further.

Jesus said, *"It is the spirit that gives life; the flesh* (which includes all the head knowledge stored inside our brains) *is useless. The words that I speak to you are spirit and life."* Jesus was definitely challenging his disciples to take a huge leap of faith. He didn't explain in a logical linear fashion what he meant; this wasn't another one of his story parables. He knew his followers would not be able to intellectually grasp what he was saying because this was a moment calling them to heart communion not head communication. All he was asking was that they trust him, even though they had no idea what he was talking about or where he was taking them.

If you think you know exactly who God is, where he wants us all to go and what he wants us all to do – or think you should know these things – then you have not entered into communion with him.

Communion is not about knowing...it's about leaping into the unknown wildness of the heart of God.

Back To Love

Mark 7: 1-8, 14-15, 21-23

The Pharisees complain that Jesus and his disciples eat with unwashed hands. Jesus calls them hypocrites, points out ways they break God's commandments and says it is what comes out of a person's mouth that makes them unclean, not want goes into it.

They were in love. Everything they did was colored by thoughts of each other and by a desire to be in communion with the other. He would bring her flowers for no reason. She would cook his favorite foods. During the day they would text loving messages to each other. They composed songs, searched out gifts, took each other on mystery excursions and read books to each other. Each one longed to know more about the other and every discovery was a treasure.

And then they got married.

Life got demanding. Children were born, finances became a struggle, days dissolved into chaotic exhausting routine and moments of intimacy became rare. If they thought of each other during the day, the thoughts were often tinged resentment over lack of help and understanding or they were worrying thoughts about obligations that needed to be met. From their days of first love's communion, they maintained a few habitual modes of communication: a quick kiss hello or goodbye and gifts on anniversaries and birthdays but even these communications often lacked forethought or a deep intention to please. Mostly they were done because they were expected.

This was their marriage. They went through the motions the best they could but very often their commitment to each other was defined by a list of obligations fulfilled: "I take out the garbage, I look after the kids, I cook the meals, I go to work, I maintain the home/vehicle, I wash your laundry, I shovel the driveway..." What began as a loving relationship full of communion and communication rooted in mutual love was eroded into a daily grind of two people going through the motions without ever looking at the other's heart or trying to discern what the other truly needed or desired. Even actions that once had real relationship significance to both of them had become obligatory, done because "We always kiss in the morning," or "We always eat out on our anniversary."

The scribes and Pharisees constantly challenged Jesus because he and his disciples didn't always follow the traditions of the elders. The traditions or obligations spoken about in this scripture were not laws handed down by Moses but were practices added over the years. When one of these traditions began, it could very well have been started by someone who really had a deep and loving relationship with God and wanted to show his or her love by being extra diligent in a matter of purification or sacrifice. It could have sprung out of intimate communion and been a living gift of communication between God and one of his beloved. It doesn't take a lot of imagination to see how others may have adopted this extra ritual because the one who began it was a beautiful and holy person and others mistakenly assumed it was the action that caused the holiness rather than the love relationship from which the action sprang. Then, as generations continued the practice, little by little the love and grace of the action was lost until it became an empty ritual, something that was mandatory but not really understood. The communion within it became totally lost.

In other words, just as it is easy to lose the effervescence of first love and continue in a relationship with actions that are devoid of any kind of communion, it is very easy to fill our spiritual lives with various traditions, prayers and actions that are empty of true communion with God. That doesn't mean these traditions are in any way bad, useless or meaningless; it simply means that, just as in any good marriage or relationship, we need to stop, review all the things we do and ask ourselves if we are depending on obligatory actions to justify and define us. Do we just keep on performing certain actions because that's what our parents did or that's what our community always does? We especially need to spend time discerning whether we rely on our actions to justify ourselves spiritually while judging others who don't seem to be quite as diligent as we are. It is right at that point that Jesus had issues with the Pharisees and scribes. He didn't mind if they wanted to wash their hands all day long but where washing and purification became more important than compassion and love and when all the washing being done was hiding hearts that were judgmental, self righteous, territorial, resentful and lacking in a true relationship with the Father, that's where Jesus put his foot down.

No outward action has value or significance in itself and outward actions can actually mislead us into thinking our relationship with God is just fine. "That is not communion, people;" Jesus was saying, "that is not a love relationship with my Father. That is a relationship with your own outward righteousness, your own opinions, your own ego and your own external image. You have made the huge mistake of thinking that what you *do* is what makes you pleasing to the Father." To that mistaken understanding, God says, "Their hearts are far from me."

The married couple who kept up with their outward obligations but allowed the communion of love to wither away could also say of one another, "His heart is far from me." or "Her heart is far from me." There is sadness, loneliness and grief in that statement. The relationship has been defiled, not by evil but by carelessness. While outward appearances were maintained, their inner hearts were allowed to become lax and they turned inward on themselves. Desert desolation set in. The same thing happens in the spiritual life.

I have a feeling this is what Jesus meant whenever he said, "Repent." He meant, "Turn around, come back to the beginning, back to your first love. Come back to me with all your heart."

Repent and...
"You shall no more be termed Forsaken, and your land shall no more be termed Desolate; but you shall be called 'My Delight Is in Her', and your land Married; for the Lord delights in you and your land shall be married. For as a young man marries a young woman, so shall your builder marry you, and as the bridegroom rejoices over the bride, so shall your God rejoice over you."(Isaiah 62: 4,5 NRSV)

Your Beloved awaits.

Love Limited

Mark 7: 31-37

A deaf man with a speech impediment is brought to Jesus to be healed. Jesus looks up to heaven, sighs, and says, "Ephphatha" which means, "Be opened," and the man is immediately healed.

It's the sigh that gets to me.

When my children were young there were many times when I could see that they were hurting inside. Like all children and teenagers they went through tough experiences such as being the victim of a bully or being pushed out of the 'in' group or having a relationship break up. The wounds were deep and real and I never felt inclined to say, "She'll get over it. No big deal," or "He's all right; it's just teen-age love. Nothing serious." There were times when I knew there were wounds but the wounded one didn't have the ability to share how they were feeling in order to accept a touch of love or words of empathy. Young guys especially don't share emotions very easily. Even when I was able to offer physical touch and words of empathy and sympathy, which are very important in themselves, I couldn't do what I really longed to do: reach into the depths of them, touch the place that was so wounded and make it all better. Life still occasionally deals blows to my adult children and my husband and I still sigh for the wounds. That's the way it is with parents and children.

It makes us sigh, not from impatience or frustration, but from love that finds itself achingly limited.

When Jesus came to earth, he accepted the condition of being humanly limited. You might argue that being able to heal the deaf and raise the dead isn't exactly being limited, but from Jesus' point of view, from how he knew the Father and what he knew his Father wanted for his people, he was very limited. Jesus was able to heal those he did because there was belief, acceptance, hope and faith there. He could not heal those who did not want healing and did not believe he could help them. (*"And he could do no mighty work there, except that he laid his hands on a few sick people and healed them. And he marveled because of their unbelief."* Mark 6: 1-6, ESV) When people didn't accept him as the Son of God he was not able to work any miracles because God will never force himself on anyone who does not want him. Ever.

Jesus gladly healed the deaf, the blind, the mute and the ill. Wherever there was even a tiny spark of faith and desire, he worked miracles. But so rarely was he able to work the miracle he desired to work the most which was the miracle of reaching deep inside and touching the inner wounds of fear, rejection, self-condemnation and blindness to the true nature of his Father.

Then looking up to heaven, he sighed and thought, "Father, if only I could reach in and touch this man's wounded spirit. If only I could open his ears to your wonderful life-giving voice telling him he is loved, loved, loved by us. If only I could touch his spiritual tongue so that words of love for you would begin to flow like honey, creating a desire within him to stay beside you forever. If only I could open his eyes to who you really are so that he would no longer see you as a distant disinterested God. I long to wash away his fear of you so he will run into your arms. If only I could change how he sees himself so he could begin to delight in his whole self as your unique creation."

I have no doubt that the sigh Jesus heaved blew through the portals of the kingdom and filled all of heaven and earth, while angels and archangels experienced intense communion with his sigh – the sigh of eternal desire.

So why couldn't he just reach inside and heal the heart of the man? He was God wasn't he? Think of how much more effective his ministry would have been if he had immediately healed the inner heart of every person he saw. It would have been so simple.

Simple? Yes. Loving? No.

God, too, has limited himself in love and he will not push himself where he is not asked, wanted or recognized. For Jesus to heal where he was not asked to heal or where recognition of need was absent would have been an act of intrusion, power and control of the sort God does not engage in – and we humans often engage in. We might argue that the good that would result would be worth it. Not to God. He wants his people to come to him freely. To heal where healing is not asked for, to change hearts when change is not perceived as something that is needed, is the act of a dictator. God is not a dictator, not even a benevolent one. No dictatorial role, benevolent or otherwise, flows out of true relationship and what God wants with his people more than anything is true relationship, a free, loving, open, joy-filled relationship. He wants the kind of relationship where you will seek him in freedom, faith and strong trust for all your inner transformation and then stick around to enjoy those changes with him, not just seek him when there's a problem. He wants to be more than the giver of all goodness; he wants to be your Beloved, someone you long to be with and someone with whom you are excited to share life and are restless if you're away from him. The tragedy is that most often we misunderstand him and turn to him only when things are rough or regard him somewhat fearfully as the Dictator and do all we can to placate him - except go to him as children and lovers.

Some people prefer to think of God as a dictator. It's so much simpler. Then all they feel they have to do is know the rules and follow them. But that's sort of like your child saying, "I know that you like me have a clean room, not leave my stuff all over the house and not challenge your rules so from now on I'm going to stay in my room. I'll keep it super clean and because I'm not moving around the house, I won't be leaving stuff around. And because we're not having actual interactions you won't have to put up with my questions and complaints." Wow. Wouldn't that be simple? Sure, there would be no growth in relationship with you or inner growth in her from interacting with you but so what? It would be immensely simple and your child would be fulfilling her obligations.

And your heart would ache because you miss your child so badly and your child is missing so much of true life.

The Lord yearns and aches for us with desire of such an intensity that no earthly father or mother will ever experience for his or her children. Instead of staying within the perceived safety of just fulfilling what we think God wants from us we need to respond to him with our own sighs of eternal longing.

"God is an unutterable sigh, planted in the depths of the soul." (Jean Paul Richter, 1763-1825)

Turn now to the God who sighs for you.

On Suffering

Mark 8: 27-35

Jesus asks the disciples "Who do people say I am?" Then he asks, "Who do you say that I am?" He begins to teach them that he must undergo great suffering, be rejected, killed and then rise again. Peter rebukes him and Jesus rebukes Peter in return. Then Jesus tells the disciples and the crowd that if any want to follow him, they must deny themselves and pick up their crosses and follow him. He states that those who want to save their life will lose it and those who lose their life will save it.

How often in your life has the phrase, *"Deny yourself and take up your cross and follow me,"* haunted you in relation to a challenging situation you were dealing with? How often did it make you feel that if you didn't choose and embrace the most difficult and hurtful path possible, you would be denying Jesus and trying to save your life instead of losing it?

In writing his gospel, Mark was endeavoring to show how the Jews at first were all enthusiastic and excited about this new Messiah who had appeared on the scene but gradually began to turn away and become disgruntled with Jesus' message. It became clear to them that Jesus was not the powerful political savior they thought he was going to be. In this week's gospel passage, Jesus is challenging his twelve disciples, and the others who were following him, to understand once and for all that his mission was not a mission that would uproot the Roman Empire, empower the Jews and set them free as a political nation.

The cross Jesus was challenging those particular followers to pick up was accepting that Jesus' mission was radically different from what they were expecting. Even Jesus' closest disciples weren't too clear about what was on the horizon and when Jesus told them in no uncertain terms what was to happen, Peter rebuked him. Jesus, in turn, rebuked Peter and basically said to his followers, "If you're looking for success, national freedom, material riches and worldly power then you'd better find someone else to follow. You won't find those things with me. What you will find with me are people and priests who will hate me, reject me and put me on a cross. This is where we're going folks."

If Jesus thought that suffering in itself was a good thing and a way to please the Father, he would not have gone around healing people. He would have instead told them all that they should pick up their crosses and deny themselves. Before he was crucified, Jesus did not seek out extra pain and suffering to validate his life or please his Father. Yes, he lived simply but he had good parents who raised him in love, he often ate well, he went to weddings and drank wine and he had good friends he loved to visit. If he was offered a place at a banquet table, he took it. If a woman wanted to massage his feet with oil, he let her. He did not practice stringent asceticism for the sake of adding more pain to his redemptive work nor did he encourage any one else to seek out pain and suffering as a way to please God.

Jesus certainly suffered before he got to 'The' cross. He was human and so he suffered hunger pangs, aching feet and cold hands. He felt the sting when others rejected him and his teachings. He grieved when his father and good friends died. He endured the loneliness of being misunderstood by his closest friends. He knew what it was like to not have enough money to buy much beyond the basics and sometimes not even the basics. Jesus suffered because he accepted his human condition and lived with it *as it was*. He didn't make the mistake of actually seeking to make it any worse than it was.

If he was saying anything to the rest of Christianity down through the ages, it wasn't that suffering is good; it was that suffering is normal. Don't try to avoid it but don't seek it out either.

Are you a follower of Jesus because you believe he will make you financially rich? Do you read these reflections because you hope I might give you a key that will make you a powerful person, one who can tell other people what to do all the time? Do you go to Mass because it will give you great status in the eyes of the community? Did you have children or do you desire to do so because you think it will make you rich? Do you feel that a successful Christian is one who has all the best in material goods and is one that other people envy?

No? I didn't think so. In fact, I have to say that all the people I talk to about their spiritual lives and spiritual desires have indeed picked up their crosses, denied themselves and have followed after Jesus through the very normalcy of their lives. Status, power, riches and success have nothing to do with why they live sacramental lives. The ordinary life of the committed Christian is full of crosses and self-denial. Just look at the mother cleaning up vomit in the middle of the night or the parents staying with their child in the hospital or the people who suffer from chronic pain or the person who can't find a job with a living wage or the couple who does not have the latest and greatest of whatever is late and great because their children need school supplies and new shoes or their income is simply inadequate or because they put money in the collection plate or because they simply don't crave the latest and greatest, preferring rather to direct their energies and money to raising children or serving the church community or helping the poor. I could go on and on about the suffering inherent in our lives as people of God – sufferings we never even think about; we just live with them and get on with life in spite of them. They're always there but we have a choice as to whether we live with them in gracious acceptance that brings transformation or in fear and resentment that increases the suffering. It is not the suffering that is valuable. It is our attitude within it.

We need to understand, once and for all, that, on its own, Jesus' suffering was not what saved the world. Millions of people, before and after Jesus, have suffered and died more horribly than he did. What saved the world was Christ's love within that suffering and the love that Jesus possessed was awesome gift and grace. "Pick up your cross and deny yourself" cannot and must not be considered a catchall theology of how to please God. Like any other scripture in the bible, it can be taken out of context and applied in destructive ways. To assume that God mandates every instance of suffering is a faulty understanding of God's true nature. To assume that anything that could bring us simple pleasure and joy is to be held suspect because we're not denying ourselves is also faulty theology. Denying ourselves pleasure and seeking out pain and suffering is actually a spiritual danger. Why? Because we are prone to keeping a score board with God and we review all the pain and suffering we've gone through and all the pleasures we've denied ourselves so we can point out to him that we're good and worthy and have 'paid the price' of being his follower. Suffering can actually be a gateway to spiritual pride.

We cannot control God or manipulate him by how we suffer and we are a people who love to be in control. We love to feel that we somehow have the power to make God attend to our needs and wants by what we do. It is a real denial of self to let go of the reins and admit we have no idea what we need. It is real self-denial to humbly recognize that life is messy, wounding and not always easy or gratifying but it's all right because we walk with a compassionate Christ. Compassion means 'to suffer with' so we walk with one who suffers with us and says to us,

"Come to me all you who labor and are heavily burdened and I will give you rest. For my yolk is easy and my burden is light."

Deny yourself. Let go.

True Greatness

Mark 9: 30-37

The disciples are arguing among themselves as to which of them is the greatest. When Jesus asks them what they were arguing about, they are silent. He tells them that whoever wants to be first must be a servant of all and he takes a little child on his lap and says that whoever welcomes such a child welcomes him, and whoever welcomes him welcomes the one who sent him.

We are so used to the Gospel narrative and to the words of Jesus we've heard time and time again that we think we understand the message when in fact, like the disciples arguing who was greatest, we haven't really absorbed the message.

By taking a little child in his arms, Jesus was still instructing his disciples that following him was going to take them down a path that was polar opposite to what they were thinking was going to happen, which was overthrowing the Romans and establishing a strong Jewish nation. They had been arguing about which of them was the greatest. This was an important point they wanted to settle because whoever was the greatest would surely have a position of honor and would have a lot of power when Jesus conquered the Romans. They just didn't 'get it' and Jesus was so patient. He knew he was teaching them something contrary to centuries of social and religious conditioning. It's not easy to suddenly understand new concepts and change your mind about something you learned from birth.

We can shake our heads at what dim bulbs those disciples were, but are we any quicker to recognize when Jesus is asking us to re-examine our own deeply rooted cultural and social conditioning that spills over into how we operate as a Christian community?

Is Jesus capable now of shocking and challenging us just as much as he shocked and challenged the disciples? Are we even open to that? Or have we gradually become so familiar and comfortable with our own sets of definitions that we have absolutely no thought that God would ever shock us by exposing how we have misunderstood his desires and intentions?

The disciples truly thought Jesus was a wonderful Messiah and they weren't wrong there. Where they were wrong was in their visions of what 'Messiah' really meant and in their expectations of where they were all going, how they were going to get there and what it was all going to look like when they got themselves there. I deliberately used the phrase, 'when they got themselves there'. They really thought *they* were going to change things in Israel. Sure, Jesus would be the leader but they would all be up there with him. He couldn't do it without them, right? He needed strong right hand men to pull this off, right? He needed their hands and feet. He needed their strong religious fervor. All they were doing on the way to Capernaum was having a serious discussion as to which of them would be his strongest right hand man. Yes, Jesus was the Messiah, but he was going to need a Vice-Messiah and a whole Ministry of Messiah Affairs. He would need advisors, councils and special committees. They were pretty sure Jesus was dependent on them to get this new era off the ground and established in a proper way.

Had Jesus allowed them to continue with those visions, expectations and wrangling about their positions, the twelve would very soon have organized themselves into an elite core group. Then their energies would have been expended in defending this core group, maintaining its power, position and vision and not allowing it to grow, expand or change – or even disintegrate if that was God's will. Their focus would have been inward on the maintenance and function of the group first and then outward on making sure the community respected their visions and their authority.

The true Kingdom servant actually has no claimed territory, no expectations that must be maintained and no agendas that must be pushed through at all cost. The Kingdom servant responds to the needs of the people. Because the servant has no position of controlling power, he or she is wonderfully free of the need to defend a position, keep control or sit in judgment. The servant is free to serve where he or she is being sent to serve – and it may be someplace doing something completely different than what that servant had done before. Or it may be doing nothing. Just because the servant has always served and ministered a certain way or in a certain area doesn't mean that tomorrow the Lord won't call that servant to do something entirely different which will once again push against and expand the servant's self-set expectations, borders, definitions and limitations.

The moment any one of us is asked to operate in a way that is polar opposite to how we were brought up, we have major meltdowns. Just talk to any married couple from two distinctly different cultural backgrounds or radically different ways of being raised as children. The challenge to back down and agree that the other's values and perspectives are a better way to go in any situation is a huge battle and most often ends in resentment and wounds within the one who loses the battle.

Eventually those disciples were sent into a life of service that none of them had ever conceived of, but in order to get there they had to go through a few years of having their perspectives completely blown apart. And it may have begun when a Shepherd King placed a child on his knee.

Whenever God changes any one of us through inner death and new life, he is profoundly changing the whole Kingdom. But if we, like those disciples, keep thinking it's an outward game plan and we have to tightly control the visions and outcomes, then no...we still don't get it.

The Unclenched Heart

Mk 9:38-43, 45, 47-48

John complains to Jesus that someone was casting out demons in Jesus' name. Jesus says that no one who is doing a deed of power in his name will be able to speak evil of him. Whoever is not against us is for us. He goes on to say that if our hands or feet cause us to stumble we should cut them off and if our eye causes us to stumble it should be torn out.

Some of the worst memories I have from my childhood are of being deliberately excluded from a group. Some of the most heart wrenching times I had as a parent were when any of my children experienced exclusion. Those of you who are parents now, or will be in the future, have experienced or will experience the same inner agony at some point in your children's growing years. Exclusion is one of the most constant manifestations of original sin and children and adults alike practice it.

The theme that is most often talked about in this week's gospel is the avoidance of sin in our lives and we are struck by Jesus' use of extreme hyperbole to get this point across. We generally receive his words as direction for our individual overall morality but in this gospel, Jesus actually seems to be talking about something in particular that wrenches the Father's heart and that is exclusion – the practice of elitism or a determination that we have the right to judge another individual or a group that doesn't play the game our way.

Before Jesus speaks about cutting off body parts that offend, he is instructing the disciples not to be so quick to judge that someone is "not one of us". The first reading follows exactly the same theme. Complaints are brought to Moses that there are people outside the camp who are prophesying. Moses responds by saying, "What's the problem? I wish you all would prophesy." In both readings we have the infant beginnings of two different religious communities and in both of them, before people even knew what was really going on, they were practicing exclusion. It's so elemental to human nature and it is as hurtful to the heart of God as it is to our hearts when our children are rejected and excluded.

One of the most destructive forces in any community, whether it's a parish, the workplace or a family, is the formation of territories. You can see it happening all the time. One group sets up its own territory, which in a parish could even be a ministry or a prayer group, and gradually this territory has to be defended and controlled. The enemy has to be identified and that enemy is often someone who suggests changes or else another group that doesn't think along the same lines. The enemy may be more conservative or more liberal, too lax or too rigid, too much into social justice or not enough into social justice... It's human nature. Watch a group of kids and see how long it takes before one or more of them say something like, "This is my room. This is my toy. This is my space. You can't tell me what to do. You're not the boss. Don't cross this line." It's very rare that communities, institutions and workplaces aren't divided into distinct groups: this ministry against that ministry, management vs. regular employees, this division against that division and this faculty against that faculty.

This is anathema to the heart of God. These attitudes of territorialism and defensiveness have absolutely nothing to do with the Spirit of God. Notice that neither Moses nor Jesus said, "Just a second. I'll check these people out and then I'll tell you if there's anything to worry about." They didn't get all threatened, alarmed and worried. Neither Moses nor Jesus were concerned about their territories. They had nothing they needed to defend.

Their egos were not on the line. When we get into an attitude of defending what we think God wants us to defend, what we are most often defending are our fragile egos. Our group or our territory has become our identity. Jesus had no need to defend himself against anyone who might act without asking his express permission because his ego was not all wrapped up in his mission.

Instead of individual people going around wondering if they should cut off their hands to avoid offending God, I propose that whole communities should be terribly worried about this. If there's a group in the body of Christ that thinks it is God's right hand group and it is always defending its territory by pointing fingers at others, then this is the hand that should be cut off before it causes offense. I have seen parishes destroyed by this attitude. I have seen individuals and groups wounded terribly which caused them to define their own territories so they wouldn't be hurt any further; then they started to point their own fingers and the whole scenario was repeated. It literally takes years, even decades, for a parish to heal from rampant territorialism. In the work place, extreme manifestations of territorialism can cause businesses to go under. Families can die from it.

I'm being very heavy about this topic but it's too important to gloss over. We do it all the time. We do it as groups and we do it as individuals. Every time we share something negative with someone about another person or another group with whom we philosophically disagree, we are practicing exclusion and building walls. We fear we will be infected by wrong ideas. We fear we will be made to feel uncomfortable. We fear we will be judged so we judge first. We fear change.

Lose the fear. Think of Jesus. Think of Moses. It's not up to us to defend God in whatever way we think he needs defending. Lose the fear. Open up. Love. It's not about who's right and who's wrong. It's about love. It's about respect. It's about acceptance, bridges and hands reaching out to each other to invite in, not keep out – open hands, not clenched fists with pointing fingers. We must lose the fear – it is destroying us.

My husband and I worked in the UVic Chaplaincy where there were 14 different faith groups sharing office space. These weren't just Christian groups; Buddhist, Moslem, Jewish, Baha'i and Sikh were some of the other faiths represented. There was absolutely no way we could all agree on our spiritual and religious beliefs. Even among the Christian faith groups there were large differences. But our differences were not what we focused on. We all strove to find what we had in common. It wasn't hard to find these things. Love. Integrity. Desire to serve God. There was no sense that anyone felt they were better than anyone else. Everyone supported each other's ministries. Everyone knew that each chaplain was completely committed to his or her own faith beliefs but defensive walls didn't need to be built. Everyone recognized that the only way the chaplaincy could operate was if there was huge respect and love for each other.

Each of us is called to search inside ourselves and see if we are harboring prejudice against 'the other', whether the other is someone of a completely different belief system or a person or group within our own parish or a family member who has chosen a path different from our own. Love *cannot* operate from behind a fortress wall. Love is not love if it requires another to change before we will love them unconditionally. God does not treat us this way and we cannot – we must not – treat others that way.

The hands must be open and the heart unclenched.

"And you shall be called 'Breach Mender, Restorer of Ruined Houses." (Isaiah 58:12, Jerusalem Bible)

Mend the breach – restore the home. We cannot survive any other way.

Growing Down

Mark 10: 2-16

Some Pharisees come and test Jesus by asking if it is lawful for a man to divorce his wife. Jesus expounds on the law of God regarding divorce.

Then people bring their children to Jesus so that he can touch them. The disciples try to make them go away by speaking sternly to them but Jesus says to let the little children come to him, because the Kingdom of God belongs to ones such as children. He tells them that anyone who doesn't receive the Kingdom like a like a small child will never enter it.

I know that the sequence in which incidents in the Gospels are written aren't necessarily the sequence in which they occurred but it in this case, it makes sense to me to have Jesus reaching out to children after being with the Pharisees.

The following is a conversation my daughter had with her 21-month-old son, Jasper but I'm going to relate it as if it was Jesus having the conversation:

Jesus: *Look, Jasper! An airplane.*

Jasper: *Fly. Moon.*

Jesus: *It's flying to the moon?*

Jasper: *Yeah.*

Jesus: *What's on the moon?*

Jasper*: Puddles.*

Jesus*: Anything else?*

Jasper*: Bananas.*

Jesus*: Anything else?*

Jasper*: Stickers.*

Jesus*: Anything else?*

Jasper*: No.*

After spending time debating law with the Pharisees, a conversation like that with a small child must have been delightful and refreshing for Jesus. In preparing to write this reflection, I felt sympathetic to Jesus' desire to have some children around him because I spent a good portion of an afternoon researching Jewish marriage, what it meant to them to be 'one flesh' and what the Jewish laws actually state about divorce. It was a *long* afternoon.

Some of it was interesting, though. For instance, did you know that the Hebrew word for 'one' in the phrase 'one flesh' is the same as the Hebrew word that is used for 'one' in Deuteronomy 6:4? *"Hear, O Israel: The Lord our God, the Lord is one."* And did you know that some Jews believed that God originally created one human being with one soul? Then he created them male and female and he divided the soul between them. They believed marriage was the coming together of two equal soul halves to make one complete soul.

And then I got into the divorce laws and I realized, once again, that we humans sure make things complicated. For the Jewish

Law, every little possibility and complexity had to be worked out and defined. What constitutes a valid reason for saying, "I divorce you"? Can a woman say it to man? What is a 'Get'? (It's a Jewish divorce document.) What happens to the dowry if a couple gets divorced? Can a man remarry a woman he already divorced once and get another dowry? The dowry issue was huge. It often was the sole thing that kept a man from divorcing his wife because she often got to take the dowry back! What a great reason to stay married. I'm sure that really pleased God.

By the time I was finished reading all that stuff, I totally understood Jesus getting indignant with the disciples for sending the little children away and why he said, "Seriously, I tell you, whoever does not receive the kingdom of God as a little child will never enter it."

We adults have forgotten how to be simple and how to receive the Kingdom with wide-open hearts full of innocence, awe and wonder. We've forgotten how to open ourselves to pure mystery and let mystery be...mysterious. Mystery is supposed to be something we cannot figure out, identify, define, label and put on a shelf but we always want to do that. We want to be completely sure, totally right and in control of all possible outcomes.

We absolutely need rules just like children need rules. Marriage and everything else in life can be messy with hurtful complications and without some guidelines it can be hard to maneuver through pitfalls and find our way back along roads that have taken a wrong turn. Having guidelines isn't the problem. The problem is when we obsess over the Law and stay there. It's like owning a beautiful light filled house with many rooms and a good solid foundation but insisting on living in the windowless basement and refusing to leave.

The law cannot show us the realms and joys that are beyond our present situation; it can only tell us when we're wrong. It does not open us to spiritual possibilities but keeps us focused on our human limitations and if we live too long focusing on just what the law says, we become hard of heart like Jesus said the Jews were. That didn't mean the Jews weren't serious about serving God; it meant they were locked into trying to justify themselves by knowing and keeping all the rules. They lost the softness of heart that comes from living by faith and believing that God is far beyond the limited perceptions of the human mind. They became seriously 'adult' and lost the capacity to envision with awe and wonder and to yearn for the mysteries of God that would lead them like children into the Kingdom.

We think we know everything we need to know about being good Christians. For the most part we know very little. If we understood how little we know it would be cause for huge celebration and freedom, for when we become comfortable with knowing nothing, we stop telling God what he can and cannot do and stop telling ourselves what can or cannot be.

We all know children are not perfect little beings. Before they can even speak they display selfish behavior and stubborn willfulness. The word "no" comes to them very naturally and very early. Children are not saints. But to them, the realm of spiritual possibility is wide and fantastic. They can see angels and are astounded by a God who is invisible but is with them everywhere. Before they are given different images, they will relate to a God who not only has a lap but also, quite possibly, has a dinosaur with him in heaven. They have no grasp of theology and therefore have not put limits on what is feasible or possible in God's eyes. They haven't broken life down into sections and subsections and they haven't learned about all the boxes we grown-ups like to keep God in.

Jean Allen

Here's a critical theological question for you. Think carefully before you answer, because the answer has serious implications.

Can your God put puddles on the moon?

Becoming Dispossessed

Mark 10: 17-30

A man runs up to Jesus and asks what he must do to inherit eternal life. Jesus lists the commandments and the man says he has kept them since he was young. Then Jesus says he lacks one thing; he must sell his possessions and give the money to the poor. The man is shocked and goes away disheartened because of his riches. Then Jesus tells his disciples that it is easier for a camel to go through the eye of a needle than a rich man to enter heaven.

This is a wonderful gospel passage, but the wonderful part of it is often overlooked because of the immediate discomfort it creates as we survey all of our material possessions and ask ourselves if Jesus really meant that we have to sell everything in order to follow him. We can certainly understand that it's easy to get too caught up in our possessions and end up in a never-ending cycle of attainment and maintenance that completely distracts us from the Kingdom life. So we wonder if we have become too attached and too focused on our material possessions. It's a good exercise to discern how attached we are to what we do have and how focused we are on what we don't have. However, don't let this very good exercise overshadow another deeply important and wonderful truth in this gospel.

The rich man proudly declared to Jesus that he had followed all the prescribed rules since he was a boy. The first clue we have that Jesus is trying to get something planted in the hearts of his disciples is planted within Jesus' reply to the man. *'Jesus, looking at him, **loved him** and said, 'You lack one thing; go, sell what you own, and give the money to the poor, and you will have treasure in heaven; then come, follow me.'* (NRSV)

Jesus looked the man and loved him. Within that look and that love was an invitation much deeper than a simple invitation to sell all his material possessions. Far more than material possessions were hindering the man from moving from a law-based spirituality to a life-based spirituality. Why would this man run up and ask Jesus what he should do to inherit eternal life if he already knew he had kept the Jewish commandments all his life and had been taught that this is what would grant him eternal life? Was he really looking for the key to eternal life or was he actually looking for approval from Jesus for his faithfulness to the law? Maybe he hoped Jesus would say something like, "Look at this man. Here is what you all should be striving for. Obviously, God loves him because he is wealthy and not only is he wealthy but he is excellent at following the law. What a guy!"

Instead, Jesus told him he was lacking one thing. Was this 'one thing' simply the action of selling all the man owned? Perhaps not. Perhaps the one thing lacking was actually letting go of all he depended upon to justify him and all the things he did to try to merit eternal life. The man went away shocked. He failed to look at the love in Jesus' eyes and he didn't allow himself to experience the true freedom of grace. All he could hear was "sell all". He was jarred to the core of his being because all Jews assumed that wealth indicated God's approval. If he was looking for approbation, recognition or a pat on the back, he didn't get it. Jesus didn't say to him, "You're great! You've done everything you need to do. I wish everybody was like you." The rich man completely missed what was in the eyes of Jesus, which was what he really needed: Jesus' unconditional love and grace. Had he looked into Jesus' eyes and seen the love there, had he understood that he was being called to leave behind the uselessness of self justification in order to receive the free gift of grace, he would have done everything possible to follow Jesus.

Jesus then commented to his disciples about how difficult it is for a rich man to enter into the kingdom of God. Was Jesus really speaking about life after death or was he speaking about becoming intimately engaged with the Kingdom of God in the present moment? In Luke 17: 20, 21, Jesus was asked when the Kingdom of God was coming and in his reply he ended with, '...*in fact, the kingdom of God is among you.*' An alternative word for 'among' is 'within'. The kingdom of God is within you.

The disciples as well as the rich man were looking for information about the afterlife and how it was possible to earn eternal salvation. What Jesus was trying to get through to them was, "I am the kingdom of God and I am here. When you look into my eyes, fall in love with me and allow me to love you, you will have the kingdom of God within you. It will be all you need. It will be all you want. I am eternal life personified."

The big question is, what is stopping any of us from living in the grace of Christ, finding all we need in him and being fully engaged in the here and now Kingdom of God? Do we seek the eyes of Jesus in every moment to see his love, or are we so concerned with keeping the proper rules and keeping a tally of everything we do for the Lord that we miss experiencing Kingdom grace right now, right where we are?

To the rich man, wealth was a sign of God's approval. What signs do we look for to indicate that we are acceptable to God? It could be that we are caught up in material possessions but I don't think that people today believe that being wealthy automatically means we have God's approval. We would do well to look at other things we think might indicate that God is pleased with our efforts. Could it be that having a successful ministry means God is on our side? Might we be placing an enormous amount of personal justification on the behavior or spiritual conformity of our children or on the number of children we have? Every time we experience God's blessing, do we immediately recall all the rosaries or prayers we have recited or how often we attend daily Mass? When we experience any kind of hardship, is there a temptation to blame ourselves for our spiritual failings, sure that God failed us because we failed him? Do we place a lot of importance on how much we know about the church, faith and scripture and feel that the more we know, the safer we will be from committing offenses against God? There's nothing wrong with any of these things – including wealth. It's our dependence on them to justify us that causes the problem. Even voluntary poverty can become a source of pride and self-justification. All these things become unhealthy when they become *our* possessions and, in maintaining our possession of them, they separate us from complete and utter dependence on the love of Christ to justify us and take us home. They become obstacles to grace.

The spiritual journey is a life long process of having our fingers pried off false security. No one is exempt. The call to let go of all that we hold onto is not a call coming from the heart of a forbidding God. It is a call from the heart of the Beloved:

"Please...look into my eyes. See the love there? That love says that I will be the total source of your spiritual validation that will get you through the gate to the Kingdom. I am the one who can navigate you through the eye of the needle."

I know it can be a shock. I know it's hard to grasp but it's true. The best way to come to him is to let go of every single one those self-justifying "possessions" and, like the children Jesus cherishes, come with nothing.

It is only Christ's grace that will carry you into the Kingdom.

29th Sunday Ordinary B

Moving On To Smaller and Greater Things

Mark 10: 35-45

James and John ask Jesus to grant that they will be allowed to sit, one at his left and one at his right, in his glory. Jesus asks them if they are able to drink the cup he will drink or be baptized with the same baptism and they say they are. The other disciples are angry with James and John so Jesus explains to them that whoever wishes to be great must be the servant of all, for the Son of Man came not to be served but to be the servant of all.

As Jesus and his disciples traveled on their journeys, they ran into a lot of derision. We know that Jesus' authority was often challenged simply because he was just a carpenter's son from the down and out village of Nazareth, ("Can anything good come out of Nazareth?") so it stands to reason that the disciples also received their share of disrespect. They must have experienced, with Jesus, the humiliation of being subtly categorized as people who were of no great value to society and felt the sting of suspicion and accusations launched at them simply because of bigoted perceptions and because of their lack of status. Very few of us make it through life without experiencing at some point the pain of attitudes that imply that we are not as valuable, influential, highly paid, educated or powerful as another, or attitudes that insinuate that because of the group, race, faith or culture we belong to, we probably share the worst traits of those who have proven themselves to be destructive within that group. The frustration and pain of being labeled and dismissed or even vilified is something that can easily undermine one's personal sense of value. It hurts because we all have a deep human longing to know we are needed by others and that others recognize our dignity and value.

James and John had exactly this same human need. They probably felt the hurt of being disparagingly referred to as "just fishermen" and dismissed as sinful, ignorant, on par with prostitutes and tax collectors, and useless for anything except catching fish. In this week's Gospel, they were seeking positions of influence and power because, being human and still very fuzzy about who Jesus really was, they may have been tempted to ease the humiliation of being categorized and dismissed by finding places of power, dignity and status where they would be respected and honored.

What Jesus understood, and they didn't, was that even if they did achieve higher and more respected positions, they would soon spend most of their time maintaining and defending those positions. Look at how the other disciples reacted to James and John's request to sit Jesus' side in his glory, which they probably assumed would be when he defeated the Romans and was crowned King of the Jews. The rest of the disciples were angry and resentful. If Jesus hadn't cut them all off at the pass, the others would have asked why James and John should have such elevated positions and then demanded equality or at least equal opportunity to apply for the same positions. Then James and John would have felt the necessity to prove that they were best suited for the positions which could have meant showing how the others were *not* suited, perhaps subtly pointing out inadequacies and faults...you can see where this is going.

I guarantee there would have been no jostling for position and no angry resentment if James and John had gone up to Jesus and said, "Jesus, we would like to be the ones who will always be responsible for digging the latrines when we're on the road." There was no glory, power or honor for latrine diggers but neither would anyone have resented them or tried to find ways to malign them or oust them from their positions. No one would have been giving them the silent treatment as pay back for being uppity. They would have been completely free to serve.

However, the action of digging latrines – or washing dishes, or changing diapers, or picking up garbage, or being at the beck and call of others or any other non-glorious way of serving the family or one's faith community – doesn't necessarily make anyone a saint. What creates holiness within these perceived lowly positions of service is love and nothing else.

As a young stay at home mother, I used to struggle daily to find and cling to my innate worth. In a world where valuable skills are rewarded with a good paycheck and benefits, being 'just' a stay at home mother can often insignificant indeed. There have been many times over the years when the culture of the world has made me feel inconsequential, not only as a stay at home mother but also as a woman. My family and faith community respected me in my role but many outside the family and Church did not. I absolutely had to find my worth and value in some way other than the way the world dictates value. I often clung to the words of a blessed spiritual teacher (Carlos Caretto), that Jesus *chose* the lowest place. It was very difficult sometimes but I now know that experiencing that place of no status was what pushed me to find my dignity and worth where it really is.

My value does not depend on what I do, how good I am, how much power I have, who respects me, how much I am paid, what status I achieve or what I accomplish. My dignity is in the eyes of the Lord. I had to find it there and allow it to feed my innermost being. Status and respect in the eyes of the world are not bad in themselves but Jesus knows that having them can blind us to the real source of our true selves. It is the lowest places, the places of service, the places of not being appreciated for who you really are that can drive you straight to the heart of God. Once you're there and once you have seen yourself reflected in his eyes, there is nothing that can devalue you and no one who can unseat you from your place. But it is a choice to go there. Desiring the place of being hidden and the place of service and love is a choice, and it is a choice to seek our value solely in God instead of in the admiration and respect of others, even of others within our own faith communities or families.

The Suscipe, the prayer of St. Ignatius of Loyola, is a powerful prayer that has had great significance for me, especially in times of struggling to know my value and worth.

Take, Lord, and receive all my liberty,
my memory, my understanding,
and my entire will,
All I have and call my own.
You have given all to me.
To you, Lord, I return it.
Everything is yours; do with it what you will.
Give me only your love and your grace,
that is enough for me.

I have often prayed, over and over, "Your love and your grace are enough for me," yearning to know his love and grace in a way that nothing could ever make me forget it – because it is impossible to embrace a lifestyle of doing small things with great love...

...unless you completely understand that you are a small one who is greatly loved.

Critical Perspective

Mark 10: 46-52

Bartimaeus, a blind beggar, hears that Jesus is passing by. He calls out, "Jesus, Son of David, have mercy on me!" Even though many sternly order him not to call for Jesus, he does so again. Jesus hears him, asks him what he wants Jesus to do for him and, when he asks to see again, Jesus heals him, saying that Bartimaeus' faith made him whole.

When we read this Gospel or others like it where someone has a healing encounter with the Lord, it is a common and very good meditation to place ourselves in the scene as the one who is receiving the healing, whether it is an emotional healing like the woman at the well, or a physical healing such as in this story of Bartimaeus, the blind man.

But I'm going to shake up the common perspective and ask you if you have ever thought of putting yourself in Jesus' place instead or imagining yourself as one of the disciples being trained to follow in the footsteps of Jesus? Do you always imagine yourself as one of the needy, one of the blind or deaf, one of the outcast or one of the leprous ones who encountered Jesus? This is certainly where we begin in our journey with Christ. But we must not stay there.

1 Peter 2:9 states *"But you are a chosen race, a royal priesthood, a consecrated nation, a people set apart to sing the praises of God, who called you out of darkness into his wonderful light."(Jerusalem Bible)*

At some point, we all need to seriously face the fact that we are not called to remain poor and needy. That does not mean to say that we should become arrogant or have an over-inflated sense of our own importance. It doesn't mean that we should never have failures, problems or needs. It simply means that we have been called to the Priesthood of the Laity – the Royal Priesthood. It means that we have been called to walk with the same dignity and authority in which Jesus walked and in which the disciples grew and flourished as the Church had its beginnings. It means that we have been chosen to be other Christs to the world and to our brothers and sisters in our faith communities.

When I first wrote this reflection several years ago, we were all shocked by the arrest of the Bishop in Antigonish who had child pornography on his computer. Before then and ever since, there were and have been many instances of priestly misconduct here in Canada and around the world. These scandals have not only caused anguish and huge trauma in the laity, but have also deeply wounded those good priests who are faithful to their calling to serve Christ and his people with all their hearts. They are wounded because the scandals have undermined the integrity of their calling in the public's eye. We feel betrayed but so do they. Fewer young men perceive the priesthood to be a desirable calling and the ministerial priesthood is overworked, heavily burdened and deeply discouraged. Many good priests and bishops struggle daily with depression and anxiety.

There are solutions but no quick fixes. However, we lay people *must* begin to grasp that we have been called to the priesthood of the laity and there is a huge need in the church for people to wake up to that call.

We all have images in our minds of an ideal priest and only a small part of these images are of one who faithfully administers the sacraments to the people. The rest of our images of the ideal priest are of a man who is full of mercy and compassion, one who listens, who has wisdom and balance, who doesn't isolate himself from the community, who has a sense of humor and can relate to the young, the old and everyone in between. Our "wonder priest" supports community events and the people who organize them. He really listens to people, hears their wounds, allays their fears, assures them of Christ's love and builds up confidence. He teaches with authority. He is always available. He inspires. He blesses. He is a walking sign of God's grace.

As a lay priesthood, we are not called to administer the sacraments but we *are* called to everything else in the above description of a great priest. Through baptism, we were anointed for this calling and we can no longer leave all those priestly attributes to the ministerial priests. It's not easy for people to suddenly stop thinking of themselves as sheep and begin to start thinking of themselves as shepherds with responsibilities as grave and necessary as the responsibilities of the ministerial priesthood but that's the journey we are all called to make as we grow to maturity in the Spirit.

It's a decision...and it's a conversion. It's a realization that at some point the follower of Christ must grow into being a co-shepherd with Jesus the Chief Shepherd. We must be willing to move from being blind or disabled sheep, to being people who have sight and mobility and who have received the graces and gifts necessary to be priests and shepherds to others who are just beginning the journey or who have suffered deep wounds.

We were anointed for this at baptism; we were anointed to live with great dignity and authority. Authority to do what? If you recall last week's reflection, it's certainly not the authority to have power over other people and to "lord it over them' or to seek positions of status. The authority we are called to is the authority to love like Jesus loved, listen like he listened, to touch others with the very same compassion as he did, to bless people, to offer insight and wisdom, to set the entangled free, to ease the guilt, to support others and to help carry the burdens. Do we really believe these things are part of our vocation as a royal priesthood – or are we content to leave it all to the parish priest and then complain when he doesn't meet our expectations?

This week, take the Sunday Gospel and find a few moments to sit quietly to meditate on the scene conveyed. Put yourself in Jesus' place. Visualize yourself responding with love and compassion to a blind man and then listen to the blind man speak to you about his needs. Listen to the wounds in his heart, as well, and to the lonely struggles he has endured because of his blindness. Feel your heart touched by the fact that he has called your name out loud even though he can't see you. Talk to the Father about him and *allow the Father to share with you his own deep love and compassion for the man*. Then listen for the Father to tell you what to do.

Jesus said, "I only do what I see my Father in heaven doing," and it wasn't always the same action in every situation. Jesus made no assumptions about what the Father wanted. That's why it's so important to develop the habit of listening to God the way Jesus listened. It's through knowing who you really are and listening to the Father with the heart of a shepherd that you can begin to discern the voice of God saying to you,

"The Spirit of the Lord is now upon you to bring good news to the poor, to heal the broken hearted, to set the prisoners free, to give sight to the blind and proclaim this a time of God's favor." (NRSV)

Listen. Perhaps you will be moved to say to someone, "What do you want me to do for you?"

Shema Yisrael

Mark 12: 28-34

A scribe hears a group of Sadducees disputing with Jesus and listens in. When he sees that Jesus is giving good answers to the group, he asks Jesus what the greatest commandment is. Jesus answers, "Hear, O Israel: the Lord our God, the Lord is one; you shall love the Lord your God with all your heart, and with all your soul, and with all your mind, and with all your strength." The second is like it, "You shall love your neighbor as yourself." The scribe affirms Jesus' answer and adds that the two commandments are more important than whole burnt offerings and sacrifices. Jesus tells him that he is not far from the Kingdom of God. None of the others dare to ask Jesus any more questions.

Imagine.

Let's imagine that the scribe in this week's Gospel was named Jacob:

Jacob stood quietly at the back of the group of Sadducees as he listened to the Nazarene answer the questions being shot at him. He let no one know he was there. He just wanted to listen for a while and he knew that as soon as he was noticed, all the focus would be turned on him and everyone would respectfully wait for him to ask questions and provide the correct answers. He wanted to hear what the Nazarene had to say. According to all the rumors, the man was a rebel with a questionable grasp on the law but Jacob had learned not to make judgments before he had all the facts before him. He was interested in truth, not in rumors rising out of jealousy and fear. So he just listened and the more he listened, the more he appreciated the Nazarene's keen insight and his obvious knowledge of the law.

When the Sadducees began to argue more with one another than with the man called Jesus, Jacob felt it was time to step in. He decided he would ask Jesus the first and foremost question that should precede all discussion of the law. The answer to this question was one that every good Hebrew child learned as soon as he could speak. If this man was a good Jew, he would immediately know the answer and he would know that he was required to only teach the knowledge that was given to him. These were the duties of a student of the law. All knowledge of the law should rest on the answer to this question – something the Pharisees and Sadducees seemed to often forget. The answer to this question was, indeed, the total foundation of Jacob's love for his God. He was passionate about it.

He raised his voice to carry over the voices of those who were arguing and debating.

"Jesus of Nazareth," he called. "I have a question for you."

The noise of the crowd died down for they recognized the voice of Jacob. He was a highly respected scribe in their district and he had taught many of them. If anyone could put this man Jesus in his place it would be Jacob with his keen insights and deep knowledge of the Law. They were excited to see how he would humiliate the Nazarene.

"Jesus, tell me. Which commandment is the first of all?"

A murmur of disappointment ran through the crowd. This was easy stuff! This wasn't a question that would trap Jesus; everyone knew the answer to that one, even an ignorant carpenter from Nazareth. Sure enough, Jesus answered fully and correctly. However, instead of covering his eyes with his right hand, which all Jews do when reciting the commandment to keep themselves from being distracted, he looked straight at Jacob and his eyes were warm and as bright as fire as he answered,

"The first commandment, Jacob, is, *"Hear, O Israel: the Lord our God, the Lord is one; you shall love the Lord your God with all your heart, and with all your soul, and with all your mind, and with all your strength."* The second is this, *"You shall love your neighbor as yourself."* There is no other commandment greater than these."

For the space of a second, Jacob was disturbed that Jesus had not covered his eyes and equally disturbed that Jesus knew his name. But as Jesus spoke, those eyes captivated Jacob and pulled him into a joyful circle of intimacy. He felt as though the passion he had always carried in his heart had been radiantly acknowledged and shared in a way he had never experienced with anyone before. So often, he had tried to pass on to his students the inexplicable love he had for the One God. He had tried to instill the same passion for the immensity of a God who encompassed all diversity in his oneness. Always, he lacked the words and the ability to fully express the love that drove him to serve his God. Yet in this brief space of time, this Jesus showed him that his passion was not only completely understood but also completely shared. And Jesus' eyes promised more...much more!

Jacob drew closer to Jesus and before he even thought of what he was saying, he replied, "You are right, Teacher."

The crowd gasped and then went even more silent with shock. Jacob had called the Nazarene "Teacher"! Jacob the erudite, Jacob the wise, Jacob the educator, Jacob the authority to whom all looked for answers and judgment had called this poor nomadic rebel "Teacher".

"You are absolutely right, Teacher," repeated Jacob. "You have truly said that *"he is one, and besides him there is no other"*; and *"to love him with all the heart, and with all the understanding, and with all the strength"*, and *"to love one's neighbor as oneself"*, — this is much more important than all whole burnt-offerings and sacrifices."

Still looking into Jacob's eyes, Jesus moved closer to him, put his hands on Jacob's shoulders and said, "You answer with great wisdom, brother. You are not far from the Kingdom of God."

One by one the crowd of Sadducees dispersed. They could not intrude and they dared not question. Who among them could question Jacob, the most knowledgeable of them all, the one who had brought them up in the ways of the Law and who was revered by everyone? There was nothing more they could do or say.

When everyone had left, Jacob simply stood there as he soaked in what was being lavished on him through the eyes of Jesus. Then he slowly pulled his prayer shawl over his head and lifted his hands to heaven.

"Shema Yisrael," whispered Jacob to Jesus. "Adonai Eloheinu. Hear O Israel, the Lord is one. And you are the One!"

God At The Treasury

Mark 12: 38-44

Jesus warns people to be wary of the scribes who covet honor and status and act for the sake of appearances. Then he sits opposite the treasury and watches people putting money in. Many of the rich put in large sums and then a poor widow puts in two copper coins. Jesus says that the widow has contributed more than all the rich people because they contributed out of their abundance but she gave all she had to live on.

A visiting priest, who was a former prison chaplain, described an incident he had witnessed one evening while at the prison giving a homily on love. It was a cold night and one inmate had arrived inadequately dressed in a thin shirt. He sat in his chair huddled and shivering. Another inmate had arrived wearing a jacket and he also had a blanket draped over his shoulders. While the priest was speaking, the inmate with the blanket walked over to the one that was shivering and placed the blanket around his shoulders.

It was such a simple gesture. Nothing hugely dramatic. It was about as earth shaking as a widow dropping a few pennies in a treasury box. Why, then, did we all feel deeply moved as the priest described this incident? If we had been asked, we may have said something about how beautiful it was to hear of a prisoner being so sensitive to the suffering of someone else and we would have been partially right. But pushed to elucidate further, we might have realized that it felt like we had been exposed to the presence of something holy, beautiful and powerful. Pushed a little further yet, we might have said, "I felt like I saw God."

Jesus deliberately sat down opposite the treasury and watched the people ostentatiously putting in their contributions. He just sat and watched. Was he waiting for a poor person to come and contribute just so he could give his disciples an object lesson? Or did he have an appointment? Perhaps the Father had said to him, "Be at the treasury. I will meet you there."

So, he watched and waited. He watched as people rich in gifts, skills and talents, as well as money, moved confidently up to the treasury and deposited their contributions. One could be forgiven for looking for the Father somewhere amongst these people. After all, he is God, King of the Universe, the source of all riches, power, gifts and glory. Would he not come in great dignity, in a mode that would cause people to stop, fall on their knees and gaze in wonder and awe? Would he not be robed in majesty and grace? Wouldn't he present himself as Power personified? That's what the people in the temple would have watched for if they were told that God was going to make an appearance.

Not Jesus.

I can see him sitting impassively as he watched the people dressed in fine robes parade by. These were the main supporters of the temple, the decision makers, the movers and the shakers, the fine upholders of the law. They were the leaders, the ones that were respected, depended upon, noticed and honored.

Then the shabby widow appeared. To most observers there, if they had deigned to look at her at all, she had three strikes against her. She was a woman. She was a widow. She was poor. In other words, in their eyes she was less than nothing. She had no money, no viable skills, no education and no husband to give her status and, what's more, she knew it. Yet, she gave freely to the temple in the sight of those who looked down on her. She supported a community that was unaware of her needs, judged her as a sinner, labeled her and ignored her. Nobody was waiting for her or impressed by her presence. But she came anyway. She came and gave the little she had to give.

Just as our hearts leapt within us upon hearing of the prisoner who shared his blanket, Jesus' heart leapt within him when he saw the widow and he said to himself, "There is my Father."

This Gospel passage is not just speaking about the important spiritual requirement of being generous with one's possessions. It is also presenting us with a stark image of a fundamental aspect of God. We are all aware that we have an obligation to give, but without the understanding of how small acts done with great love have the power to make God present in our world, we remain limited in our capacity to experience his presence or help others experience him. Giving in love opens up holy spaces in our lives where God can be totally present to us and to those around us.

We have a terribly difficult time shifting our minds away from the world's definition of value and effectiveness. We think in terms of important acts with tangible results. We value quantifiable outcomes that proclaim a program's or a person's effectiveness. Grand actions are fine but they are not necessarily evidence of the presence of God and they certainly are not evidence of our own intrinsic worth.

The Father's whole nature could be witnessed in the widow – and in the prison inmate. It is God's nature to come and generously give all he has to a world that does not desire him, recognize him or value him. In love he pours out more than just a portion of his abundance; he pours out everything he has and everything he is. Even Christians often don't fully realize how personal that outpouring is, because many lack a face-to-face experience with the God of generous love.

How can you experience the living presence of God? Give. Give with love and do it often. It doesn't have to be money; in fact, money is often the least personal way to give. It doesn't have to be big. Give assistance. Give a word of praise or encouragement. Give a hug. Give recognition. Give a meal. Give company. Give gratitude. Give support. Give whatever you can wherever you can – but give it with great love. Before long you will know that God is indeed with you. You will see him beaming at you in small places and you will encounter him in the people you serve.

When our son had an accident, my husband went to help him and his wife look after their four small children, two of whom were seven month old twins. My husband went with the mindful intention of lovingly serving the family in any way he could. He babysat, changed diapers, fed babies, drove kids to school, cleaned, shopped and did whatever else was needed and he did it all with conscious intentional love. Later he said that whenever he would go to get the twins out of their cribs, they would give him huge happy smiles. With tears in his eyes he said, "It was as if God was smiling at me."

Fill your life with small acts done intentionally with great love and you will see God himself smiling at you in the sacred spaces you have opened up.

It's the way he comes.

At The High End

Mark 13: 24-32

Jesus is speaking about the signs that will accompany the end times. He says that heaven and earth will pass away but his words will not pass away. He states that no one knows when these things will happen; neither he nor the angels know the time. The only one who knows is the Father.

Just in my lifetime, there have been several predictions that the end of the world was about to take place. In the book "The Late Great Planet Earth" (1970), the author, Hal Lindsey, predicted that human history would end in the 1980's. This book was even on secular best-seller lists. There have been a few instances in the past two or three decades where large groups of people have gathered at certain places in the world to watch the end of the world take place and the latest well publicized prediction of the end of the world had people selling all their worldly goods in preparation. Obviously, nothing came of these predictions.

I have my own pet theory about the end times, one that has little basis in anything, really. I just think it would be amusing if my theory were true. I think there's a good chance that even if someone gets it right and accurately predicts the date on which the world is to end, God will change the date. God said through Isaiah: *Now I am revealing new things to you, things hidden and unknown to you, created just now, this very moment, of these things you have heard nothing until now, so that you cannot say, 'Oh yes, I knew all this.'* (Isaiah 48: 6-7 NRSV)

God does not want us getting so caught up in seeking esoteric knowledge that all our attention is focused on disaster, whether it's political, social or natural events. He wants our focus and attention on hope and faith and on walking with him in the moment. Even though he calls us to be concerned for and compassionate towards the world around us, he doesn't call us to become cynical and despairing. And isn't the very act of looking at current events and predicting the end of the world an act of despair? "Things are so bad that Christ must be getting ready to come again to wipe the slate clean."

One could easily think Jesus was advising all of the disciples to pay attention to signs of the end times and to expect them soon when he said, *"...this generation will not pass away until all these things have taken place."* Some theologians feel that he was either referring to the destruction of Jerusalem in A.D. 70 or that 'this generation' refers to the spiritual generation of all Christianity. Some think that Jesus meant that once the end times begin, everything will happen very quickly – within a generation. Whatever he meant, he also said that no one, not even he, knew when these things would take place. No one, Christian or otherwise, has insider knowledge of the future and they will not be given that knowledge.

To me, the key sentence in this week's Gospel is: *"Heaven and earth will pass away, but my words will not pass away."* The words of Jesus are full of life and hope that will endure no matter what cataclysmic events are taking place either in the world or in our personal lives. While we have to deal with tragedy and endeavor to mitigate our own destructive actions or those of society in general, we are still called, above all, to focus on our hope in Christ who is The Word of Hope. We need to cling to what God says to us in Jeremiah 29: 11-14 (NLT): *"For I know the plans I have for you," says the Lord. "They are plans for good and not for disaster, to give you a future and a hope. In those days when you pray, I will listen. If you look for me wholeheartedly, you will find me. I will be found by you," says the Lord. "I will end your captivity and restore your fortunes. I will gather you out of the nations where I sent you and will bring you home again to your own land."*

It is easy and it is entirely human to focus on the negative and the destructive. This is true whether we are looking at the state of the environment or the social and political world, or whether we are focusing on our personal lives. It is easier to pinpoint all that is wrong than to have faith in the Lord of All that is Right. It is much easier to look for injury, failure, doom and destruction than it is to have faith in the One who heals, builds and creates in the midst of chaos. In the short term it often feels more emotionally satisfying to criticize the world and the people who run it or ruin it; it feels like we're more in control if we can spot everything that is wrong. I am not saying we shouldn't do all we can for the environment or work to build a just society. I am not advocating going into denial in relation to things that need to change in the world or in our own lives. All I'm saying is that as Christians, we are called to first grasp hope and faith in the God of all power before we are called to grapple with the problems of a humanity so full of weakness and need. Was there some other reason Jesus came and died on the cross? I don't think so.

In the first reading from Daniel this week, it says, *"Those who are wise shall shine like the brightness of the sky, and those who lead many to righteousness, like the stars forever and ever."* (NSRV) It is wisdom to seek to understand what God meant when he said, *"For my thoughts are not your thoughts and my ways not your ways. Yes, the heavens are as high above the earth as my ways are above your ways, my thoughts above your thoughts."* (Isaiah 55: 8, 9, NSRV) We see doom and gloom, but wisdom knows that God does not see things as we do. God's vision is not limited or short sighted like ours. When we think all is lost, wisdom says God knows what is on the verge of being found. When we think everything is going to hell in a hand basket, wisdom says that Jesus went to hell and brought it all back in a treasure chest.

Jean Allen

When we think society has lost all sense of morality and justice, wisdom says that God's Truth and Justice was nailed to a cross and won the victory for all eternity.

You've heard the old adage, "Don't believe everything you read." We need to add to that, "Don't believe everything you think."

St. Paul said: *"And I am convinced that nothing can ever separate us from God's love. Neither death nor life, neither angels nor demons neither our fears for today nor our worries about tomorrow—not even the powers of hell can separate us from God's love."* (Romans 8: 38,39 NLT)

Amen and amen.

444

No Usurping Allowed

John 18: 33-37
Pilate questions Jesus as to whether he is the King of the Jews. Jesus says that his Kingdom is not from this world. Pilate again asks if he is a king and Jesus states that he came into the world to testify to the truth and everyone who belongs to the truth listens to his voice.

Jesus: the King, the 'Ancient of Days', given glory, kingship, dominion and power over heaven and earth. Jesus: the Lord, robed in majesty. Jesus: the Ruler over all rulers, the Alpha and Omega, the one who is worthy to receive power, divinity, wisdom and strength. Jesus, whose dominion is an everlasting dominion...

Now...where's that dominion? If Jesus is a king, he's got to have a kingdom, right? Is it heaven, the place we go after we die? If we commit our lives to Christ and follow him in faith, is his Kingdom our reward for being good followers on earth?

That makes sense except for these verses from scripture and phrases from the Mass: (All Scripture: NASB)

But **seek first His kingdom** and His righteousness, and all these things will be ɩadded to you. (Matthew 6: 33)

"The time is fulfilled, and **the kingdom of God is at hand**; (Mark 1:15)

To you has been given the mystery of **the kingdom of God**; Mark 4:11)

'With what can we compare the **kingdom of God**...(scattered seed, mustard seed, yeast, something that can be seen, a lost coin, the pearl of great price etc....)?' (Gospel parables)

"Permit the children to come to me; do not hinder them; for **the kingdom of God** belongs to such as these. Truly I say to you, whoever does not receive the **kingdom of God** like a child will not enter it *at all*." (Mark 10: 14,15)

'You are not far from the **kingdom of God**.' (Mark 12:34)

'Blessed are you who are poor, for yours is the **kingdom of God**.' (Luke 6:20)

'For the **kingdom of God** is not eating and drinking but righteousness and peace and joy in the Holy Spirit.' (Romans 14:17)

'Let us pray for the coming of the **kingdom** as Jesus taught us.' (Liturgy of the Mass intro to Lord's prayer)

'Thy **kingdom** come, thy will be done on earth as it is in heaven;' (Lord's prayer)

'...and grant us the peace and unity of your **kingdom**,' (Liturgy of the Mass, prayer before sign of peace)

'For, in fact, the kingdom of God is within you.' (Luke 17:21)

In other words, the kingdom is not only something that is to come; it is now, it is real and it is something we are called to search for diligently. It is not of or from this world. It's not simply an attitude, theology or a set of beliefs. It is a Kingdom: a *realm* that is under the control of a particular person, in this case, Jesus. And even though we cannot behold this kingdom with our physical eyes, we are told to believe in it, search for it, pray for it to come every day, believe that it has been given to us and act as if we are full citizens of this realm. We are also told exactly where it is, in case we get befuddled. ***For, in fact, the kingdom of God is within you.'***

We are also given signs that we can look for so that we can know if we are indeed dwelling in the Kingdom of God. Go to scripture and look up the parables where Jesus begins with, "The Kingdom of God is like..." St. Paul says that the kingdom of God is righteousness, peace and joy in the Holy Spirit, and the Mass reminds us that the Kingdom is a kingdom of peace and unity. Right now. Not after we die. Not after the world ends. *Now.*

Scripture tells us that only those who are like children can enter the kingdom. Children in Jesus' time were completely powerless so only those who have no interest in power struggles will find it easy to enter and stay in the Kingdom – because they know there's already a King in the Kingdom. There's just one king and it isn't any of us. When we engage in unkingdom-like behavior it is much the same as playing 'King of the Castle', a game where we struggle to make ourselves higher by casting others down. We never get booted out of the Kingdom for such behavior; when we choose to play King of the Castle, we simply make a choice to leave the Kingdom.

The moment we try to be king by walking in anger or walking with the intention of setting up and defending our own territories and agendas, we have left the kingdom. There's already a king in the kingdom. He is the King of unity and peace.

The moment we try to be king by taking resentment against people and situations and criticizing and complaining, we've left the kingdom. There's already a king in the kingdom and he has mandated that we should maintain a right spirit and walk in peace and joy.

The moment we try to be king by looking for honor, respect, recognition and appreciation from others, we've left the Kingdom. There's already a King in the Kingdom and only he is the one who is worthy of all honor and glory.

So, what is our role in the Kingdom? Who are we when we're at home? The second reading this week gives us a straight answer: "To him who loves us and freed us from our sins by his blood, and **made us to be a kingdom, priests serving his God and Father**, to him be glory and dominion forever and ever. Amen." (NRSV)

We are priests in this kingdom – not kings. We serve, mentor and mediate – not rule.

This kingdom is real, not a myth from a different age. It would be more accurate to say that the material world we live in with all its misguided ways of perceiving reality and truth is the myth or at least a sad and totally inadequate reflection of reality. "We see through a glass darkly," says St. Paul. We are priests of the Kingdom and one of our priestly duties is to make the reality of the Kingdom present to a world steeped in illusory desires and needs. It is our role to reflect hope, joy and peace to a world lost in hopelessness and immersed in hopeless power struggles. But we cannot do that if we don't live in the kingdom with the King as much as possible. You can't represent what you don't know. You can't offer what you don't have.

"Seek first the Kingdom of God," says Jesus, "and you will be given everything you need." In every present moment of every day, we are called to seek the kingdom, place ourselves within in it, don the robes of righteousness and walk as priests who belong to a different world and a different order. What is that like in reality? It's just like Jesus who walked according to a different order than that of the world. Our High Priest and King is a personal mentor to each one of us. Jesus is the only king in all of history who is willing to walk intimately with each of his subjects while saying to them, "This is the way...walk in it." When we seek the peace, truth and reality of his Kingdom in every moment, we will become increasingly familiar with his voice until:

"Your eyes will see the king in his beauty and you will behold a land that stretches far away." (Isaiah 33:17 NRSV)

Kingdom after note: If you are like myself and most human beings, when you were reading the part where I was describing actions and attitudes that are not part of the Kingdom, there were people that immediately came to your mind: perhaps your spouse, a friend, a child, a Religious, someone you work with in a group in your parish or a community leader.

No, no, no! Not allowed! No doubt, there are many people you know who create wounds and chaos by behavior that doesn't reflect Kingdom values but you are called to examine your own behavior, *not* the behavior of others. In fact, as soon as you begin to identify and point your finger at others who have failed to act as true Kingdom dwellers, you are endeavoring to be a king and are moving yourself right out of the Kingdom. The Kingdom already has a King and he is the King of unconditional love and acceptance.

YEAR C

The Advent Pilgrimage – Week 1

Luke 21: 25-28, 34-36

Jesus warns people to be on guard and not to let their hearts be weighed down by the cares and dissipation of the world so that the end times do not catch them unawares. When all the signs are manifested, then they will see the Son of Man coming in a cloud with power and great glory. Then their redemption is drawing near.

Advent:
"Arrival, appearance, emergence, materialization, occurrence, dawn, birth, rise, development, approach, coming."
Advent originates from the Latin 'adventus (arrival) and 'advenire' (to come).

I especially love the words "emergence, dawn, birth and rise". They are words filled with such an immense promise of something startlingly new, something never seen before, something that will rock people off their staid and stale foundations as happened when Jesus first came to earth. They are words of high pilgrimage. They are words that have serious consequences.

It's not all that hard to use those words in the context of Jesus and his amazing birth, his incredible life, his heart wrenching death and universally explosive resurrection. But would you ever use any of those words in the context of your everyday spiritual life? Emergence? Dawn? Birth? Rising up? Advent challenges you to not only acknowledge that Jesus came for the world and will come again for the world, but also to remember he came for you, comes for you and will come again for you – and that's just in the next two minutes. Jesus never stops coming. Ever. His whole nature and his eternal desire is to come to us, but...

We stop anticipating. We get caught up in our daily struggles and forget that we're on a pilgrimage. We forget that the spiritual pilgrimage doesn't march forward in the way the natural life does; it goes deeper and higher. And we forget to expect the one who comes. We stop watching for him so we rarely encounter him face-to-face.

We stop waiting in anticipation because we feel we have been disappointed so often. We have so many preconceived ideas of what it will feel and look like when he comes that we become spiritually disheartened when our expectations and desires are not met. We pray for something and the answer doesn't seem to come. We try to place ourselves in his presence but it feels like a failed experiment. Then we start to feel guilty because we think we're not good enough or that we don't spend enough time in concentrated prayer and maybe that's why he doesn't seem to come. Days, weeks and months go by and prayer feels dry and unproductive. It's as if we're talking to ourselves. Pilgrimage is the last word we'd use to describe our spiritual life.

I'll bet every one of you could easily identify something you are waiting for. Perhaps you're waiting for healing, healing for a relationship or a loved one who's struggling. Perhaps you're desperate for a physical healing. Maybe you're waiting for change: a change in your life circumstances or a change in your ability to deal with certain people and situations. You may be waiting for a spiritual breakthrough – something that will suddenly reveal to you all you feel you've been missing in the spiritual life. You could be waiting for guidance and direction for a tough decision. We are all waiting for something and waiting is very difficult. What we don't often realize is that waiting is a vital, beautiful and deeply spiritual activity. Waiting is prayer. Waiting is pilgrimage.

The reason we don't recognize waiting as a way of going deeper in the spiritual life is because we are too influenced by the world's perception of value. There is no doubt that 'doing, accomplishing and moving forward' are essential to surviving in the world but when 'doing and accomplishing and moving forward' are applied to our spiritual life, we are apt to get the horse before the cart. It becomes very difficult for us to remember that God is in control and that God is the beginning and the end; he is the creator and we are the created. When we realize that we have no control over God or his visions for our lives, when we understand that our goodness or lack of goodness is not what motivates God to come to us and when we know that he comes simply because he loves us too much not to, all that's left to do is wait.

Waiting is pilgrimage. It means letting go and engaging fully in life without knowing what the next moment is going to hold. It means understanding that we cannot wrangle, manipulate and control things in order that something we think is good and right will happen. It means being created beings in front of the one and only Creator. It means being poor, and spiritual poverty is something that is terribly difficult to comprehend in a world that pushes us to do, accomplish, attain, possess, move forward and control. Simply waiting for the coming of the Lord is the action of one who is very poor in spirit. But... *those who trust in the Lord will find new strength. They will soar high on wings like eagles. They will run and not grow weary. They will walk and not faint.* (Isaiah 40:31 NLT)

In scripture, there are four Hebrew words that translate as "wait": qavah, yachal, damam and chakah. The translations of these words are: *to bind together (like strands of a rope), look patiently, tarry or wait, hope, expect, look eagerly, trust, wait expectantly, to be dumb, grow silent, be still, long for.*

Waiting is not just putting in time twiddling your thumbs. Waiting in the spiritual life is a critical part of prayer and growth. It is staying in the moment and completely letting go of the need to be in control. If you resist entering into the pilgrimage of waiting, you may have a slightly mistaken idea of what the spiritual life is all about. Even God – especially God – waits.

"But the Lord is waiting to be gracious to you, to rise and take pity on you, for the Lord is a just God; blessed are those who wait for him." (Isaiah 30:18)

Not only is there is a blessing on all who wait for God but he, too, is engaged in waiting – longing for us, longing to be kind to us, rising up so that he can have mercy on us. Out of his silence he emerges or rises like the dawn out of darkness – for us. Always for us.

There is mystery and freedom in waiting, in being entwined with the Lord in longing, hope and trust, and expecting him in eager stillness or still eagerness. We are encouraged so many times in scripture to wait - there must be something extremely powerful in this holy activity. *"Wait for the Lord; be strong, and let your heart take courage; Yes, wait for the Lord."* (Psalm 27:14) Wait for him to come. Watch for him. To do otherwise is utter futility.

Be still. Advent is the pilgrimage of waiting. Make quiet your anxious heart. Breathe softly.

Do you hear it? Someone is coming...

The Advent Pilgrimage – Week 2

Luke 3: 1-6

The word of God comes to John in the wilderness. He begins his ministry of repentance and baptism fulfilling Isaiah's prophecy of a voice crying out in the wilderness, "Prepare the way of the Lord…"

Ever wonder how long John was in the desert? A few months? A year or two? For a long time I never even thought about this. Every year during Advent, the wild, passionate and totally committed John would suddenly arrive on the scene, a voice crying out in the wilderness, "Prepare the way of the Lord!" It wasn't until I began to utterly appreciate the astounding beauty of the spiritual desert that I began to contemplate what John may have gone through in the desert before he heard the voice of God speak to him.

Scripture doesn't really say how long he was in the desert but Luke 1:80 says this:
"And the child kept growing and becoming strong in spirit, and he was in the wilderness until the day he was revealed to Israel."
Some authorities believe that John went out into the wilderness as a boy. So, what was he doing all that time besides hunting locusts, sewing together animal skins and discovering the best places to find wild honey?

Probably waiting.

In the last reflection I spoke about how waiting is a holy and beautiful prayer but I was aware that what I said wasn't enough. It's a good thing there are four Sundays in Advent because waiting is a big topic and simply recognizing the spiritual value and validity of waiting won't get us through some of those long

457

periods of waiting in our lives. Waiting can be grindingly boring or it can be full of aching grief. At times it can be filled day after day with frustration, anxiety, stress or a sense that if you have to endure something for another moment you will scream. At other times, life just takes over and we get busy with all the things we are normally busy with until we suddenly realize it has been a very long time since we thought much about the Lord or about our spiritual health and we become conscious of the fact that we have lost touch with who we are and who he is. Then we begin to wait ourselves back to him. Waiting has as many tones, shapes and nuances as there are people who are in waiting. But what happens during waiting? What happens to us?

Anne (not her real name) had become pregnant, which was a longstanding desire of hers, and then she suffered an early miscarriage. This was heartbreaking for her but was also a time of great grace. Some time after that miscarriage, Anne wrote to me:

"Recently I had a feeling that I was pregnant again. This was not planned but what I felt about the possibility was: peace. If I wasn't pregnant, I felt peace about that too. I was surprised in some ways to feel this way. Most women who have miscarried find they cannot escape the heavy fear of miscarriage in subsequent pregnancies. But I felt like I had so much trust, because I knew that Christ would come to me no matter what. Through the spiritual experience of my last pregnancy and miscarriage, I was led to patience. I didn't feel this urgent need to know if I was pregnant again and I didn't feel this urgent need to make it through the first trimester if I was."

Anne was given a gift, one that all of us can receive little by little through our times of waiting on the Lord. She called it patience and patience is definitely part of it. I call it detachment.

Before I go further I need to make something particularly clear. Anne received a gift from God. She received grace and this gift was not dependent on her goodness or on her spiritual acuity. She definitely is a spiritually committed and aware woman and this gave her the ability to recognize the gift and to recognize the pilgrimage opened to her. However, she was not given a 'magic key' that would automatically make all her future times of waiting, whether for a child or anything else, easy and peaceful. What she did receive was a glimpse of what God was shaping within her and had in store for her if she continued to pay attention to her spiritual prayer of waiting.

The word 'detachment' can sound cold and distant, as if you don't care and emotions can't touch you. This is not what God's gift of detachment gives us. Anne certainly did care about whether there was a baby forming in her womb and experienced joy over the prospect. She was not given the grace to be "I don't care" detached; she was given the grace to be "My God does everything perfectly and carries me and all I hold dear in the palm of his hand" detached. We all long to have this kind of detachment: a deep and unmovable trust that whatever happens, the Lord is Good, Good, Good. It is an unshifting knowledge that no matter what our outer desires are, the only thing we really want is for him to be the creator and lover of our lives.

Our heads know we should be that trusting but we are human and trust does not come without effort. When the world and the people around us are capable of letting us down so easily, frequently and painfully, it's no wonder we struggle to find the ability to trust the Lord. He doesn't chastise us for our lack of trust; he simply sets about the task of forming trust within us and that formation is the pilgrimage called 'waiting'.

Waiting eventually strips us. It strips us of all the devices we use to try to make things happen. Waiting is the only thing that will utterly convince us of our own poverty because once God holds something back there is nothing on earth or in the universe that can release it. Nothing can happen, nothing can become alive, nothing can grow, nothing can come to a realization, nothing can be made whole and nothing can become pliable, open and willing until God says, "Now." Through waiting, we come to realize how small we are – and conversely, how great he is. And don't try the old trick of saying to God, "O.K. I'm small and you're great. Now please give me what I desire." He is the potter and you are the clay, and he knows exactly where you are in the process of formation. He reads your heart, not your lips.

Let's get back to John. Before he came to know his Name - "A Voice Crying Out In The Wilderness" - and before he could move out of the desert in certainty and power, he waited – for years. He waited, listened and waited some more. He learned the depth of power of the God who could move the wind and shift the sand. He listened to a Voice that sounded like locusts and discovered less and less need to feed on his own inner voices and his own words. He drank of the Spirit who was like honey to his parched soul and knew that movement and direction was no longer his to decide. He waited and watched a seemingly unchanging and empty horizon until he lost his own desires and became filled with God's desires. He pondered twisted roots and the miracle of a blade of grass in a waterless land and grew into the knowledge that the Messiah had come. John learned to wait. He learned to listen. He learned to see. He learned in ways he never could have learned on his own. And then, through the distant and lonely cries of a wild animal in the night, God whispered to his soul, "It is time. Go." Then John rose up with fire in his soul and before he even came to God's people, he was compelled to cry out to the desert, to the locusts and wild animals, to the howling wind and the night stars, "Prepare the Way for the Lord! Make his path straight. Build a highway for our God!" He could not contain the fullness of all that he had been waiting for. He had to shout it out even when there was no human to hear.

Whatever God has in store for you, whether it's filling your valleys, straightening your paths or smoothing the roughness, the Pilgrimage of Waiting is breathtaking. God will take your breath away – and then fill you with his own.

Worth its wait in gold.

3rd Sunday in Advent C

The Advent Pilgrimage – Week 3

Luke 3: 10-18
John explains to the people what they must do to repent. They all wonder if he is the Messiah but he tells them that there is someone coming after him who is more powerful than he, one who will baptize them in the Holy Spirit and in fire.

So, you're in the desert waiting. You know that waiting is prayer. You know that waiting simplifies and shapes you, that the Lord is the creator of all the inner transformations you are going through and that he is bringing you to a place of simply wanting his will to be yours. But, somehow, it feels like there's more. There's something within each one of us that urges us to respond to the good news that the Messiah is here. We come to the river; our hearts are filled with expectation and our spirits yearn for our Messiah. How can we find him?

Give thanks. Rejoice.

The third Sunday of Advent is Gaudete Sunday, (gaudete: rejoice), which is such a fitting theme for those who are on the Pilgrimage of Waiting because rejoicing in and giving thanks to God is a critical part of the desert journey. When we make praise and thanksgiving an integral part of our communication with God, we are not only giving him what is rightly his, but we are also continually reminding our hearts, minds and spirits that he is God, the one who does all things well, the one who creates and renews, the one who gathers, blesses, protects, redeems, lifts up, fills up, forms and directs. Scripture is filled with exhortation to give praise to God and it's not only because God is good; it's also because the actions of praise and gratitude create change within us. They redirect our focus away from the self with all its negativity and make us focus on Goodness himself.

It isn't always easy to give thanks. There are many times in our lives where we're struggling with wounds and hard situations and giving praise to God seems extremely difficult to us. And we're right. It is very difficult, more difficult, say, than giving up coffee or chocolate for Lent. It can be far more difficult than sharing our extra coat, providing food to someone, acting with justice or being satisfied with what we have. All these things can be real challenges but giving thanks in the middle of being swamped with resentment or when we're feeling overwhelmed by life's demands or when we've lost someone or something and we are filled with tearing grief, is almost like giving up a part of ourselves that is too hard to let go of. Praising when everything is going well is easy. Giving thanks when it feels like there is absolutely nothing to be thankful for is...sacrifice.

St. Paul says it in Hebrews 13:15 (ESV): *Through him, then, let us continually offer a sacrifice of praise to God, that is, the fruit of lips that acknowledge his name.*

He also says in 1 Thessalonians 5: 16-18 (ESV): *Rejoice always, pray without ceasing, give thanks in all circumstances; for this is the will of God in Christ Jesus for you.*

I'm certain that you have often said to yourself and to others, "I just want to know God's will for me." In spite of all the uncertainties that surround you, you can rest assured that no matter what is happening you can always know his immediate will for you is that you stay in the moment and offer a sacrifice of thanksgiving and that you do so continually. Why would he want that? Because he is egotistical and just wants to hear you sing his praises even though you're going through such a rough time? No. The reason is because God dwells within the praises of his people and he dwells in the present moment. He wants you to become more and more aware of his indwelling. When you give thanks you are turning to him and to everything he is.

Through the repetition of gratitude you slowly open yourself to the awareness of his presence. When you give thanks, you actively place yourself in his presence and you consciously turn away from things like fear, resentment, cynicism, complaining and living in the future or the past. You are repenting, which means turning away. The negative thoughts and emotions we have are like tempting pits and potholes in our desert highways, holes that we dig, jump into and then can't get out of. When we're in one of these pits, it's almost impossible to see good news of Jesus or to believe that he is the author and finisher of our faith (Hebrews 12:2). Did you get that? Jesus is the *author* of our Faith – and the *finisher* of it. But if we want to open ourselves to having him create and form our faith, we need to look at him in the present moment and profess his goodness in our lives. We need to be in praise mode.

Psalm 68:4 (ESV) says, *"Sing to God, sing praises to his name; lift up a song to him who rides through the deserts."*
When we give thanks, we are opening a highway between our hearts and God's heart, smoothing the rough parts, leveling the mountains, filling the valleys and straightening out the crooked. *"A highway shall be there and it shall be called a Way of Holiness."* (Isaiah 35:8 ESV)

We are not talking 'magic key' here. Praise is not an action that forces God to do what we want him to do; it is an action opens our inner eyes to God acting in our lives – something we often miss because of our set expectations. A friend of mine, who is a woman of thanksgiving and gratitude, traveled to Switzerland and when it was time for her to return, she discovered she had lost her passport. The next several days were very frightening for her as she went through the convoluted process of trying to get home, dealing with officials who often didn't speak English and doing everything in a strange city with no one to guide her. Her praising spirit didn't make it all easy – she still had to do what she had to do and struggle with confusion, fear, uncertainty and setbacks etc. But she kept recognizing the hand of God subtly helping her on her way. She recognized angels who helped her and minor miracles that graced her on her way. Long after she arrived home, she was still awed by the presence of God on that journey. What she saw as miracles and angels, other people might have judged as random coincidences. Through her spirit of thanksgiving, she was able to keep connected to the Lord and recognize that he was caring for her, and her faith was fed and shaped.

There is a Latin tag that says: Gratitudo est lingua angelorum. Gratitude is the language of angels. When we practice gratitude, praise and thanksgiving we are in great company. The angels themselves join us in great delight.

For your prayer and contemplation time, I gathered a few passages of scripture that speak of praise – a very few, as there are over four hundred. For this meditation, I have not included the scripture references, which would break the flow. Read through slowly and meditatively and allow God's word to penetrate your heart about the importance of praise and thanksgiving: (all quotes from ESV)

Offer to God a sacrifice of thanksgiving, and pay your vows to the Most High...Those who bring thanksgiving as their sacrifice honor me...Let us come into his presence with thanksgiving...For this I will extol you, O Lord, among the nations, and sing praises to your name...Sing to him, sing praises to him...tell of all his wonderful works...I will be glad and exult in you; I will sing praise to your name, O Most

High...Be exalted, O Lord, in your strength! ...We will sing and praise your power...Yet you are holy, enthroned on the praises of Israel...I will tell of your name to my brothers and sisters; in the midst of the congregation I will praise you...Rejoice in the Lord, O you righteous. Praise befits the upright...I will bless the Lord at all times; his praise shall continually be in my mouth...He put a new song in my mouth, a song of praise to our God...Lord, open my lips, and my mouth will declare your praise...Because your steadfast love is better than life, my lips will praise you...My soul is satisfied as with a rich feast, and my mouth praises you with joyful lips...rooted and built up in him and established in the faith, just as you were taught, abounding in thanksgiving...Devote yourselves to prayer, keeping alert in it with thanksgiving...Amen! Blessing and glory and wisdom and thanksgiving and honor and power and might be to our God forever and ever! Amen...

And, of course...

**From the rising of the sun to its setting,
the name of the Lord is to be praised!**

Rejoice. The one who is more powerful than you is here.

The Advent Pilgrimage – Week 4

Luke 1: 39-45

Mary goes to visit Elizabeth and when Elizabeth hears Mary's greeting, she is filled with the Spirit and exclaims, "Blessed are you among women and blessed is the fruit of your womb." She says that when she heard Mary's greeting, her child leapt in her womb and she proclaims that the one who believed that there would be a fulfillment of what was spoken to her by the Lord, is blessed.

Mary...Our Lady in Waiting.

In this week's gospel, we get the understanding that the pilgrimage of waiting is not necessarily a time of doing nothing. It is often a time of being sent and of offering ourselves for the blessing of others. We see what a generous heart Mary had as we read about her traveling to be with Elizabeth for the last three months of Elizabeth's pregnancy. Elizabeth was not a young woman anymore and having Mary there to help her was truly a blessing. It was a very loving act on Mary's part.

But there were a couple of other reasons for Mary to visit Elizabeth at that time. The first pertains to what the angel spoke to Zechariah about John. Among other things, the angel said, *"...even before his birth he will be filled with the Holy Spirit."* Now, look at what it says in this week's gospel: *"Elizabeth was filled with the Holy Spirit..."* and *"...as soon as I heard the sound of your greeting, the child in my womb leapt for joy."* During her waiting, God used Mary to bring Christ to John and Elizabeth for their blessing and infilling.

 The other very important reason for the visit was so that Mary, too, could receive a gracious and badly needed blessing from

God.

We all know this was not an easy time for Mary. She was waiting, but not just for the birth of a son. She was waiting for God to work everything out even though he had put her in a position of shame, a position where her sanity and morality were in question and a position that could have held dire consequences for her. Her waiting called her to engage in huge trust. From our perspective, having heard the story so often, it's difficult for us to imagine the kind of trust she had to have to believe God would indeed work it all out according to his purposes. She had to place herself completely in God's hands every moment of the day because there was nothing she could do to justify herself or to prove to others that she was not "shoddy goods". Mary's whole identity, inner worth and validity were completely dependent on God's love and approval. She could no longer depend on anyone or anything else to indicate that she was a good and trustworthy woman. The law condemned her and the man she was betrothed to pitied her but was not convinced of her innocence. In a time when women were in no way valued by society, entrusting one's total worth to God was a risky business. The loneliness of her heart must have been intense. Have you ever cried out to the Lord to send you someone who would understand who you are and who would affirm your inner dignity and value? Have you ever faced a situation where others are questioning your integrity and worth? Have you ever been terribly lonely even though you're in a relationship or part of a community? Have you ever felt that you have been denied normal dreams and expectations that others have been allowed to realize?

Mary's visit to Elizabeth was a gift from God to Mary as well as to Elizabeth and John. Through her obedience in going to Elizabeth, she was given unexpected outside confirmation that all the angel had said to her was true. Elizabeth greeted her with, *"Blessed are you among women, and blessed is the fruit of your womb. And why has this happened to me, that the mother of my Lord comes to me? For as soon as I heard the sound of your greeting, the child in my womb leapt for joy. Blessed is she who believed that there would be a fulfillment of what was spoken to her by the Lord."*

That greeting was a blessing that Mary desperately needed to hear. It was such a balm to Mary's spirit and such a confirmation of all she had been struggling to hold on to that her heart was immediately filled with high praise, praise we now call the Magnificat. We don't often stop to think about what that praise might have been expressing for Mary. As well as being an expression of the greatness of God, it was a prayer of deep relief and a prayer of exultant gratitude that God would know how much she needed this confirmation and affirmation. Through Elizabeth's prophetic greeting, God said to Mary, "You are blessed because you have continued to believe even though belief has been hard, rocky and lonely and you have had to struggle to hold onto your one and only true foundation. I am the one who fills you and validates you. I am your vindication and your justification. I am your Beloved and you are mine. I am your past, your present and your future. I am your all in all. I AM."

Waiting can be painful. When we are waiting, it is easy to lose sight of what it is we are actually waiting for and even easier to begin to seek people, things and activities we think will fill up the empty aching places in our hearts. Like Mary, we are waiting for Jesus to come. And like Mary, we need to open our hearts to hear God's Word telling us that he delights in our belief, especially when belief is hard. We need to be open to hearing him say, "Thank you for bearing my son within you even though others sometimes condemn you for it. Thank you for holding my son close to your heart even when it's lonely and frightening. Thank you for believing in me even when others don't believe in you."

Like Mary, your moment of encouragement from the Lord may

come when you bring Christ to someone else. You might be sent to someone in your family who also is in need of encouragement or needs the balm of love and forgiveness. You could be sent to someone outside of your family who is lonely or someone who is struggling with grief and discouragement.

Wait...but be ready to be sent. Just like Mary...

...Our Lady in Waiting.

Old Dispensations

Matthew 2: 1-12
The magi follow the star to find Jesus.

Epiphany can be beautiful but in the end it must be disturbing. If our pilgrimage towards the manifestation of the Light For All People raises no blisters or perturbing questions and doesn't fill us with an awareness of our own distorted shadows, we may not have been moving toward the light at all – or moving period.

There is a well known poem by T.S. Eliot titled, "The Journey Of The Magi", which I cannot include here because of copyright law but is readily available on the Internet if you wish to read it. Eliot, through the voice of one of the magi, describes the loneliness and hardships of the journey as their entourage followed the star. The account is filled with jarring images that foreshadow the life and especially the death of Christ. Eliot's magus suggests that this particular birth contained all the elements of a harsh death, and that he did not leave the scene of the nativity full of peace and joy but went back to his own country no longer at ease with what he calls 'the old dispensation'.

We all have old dispensations, which in this context means orders or systems. We all have ways of doing things and of perceiving how our lives must progress, and one of the things God will consistently do is disturb our old dispensations, if we allow him. If we believe in scripture, we have to believe in this disturbance. Throughout the whole bible, in the Old and the New Testament, people were forever being moved out of old ways and being challenged to change and move on. From Noah, Abraham, Jacob and Moses, through King David and the prophets, and right on through to Mary and Joseph, Christ, the disciples and the newborn community we read about in Acts, God's people were continually being moved past the old orders and dispensations. There is nothing in scripture to suggest that once the Apostles instituted the new Church, God would sit back and say, "O.K. That's it. No more. Done."

A New Covenant does not mean the destination was reached; it just means the journey was given new hope, new life, a new understanding of the nature of God and a new awareness of the Spirit, who is our mentor and guide. Two thousand years after Christ's death, we are still moving and changing, as a church and as individuals. It's often deeply disturbing. No one is exempt but anyone is free to opt out.

The beauty of Epiphany comes when we finally grasp that the Light that shines for the whole world will always draw us further in and will never ever stop challenging us. That means that one should never feel anxious about not having 'arrived'. There is no final arrival until physical death comes and we are absorbed into the full Kingdom of Christ. There is no point where all the lessons have been learned, all the laws have been conquered and all that's required is to coast into the harbor. This is not about lessons or about rules or destinations; this is about allowing the Light to keep leading us onward in ways we can't always conceive of. When we achieve one destination, what we usually find is a conundrum, a crossroad and a push to keep on going on a completely different route.

Yes, the Light leads us to personal new births but it also leads us to personal deaths. Then it leads us to personal resurrections and even then we must keep picking up the staff again and move on. The spiritual life is a pilgrimage and we will carry on making this pilgrimage together, encouraging one another through the sharp winds of cold reality.

We are all Magi on a disturbing journey.

Authentic Identification

Luke 3: 21-22
John baptizes Jesus. After his baptism while Jesus is praying, the heavens open, a dove descends and a voice says, "You are my Beloved Son and with you I am well pleased."

Excerpt from the second reading, Titus 3: 4-7 (ESV)
But when the goodness and loving kindness of God our Savior appeared, he saved us, not because of works done by us in righteousness, but according to his own mercy, by the washing of regeneration and renewal of the Holy Spirit, whom he poured out on us richly through Jesus Christ our Savior, so that being justified by his grace we might become heirs according to the hope of eternal life.

Here's a good question for the beginning of the New Year:

Who are you?

Can you answer this question without referring to any other person in your life or to any of your life circumstances or past experiences? Can you say who you are without alluding to your spouse, your children, your job, your vocation, your role(s) in the church or community or any of your gifts, skills or past achievements and failures? Can you find the answer with no absolutely no reference to present circumstances or future possibilities, good or bad?

Tough question, huh? Yet, it is the single most important question in the spiritual life and the one question most people have huge difficulty answering. We learn to measure and identify ourselves according to the expectations of the world, our families, the church community, our employers and our peers. We learn to judge ourselves according to how well we live up to or fail to live up to all these subtle but strong assumptions, and most people spend their lives grappling constantly with the expectations of others, resenting them, fearing them and feeling trapped or condemned by them. Everyone I speak to is struggling with who they really are, whether they know that's the essential question or not. Everyone yearns for the answer.

The readings for this Sunday have to do with baptism – Jesus' and ours. In order to begin to grasp the answer to the question of who you really are, it is important to understand that your baptism and Jesus' baptism are deeply connected. No ... 'connected' is the wrong word. It's more like your baptism is completely enfolded in Christ's baptism the way a baby is enfolded in the womb of the mother. All the power inherent in your baptism is drawn from the heaven and earth-shaking instant when Jesus went down into the waters and then burst forth out of them, anointed to begin the working out of all he was called to. In this moment, he heard something the rest of us long and ache to hear. He heard the Father speak his Name: "You are 'My Son, the Beloved'." And before he even began his ministry, he heard the words we all subconsciously yearn to hear: "With you I am well pleased."

The Father wasn't just saying something nice and caring to Jesus nor was he particularly concerned that others hear the Naming and understand it. This was something crucially intimate between Jesus and his Father; it was the foundational basis of EVERYTHING Jesus said and did from that moment on. After his baptism, Jesus went into the desert where there were no people, no family, no jobs, no past experiences, no vocations and no roles to play – in other words, none of the things we all normally depend on to define us – and when Satan turned up to tempt Jesus, Satan got nowhere because Jesus *knew who he was.*

It is significant that in the two places in scripture where we are privy to hearing the Father speak to Jesus, he didn't say, "You are the Christ. You are the Savior," or "This is your Messiah. Hear him." He simply spoke of Jesus' relationship to him. "You are my Beloved son," and "This is my Son, the Beloved. Hear him." The knowledge that he was God's Beloved permeated Jesus' whole being. He didn't need anything else to build up an inner sense of himself or his identity; he didn't need the approval, acceptance or admiration of other people and he especially did not need Satan's offerings of experience, power and status. In knowing he was the Father's Beloved, he had everything he needed in order to be and do everything he was called to be and do. He lacked nothing and he knew it.

So, what does all this have to do with our own baptisms and us? You might say, "Of course the Father called Jesus his Beloved Son but how does that define me? How does that tell me who I really am?"

Does the following sound familiar?

Father, God of mercy, through these waters of baptism you have filled us with new life as your very own children.

(Name), you have become a new creation, and have clothed yourself in Christ. See in this white garment the outward sign of your Christian dignity.

Dearly beloved, this child has been reborn in baptism. He (she) is now called the child of God, for so indeed he (she) is.

That's from the Catholic Rite of Baptism. From the waters of baptism, you rose up in Christ, clothed in him – completely enfolded in him. When you were baptized, you rose up dignified, beautiful and loved. When you were baptized, the Father looked on you and beheld his firstborn son, Jesus. When you were baptized, God the Father looked at you and said, "You are my Daughter/Son, my Beloved. With you I am well pleased."

Yeah...but that was then. What about now? You're not an innocent little baby anymore (if you were the recipient of infant baptism). You've muddied your boots quite a bit since you were baptized, right? That brand new creation, all washed and lovely, has become a bit moth eaten around the edges with lots of big and little pockmarks of sin and failure and inadequacy. Right?

No doubt you've made mistakes and taken wrong paths. Your ego and its neediness have most likely dictated your actions and reactions far more often than you'd like. But the Father sees beyond and through the muck. He sees his Son and he sees the ultimate beauty of who he called you to be and who you were created to be from the beginning. Your greatest sin may be that you don't believe in and accept his approval and that you are more likely to turn away from his love and his pleasure, thinking that it will please him if you just focus on your natural unworthiness. By doing that you keep yourself from moving into the joy and freedom of being a son or daughter of the living God.

Do you want to know the 'secret' to living a full spiritual life? It is understanding that being an expert at sin identification is not what heals you. Beholding who you are really called to be and walking in the beauty and promise of your Name is what will heal you. But you can't behold who you are if you won't believe you are so much more than all your petty reactions, selfish desires and desperate need for control.

Your baptism was and is an immense gift. It was the gift of new life. Do you have any idea what 'new life' means? Is it just a trite phrase you've heard way too often? New life is new life. It's life that's radically different from the old battered kind of life the world offers you – the life that caught you early and still holds you in its painful grip. The old life of the world offers unfulfilled desires, illusory promises, painful disappointments, random but heavy expectations and the suffering of a chronically ill ego, but you, Beloved, have been called to a *new* life and a new Name. Once you even glimpse who you really are, the healing will begin.

All good parents have the desire to instill in their children a deep and healthy sense of self worth. I have never met any parent who desires that their child will become someone who can't leave mistakes behind, who berates himself all the time for not being the perfect child or who is miserable in her own lack of capacity yet has no ability to move beyond those limitations. Every balanced parent wants his or her own child to be healthy, strong, confident, effective and full of the joy of living.

Why would God be any different? *"If you then, imperfect as you are, know how to give good gifts to your children, how much more will your Father in Heaven give good things to those who ask Him!"* (Matthew 7:11 ESV) The Father is waiting for you to receive new life. He is waiting every moment of the day to have you turn to him, to see his love and delight, and to hear him say, "My Beloved!"

Once you hear that and once you finally believe it so that you laugh with joy because of it, you will begin to know that God is your whole definition and everything you believed about yourself up to that point was a false definition with no basis in the reality of your baptism. When you see the delight and love in God's eyes, it will be the only definition you will ever need or want. He is where you will find all your value, worth and identity. He is where your new life begins.

The reason you will never find your identity in relationships, things, roles, vocations or even dogmas in this world is because nothing in this world can ever perfectly fit the real you, the you whom God created you to be. Everything you normally seek to find your identity in is just a poor shadow of the real thing. Through baptism, you were given the only garment that will ever fit you perfectly; you were clothed in Christ and made *identical* to Jesus. He is your identity and your Name. He is the reason the Father beholds you and says, "You are my Beloved. With you I am well   pleased!"

Jesus knew who he was. His inner life and power did not come from being Messiah, Healer, Sacrificial Lamb or Savior. It came from being Absolutely Beloved.

It's good year to find out who you are.

2nd Sunday Ordinary C

The Plan

John 2: 1-12
The wedding at Cana.

For many years this gospel story was a bit jarring to me. I found it hard to reconcile what I had been taught about Jesus' role as the Son of God, walking tightly with God's plan of salvation, with how he is portrayed in this story. He indicates that his hour has not yet come to reveal himself but when his mother ignores his protest, expects him to act and doesn't even discuss the issue with him, he disregards his stated time line and performs a beautifully loving miracle. The whole story, in my mind, just didn't fit with the idea that God has an agenda with every second planned and orchestrated from A to Z. Jesus, of all people, should have been much more aware of the importance of staying with the program.

When I was younger, there were so many times when I was in a situation where I was trying to discern God's plan for my life, intensely frustrated because if I knew what his will was, I would absolutely do it – but God wasn't giving me any clues at all. It felt like I was out there hanging in the wind and sometimes I felt that I must be spiritually dense; otherwise I would have known exactly what he wanted me to do.

We do feel a kind of security in believing that God has a detailed moment by moment plan for our lives but then we wonder about and agonize over how much power we have to derail his plans by making a wrong choice. When Jesus said, "Oh, what the heck. I might as well change their water into wine and make my mother happy," did he knock God's plan and timeline completely out of whack? When we are faced with a few different options for our

480

lives and we try to make sure each option is moral, just and true to our faith but we're not getting any leads as to which path we should choose, can we really make a choice that totally screws up 'The Plan'? This is a key question that everyone struggles with. We honestly don't want to make a wrong decision and the full intention is to do God's will. Everybody probably has this mental image of God sitting in heaven, slapping his forehead and groaning, "Oh shoot! Wrong guess. BZZZZZZ! Game over!"

Perhaps God doesn't have an A to Z plan. Maybe he just has destination points and there are many ways we can arrive at those destinations without in any way upsetting 'The Plan'. We need to stop and ask ourselves what God wants for each of us. He wants us to experience forgiveness and give it and he wants us to have life and have it abundantly. He wants us to love him, be loved by him and to share that love with everyone we encounter. He wants us to act with justice and mercy. He wants us to be willing to change, grow, take risks and learn who we really are. I think the reason he doesn't immediately show us 'The Plan' every time we try to discern a direction is because we humans are too prone to rigidity. We can get so carried away with plans and directions that we forget about living in the moment and responding to him in the fullness of each moment, which is where he lives, acts and has his being. When we become rigid, we fear the future and we become scared of taking risks. And when we really think about it, walking with the Lord of the Universe is a huge risk. We might find ourselves on an unfamiliar and perhaps uncharted course. We might be challenged to let go and grow. We might have to (shudder) change our minds. We might be faced with things we'd rather not face. We might feel lost.

Most people have a GPS (Global Positioning System). What an awesome tool it is. You just enter in an address and a voice tells you exactly what direction to head, which roads to take, what turns are coming up and then, when it's time to turn, it lets you know. Usually I have no problem following the GPS's verbal directions but occasionally I get confused, such as when there is more than one exit or there's a lot of traffic or I am mentally drifting, and the turn comes before I expect it so I make a completely wrong turn. Before I had GPS this would have been a tense situation because I would be on a wrong road heading in the wrong direction with no idea how to get back to where I should be on the journey. But now the GPS just says, "Recalculating," and then it immediately guides me along a route that gets me back to where I should be.

GPS makes the journey more enjoyable. I'm not afraid of making mistakes and losing my way. I am no longer afraid of those wrong turns and missed exits. I relax. I see more. I can also make a spontaneous decision to take an interesting road because I know the GPS will always get me back on track.

In the spiritual life, we also have GPS. God's Positioning System. If you make an unexpected turn, like Jesus did when he changed water into wine, God says, "Recalculating. Enjoy the detour. Learn something. There's some good stuff on this road too. Here's what we'll do; we'll change those jars of water into wine. It's a merciful and loving thing to do and you'll learn more about your gifts and the powers I have anointed you with. Good call. I love you!" The appropriate response to our Spiritual GPS is to trust that God actually has the power to get us to where we need to go and that he will do it in his own good time. Knowing we have a Spiritual GPS allows us the freedom to focus on what the Lord is *really* asking of us. Micah 6:8 put it very well:

He has told you, O people, what is good. And what does the Lord require of you? To act justly and to love kindness and to walk humbly with your God. (NRSV)

Jesus had a destination. The cross. But everyday Jesus had to make choices as to what road he would walk down, what group he would teach, what wedding he would attend, what town he would stay in for a few days and with whom. Those details weren't the critical parts of Jesus ministry. The important and life changing parts were how he acted with justice with each person he met, how deeply he loved mercy and how he poured it out on all the people he encountered. He was so humble that he walked *moment by moment* with his Father, not demanding a preview of a whole detailed plan but watching and listening each moment to what his Father was asking of him, fully trusting that the Father would lead him to where he needed to be, when he needed to be there, and would provide the power and grace necessary for each moment on the way.

"I tell you the truth, the Son can do nothing by himself; he can do only what he sees his Father doing, because whatever the Father does the Son also does." (John 5:19 NIV)

It would seem that after he spoke to his mother at the wedding in Cana, Jesus turned to his Father and saw water being turned into wedding wine. Perhaps he also saw a body on a cross, pouring out the wine of life. Then, maybe he felt the explosive joy of the heavenly Bridegroom at a wedding feast to end all wedding feasts.

He started to say no. He started to say it wasn't in 'The Plan'. He could have kept rigidly to the schedule, as he understood it.

But, apparently, in the Father's eyes, Love trumps Plan.

The Real Truth About You

Luke 4: 14-21

Jesus stands up in the synagogue to read the scroll of the prophet Isaiah. He reads the place where it is written, "The Spirit of the Lord is upon me to bring good news to the poor, to proclaim release to the captives, to give sight to the blind, to set prisoners free and proclaim the year of God's favor". Then he says to the people, "Today this scripture has been fulfilled in your hearing."

It's sometimes easy to just skim over the Gospel readings simply because they are so familiar. Take this week's passage, for example. You might have read it and perhaps had a few fleeting thoughts about how much courage it took for Jesus to announce to those listening that he was the one who was the fulfillment of that scripture reading. Perhaps you briefly pondered on how dangerous it was for him to make such a statement because he was openly inviting judgment. It may have struck you that he was making himself totally vulnerable to people who had known him all his life and he was giving them the opportunity to either condemn him for being incredibly arrogant or accept him completely as one who was telling the truth.

I don't know if you realize it or not, but each time you read this scripture you, too, are called to make a judgment as to whether Jesus was arrogantly deluded or if he was revealing the truth. You can either reject what he said or you can accept it. Most likely, right now you are saying, "Of course I accept it." Good. Now, I want you to go back to the above scripture and read it again, only this time I want you to imagine that instead of Jesus reading the scroll, you are. Every time the word "me" occurs, it means you personally.

Do you accept that or do you reject it? If you imagine yourself in that scene and you are the one claiming an anointing, would you feel you are being arrogant and delusional – or would you be stating the truth? How comfortable would you be about stating that truth in public? The truth was that Jesus definitely had been anointed by God to bring good news to the poor and to proclaim release to the captives etc. If, for the sake of being humble, he had proclaimed anything less than what he did or if he had said anything that would indicate that he didn't feel he should assume that this was a role meant for him, he would have been practicing false humility. Christ's claim to be the fulfillment of Isaiah's scripture passage was true humility; it was full acceptance of who he really was and full acceptance of what he had been anointed to do. No more, no less.

Up to the beginning of his ministry, Jesus had spent his life listening to the Father speak his name and he had to come to terms with his true identity. To us, the name 'Jesus' is synonymous with his Messiah identity but in actual fact, the name 'Jesus' was an extremely common name in those days. Jesus heard far more than just his given name being spoken by the Father. He heard Names that spoke of who he was created to be and he had to accept these names. This acceptance was not based in arrogance but in humility. In fully accepting all he was called to be, he was doing what his Father required of him: walking humbly with his God. (Micah 6:8)

There is an inclination in all of us to allow ourselves to be less than who we really are. We think that everything Jesus did and said was more possible for him than it is for us because he was God incarnate. We feel he was filled with all these graces and blessings that we don't have access to, so we can't hope to be completely one with his identity, his mission and his ministry.

Scripture says differently. In Philippians 2:5 (NRSV), Paul said,

"Let the same mind be in you that was in Christ Jesus." In John 14:12 (Jerusalem), Jesus said, *"I tell you most solemnly, whoever believes in me will perform the same works as I do myself; he will perform even greater works, because I am going to the Father."* The Mass, too, acknowledges that we have access to all the same graces Jesus had access to: *"Almighty God, we pray that your angel may take this sacrifice to your altar in heaven. Then as we receive from this altar the sacred body and blood of your Son, may we be filled with every grace and blessing."* Or how about: *"By the mystery of this water and wine may we come to share in the divinity of Christ who humbled himself to share in our humanity."*

We know scripture says that Jesus experienced all the temptations that we do. He would definitely have been faced with the temptation to downplay his own importance, his relationship to the Father and what he felt the Father was calling him to be and do. He would have been tempted to practice false humility. "Who do I think I am? I'm nothing special, just a carpenter from a poor village. My mother thinks I'm special but all mothers think their sons are special. It's true, I keep having these inner yearnings toward people around me and I feel such love and compassion for everyone I meet. I ache to be able to lift up their hearts and give them hope because they are all so amazingly precious. But I can't just claim the authority to go around blessing and healing or speaking about how wonderful the Father is. I'm just plain old Jesus from Nazareth and they know it. They would think I'm trying to make myself more important than I really am."

Jesus had to deal with this temptation. He had probably heard and read that particular scripture from Isaiah many times and perhaps each time he heard it, a huge desire would stir within him, and perhaps each time it was a little stronger than the time before. Eventually he had to pay attention. He had to go to the Father and ask, "Does this mean me?" He had to decide if he was going to believe it and accept it and if he did decide to accept it, what then? He would have had to tell the Father, "I believe you are calling me and I will trust you to take me where I must go and to lead me moment by moment. I open my whole being to you."

Through baptism and confirmation, you, too, have been anointed. The Holy Spirit was given to you and continues to be sent to you to stir, anoint and move you just as he came to Jesus to stir, anoint and move him. Ignoring or downplaying this aspect of your spiritual life might feel to you like you are being humble. There is a great temptation in the spiritual journey to pay more attention to one's sinfulness than to the freedom and calling we have received through Christ's sacrifice. There is a mistaken sense that if we pay a lot of attention to how bad we are, the Lord will be pleased because we aren't being proud and arrogant about ourselves.

False humility.

It is absolutely true that you are broken, that you make mistakes and that you often have need of God's forgiveness and reconciliation. However, if you ignore the stirring of God's Spirit within you and lack the courage to acknowledge that you are a beloved of the Father, are called to the Royal Priesthood, are clothed in Christ, can actually access the same mind Christ had, are filled with the exact same dignity and authority of Christ and have a Name and a unique calling no one else can fulfill, then you are being tempted to define your worth through false humility by false voices in your head.

We all need to continually contemplate these questions:

1. By Name he has called me. What is my Name? Who am I?
2. What was I chosen, anointed and sent to do and be?

3. Do I really accept and believe this? (Am I prepared to practice true humility?)

Several years ago there was a hymn titled, "Here I Am, Lord" (Dan Schutte, 1981) that became very popular. It was very significant that this song seemed to touch almost everyone in a very deep place. Go on the Internet or get a copy of a songbook and revisit all the lyrics of this song and recall how, when it first started being sung, it seemed to stir something within you whenever it was sung. Contemplate the message and the meaning and try to grasp that God really is calling you in the night, longing for you to recognize his voice and hear the name he chose especially for you. Pray for the grace to be able to accept that it is definitely you he is calling and that you, truthfully and in all humility, are allowed to say,

"The Spirit of the Lord is upon *me*. He has anointed *me*. He has sent *me*..."

Kingdom Grace

Luke 4: 21-30

After Jesus tells the people that the scripture from Isaiah, ("The Spirit of the Lord is upon me...") has been fulfilled in their hearing, they are amazed at the gracious words coming from his mouth and ask if this is not Joseph's son. Jesus says that a prophet is never accepted in his own country. The people become enraged, drive him out of town and try to throw him off a cliff, but he simply passes through the midst of them and goes on his way.

One of the most beautiful words of all time is "gracious" and my favorite images of Jesus are those of a gracious man and a gracious God. In this Gospel, everyone was 'amazed at the gracious words that came from his mouth'. One would wonder what kinds of words they were used to hearing. Condemnation? Judgment? Words that belittled them? Words that evoked fear, anxiety and guilt? At first they spoke well of him and then, because Jesus knew how their minds would rationalize away any possibility that he could be a source of grace, he short circuited them by telling them where their thoughts were heading and they ended up wanting to hurl him off a cliff. He knew they would ultimately reject him, not only because they thought they knew who he was but also because they didn't think he had appeared to them the way a Messiah should appear.

Jesus reminded them of how the prophets Elijah and Elisha, at two different times in Jewish history, were only able to perform miracles for foreigners, even though there were Israelites who were also suffering. This was a pointed statement about the Jewish people's lack of openness to receive God's grace and favor. He knew that even if he did perform some miracles for them, their attitudes wouldn't change. They were too hung up on their own perceptions and too busy feeling threatened to accept the profound simplicity of grace and love.

We, too, need to constantly revisit our perceptions of who God is to see if we have the inner freedom to accept that our God is indeed gracious and that he wants to be gracious to us.

In order to understand the graciousness of Christ, it might help to bring it down to our level and explore what it means for anyone to be gracious. We have all run into people whom we would define as gracious. Gracious people are those who are deeply aware of other people. Authentically gracious people are people who know so well they are loved and valued by God that they are able to stop thinking of their own needs and agendas and are able to completely appreciate the people they encounter. Because they do not require recognition from others to tell them how worthy and valuable they are, they are able to fully value others and focus on them. They listen. They are compassionate. They appreciate the good and the true. They build others up. They make others the center of their attention. They offer hope.

I want to emphasize that authentic graciousness is not just a type of outward action, though it encompasses that. It is outward action built on an inner conviction of being loved, on believing in one's priesthood and on knowing one has been called, anointed and sent. Gracious people make an impression. They leave us wanting to be in their presence more. They exude a peace and an inner certainty we would all love to have in our lives.

Jesus was a gracious man. He knew who he was and who he was called to be. He was convinced of the Father's love for him and convinced that the Father's love was for everyone. He had no anxiety about his own needs and status but was completely aware of the needs of those around him. This made him an extremely attractive and fulfilling person to be around – except for those who thought they knew him. They couldn't get past their rational minds or their religious expectations. Even though they found him engaging at first, they refused to even consider the idea that their judgments and religious expectations might be wrong. They could not receive his grace.

They demanded miracles to prove something to them but, as I mentioned before, Jesus knew that miracles would not make a difference. Why? Because if they could not even respond to the graciousness of God, they certainly weren't going to respond to miracles. Being connected to a gracious God means being in a love relationship with him and it is this gracious relationship that changes people on a gut level, not miracles.

But *we* know who Christ is and *we* don't block radical inner change because we're a little too rational and have set-in-stone religious expectations about the Messiah...do we? Unfortunately we do. The difference with us is that, generally, it's not Christ we want to hurl off a cliff – it's ourselves. We know ourselves too well. We have grown up with this very human person called "Me" and cannot even begin to believe that this less than extraordinary person, so similar to every other ordinary person, could be graciously and unconditionally accepted and loved, let alone be called to be an Anointed One. We are too afraid to let go of religious perceptions that have taught us that we are simply ordinary, mucked up sinners – and nothing else.

God can (and does) throw miracles our way constantly but there often remains a huge inner resistance to opening up to astounding grace. Miracles are wonderful things and are like precious reminders of his presence and love but if we review the large and small miracles that have come our way through our lives, we would have to admit that they are not what fill us up or heal us inside. We still succumb to the temptation to throw ourselves off a cliff rather than cast ourselves into the gracious arms of the Father.

There is only one thing that will fill you and heal you deeply and that is looking into Christ's eyes, allowing yourself to see Grace Without Borders and completely accepting that it's meant for you, as you are, where you are. That's what grace is. A truly gracious person does not require another person to shape up or change in order to receive the gracious person's attention, approval and love. Rational thinking tells us that we're unworthy and that we're failures. Rational religious thinking will deny who we really are and throw us off a cliff in a rage. Grace is completely irrational. Grace is unconditional. Grace cannot be earned; it can only be received with gratitude.

Grace is the display of love's beauty.

The Grace of our Lord Jesus Christ, and the love of God, and the communion of the Holy Spirit, be with you all. Amen.

Leaving Your Boat Behind

Luke 5: 1-11

Jesus is speaking to the crowd, which is pressing in on him. He sees two boats on the shore where the fishermen are washing their nets, so he asks them to put a boat out a little way from the shore and he speaks to the people from there. After, he tells Simon Peter to let down his nets for a catch. Peter replies that they fished all night and caught nothing but says they will do it if Jesus says so. They catch so many fish that their nets start to break and they need help bringing in the haul. Peter tells Jesus to go away from him for he is a sinful man. Jesus says not to be afraid because from now on he will be catching people.

There is not a person among us who can't relate to the bone-weariness of Simon Peter, James and John. They had been out all night fishing, had put in a lot of hard work and had nothing to show for it except extreme exhaustion which was made deeper and heavier by failure. They had families to support and perhaps they had debts they needed to repay. They probably had customers who might be tempted to go elsewhere for their fish. They needed to catch fish.

They weren't just tired; they were stressed out and probably a bit short tempered. Then this stranger had the gall to come up to Simon Peter and ask him to put aside the necessary work of cleaning the nets in order to take him out in the boat so he could speak to the crowds. I wouldn't be surprised if Peter didn't feel very gracious about this request.

After Jesus finished speaking, even if Peter had been fascinated by what Jesus was teaching, he probably wasn't prepared to have Jesus turn to him and tell him to go out deeper and let out his nets. Think about it. If Peter knew anything about Jesus, he would have known that Jesus was a carpenter, not a fisherman. Who did this guy think he was to tell him how to do his job? I wonder if Peter was tempted to say to Jesus, "Why don't you just go home and build a chair or something? Maybe you should go back to Nazareth and take care of your Mother. She's a widow. Why don't you do your job and take care of your own responsibilities instead of trying to tell me how to do my job? We are professional fishermen. We were out there all night. THERE ARE NO FISH!"

Even if Peter didn't say all of this out loud, Jesus would have known exactly what he was thinking and feeling but Jesus didn't back down. "Go deeper. Let out your nets."

Within a short period of time Peter, James and John pulled in enough fish to support all their families, pay their debts and satisfy their customers' needs abundantly, and probably there was enough left over to give some away to the poorer families nearby. Perhaps Peter was amazed, awed and utterly ashamed over his reluctance to obey Jesus and for his mean and miserly thoughts about Jesus. It was as if the miracle of the abundant catch was Jesus' answer to every cranky thought Peter had entertained about Jesus.

'Go away from me, Lord, for I am a sinful man!'

What does Jesus say? "That'll teach you to judge me! So, you think you know what I should be doing? Do you know who I am? Do you think you know the score better than I do? You think I don't know your doubts about me or about your reluctance to follow my instructions? I know the thoughts of your heart and you'd better shape up or (excuse the pun) ship out!"

No, he does not say anything like that. Jesus says, "Do not be afraid." He may have added, "Weariness and discouragement makes you fearful and fear makes you tight and tightness makes it hard to open up and go beyond what you think you know. Do not be afraid. Don't be afraid of a future defined by your past experiences. Stay with me in the present moment. Don't be afraid of your natural broken limitations. I am calling you beyond that and above that. Stay with me, listen to me speak your True Name. From now on you will be Fisher of People."

When you think about the Lord calling you by name, what are you afraid of? Are you afraid of what God might ask of you? Are you afraid of getting in too deep? Are you afraid of acting bigger or more capable than you really are? Are you afraid of your weakness, your failures or your lack of faith? Are you afraid of your own sinfulness? Are you afraid of God?

Jesus says, "Do not be afraid."

Like Peter, all of us need to accept that we don't often feel completely prepared for or capable of doing whatever the Lord calls us to be. It's true that 'the Lord doesn't call the equipped; he equips the called,' but always, there is first a call from him to take a risk, move our boat out deeper, away from what we *think* we know and push out into unknown waters, even though it seems like a waste of time.

After Jesus filled their nets, Peter was afraid. Peter told the Lord to go away. Peter thought he was too ordinary, too sinful, too messed up and too ignorant to be in the presence of someone so amazing and so powerful. But, when Peter said, *'Go away from me, Lord, for I am a sinful man,'* do you know what Jesus heard? He heard a tiny grain of faith, even though it was weak, anguished and filled with uncertainty. Peter had called him,

"Lord". For Jesus, that was more than enough. Nothing else mattered.

Notice that Jesus began his relationship with Simon Peter by getting into Peter's boat and allowing Peter to use his natural skills and abilities to serve him. It was his request to get into Peter's boat and he generously rewarded Peter and the others by blessing them with great abundance for their service to him. But also notice the last words in this Gospel story: *"When they had brought their boats to shore, they left everything and followed him."* Though they had served the Lord well and the Lord had blessed them for it, the time had come for them to leave behind their own little boats, their own natural knowledge, skills and abilities. They had to leave behind all that was their security and all that they realistically had to offer God. They had to listen for their Names and follow Jesus with absolutely nothing of their own to fall back on.

Just like Peter, we are weary broken people living in a tired and broken world. We are often afraid, discouraged, wounded, toiling in the night and waiting for the dawn so we can just wash our nets and go home. But just as there was someone waiting for Peter, there is someone waiting for you to leave behind your own little boat of self-definition and go with him to begin to find out who you really are and what is the Name *he* calls you by.

"Do not be afraid."

The Second Adam

Luke 4: 1-13

Jesus, full of the Holy Spirit, is driven into the wilderness for 40 days and is tempted by the devil.

Throughout Lent, I'm going to focus on aspects of the Gospels that highlight the amazing things that Jesus accomplished for us with so much love, to give us free access to the Father. In the midst of a busy life full of small and big demands, wounds, worries, unmet desires and immensely tough inner challenges, it's so easy to lose touch with the full reality of Jesus and what he really did for us – for you, actually. Instead of using the pronouns 'we' and 'us' this time, I am going to write to *you*. It is too easy to feel lost and anonymous in the crowd of 'us and we'. If you were the only person in the world, Jesus would have still died for you. You matter very much.

Near the end of the Ash Wednesday reflection at the back of this book, I encouraged you to ponder on the line from the Exultet: "O happy fault, O necessary sin of Adam, which gained for us so great a Redeemer!" The story of Adam and Eve is a story that astutely explains the propensity of human beings to desire control and autonomy over their lives and to live according to their own needs, wants and twisted perceptions rather than living harmoniously in God's love and order. Genesis says, *"Now the serpent was more crafty than any beast of the field which the Lord God had made."* Another translation says the serpent was the 'subtlest' of any beast. I like the word 'subtle' better because it is with great subtlety and deception that Satan used God's own words and twisted them in order to manipulate Adam's and Eve's desires. The fault that the Exultet speaks of is the failure to listen to God and trust in his words of Life. This failure stripped Adam and Eve of their innocence. It laid them naked to their own inadequacies and made them acutely and humiliatingly aware of this nakedness. You have probably had many times in your life when an awareness of a sin created a deep, embarrassing and hurting disturbance in your spirit and made you feel naked, anxious, vulnerable and scared - scared of your own inadequacy to always do the right thing and scared of your consistent inability to change yourself. You were miserable because you just couldn't fathom how God could love you or even like you. You were desperately in need of a savior!

One of Jesus' myriad of beautiful names is 'The Second Adam." In this week's Gospel, after he had been baptized and heard the Father's words, "This is my beloved Son in whom I am well pleased," Jesus was led into the desert where he, too, was confronted by "the subtlest of all beasts." Again, Satan tried to thwart God by using God's own words to manipulate the second Adam just as he manipulated the first Adam. He wanted to strip Jesus of his innocence and lay him naked, humiliated and blemished before God.

The temptation of Jesus in the desert wasn't just an occurrence to show you that Jesus resisted temptation, so you should too. The temptations were an eternally mysterious, deep and necessary part of God's total plan to bring you back to the Garden of his love. By resisting Satan's attempts to manipulate and corrupt him, Jesus began the journey toward your full redemption. Where Adam and Eve failed and gave in, Jesus succeeded and held strong. Where Adam and Eve lost their humble innocence in the enthronement of Self as lord, Jesus professed and re-established the Father's Kingship over all, especially over self-desire, self-control and self-aggrandizement. Where Adam and Eve felt the full humiliation of their nakedness and vulnerability, Jesus sanctified the waters of Baptism to cover your nakedness, (as *many of you as were baptized into Christ have clothed yourselves with Christ.* Galatians 3:27), then he resisted Satan and established the true security of the Lordship of the Father. Through this intervention, he reclaimed the deserts of your inner self to re-establish within you the Garden of the Lord, the Kingdom.

Jesus went into that desert for you. He went to the desert in your place. It was the beginning of the end of your naked vulnerability to the condemnation of sin. Jesus, the Lamb of God, was exposed to the evil one and remained unblemished - and we know that only an unblemished lamb was allowed for the Jewish sacrifices. Throughout the whole of the Old Testament the unblemished sacrificial lamb was a foreshadowing of how Jesus would bring you back home, back to the garden and back to his heart, back to your true self and back to the Father's arms.

But he didn't do this in some sort of Godly isolation, a super hero ten times removed from you and the other multitudes of sinful wretches. When looking at the crucifix at your church or when you see artists' renditions of the suffering Christ, it's easy to forget that Jesus is your brother. He is your big brother who, because you were lost, came to earth in order to bring you home. He came to slay "the subtlest of beasts" so you could follow him home in safety. Paul says in Romans 8: 29 (ISV): *"For those whom he foreknew he also predestined to be conformed to the image of his Son, in order that he might be the first of many brothers and sisters,"* and in Galatians 4 (ISV) he says: *"But when the appropriate time had come, God sent his Son, born by a woman, born under the Law, in order to redeem those who were under the Law, and thus to adopt them as his children. Now because you are his children, God has sent the Spirit of his Son into our hearts to cry out, "Abba! Father!" So you are no longer a slave but a child, and if you are a child, then you are also an heir because of what God did."*

A slave belongs to a master and is obligated by law to follow and obey, usually in fear of harsh punishment for mistakes. The relationship between a Father and his children is a relationship of love, trust and forgiveness of the type we witness in the story of the Prodigal Son. If you forget the love, if you forget who Jesus is, what he actually did and why he did it, then you slip back into the slave relationship where unresolved guilt creates within you huge condemnation and fear of reprisal. That's exactly what Jesus came to save you from.

Can you believe it?

The Way Out

Luke 9:28-36
The Transfiguration.

In my last reflection, I wrote about Jesus being the second Adam and about the significance of his time in the desert in relation to God's whole plan of redemption for you. This week's Gospel, the very familiar account of the Transfiguration, is brimming over with significant signs of a plan of salvation that had been moving towards the person of Jesus since the beginning. The parallels between Jesus and Moses and Elijah are too many to cover in a short reflection; it's a whole bible study in itself. What I'm going to focus on is one significant word in this scripture passage: 'Exodus'.

They appeared in glory and were speaking of his exodus...

Instead of the word 'exodus' in other translations, you will often read 'departure' or 'death' but 'exodus' is a more accurate translation. Exodus means 'a way out of'. Naturally, whenever we hear the word exodus, we think of Moses leading the Israelites out of slavery in Egypt and it's not hard to see where things are going here: Jesus is the second Moses and he came to lead God's people out of slavery. Moses and Elijah were discussing with Jesus his imminent death on the cross - the ultimate 'Way Out' or Exodus for the people of God.

In scripture, Egypt is symbolic of the world – worldly passions, worldly desires and worldly values, which are passions, desires and values not based on God's precepts. Egypt is a broken world, a world where the fall of Adam is played out daily. People are enslaved in this world where ego reigns supreme, control is coveted and people are wounded and broken. Just as Moses challenged the Pharaoh and led the Israelites out of slavery, so Jesus came to challenge the ruler of this world and lead his people to freedom.

There is a tendency to smile at Peter for wanting to set up tents for Jesus, Moses and Elijah but in fact, Peter was responding in a deeply respectful way to what he was witnessing. He wasn't suggesting they all stay on the mountaintop, camp out, sing praise and worship songs and have a wonderful time. He was suggesting that they build structures equivalent to the Jewish "Tent of Meeting" which was a holy place for the presence of God to rest, a sanctuary or a tabernacle. Peter wasn't far off the mark. He recognized that the God of Israel was indeed present when he saw that *the appearance of Jesus' face changed, and his clothes became dazzling white.*

In the old Testament, someone else's face changed in the presence of God and became so brilliant that he had to wear a veil so the people could look at him: Moses. Peter understood that something awesome and mighty was taking place and he wanted to treat it with great reverence and respect. When he made his suggestion, a cloud covered them all. In the Old Testament, a cloud signified the presence of God, as did brilliant light or the 'shekinah glory'. Out of the cloud, God's voice was heard saying, *'This is my Son, my Chosen, listen to him!'* Was God just giving Peter some general guidance, similar to how a parent might admonish a wayward child? "Smarten up...listen to your master!" I don't think so.

Moses mediated between God and the Israelites and brought to the people the Covenant God wanted to make with them. In Peter's Jewish experience, an appropriate, faith filled response to what he was seeing would have been to build a Tent of Meeting, a place where God could reside and which would be similar to the building that housed the Ark of the covenant (a wooden chest containing the tablets with the 10 commandments). However, Peter didn't yet fully understand that Jesus wasn't just a prophet like Moses and Elijah. He didn't realize that Jesus himself was now the Ark of the Covenant and that Jesus himself was now the true Tent of Meeting, the Tabernacle and the Dwelling Place of God. Within Jesus was a new Sanctuary and this sanctuary was to be totally accessible to all God's people, not just to the Jewish High Priest once a year. God was saying, "Listen to my Son and he will reveal to you my true dwelling place. He will reveal himself. He is not just bringing a New Covenant to you. He *is* the New Covenant."

So, what does all this have to do with you personally, over 2000 years later? How can all this ancient history have an impact on your life right now? Perhaps we need to review what a covenant is. A covenant is an agreement that brings about a relationship of commitment. The key word here is 'relationship'. That's a two way street. Certainly, you are committed to the Lord but you need to realize that the Lord was the first to make a commitment and he wants to have a relationship with you. That is a covenant. It's two parties making a commitment to each other. Marriage is a covenant. If it makes it easier to grasp, you can rightly assume that God wants to marry you; he wants to have a love relationship with you. He wants you to be his bride. You need to accept that and reciprocate in order to seal the covenant. A covenant does not take place if only one person is fully committing to the relationship. God is always fully committed. Are you?

The old covenant of the Old Testament was a legal covenant, a commitment based on law and a physical submission to the law. Circumcision, sacrifices, following the letter of the law and punishment for breaking the law were the basis of the old covenant. The New Covenant is a commitment based on the heart and the spirit of the law, not the letter. God was not satisfied with the old covenant based on law but it was what the maturity of the people could handle.

My husband and I have four adult children. When they were growing up, we surrounded them with rules. We didn't enjoy being rule enforcers but they needed that. Our love for them had to include definitive laws to help them grow. They didn't have the maturity to grow up without guidelines. Now that they are adults, what they learned by law as children is an integral part of who they are. We no longer have to lay down rules for them to be responsible people of integrity; it is now part of their natures and characters to be that. They *want* to be responsible good people. We now have relationships with them not based on enforcing rules and giving directions but on enjoying them totally for themselves and delighting in who they are. God always had in mind the day when his people would be mature enough for him to establish a New Covenant of love with them.

"The day is coming," says the Lord, "when I will make a new covenant with the people of Israel and Judah. This covenant will not be like the one I made with their ancestors when I took them by the hand and brought them out of the land of Egypt. They broke that covenant, though I loved them as a husband loves his wife," says the Lord. "But this is the new covenant I will make with the people of Israel after those days," says the Lord. "I will put my instructions deep within them, and I will write them on their hearts. I will be their God, and they will be my people. And they will not need to teach their neighbors, nor will they need to teach their relatives, saying, 'You should know the Lord.' For everyone, from the least to the greatest, will know me already," says the Lord. "And I will forgive their wickedness, and I will never again remember their sins." (Jeremiah 31:31-34 and Hebrews 8: 8-12 NLT)

God is in love with you and never at any point did he want anything to block your way to his heart. Jesus came and parted the waters of slavery so that you could have a way out of the wastelands of your Egypt and live face-to-face and heart-to-heart with your God.

Jesus became, for us, the Second Adam, the Second Moses, The Way Out and the New Covenant.

It just gets better and better.

Of Fruitful Trees and Negative Ions

Luke 13: 1-9
The parable of the barren fig tree which the master wanted the gardener to cut down. The gardener wanted to dig around it and put manure on it for a year to see if would bear fruit. If not, then he would cut it down.

John 4: 5-42
The woman at the well.

Which Gospel you hear this weekend will depend on whether there are catechumens in your parish. For the catechumens who have gone through the Rite of Election, this is a "time of scrutiny, a time of self searching and repentance and a time to bring out, then strengthen all that is upright, strong, and good." (From the RCIA Document). All Catholics are encouraged to engage in this time of scrutiny.

At first glance, the two Gospels are disparate in theme. In the first, Jesus is sternly warning people that unless they repent they will suffer the same fate as some Jews who were killed by Pilate or others were killed when a tower fell on them. Then he tells the parable of the fig tree. In the second Gospel, Jesus is speaking to a Samaritan woman and offering her living water. He doesn't warn her that unless she repents she will suffer death and punishment. He is gentle and compassionate in his interaction with her.

The Fruitless Fig Tree
The reason I'm focusing on the parable of the fig tree that bore no fruit from the first Gospel is because of our natural propensity to hear condemnation and not hear the solution. It would be so easy to listen to that reading, squirm inside at the "hellfire and

damnation Jesus" and miss what he was really saying to the people. The owner of the fig tree feels the tree is useless and wants to cut it down. But the gardener wants to work with the tree and fertilize it and bring it back to health. He wants to save it. The gardener wouldn't have suggested that if he thought it was a useless exercise. In this parable, Jesus is the determined Gardener. He was telling the people that no matter who they were, Pharisee or prostitute, they needed to repent. Just because some Jews suffered and died in different circumstances didn't mean they were more sinful than the ones Jesus was talking to. Everyone is broken. As Paul says in Romans 3:23 *"We have all sinned and fallen short of the glory of God."* In telling the parable of the fruitless fig tree, Jesus was saying that if they turned to him (repentance), he would be the one to heal them and make them fruitful in spite of the fact that they had *all* fallen short.

The emphasis and focus in Jesus' mind was on turning back to God and on forgiveness, not on the sins committed. This emphasis is actually part of the Jewish doctrine. The Talmud holds that a repentant sinner attains a more exalted spiritual eminence than one who has never sinned. Chew on that one for a while.

So, Jesus is the Gardener, the one who desires to tend and feed your roots and bring your dead branches back to life. Your responsibility is to turn to him with a true desire to be changed in mind and heart. You are called to allow the Gardener to do his job, a job that also entails delicate transplantation. He's going to get you back to the garden if it kills him.

And it did kill him.

The Woman at the Well
Living water: a term we've heard so often that it has ceased to have great meaning in our lives. Perhaps because water is

generally so readily available to most of us, we tend to forget the crucial value of water to all life. But even if we in the first world do have distinct memories of how hard it was once when the pipes were frozen or when there was a drought in our area and we had to conserve water, these memories don't always translate over to the spiritual life so that we can truly appreciate that Jesus came to earth in order to be Living Water for us.

Living water: the opposite of stagnant water. Living water: healthy water that burbles and flows. Living water: water that pounds and shapes, tumbles and shakes and is turbulent, alive, clear and clean. It is water that not only sustains the life near it but also, more importantly, sustains the life within it. We are meant to be within it, not just near it.

The way we experience sacramental water in church is a simple and easily understood sign of something that is, in reality, much more abundant and overwhelming. Jesus came to submerge us in unfathomable oceans of Living Water. Moses struck the rock as God instructed him and good water came gushing out of it. Jesus, the second Moses, didn't just strike a rock – he became The Rock out of which water gushes for his parched people. Jesus met the woman at the well of Jacob, a well, legend says, where water gushed to the very top and overflowed so that people didn't have to let their buckets down deep and work hard to draw it up. How appropriate that Jesus should speak of Living Water at this well.

I love to walk by the ocean, preferably where the waves are rolling and pounding. I always come away feeling refreshed and more relaxed. It always felt to me as if the ocean had the power to untie knots. Then I discovered that the ocean actually does have that power. It's a scientific fact that bodies of moving water – rain storms, the ocean, rivers, waterfalls, fountains etc. – create negative ions and negative ions have the capacity to alleviate minor depression, relieve stress, improve immunity and are essential to high energy and a positive mood. If Jesus came to earth today and was speaking to us about himself, he might very well say, "I am the Negative Ion." Or perhaps, "I am that I Am Ion."

The psalmist in Psalm 46:4 (RSV) says, *"There is a river whose streams make glad the city of God, the holy habitation of the Most High"* and verse 10 says, *'Be still, and know that I am God!'* The gladness of the River of Living Water is easily missed because it's so hard to be still long enough to be immersed in the river and long enough to hear the voice of the Lord say to your heart, *"You are my Beloved. Come and jump into me. Let me flow into, around, over and through you. Let me soak your roots in my love and forgiveness so that your branches will bear new life and good fruit."* Sometimes you forget that not only do you have permission to wade into his cleansing waters but you are also invited to jump into the deep end and get completely drenched. Often, Christ's followers can be seen off to the side of the river scrubbing themselves and trying to clean themselves up, an activity which is pretty much equivalent to scrubbing off multiple, heavy layers of encrusted dry mud with a damp cotton swab when Christ has got torrents of water to do the job and do it completely. That's why he's there – to wash you and make you clean in his love. You can't do the job. No one can.

Jesus came, for you, to be the second Adam, the second Moses, the New Covenant, the Way Out, the determined and stubborn Gardener, the Rock, your Ocean of Living Water and your Stream of Gladness.

What a God!

Turn On The Light

Gospel Acclamation:
"I am the light of the world; those who follow me will not walk in darkness, but will have the light of life." (John 8:12, NRSV)

Excerpt from the Gospel for the second Scrutiny, (John 9: 5, NRSV)
"As long as I am in the world, I am the light of the world."

Verses 35 - 38:
Jesus said (to the man healed of blindness), 'Do you believe in the Son of Man?' He answered, 'And who is he, sir? Tell me, so that I may believe in him.' Jesus said to him, 'You have seen him, and the one speaking with you is he.' He said, 'Lord, I believe.' And he worshipped him.

By saying he was the light of the world, Jesus made an enormous claim. He was not just claiming to be one who was an extraordinarily good person or a sensitive prophet; he was establishing himself as a dwelling place of God and the Word of God. To the Jews, fire and light indicated the holy and awesome presence of God. No wonder those Pharisees were incensed with him.

We looked at Jesus as the second Moses so let's look at a few places where fire and light were significant signs of God's presence in Moses' life. Last week, one of the first readings was about Moses and the burning bush. The fact that the bush was burning was not significant in itself because dry bushes often spontaneously ignite in the heat of the desert. What caught Moses' attention was that it was not being consumed like it would be in an ordinary fire. The fiery light was the living presence of God and Moses was instructed to take off his sandals for he was standing on holy ground.

Another light filled indication of God's presence throughout the Exodus was a pillar of fire that led the Israelites through the wilderness. By day, it was a pillar of cloud (another sign of God's presence) and at night, a pillar of fire. God directed Moses and the people to build a Tent of Meeting or a tabernacle for his presence and when the pillar of cloud and fire rested on the tabernacle, the Israelites stayed where they were and when the cloud and fire moved on, the people moved on. So, the light not only assured them of God's presence and blessing, it also guided them safely through the wilderness.

As well as associating light with the presence, the leadership and the living word of God, the Jews also connected light with the coming of the promised Messiah. They were taught that the name of the Messiah would be "Light". When Jesus said, "I am the Light of the World", he was proclaiming that he was the Messiah. There was no ambiguity in the Pharisees' minds that he was claiming to be the Holy One of God.

The coming of the Messiah, the Light, had enormous implications for the Jews. To them it meant they were to be saved from political bondage and be raised up as a free and victorious nation. We now know that Jesus didn't come to save them from the bondage of Roman domination; he came to save us all from the bondage of brokenness. These are all familiar concepts and they roll off the tongue almost glibly. What you need to determine is, what does Jesus being the Light of the world mean for you personally, today, in the midst of your family concerns, challenging relationships, deep inner wounds, anger, frail health, career struggles, loneliness and way too many demands on your time and on your emotions? Where is the Light in your life right now? Is his light a constant reality for you?

Jesus healed the blind man and this was wonderful for the man. He was given the ability to see as every other sighted person could see – by the natural light of the world. He was probably floating on air with his sudden ability. There were so many possibilities and adventures awaiting him. Eventually, though, sight would become less extraordinary to him. He would get used to living in the blessings of all that light and become less and less excited by it. He would find that even though he could see, people could still irritate him and give him grief. Life would still carry a lot of wounds and challenges. They would be different challenges from when he was blind but challenges none-the-less.

The blind man was gifted with natural sight but he needed more. Jesus found him again and completed the healing. He asked the man, "Do you believe in the Son of God?" It was necessary for the man to profess directly to Jesus, "Lord, I believe," and then worship Jesus face to face.

Saying "I believe in you, Jesus," and then worshipping him is often an act of the will and an act of sheer faith but they are acts that are very necessary to "keeping the flame alive in your heart" as we are exhorted in the rite of baptism. "I believe in you, Lord. You are my Light and I worship you," are words your heart needs to speak often. Don't wait for Mass to say these words. Don't just allow rote prayers to say them for you. Pray them when you wake up, pray them in the car, say them as you go about your daily work or recreation and pray them before you go to sleep.

As you pray them, take a few seconds to decide what those words actually mean at that moment. Do they mean you are dependent on him to reveal his presence to you in your life? Do they mean that you acknowledge that your perceptions and expectations may be faulty and you need his light to open you up to his own depth of sight? Do they mean you want to walk with him as closely as you possibly can because he is the light and without him, you are in the dark? How willing are you to allow his incisive light to penetrate your whole life, moment by moment?

Jesus came, for you, to be the second Adam, the second Moses, the New Covenant, your Way Out, the determined and stubborn Gardener of your fruitfulness, your Ocean of Living Water, your Temple of God's holy presence and the illuminating Light in your heart.

This is a God worthy of worship!

"But to you who worship my name, the sun of righteousness will rise with healing in its wings; (Malachi 4:2, NRSV)

Worship him now. Don't ever stop.

The Life Choice

John 11: 1- 45 (Third Scrutiny) verses 17-27
Jesus raises Lazarus from the dead.

If anyone asked you, "Do you believe in life after death?" your answer would be, "Absolutely!" That belief is a basic and foundational tenet of our Christian faith. As St. Paul said, "If for this life only we have hoped in Christ, we are of all people most to be pitied," (1 Corinthians 15:19 NRSV) meaning that if Christ did not rise from the dead, all our hopes and beliefs are pretty silly.

But what if someone asked you, "Do you believe in life *before* death?"

Life after death for most people is a somewhat unreal far away concept, something that's going to happen down the road sometime. There certainly are times when the reality of death hits home such as when someone you love dies or when you have a close call where death could have been the outcome. Unless you are very sick with a life threatening illness, you don't live with the reality of death and resurrection on a daily basis.

In the gospel, Martha was dealing with the reality of death. When she met Jesus, like all of us when we find ourselves in very painful circumstances, she wanted to blame him. *"Lord, if you had been here, my brother would not have died..."* But, because of her relationship with Jesus, there was something within her that nudged her toward a further expression of her developing trust in him. *"But even now I know that God will give you whatever you ask of him."* She wasn't necessarily indicating that she expected Jesus to raise Lazarus from the dead; she was just expressing her faith that he loved her and would be there for her and Mary no matter what. When Jesus said, "Your brother will rise again," she didn't assume he meant immediately. She thought he was talking about the belief the Pharisees held – and which she obviously held as well – that eventually everyone who died would be resurrected.

Then Jesus said something to her that you need to pay close attention to. He said, *'I am the resurrection and the life. Those who believe in me, even though they die, will live, and everyone who lives and believes in me will never die. Do you believe this?'*

Note that Jesus did not say, "I *will be* the Resurrection." He said, "I **AM** the resurrection." He had not gone to the cross and died yet; that was still in the future. He was telling her that right in that present moment he was her resurrection and life as well as Lazarus's. He was saying to her that everyone who believes in him will live. Then he said that even if they die, they will live. Death is not the prerequisite to Resurrected Life. Belief is. Resurrected Life is yours right now if you believe. This is not a "somewhere down the road" theology. This is present moment, right now, every day of your life theology.

In last week's gospel, Jesus told the healed blind man that he was the Light of the world. Then he asked the man, "Do you believe in me?" In this week's gospel, Jesus tells Martha that he is the Resurrection and the Life. Then he asks her, "Do you believe?" He knew Martha well. He knew what she believed and didn't believe. So why did he ask her? Because Martha needed to speak it. She needed to look into his eyes and say, "Yes, Lord, I believe." The blind man who was healed needed to look into Jesus' eyes and say, "Lord, I believe." Jesus once asked his disciples, "Who do you say that I am?" Jesus didn't need to hear what his disciples thought. The disciples needed to speak it.

You need to do that. Every day you need to take time to look at Jesus through the eyes of faith and say, "Today, Lord, you are my Resurrection. Today you are my life. Yes, Lord, I believe." You need to affirm that he is your Lord and that he is the one who will bring life to every moment that feels like death.

Paul says in Romans 6:3,4 and 8 (NRSV):
Do you not know that all of us who have been baptized into Christ Jesus were baptized into his death? Therefore, we have been buried with him by baptism into death, so that, just as Christ was raised from the dead by the glory of the Father, so we too might walk in newness of life.
... if we have died with Christ, we believe that we will also live with him.

You are called death and resurrection...*before* you die. Every moment of every day is an opportunity of choice. You can seek the giver of Resurrected Life or you can fumble along in the death-walk of your own ego.

You need to come back time and time again to this incredibly important basis of our whole faith and you need to ask the question, "Do I believe in Life before death? Am I daily seeking the One who will show me what it means to live a Resurrected Life?"

Jesus came, for you, to be the second Adam, the second Moses, the New Covenant, your Way Out, the determined and stubborn Gardener of your fruitfulness, your Ocean of Living Water, your Temple of God's holy presence, the illuminating Light in your heart, your Resurrection and your Life.

Do you believe it?

The Passion of a Passionate God

Excerpts from the Gospel Reading (NRSV)

- *Then Pilate said to the chief priests and the crowds, "I find no basis for an accusation against this man."*

- *Pilate then said to them, "You brought me this man as one who was perverting the people; and here I have examined him in your presence and have not found this man guilty of any of your charges against him. Neither has Herod, for he sent him back to us. Indeed, he has done nothing to deserve death."*

- *A third time Pilate said to them, "What evil has he done? I have found in him no ground for the sentence of death."*

- *The other criminal rebuked the first and said, "...we are getting what we deserve for our deeds but this man has done nothing wrong."*

- *When the centurion saw what had taken place, he praised God and said, "Certainly this man was innocent."*

Jesus is your Paschal Lamb.

The term "Paschal lamb" refers to the Jewish Passover in Egypt where God instructed the Israelites to kill an unblemished lamb and put the blood of the lamb on the lintels of their doorposts. The angel of death would see the blood and 'pass over' that household. The Israelites were also instructed to make sure that every member of the household consumed at least a small portion of the roasted lamb.

From the long Gospel reading of the Passion, I pulled out the above passages that speak of the innocence of Jesus because the unblemished lamb of the original Passover was a foreshadowing of the sacrifice of Jesus, your paschal lamb. Jesus went to the cross, unblemished, so his death could in no way be construed as just punishment. It was innocent blood that was spilled on your behalf. Because of your baptism where you died with Christ, and because of your belief in Jesus, the blood of the lamb has marked your spiritual 'lintels'. You are identified as God's chosen, one who is saved from the power of sin and death.

Wow.

The parallels between the first Passover and the death of Jesus astoundingly show that God was always thinking of your salvation from the beginning. But there are other parallels not often emphasized. Here are a few:

- According to the law, the Jews were to select their sacrificial lamb on the tenth day of the first month, four days before the actual sacrifice. According to John, Jesus entered Jerusalem on the tenth day of the first month. The people then acclaimed him as their Messiah. He became the 'Chosen Lamb' on the exact day the Passover lambs were traditionally chosen.

- When Jesus and his disciples sat down for the Last Supper, (Seder) it was the beginning of the 14th day of the first month. In Exodus (12:18) God instructs the Israelites to sacrifice a lamb at twilight on the 14th day of the Jewish month of Nisan, before the sun sets. Though the biblical day begins at sunset, they were having their Seder meal early because Jesus knew that when the rest of the Jews were having their Seder meal, he would be dead and buried. At the last supper, Jesus instituted the Eucharist. "This is my body...this is my blood..." All those who were present at the last supper partook of a small portion of the sacrificial Lamb, Jesus, just as the Jewish people would be partaking in the sacrificial lamb at their own Seder meals.

- When Jesus was nailed to the cross it was the third hour, the hour when the first male sacrificial lamb (the Tamid) was slain in the temple and its blood collected to sprinkle on the altar.

- When Jesus died, it was the ninth hour, the hour the rest of the sacrificial lambs chosen by Jewish families and communities were ritually slain in the temple.

- During the Passover, Jerusalem was filled with thousands upon thousands of Jews singing and reciting the traditional Hallel psalms (113-118). Their voices would have been heard outside the city walls. While Jesus hung on the cross, those who stayed with him would have heard phrases like, ***"The cords of death entangled me . . . I suffered distress and anguish. Then I called on the name of the Lord: 'O Lord, I pray, save my life!'... I kept my faith, even when I said, 'I am greatly afflicted'... precious in the Sight of the Lord is the Death of his Righteous Ones . . . Open for me the Gates of Righteousness . . . The stone the builders rejected has become the cornerstone... Blessed is the one who comes in the name of the Lord."***

- A ritual instruction for the preparation of the Passover lamb was that no bones be broken. After Jesus had died, the soldiers came and broke the bones of the two men on either side of him but when they came to Jesus, they saw he was already dead and so they didn't break his bones.

> Psalm 34:20 also states, *"...taking care of every bone, the Lord will not let one be broken."*

In these modern times, it is difficult to relate to the idea of sacrifice. It seems so bloody and primitive. Surely all of us, at one time or another, secretly or out loud, have wondered how a loving God could demand his 'pound of flesh' and send his son to die. And right there is where the mistake is made. We envision God the Father in heaven, sorrowfully watching from a distance, observing his only son die on a cross. It was tough but it had to be done. "This hurts me more than it hurts you," type of thing. We forget that Jesus kept emphasizing to his disciples, "The Father and I are one. If you have seen me, you have seen the Father." Where was the Father when Jesus was on the cross?

On the cross with him.

The mystery of the oneness of the trinity means that because of his huge love for you, God sent *himself* to die for you in order to become the 'once and for all' sacrifice. There was no "You go and I'll stay here and watch." It was, "Let's go and bring our children, our brothers and sisters, home."

Throughout the Old Testament, God kept telling his people that burnt offerings and sacrifices were not what pleased him. What pleased him were love, mercy, compassion and humble hearts. So, why would he have created laws requiring sacrifice if it wasn't what pleased him? It was because God always works with his people within the capacity of their understanding, and he continues to do so today.

Having lived in Egypt for over 400 years, the Israelites were totally used to the idea of sacrifice to appease the gods. It was culturally acceptable to them. After he took them out of Egypt, God instituted very tight laws that specified what could be sacrificed: animals, birds and produce, etc. But not people! These ancient Israelites had been exposed to cultures where slaves, babies and virgins were regularly sacrificed to keep the gods happy and that seemed normal to them. God was moving them out of that kind of despicable idea of sacrifice and away from the perception that he could be that kind of God.

As a young nation the Israelites needed strict laws to teach them the way to live morally upright lives, just as young children need very clear rules and standards to teach them the right way to live. But the people as a whole just could not get their heads around the idea that their inner hearts and the actions that come from a willing and loving spirit were what blessed God, not the sacrifices. They kept falling, just as we do today, into following the letter of the law. The "good" Jews were impeccable in their observance of the law. They made all the proper sacrifices, said all the proper prayers and observed all the proper feast days. But God agonized over them because "their hearts are far from me."

The death of himself, the unblemished lamb, on a cross was the complete end to useless ritual sacrifice, sacrifice that did nothing to cleanse the heart. It was the beginning of a new relationship with God, a New Covenant based on outrageous passionate love, not on blind, dead law. Even the sacrifices of non-Christian Jews came to an end as the temple in Jerusalem was destroyed relatively shortly after the death of Jesus. To this day there are no bloody sacrifices being offered on behalf of the Jewish people.

You belong to a God who never lets go and who will do *whatever it takes* to rescue you and get you home.

Jesus came, for you, to be the second Adam, the second Moses, the New Covenant, your Way Out, the determined and stubborn Gardener of your fruitfulness, your Ocean of Living Water, your Temple of God's holy presence, the illuminating Light in your heart, your Resurrection, your Life and your paschal Lamb.

Hold the Lamb. Feel that perfect love.

First Morning

Whenever I think of Easter, my first images are not of disciples discovering an empty tomb or Mary encountering angels and the 'gardener'. I don't immediately think of the two men on the road to Emmaus being joined by the engaging stranger. I don't think of words like, "He is not here but has risen" or "Woman, why are you weeping? Who are you looking for?" As wonderful as they are, the accounts of the disciples discovering that Jesus was not dead after all are not what excites and stirs my spirit.

Instead, I hear in my imagination an immense and intense CRACK! It's the sound of a sudden thunderclap overhead or the trunk of an ancient gargantuan tree suddenly fracturing in two in a strong wind or the report of a thousand rifles being shot simultaneously. It's not a crash. It's a sharp, immediate sound that's over as suddenly as it began except for the reverberating echoes down through eternity. It is the crack of Resurrection. It is the power of death being snapped.

Then I see Jesus sit up. Even though it's still dark, there is light around him. He begins to laugh. The pain and fear is gone, the knots in his stomach are untied, the relief is overwhelming and pure golden joy cascades over him. The world is not yet awake as he moves out of the tomb but along the horizon is another kind of crack – the crack of a dawn just beginning. I see Jesus walking through the gardens and all he wants to do is breathe. He takes in deep, marvelous and unobstructed breaths that are free of tension or care. If he had a bike, he would ride it. He would glide, carefree and excited down silent paths and through still olive groves. As it is, he walks, almost floats, without the heavy restraint of the worldly gravity of sorrow, pain and fear. He praises his Father but not with words. By breathing, he praises.

By delighting, he praises. By allowing excitement and anticipation to well up inside, he praises. There are no words that can do justice to his praise.

He stops on the top of a high hill and gazes down on a sleeping Jerusalem. The heaviness of the people is visible to him. It's like a miasma of fear, uncertainty, suffering, anger and anguish seeping through the hushed streets, too heavy to rise or dissipate. He knows where his disciples are hidden, unable to sleep in their confusion and pain. He knows because he can see all things clearly but he also knows because their terror has a suffering color of misery different to the rest of the unaware population. He is touched by their suffering and wishes he could hold them and let each one experience just how glorious this dawn really is.

But it's all right. Soon they will know. Soon.

Then, on that hill of dawn stillness, the heavens break open and Jesus is immersed in the company of heaven singing his Names. His Names flow down on him and envelop him like a warm bath of sunlight, buoying him up and washing away the last vestiges of the heavy earth. Names like:

Alpha; The Anointed One, Carpenter, Beginning and the End, Express image of God's person, One and Only Begotten, Gift of God, Merciful High Priest Bridegroom, Bright and Morning Star, Anchor, Captain of our salvation, Chief among ten thousand, Child, Consolation of Israel, Almighty, High Priest, Cornerstone, Apostle, Counselor, Redeemer, Creator of all things, Foundation, Daysman, Blessed, Branch, Sanctification, Helper, Glory of God, Deliverer, Ancient of Days, Balm of Gilead, Door, Emmanuel, Shiloh, End of the Law, Faithful, True, First and the Last, Commander, First begotten of the dead, Brightness of God's glory, Altogether Lovely One, the Christ, Firstborn, First fruits, Fountain, Our Passover, Friend, Fullness of the Godhead, Word,

Good Master, Governor, Great High Priest, Righteousness, Guide, Head, Son, Servant, Heir of all Things, Hiding Place, Holy Child, the Just, Horn of salvation, Beloved, I am,

Jesus

Intercessor, Judge, Dayspring from on High, All in All, Just One, King, Lamb, Lawgiver, Savior, Hope of Israel, Master, Vine, Mediator, Propitiation, Chosen of God, Mercy, Messiah, God, Mighty God, Desire of all nations, Minister of the Sanctuary, Sower, Forerunner, Offering, Stone, Root of David, Testator, Ointment Poured Forth, Life, Bread, Arm of the Lord, The Great Amen, Angel of the Lord, Our Peace, Physician, Day Star, Rod, Power of God, Quickening Spirit, Ransom, Comforter, Refuge, the Life, Sacrifice, Plant of Renown, Kinsman, The Same now and forever, Shepherd, Star, Rock of Salvation, Light, Lion of the tribe of Judah, Sun of Righteousness, Prophet, Surety, Teacher, Lord and Savior, Tender Plant, Resurrection True Bread, Truth, Way, Wisdom, Shadow of a great Rock, Father of Eternity, Wonderful, Omega, Author and Finisher of our Faith,...

His Names seem to go on for an eternity, pouring over him like a river of truth and grace and, in answer, he begins to sing the names of all of his beloved, past, present and future. You're not even born but he names you and calls you. He calls you as an extension of himself, names you as someone who flows out of himself. Because his name, Jesus, is the Name above all names.

"Speak the Word and we shall be created."

Eventually, the rest of the world that sleeps the sleep of death will know about the resurrection too, but it won't be as easy to identify as the natural sun rising in all its glare and heat. His resurrection will appear dawn-by-dawn, moment-by-moment, stillness-by-stillness, and tomb-by-tomb. Each spiritual death will bring a sharp crack of death being broken and a soft crack of dawn breaking on the horizon and a name being called.

This is my imagination of Easter but it's not an imagining based on pure fantasy. It's based on the resurrections I have experienced in my life, the moments where I passed from heaviness and death into a gracious crack of new light. It is based on the knowledge that Jesus has sanctified all my tombs and the tombs of all his people. They are no longer graves of imprisonment but portals to the kingdom through which we can see the creeping light and hear the echo of our spiritual names.

I pray for you a holy and blessed Easter. Slip through the crack of your tomb and join him on the silent hill. He is calling you and would love to see you.

"Do you not know that all of us who have been baptized into Christ Jesus were baptized into his death? Therefore we have been buried with him by baptism into death, so that, just as Christ was raised from the dead by the glory of the Father, so we too might walk in newness of life.

*For if we have been united with him in a death like his, **we will certainly be united with him in a resurrection like his.** We know that our old self (the ego) was crucified with him so that the body of sin might be destroyed, and we might no longer be enslaved to sin. For whoever has died is freed from sin. But if we have died with Christ, we believe that we will also live with him. We know that Christ, being raised from the dead, will never die again; death no longer has dominion over him. The death he died, he died to sin, once for all; but the life he lives, he lives to God. So you also must consider yourselves dead to sin (of the ego) and alive to God in Christ Jesus."* (Romans 6: 3-11, Easter Vigil Epistle, NRSV)

Thomas

Peace be with you, Brother Thaddeus,

Once more, I need to express my gratitude to you for staying in the village with our mother and caring for her when I know you ache to be with me here in Jerusalem. When I left home to follow the Master, I promised you I would get word to you as often as possible – I'm sorry that it has been a very long time since the last letter when I told you about the Master bringing Lazarus back to life. So much has happened since then. I need not tell you everything since I know the news of his death by crucifixion has reached believers in the villages closer to Jerusalem. I have not forgotten you and I know that you must be in great pain and grief. It has been a terrible, terrible time for everyone. I cannot even begin to convey to you what it was like here, in the midst of it all. However, maybe this letter will make up for my long silence.

Those of us here in Jerusalem have been in hiding. We were terrified that the Priests would decide that Jesus' followers should also be put to death in order to completely stamp out his influence. We quickly found a safe place far from Golgotha but because of our haste we did not have any food. We knew someone had to go out or we would die of starvation but our fear was so great that no one would volunteer.

I was sitting on the floor, trying to be invisible, listening to the others argue as to who should go, when a memory flooded my mind. It was different than simply remembering an incident. It was almost as if I was inside a vision, feeling what I felt and saying what I said at the time. I remembered when Jesus told us he was going back to Judea because Lazarus had died. We all tried to discourage him because it was so dangerous but Jesus always seemed to know exactly where he was going and what he was going to do. When I saw him turn from us and start off down the road on his own, my heart couldn't stand it and I said to the others, "Let us also go, that we may die with him."

When that memory flooded through me, my shame was so intense that it was all I could do to keep from crying out. I was the one who had suggested we go with him and I was so full of brave words. Now, here I was, cowering in a corner. We had all run away at the first sign of trouble; we hadn't been the least willing to die with our Master. Now we were arguing and acting like frightened children, not even willing to put our lives at risk for some food.

I couldn't stand it. I jumped up and yelled, "Everybody just shut up! I'll go!" and, without even checking to see if it was safe, I barged out and slammed the door shut behind me. I could hear them quickly locking the door behind me.

I spent some time going to the homes of a few believers who were generous with their food but were relieved when I left, not wanting the authorities to see them consorting with me. When I returned to our safe house, the others saw it was me and quickly let me in but I could not believe the difference in their faces. I was expecting them to be grateful and fall on the food I had brought, but no. They were too excited and too busy laughing and slapping each other's backs. Peter pulled me to the side and said, "Thomas! We saw him! He came right in here even though the door was locked. He was suddenly standing right over there and he said, 'Peace be with you,' as if nothing had happened." Peter grabbed my arms and started swinging me around, yelling, "He's alive, Thomas! He's alive and he was here!"

I roughly pulled away from Peter and said, "Be quiet, you fool. They'll hear you in the street. What is wrong with you? You say you saw him? Well, good for you. But unless I see the mark of the nails in his hands, and put my finger in the mark of the nails and my hand in his side, I will not believe." I turned away from him, sat down on the floor and refused to look at any of them. My heart was stinging with confusion, hurt and total resentment. All I could think was "Why? If the Lord was really alive, why did he wait until I was gone to appear to everyone? Why was I left out?" I didn't know if I believed them or not, but they were so joyful and they had no reason to make up such a story. I was utterly miserable.

As I listened to them discuss his appearance, my resentments still rankled but I also became bothered for another reason. The way they were talking, you'd think things were just going to keep on going the way they always had been. They were talking about finding him and discussing how they could get him out of Jerusalem without being seen. They even talked about how they could disguise him. They were talking about going with him to Egypt, maybe, or perhaps even farther, taking his message to other lands and waiting until things settle down here in Jerusalem.

The more they talked, the more I doubted the whole reality of the situation. If our Lord had really died and was now really alive, everything was changed. Could they not see that? They weren't thinking straight. If he could really appear in a locked room and leave the same way, he had no need of them to help him to evade the authorities. He had no need of them at all. My mind was swirling with possibilities of what this all meant and I could hardly believe it or keep it all straight. Things that Jesus said when he was with us kept coming back to my mind, especially one thing he said to me at the last meal we had with him. When I remembered his words, it was as if the heavens opened up and rocks fell on me:

'I am the way, and the truth, and the life, Thomas. No one comes to the Father except through me. If you know me, you will know my Father also. From now on you do know him and have seen him.'

"You do know him and have seen him..." These words kept running through my head over and over. He said that if I knew him, then I knew the Father. That meant I know God since I knew Jesus. Jesus was God. If he is alive now then...Jesus *is* God. He really is God.

For days these thoughts kept looping through my head until I thought I would go crazy. I doubted my reasoning and I doubted my sanity.

Then early one morning, as we were putting away our sleeping mats and dreading another long and tedious day, he was suddenly there. I saw him before anyone else. He was looking directly at me with the most loving look in his eyes and I knew without a doubt that he knew exactly what I had been struggling with all week. Not only did he know but, somehow, I also realized that he was the source of all my thoughts. He was the one who brought the memories back to my mind.

He opened his robe, held out his hands and invited me not only to touch him but to also enter deeply into his wounds. It was as if he was opening a gate to me. I know he didn't say anything out loud but in my head I heard, "If you know me, Thomas, you know my Father. My Father and I are one. You are right. Nothing is the same anymore. There are no longer any walls or doors that have the power to keep me away from my people. There are no longer any walls or doors that can keep you away from the heart of God. Do you know me, Thomas? Do you know who I am?"

I fell to the floor and wept, "Yes, Master, I know you! You are my Lord and my God. You are God. You are *my* God. You are ho Theos*...I KNOW you!"

The Master is alive, Thaddeus! I have seen him. I walked through his wounds into utter freedom. There are no more walls or doors that can keep him out. There is no distance between him and any one of us. And he gave me a message for you. He said, "Have you believed because you have really seen me? Blessed are those who have not seen yet have come to believe. Tell my brother and yours, Thaddeus, that I will come to him very soon."

There is little else I can say, my brother. Wait for him. He is coming. He is ho Theos, he is alive and he is coming to you. Believe it!

Through his most precious wounds,
I am your twin,
Thomas.

*After the Resurrection, Thomas was the very first person to call Jesus, 'Ho Theos', which means "The almighty God". In other words, he was the first to recognize the absolute divinity and Godhead of Christ, an understanding that the other disciples had not yet come to.

Transitioning

John 21: 1-19

Simon Peter and the other disciples decide to go fishing but they caught nothing that night. Just after dawn Jesus calls to them, "You have no fish, have you?" When they answer that they didn't, he tells them to cast the net to the right side of the boat and they catch so many fish they can't haul the net in. Peter recognizes Jesus and jumps out of the boat to go meet him.

Later, after breakfast, Jesus asks Peter three times if Peter loves him. When Peter affirms that he does, Jesus tells Peter to feed his sheep.

Change can be immensely exciting but it can also be terribly difficult. Change is wonderful in the way it brings new experiences, new skills, new interactions and new ways of beholding God, others and yourself. What is difficult about change is that there is often a transition period, a period in between the old and the new where it can feel like everything is just on the edge of unraveling. It can be terribly lonely and filled with uncertainty. Even if the change was one that was longed for, the challenges within transition have the potential to make one ache for the familiar ground of what was before. In the transition desert it is difficult to maintain a vision of the rightness of change. It's easy to feel self-doubt and wonder where God is. People can be forgiven for trying to recreate the familiar within the new circumstances where the spiritual landscape is strange and old routines have been upset.

The disciples in this gospel were in transition. They had seen Jesus, knew he was alive and knew everything had changed – again. You'd think that after three years of following Jesus they would be used to profound change and used to handling exceedingly unfamiliar situations, but this was radically different to anything that had happened previously. Before he died, Jesus was with them in the flesh, all the time. Even when all sorts of boggling, exciting and challenging things were happening, Jesus was their constant. They knew they could come to him face to face, ask him questions and get answers, even if they didn't understand a lot of the answers.

So, as joyful as they were to know that Jesus wasn't dead, it was still very confusing to know how to proceed. Jesus was alive but where was he? They couldn't just turn around at any given moment and say, "Hey, Jesus. What did you mean when you said...?" They were probably remembering all the times of immediate contact they had enjoyed with Jesus in the past and how they squandered it and took it for granted. Maybe they were reminiscing about laughter in the evenings as they sat around the fire with Jesus or the times when they all walked along the roads between villages, singing the psalms together. What they wouldn't give to go back to those halcyon days of walking day by day at Jesus' side! Now, even though they knew Jesus was alive, there were moments of overwhelming homesickness for the days when things didn't seem so complex and spirituality didn't seem to demand so much faith and courage.

We've all been there. Radical change is a part of life as we move through changes of vocations, jobs and living spaces. We face unknown situations, strange people or unfamiliar cultures or traditions. Children are born, relationships change or perish, loved ones die, responsibilities shift and roles switch. We've all been faced with unsettling and sometimes deeply painful radical change, so we can all totally relate to what Peter decided to do.

Go fishing.

Fishing was what Peter knew. Before Jesus came and called his name, Peter was a fisherman and when he was fishing, he was in control. He knew how to handle the boat, he knew how to deal with the nets and he was at home on the water. So, in his loneliness and confusion, he turned back to the familiar and the known. It probably felt very comforting to be in that boat doing exactly what he knew how to do but after a while something became very apparent. No fish. All night they fished and caught nothing.

In the spiritual walk with Jesus, you can't go back. No matter how uncomfortable the present feels and no matter how murky and confusing the future looks, you can't go back – not if you desire to grow and flourish. Not if the Lord is calling you by Name.

Jesus appeared on the shore and said to them, "Children, you have no fish, have you?" He was so gentle and so loving. He knew how they were grieving for the past and he didn't blame them one bit. He told them to cast their net on the right side of the boat and he filled the net to overflowing, just like he did when he first called them to follow him. It was a gift but also a lesson. "Unless the Lord builds the house, they labor in vain who build it." Unless the Lord sends you fishing, it's probably not going to do much good to look for the old boats to go fishing.

At one time, Jesus filled Peter's nets and then told him that from then on he would be a Fisher of People. Later he told Peter he would be a Rock for his Church. On the shore of the Sea of Tiberias, he told Peter three times to feed his lambs and sheep. He was telling Peter he was a Shepherd. "Unless the Lord builds the house..." Unless the Lord speaks your name –Fisher of People, Rock, Shepherd, Voice in the Wilderness, Warrior, Counselor, Teacher, Breach Mender, Builder, Comforter etc.– your self determined labor will distract you and keep you busy but your nets will be empty. In times of transition you need to learn to wait for the Lord and listen for the Name he calls you by.

We are allowed to grieve for the past for a while; indeed, it is healthy and good to grieve over, love and honor all that has shaped us so far. It is part of the dying and letting go process. But we must not forget that where we are ultimately moving is forward into *new* life and 'new' means 'unknown'. When we read this week's gospel, it is hard to ignore the fact that any change that brings new life involves taking risks. Nobody can deny that completely trusting in God when the unfamiliar threatens to swamp us and overwhelm us is very risky. The risk lies in the fact that when something is new it cannot be easily visualized, controlled or actualized by us. Only the Lord can create what is truly new. What we tend to create is a rehash of what we've always known.

Don't go back.

The Voice

John 10: 27-30

Jesus says that his sheep hear his voice. He knows them and they follow him; they will never perish. What the Father has given him is greater than all else and no one can snatch them out of his hand.

In a previous reflection, I wrote about sheep hearing the shepherd's voice so I'll just remind you of the particular significance of Jesus using this analogy. In Jesus' time, shepherds would bring their flocks to a walled enclosure to keep them safe at night. In any one enclosure there would be several flocks belonging to different shepherds and there was no effort to keep each flock separate from the others. One would think there would be complete chaos in the morning as the shepherds tried to sort out their own sheep from all the others. Not so. Each flock intimately knew the voice of its own shepherd. Each shepherd would simply call the sheep by their names; his sheep would hear his voice and follow him. Sheep are not particularly bright animals so this voice recognition was not due to their high intelligence. It was due to the fact that a shepherd spent so much time with his flock and spoke to each one by name so often that the sheep learned to distinguish his unique voice from other voices.

Jesus said, "My sheep hear my voice. I know them, and they follow me." A shepherd *knew* his sheep. This indicates a shepherd who interacted daily with each individual animal. From the moment a lamb was born, the shepherd became intimately involved with it. He named it and called it by name from then on. He came to know that sheep's character in the same way parents know their own children's natures and proclivities.

In John 10: 3-5 (NRSV), Jesus says, *"He calls his own sheep by name and leads them out. When he has brought out all his own, he goes ahead of them, and the sheep follow him because they know his voice. They will not follow a stranger, but they will run from him because they do not know the voice of strangers."*

It's important to establish how much individual care and attention a shepherd lavished on each of his sheep in order for us to really appreciate what Jesus is saying in this week's Gospel. It's not always easy to hear the passion of Jesus in the Gospels. It often sounds like he's just giving a short religious dissertation because the writers were simply trying to record important events and get the words of Jesus written out so they would not be forgotten. They weren't writing exciting novels full of descriptive prose that could give readers an idea of the depth of Jesus' spiritual determination and his fiery love for his people. But when I read the words, *"No one will snatch them out of my hand,"* I want to add an exclamation point in there. *"No one will snatch them out of my hand! Just let them try. I would die rather than let my sheep be led away by a stranger."* Any parent reading this will understand the intensity of what Jesus is saying. "Don't you touch my child! Don't even think about it!"

And then Jesus says something incredibly wonderful. "What my Father has given me is greater than all else..." *Greater than all else.* What is he referring to? What's greater than all else?

You.

To Christ, you are more precious than anything else in the universe. *Greater than all else*...you are worth more to him than you can imagine.

You all know this. Intellectually you know it because it's the basis of our faith. If he didn't particularly care about you, he wouldn't have gone to the cross for you. But it's difficult sometimes to let that knowledge filter down to the heart level to the degree that you walk in continual love and gratitude that you have such a Shepherd who knows you personally by name. When the knowledge remains head knowledge, it's easy to abandon the relationship little by little. You start to forget that Christ has a voice that you can listen to and come to recognize and wait for with anticipation. You forget that your relationship with Christ is not a relationship between you and some words on a page or between a boss and a slave, but is a relationship between the Lover and the Beloved. When you lose sight of the truth that he is always coming to you and calling you by name, you can become forgetful of his immediate and tender concern for every aspect of your life.

How do you know when you are hearing the voice of your Shepherd? That is, unfortunately, a complex question because we are all vulnerable to many inner and outer voices, which can be hard to sort out and identify. A partial and helpful answer would be to determine some of the things that are *NOT* the voice of the Shepherd:

1. The voice of the Lord does not condemn. If there is something unbalanced or wrong in your attitudes or life directions that he wants you to realize, his voice brings conviction, which is much different than condemnation. Conviction allows you to see what's wrong and gives you the desire, courage and grace to change. Condemnation puts chains around you and keeps you in a mode of anxious self-loathing and shame. (*So now there is no condemnation for those who belong to Christ Jesus. And because you belong to him, the power of the life-giving Spirit has freed you from the power of sin that leads to death.* Romans 8: 1, 2, NLT)

2. The voice of the Lord is not a demanding voice coldly pronouncing, "you should..." His voice is a voice of loving affirmation and animation. It is a voice that inspires action born of love and desire, not guilty action that comes from the pressure of someone constantly nattering, "You should..." Whose voice is that, anyway?? A parent's? A teacher's? A partner's? A priest's that you knew a long time ago? Old voices are so effective at blocking Christ's voice.

3. The voice of the Lord is not impatient. *We* have critical timetables and schedules; God does not. If you're not sure if God is saying something to you or directing you somehow, wait. Wait, pray and stay open to clarification. Very often, it's your own preferences, attitudes and perceptions that cause you to think, "I have to do this RIGHT NOW or all will be lost!!"

4. The voice of the Lord is full of wisdom. This is wisdom that is beyond your natural wisdom based on past experience. The Lord can use your past experiences but very often, those experiences are so tainted by fear, mistrust and wounds that it's not wisdom at all; it is self-protection.

5. The voice of the Lord is quiet. God does not batter his people with noisy clamor. We do that to ourselves. The world and the media do that. If your life is totally filled 24/7 with busyness, chaos, madness and noise, it will be difficult to come to know the sane, quiet but gently authoritative voice of God within. He will not harangue you into obedience. He will not mercilessly drive you to action. In Jesus' time, the Shepherd *led* his sheep. It was the butcher who drove the sheep.

This certainly is not a comprehensive look at what the voice of the Lord is like but it's enough to give a head start in untangling all the broken voices in your head to see if you can find the long strong silver strand that is the Shepherd's living and life giving voice. If Jesus said, *"My sheep know my voice..."* then it is certain that he wants you to discover his unique voice and learn to be able to distinguish it from all the others.

The Shepherd is calling your name right now. But can you hear him?

5th Sunday of Easter C

Original Love

John 13. 1, 31-33, 34-35
After the Passover, Jesus knows his hour is coming and he loves his disciples to the end. After Judas leaves, Jesus says he will be with them only a little while longer. Then he gives them a new commandment to love one another, just as he loves them, for this is how the world will know that they are his disciples.

"Just as I have loved you…"

We give love the way we have experienced love. For most of us, that would mean our parents formed our perceptions of what it means to love. Some had parents who were struggling with their own wounds and failures and didn't show love very well or very consistently. Others had parents who showed love by being permissive and refusing to set boundaries. Some had parents who showed love by being critical and heavy handed. Others had parents who were emotionally healthy but still made their own mistakes in loving just because they were human. In other words, we all have completely inadequate perceptions of what it means to be loved by Christ. It doesn't matter how wonderful one's parents are, or were, human love can never form a complete basis for understanding of Christ's love. Human love will always be inadequate.

Even when there are occasional experiences of wonderful unconditional love from another person, it is generally not quite enough to give anyone a true sense of Christ's love for us, because on a day-to-day basis, we all learn from the time we are infants that we gain approval by how we act. The whole world operates on merit and it's not surprising that we often equate love with the approval we receive for doing good things.

"What an awesome child you are...you ate all your peas!"
"You shared your toy with your friend. That was wonderful."
"You got straight A's this term. I am so proud of you!"
"You are a responsible and effective employee. We're giving you a raise."
"You did a superb job of running that committee. Thank you."

There's nothing wrong with praise and approval from parents, partners, teachers, friends and employers but it does mean that in order to even begin to grasp the kind of love Jesus was talking about in this Gospel, we need to push ourselves beyond all the boundaries of what we've always thought and challenge our ultimate perceptions of what it means to be loved by Christ and to love just as he loves.

So, how did Jesus love his disciples? We could say, "unconditionally," since if there was a way to fail or a wrong thought that could be expressed, those disciples found it. So, it's a logical conclusion to think that unconditional love means loving someone 'in spite of' not 'because of'. That's moving closer but it's still inadequate when trying to comprehend Christ's love. Usually when we attempt to practice unconditional love in any situation, it means that we have first made a judgment as to whether that person is deserving of being loved and then, finding he or she isn't deserving, we decide to love them anyway. That's better than love that's based solely on merit but it's still not Christ's love.

Christ loves us with First Love or Original Love. Christ loved us before there was any such thing as sin and failure. *"Blessed be the God and Father of our Lord Jesus Christ, who has blessed us in Christ with every spiritual blessing in the heavenly places, just as he chose us in Christ before the foundation of the world to be holy and blameless before him in love. He destined us for adoption as his children through Jesus Christ, according to the good pleasure of his will, to the praise of his glorious grace that he freely bestowed on us in the Beloved."* (Ephesians 1: 3-6, NRSV)

He knew you before the foundation of the world. He thought of you and spoke the Word that is you. When you think of yourself, you might think of a few good and positive qualities but very quickly your mind will slide into all those failures, wounds and broken areas of your life. That is most often what you think of when you think, "I am…" You find it difficult to love what you see as yourself and so if you think you are accepting God's unconditional love, it's always an 'in spite of' love that you are accepting. It is so rare for the human mind, heart and spirit to conclude that any of us might be a whole that is far greater, far more wonderful and exceedingly more beautiful than the sum of the parts that we usually focus on. And rarer still is it for us to consider that there may be a 'me' that is unblemished, full of grace, clothed in dignity, bestowed with priestly authority, love and compassion, a 'me' who looks an awful lot like Christ.

Jesus loved those disciples with Ancient Love, or Original Love. He loved those men and women with the same love with which he loved them when he created them and *knew* them before the foundations of the world. It was not 'in spite of' love. It was deep love for the amazing reality of their True Selves – a reality so removed from their self perceptions that they had to stumble, fall and fail terribly in order to be able to finally grasp that, *"… we are God's masterpiece. He has created us anew in Christ Jesus, so we can do the good things he planned for us long ago."* (Ephesians 2:10, NLT)

How, then, can you even begin to love others as Christ has loved you? There is only one way: by seriously and unceasingly searching for who you really are and recognizing that who you have been thinking you are is not you at all; it is a false front built up since you were an infant, a persona (Greek for 'mask') that you built up to protect yourself from danger and wounds but which has rarely protected you at all. This mask is where all your sins, wounds and failures reside. It is False Self. Christ came to earth, did all that he did, died and rose again so that you could be released from False Self, come home to who you really are and fully experience Original Love.

You cannot truly love unless you have experienced true love. Once you have experienced Christ's authentic love, you will fall in love with the creation that is you. It is only then that you will know that everyone else was also created as incredible works of art and you will love others as Christ has loved you and as you love yourself.

This, brothers and sisters, is true redemption – to be brought back to the garden of the self that has been there since before the foundations of the world. Then and only then will you be able to love as Jesus loves.

It's the whole point.

Awakening To True Self

John 14: 23-29
Jesus is speaking to his disciples, explaining that those who love him will keep his word and he and the Father will make their home with them. He says that the Father will send the Holy Spirit who will teach them everything. "Peace I leave with you; my peace I give you, but not as the world gives peace," he says, and tells them not to let their hearts be troubled or afraid.

In the last reflection (Original Love) I mentioned True Self and if anyone pondered upon the reality of True Self and False Self, there may have been some questions about how to find that wonderful True Self that is within. Any questions about True and False Self are pivotal because when Jesus talks about giving us peace that's different from the kind of peace the world gives, True and False Self absolutely come into play.

The world promises peace to False Self and it is from the vantage point of False Self that we are most often looking for peace. It is within False Self that all of our anxieties, anger, wounds, failures, negativism and brokenness reside. But Jesus says he does not give peace as the world gives peace. He does not give peace or promise control to the false fronts or the personae that we have built up over the years or to the ego we constantly deal with. If our hearts and minds are continually hanging out with False Self in all its needs and brokenness, we will find very little peace. There may be the odd moment of peacefulness but usually it doesn't last too long, and then it's back to struggling with all the old struggles – again and again and again.

False Self seeks the approval of others, is easily offended, is proud, is locked into its own opinions, has many fears and anxieties, is self judgmental and critical of others, can't let go of old resentments and has so many desires and insecurities that it scrambles to maintain control, however it can wherever it can. Any threat to its sense of being in control is a huge threat to be eradicated in any way possible. One doesn't need to be a recognized control freak to have the need to be in control. Every anxiety we carry is the fear that someone or something will hurt us and diminish us so we strive to gain some sort of control as a means of self-protection. Even many of our spiritual self-disciplines are rooted in the need for the False Self to get everything under control and we end up with False Self trying to change and control False Self. Now that's one losing battle!

Jesus does not promise peace to the False Self because it's not who we really are. You may recall that after Jesus spoke these words about peace, the disciples did not immediately start walking in this peace. Throughout the crucifixion and the days that followed, right up until Pentecost, they were confused and terrified. Even when they knew Jesus had risen and was alive, they still hunkered down in locked rooms for fear of the Jews. Not a peaceful existence.

Their False Selves were still in full gear. They were afraid, full of guilty self-recrimination and were anxious about an uncertain future. Note that they were totally committed to Jesus and were ecstatic that he was alive, but until the Holy Spirit came to them and revealed their True Selves to them, they were riding the emotional roller coaster of False Self. We are all familiar with the radical change that came over them after Pentecost. These were different men and women. That wounded shell of False Self was broken, leaving them face to face with everything Jesus had always known them to be since before the foundations of the world. They saw their True Selves and there was no holding them back. It was only then that they finally understood the peace that Jesus had been talking about. It was not the peace of physical safety or of total future certainty. It was not the peace of knowing everything was in their control. It was not the peace of being approved of by other people. It was the peace of knowing that who they really were was completely loved and approved of by God. They needed nothing else. They did not need complex inner defense systems. They did not need to have anyone else's respect, admiration or approval. They didn't need insurance plans. They had seen who they were and they had experienced God's complete love for all that they were created to be. It was enough. It was more than enough.

But the question still remains for all of us: how do we become connected to our True Selves when all we can see is the self that's full of anger, anxiety and failure, that self that scrambles to bring everything under control whether it's sinful inclinations, guilt, resentments, irritating people or wounding circumstances that threaten to overwhelm?

It helps tremendously to actually accept and believe you have a True Self, a self that is who God created you to be, a self that is full of dignity, faith and compassion, a self that is separate from that false front you have maintained for so long. This True Self delights in God and is utterly familiar with the fact that God delights in it. This self is still reveling in the affirmation of its full nature at baptism and will continue to revel in it for all of eternity. This self has the authority of a priestly being and exists in order to be blessed by God and then share that blessing with everyone around.

Is there scriptural basis for True and False Self? You bet. Paul often talks about the flesh, another name for False Self. But take a look at this passage from Romans 7:16-20:

"When I act against my own will, that means I have a self that acknowledges that the Law is good and so the thing behaving in that way is not my self but sin living in me. The fact is, I know of nothing good living within me – living, that is, in my unspiritual self – for though the will to do what is good is within me, the performance is not, with the result that instead of doing the good things I want to do, I carry out the sinful things I do not want. When I act against my will, then, it is not my true self doing it but sin which lives within me." (Jerusalem Bible translation)

It might take some faith on your part to visualize that True Self within you but it's not as if you've never experienced your True Self. Every time you've offered real compassion when it would have been easier to turn away, your True Self was active. Every moment of grace where you sensed the bottomless love of God, True Self was stronger than False Self. Every instance where joyful gratitude welled up in your heart, True Self was peering through the chaos like the sun through the clouds. Every time you blessed someone else in word or action and didn't need or expect gratitude, True Self was dancing with God.

It's all very well to recognize the existence of True and False Self but what then? How can this realization lead us to a spiritual journey that's more connected to True Self than to False Self? How can we begin to free our real selves from the dictates of that protective false front that we have lived with since we were infants? Or, as Paul says in Romans 7:24, *"What a wretched person I am! Who will rescue me from this body doomed to death?"*

Thanks be to God through Jesus Christ our Lord we have been given the light of the Holy Spirit and what better time to see how this light can free us from False Self than in the following weeks as we celebrate Christ's ascension and then prepare ourselves for the great feast of Pentecost.

Stay tuned…

True Self and the Wounded Warrior Part I

Luke 24: 46-53

Jesus opens the disciples' minds to understand the scriptures concerning his death and resurrection. Then he instructs them to stay in the city until the Holy Spirit comes to them. He blesses them and while he is doing so, he is carried up to heaven.

Then what if you were to see the Son of Man ascending to where he was before? It is the spirit that gives life; the flesh is useless. The words that I have spoken to you are spirit and life. (John 6: 62, 63, NRSV)

I included the above passage of scripture from the Gospel of John because it clarifies something about the wondrous significance of the Ascension. Before Christ could send the Holy Spirit, he had to ascend to God to re-assume his place as the Lord of all and the *all in all*. Up until the moment the Holy Spirit descended on the disciples after the Ascension, Jesus had been teaching limited minds. *"Then he opened their minds to understand the scriptures..."* For three years his followers had listened to his words, receiving them through the lenses of their flesh and limited understanding, and Jesus was fine with that even though they had a very difficult time knowing exactly what it was he was talking about. He was building a foundation within them for the future.

What he really loved about them was not their intellectual grasp but their devotion to him and their willingness to stay with him even though his words didn't always make sense. All along he could see what they couldn't even begin to conceive; he could see their True Selves and he could see them receiving the gift of his own awesome, all pervading Spirit at Pentecost. He knew that when that happened they would 'get it'. They would comprehend who they really were on levels higher and deeper than what their flesh and finite minds could ever begin to comprehend.

"It is the spirit that gives life; the flesh is useless." Flesh: False Self, Ego. Maybe a better term that doesn't have such negative connotations is "Wounded Warrior". For most people, the Wounded Warrior is less this selfish controlling monster than it is an entity that has tried from birth to protect one from wounds and keep one safe. Wounded Warrior has tried to be strong and protective but it is absolutely and utterly useless when it comes to living out the fullness of the spiritual life. Yet it is what is most often turned to, listened to and heeded when it comes to trying to live the spiritual life.

Even very spiritually oriented people, people who desire with all their hearts to live lives pleasing to God, are often unknowingly caught up in the Wounded Warrior's interpretation of how best to achieve that life. There can be this great desire to clean up one's faults and be the kind of Christian one feels one should be but Wounded Warrior is still ends up in charge.

Wounded Warrior sees those faults. Your Wounded Warrior, in its need to be in full control, acts out the roles of accuser, arresting officer, jury, judge and jailer. It feels that if it judges itself, sentences itself and carries out the discipline it has decided upon, it will be safe. Your Wounded Warrior hopes God will see that it is trying to be in control of all the sin and brokenness and he will be pleased.

So...how's that working out for you?   *Not!*

Not well, I would guess. However, the voice of the ego's Wounded Warrior is a loud and insistent one and it has been voraciously active all your life. It's the product of original sin. I have a theory that the Tree of the Knowledge of Good and Evil in the garden of Eden with its forbidden fruit, could have been called "The Ego Tree'. And we have become completely used to living with our Wounded Warriors. Life with it seems normal and true.

A friend of mine wrote this to me: "All too often I listen to voices of guilt or condemnation without even asking "Is this my Shepherd's voice?" Seems like a no brainer but the more I listen to such a "voice" the more it becomes familiar and the less I even question it - almost as though I've given it authority."

Would you recognize your True Self if it stood in front of you and smiled compassionately at you? Maybe not, unless you have become very comfortable with the idea of a separate and whole True Self. The thing is, the Wounded Warrior is completely convinced it *is* the true self – the total reality of who you are.

Jesus said, "The flesh is useless. It is the Spirit that gives life."

Through baptism your True Self is deeply connected with the Spirit. It just is. Your True Self is a gift that is always within you and will never be taken away, but neither will it ever intrude upon you. Just like everything in the authentic spiritual life, seeking True Self is a risk because it means not believing everything the Wounded Warrior tells you about yourself. Tell me honestly – does it not feel safer and less risky to believe what Wounded Warrior tells you about all your faults and sins (the knowledge of good and evil?) than to believe that there is a self within you that looks like Jesus, a self that sees the best, is compassionate, full of love, pure, dignified in its inherent authority, knows it is deeply approved of and is delighted in its own reality because it's a reality created by God? Does that sound almost 'new agey'?

The eternal Father said, "And if anyone should ask me what this soul is, I would say: She is another me, made so by the union of love."

Does that sound a little like a new age perspective? It's from St. Catherine of Sienna, a doctor of the Church.

Let see what else she said:

"God was made human and human was made God."

"The soul is in God and God in the soul, just as the fish is in the sea and the sea in the fish."

"We've been deceived by the thought that we would be more pleasing to God in our own way than in the way God has given us."

Perhaps St. Francis might convince you.

"We are all in mourning for the experience of our essence we knew and now miss. Light is the cure, all else a placebo. Yes, I will console any creature before me that is not laughing or full of passion for their art or life; for laughing and passion— beauty and joy—is our heart's truth, all else is labor and foreign to the soul." (Our Need For Thee. St. Francis of Assisi.)

St. Francis seems to imply that somewhere in our eternal history we knew our True Selves. *"...our essence we knew and now miss."* Ancient and modern mystics are ones who have met their True Selves. That's what gives them the capacity to be all that they are. Their actions, devotions and convictions flow out of knowing the real truth about themselves and knowing God through that truth. Not the other way around.

As familiar as we are with our Wounded Warrior's ways and perceptions, listening to it is "labor and foreign to the soul".

Wouldn't you rather be at home?

I try to write only a certain amount in each reflection because if it gets too long, people find it hard to take the time to read and take it all in. The next reflection is Part II of this Sunday's Gospel.

It's that important.

True Self And The Wounded Warrior Part II

(The following is the second part of a two-part reflection for ascension. If you have not yet read "True Self and the Wounded Warrior Part I", go to the previous reflection.)

True Self is full of love, joy, peace, patience, generosity, faithfulness, gentleness and goodness. True Self is patient and kind; it is not envious, boastful, arrogant or rude. It does not insist on its own way; it is not irritable or resentful; it does not rejoice in wrongdoing, but rejoices in the truth. It bears all things, believes all things, hopes all things and endures all things. True Self's entire focus centers on whatever is true, honorable, just, pure, pleasing and commendable and if there is any excellence and if there is anything worthy of praise, these are the things True Self thinks about. (A paraphrased composite of Galatians 5:22, 1 Corinthians 13:4+ and Philippians 4:8)

The above is a partial description of the True Self who dwells within you, apart, separate and undefiled by controlling Wounded Warrior. It is the part of you that was baptized in Christ, buried and resurrected with Christ, clothed in Christ and filled with the gift of Christ's Holy Spirit. It is the Pearl of Great Price, the Lost Coin and the Treasure in the Field. It is worth everything you have to believe in it and find it because it shares in the very nature of Christ.

In contrast, the Wounded Warrior, which endeavors to keep everything under its own control, is composed of limited love, despondencies, anxieties, impatience, selfishness, controlling tendencies, anger and sometimes hurtful actions and reactions. It has the capacity to be cutting instead of kind, is a little envious when others succeed where it has not and protects itself from its own perceived diminishment by pulling others down publicly or privately. It often insists its way is the only way and when it doesn't get its own way it becomes irritated, angry, resentful and sometimes very anxious. There are times when it is rejoices to see all that's wrong and once it has perceived something wrong, it doesn't try very hard to find truth, goodness or the commendable and excellent. It's pretty happy to pay attention to just the shortcomings. It may seem committed to service but needs others to appreciate that service.

The Wounded Warrior will bear things for a short while but then it becomes frustrated. It tries so hard to believe in the power of Christ but its eyes are always being pulled over to the negative, the bad, the ugly and the offensive. Its hope is always being eroded by thoughts of the past and future. Staying in the Present moment feels like being out of control. Wounded Warrior feels it has more control if it is rehashing the past and casting fishing lines into the future.

Wounded Warrior focuses more naturally on what it thinks is false, dishonorable, untrue and unjust, especially if it perceives these things in other individuals, groups or situations. It thrives on the 'us against them' mentality because it feels better when it thinks it's right.

In spite of all its self-protective mechanisms, it has been terribly wounded by life, others, and itself. These wounds are very real and often deep, and that's why the Warrior has so many defense mechanisms. It is trying to protect the wounds. When it feels challenged or diminished by anything or anyone, it fights desperately to keep itself from further diminishment and pain. The Warrior is so convinced it is totally right in whatever it perceives that it refuses to let go, because that feels like further diminishment and further loss of control.

Everyone is familiar with the story of Jesus visiting Martha and Mary. Martha is very busy doing what she thinks is her duty and Mary is sitting at Jesus' feet. Martha tells Jesus to make Mary get up and help her but Jesus says to Martha that she is distracted by many things, and that Mary has chosen the better part. (Luke 10: 38-42)

Wounded Warrior is a Martha. True Self is a Mary. Martha had Jesus right there with her – she welcomed him in - and it was her intention to serve him but in her need to do all the right things, follow all the traditions and have everything go the way she thought it all needed to go, she could not be present to who he really was. Instead, all she could see was what she thought was her duty and when it didn't seem that her agenda was rolling along smoothly, she projected her resentment onto her sister and blamed her. She probably secretly resented Jesus for seemingly not seeing that she was struggling and burdened.

Martha was very similar to most of us in that she treated Jesus as an honored guest but felt her performance, as a servant, was the true reflection of her value and worth. Mary simply saw Jesus as a Beloved, someone she wanted to be close to and spend time with. She wanted to soak in his whole nature and drink in his words. While Martha was finding her identity in traditional rules and roles, as well as in her own performance, Mary was finding her fulfillment at the feet of Jesus. It's a distinction we must pay attention to when building an awareness of the Wounded Warrior identity.

Note that Jesus did not attempt to soothe and heal Martha in her role of being a Wounded Warrior. Instead he invited her to leave that place and come to the same place Mary was sitting.

I have given you relatively in-depth (but still partial) descriptions of the characteristics of True Self and of the Wounded Warrior because next week I am going to describe to you a 'way' to begin to let the Warrior rest and to allow True Self to become more and more operative in your life. In this Way, awareness and recognition is crucial.

So, for the next while, see if you can be aware of when the Wounded Warrior is rising up in self-protective mode. That's all – just try to recognize it. *Do not try to deal with it or castigate yourself when you see it.* Don't ridicule it or judge it. This is very important! Just recognize it and say, "There is my Wounded Warrior in action." If you want, you can endeavor to recognize what the Warrior is trying to protect, but that's all. This is simply an exercise of recognition and awareness, not a self-recrimination exercise. When self-condemnation kicks in, that's actually the Wounded Warrior taking over and saying, "I've got to get this under control." It doesn't work. Never has. Never will. Try to be aware that the Warrior is not who you really are and is not who God sees.

This is *not* an exercise of ignoring your sins and failures or saying they are not real. This is a journey of discovering their source as well as discovering the real source of spiritual life and power within you.

"The flesh is useless. It is the Spirit that gives life."

We've believed in the authority of the Wounded Warrior for far too long.

It's time for a change of administration.

The Awareness Choice

John 14: 15-26 (Alternative Gospel for this Sunday)
Jesus says to the disciples that if they love him they will keep his commandments. He will ask the Father to send the Holy Spirit to them. Then he says that those who love him will keep his word and the Father will love them and both he and the Father will come to make their home with them.

Jesus often spoke to the people using parables and images because it made it easier for people to envision what he was talking about. So now, to open to you a way to allow the Wounded Warrior to fall away little by little while True Self becomes stronger and more apparent, I am going to invite you to use your imagination to visualize an inner landscape where the Holy Spirit dwells.

Imagine that within you is a high Tower. This Tower is not a heavily guarded and fortified Tower but, rather, a Tower of beauty and light. At the top of this Tower is a dwelling place, open and spacious. From this place it is easy to view the surrounding countryside where there is a flowing river, grass, trees and plants in lush abundance and off in the distance, the ocean and mountains – whatever natural surroundings speak to your heart. This vista, when viewed from the Tower, offers a sense of peace and life. One can breathe in the Tower.

In this Tower dwell four Beings in loving community. Three of them are the Holy Trinity. The fourth is your True Self. The Tower is warm with the joy of the relationship that the four of them delight in. True Self is smaller than the other three but it is obviously an offspring of the Trinity. The resemblance of True

Self to the other three is remarkable and the Trinity interacts with True Self as a welcome and beloved member of the family.

Looking out of the Tower, one can see an area in the not too far distance that mars the landscape. From the Tower it looks like a battlefield. The earth is pockmarked, scorched and dry. Plants have been trampled and trees uprooted. Around the perimeter of the area are rolls of barbed wire and in the middle of the compound one can see a weary and lonely figure surrounded by implements of war and struggle. It is the Wounded Warrior.

In all of this there is another entity that I will call Awareness. The Wounded Warrior never visits the Tower but Awareness does. It doesn't get there often as it would like but whenever it does it is amazed at the quality of the Light and it revels in the peace it discovers. However, very soon it sees and hears the Warrior rising up to do battle with another challenger, and it immediately heads back to the compound. The life it found within the Tower becomes a hazy memory and it forgets how to get there. The Warrior convinces Awareness that the Warrior is the True Self, that the battles it engages in are crucial and that the battles are the only way to make itself worthy enough to gain access to the Tower. So Awareness stays with the Warrior, longing for the day when it will be free and good enough to once again access the peace of the Tower.

I have set the scene of a landscape that we all share. We all long to dwell in the Tower but the battles of the Warrior consume us and pull us away and, as a people, we have lost the understanding that the Warrior can *never* win the war. The Warrior can never open the way to the Tower; it will simply continue to fight and defend, as well as be a provocateur. If there is no battle it will often create one.

How can Awareness become free of the Warrior?

It is simple. But it isn't easy. It's through choosing to believe that the Tower is its rightful dwelling place, that access to the Tower is free and open, and through finding the courage to believe that the True Self is fully alive and fully formed within that Tower. It is through choosing True Self over the Wounded Warrior.

No, it's not easy. The Warrior is one strong being – a bit of a giant in its own right – and walking away from it is not effortless because, for some reason, we would all rather fight battles than dwell in peace. We are more comfortable living with negativity than freedom. Awareness needs to get to that Tower and make continual choices to stay there even when there are battles and skirmishes on the front lines. It needs to stay there long enough to experience the power that the Tower dwellers can have in diminishing the Warrior's false sense of its own importance, as well as experience the Trinitarian power to heal the sources of the Warrior's battles. If Awareness does not experience these things, it won't be able to withstand the Warrior's frequent and strident calls to battle. Awareness needs to stay in the Tower under the protection of True Self and the Trinity, in order for them to deal with the Warrior.

So, imagine yourself in the Tower as your True Self. You are there in all your priestly authority and compassion. You are a Being fully in love with the Trinity, fully loved by them and you are there as one who has found everything you have ever wanted. You bask in Trinitarian love and wisdom and your Awareness knows True Self is deeply connected to all that the Trinity is and does.

Suddenly a battle cry goes up from the compound of the Warrior. There is a threat or a challenge to the Warrior and your Awareness wants to rush to the battle. But this time you resist. It's very difficult but you withstand the pressure to go out and fight. Instead you stay with your True Self in the Tower with the

Holy Spirit by your side and all of you watch the Warrior. All you do is observe it closely. The Tower is, in fact, an Observation Post. As you observe, True Self might speak to the Holy Spirit about what it is seeing and perceiving.

"The Warrior is angry because it feels threatened and is anxious that it will be overcome and diminished. It is scared it will lose again. It is scared that its needs will be pushed aside for what someone else wants. It is scared that if it lets go of the battle something worse will happen or it will be blamed or it will not have enough. It fears censure and ridicule. It fears God's disapproval. It fears further loss. It fears that if it stands down someone or something else will gain control."

True Self and the Awareness of True Self do not condone the Warrior's battles but neither do they judge or condemn them. Neither does the Holy Spirit. Together they simply observe the Warrior with compassion. They recognize the futility of the battle but there is no derision for they also recognize that the Warrior thinks it is defending the Tower – a Tower that needs no defense because it is home of all the power, light and life that the Spirit brings.

As they all observe the Warrior with love and compassion, something amazing begins to happen. It's as if the love and compassion become a ray of light and that ray of light shines directly on the Warrior. The Warrior feels the light more than sees it and it hesitates. It goes to continue the battle but something doesn't feel right anymore. The more the light shines on it, the more the Warrior begins to feel that the battle isn't quite as important as it thought it was.

In the Tower, the more Awareness stays with True Self and the Spirit, observing and having compassion on the Warrior, the more Awareness and True Self merge into one and Awareness begins to be acutely conscious of the presence of the Holy Spirit and the Father and Son in the Tower. The Warrior's battle becomes less and less of an issue and the joy and peace of the Trinity starts to flood through the Awareness of True Self.

Sounds too easy, doesn't it? Well, again I need to emphasize that the difficulty comes in the choice to go to the Tower and stay there. It's a choice that will have to be made time after time, moment by moment, day after day. After all, Awareness has lived for a long time with the Wounded Warrior and is used to living on the battleground. The battleground feels normal and often it feels absolutely right. New habits have to be developed through belief and choice: believing that the True Self exists and choosing to go to the Tower and stay there, choosing to observe with the light rather than fight with the Warrior.

At first it will be very difficult to keep choosing to go back to the Tower, especially if a battle flares up before one is even aware a battle was coming. It's not an easy task to leave the Warrior when it's in full rage. Don't be discouraged. Leave and go to the Tower whenever you can. The more you practice observation and experience the power within the Tower, the easier it will become to make the choice to go. You will also become aware that the power that dwells in the Tower is an extensive power. Many have experienced changes in their circumstances just by dwelling in the Tower as True Self and observing the Warrior. But those kinds of changes are up to the Wisdom of God and True Self is content to trust in whatever the Trinity wants to do.

Please be aware that if, while you're in the Tower, you find yourself kicking yourself or condemning yourself for the antics of the Warrior or feel as though you should wrestle Warrior to the ground to get it under control, you have actually left True Self and gone back to the Warrior. The Warrior is back in control. With the Warrior it's always about control and making things right no matter what. With the True Self, it's always about staying with the Lord, fully trusting in him in the present moment.

The next reflection continues on this theme.

Meanwhile, let's see what a couple of Saints and the scriptures say about all this:

We are all in mourning for the experience of our essence we knew and now miss. *Light is the cure, all else a placebo.* (St. Francis)

"A single sunbeam is enough to drive away many shadows." (St. Francis)

"Be who God meant you to be and you will set the world on fire." (St. Catherine of Siena)

"Love transforms one into what one loves." (Catherine of Siena)

"Live as children of light— for the fruit of the light is found in all that is good and right and true. Try to find out what is pleasing to the Lord. Take no part in the unfruitful works of darkness, but instead expose them. For it is shameful even to mention what such people do secretly; but *everything exposed by the light becomes visible, for everything that becomes visible is light.* (Ephesians 5: 9-14 ESV)

I pray that, according to the riches of his glory, he may grant that you may be strengthened in your inner being with *power through his Spirit*, and that Christ may dwell in your hearts through faith, as you are being rooted and grounded in love. (Ephesians 3: 16,17, NRSV)

You were taught to put away your former way of life, your old self, corrupt and deluded by its lusts, and to be renewed in the spirit of your minds, and to *clothe yourselves with the new self, created according to the likeness of God in true righteousness and holiness.* (Ephesians 4: 22-24, NRSV)

For I delight in the law of God in my inmost self, but I see in my members another law at war with the law of my mind, making me captive to the law of sin that dwells in my members. Wretched man that I am! Who will rescue me from this body of death? Thanks be to God *through Jesus Christ our Lord*! (Romans 7: 22-24, NRSV)

But if it is by grace, it is no longer on the basis of works (battles?); otherwise grace would no longer be grace. (Romans 11:6, NRSV)

Remain in me, and I will remain in you. For a branch cannot produce fruit if it is severed from the vine, and *you cannot be fruitful unless you remain in me.*
(John 15: 4,5, NLT)

Did you receive the Spirit by doing the works of the law – or by believing what you heard? Are you so foolish? *Having started with the Spirit, are you now ending with the flesh*? Did you experience so much for nothing?—if it really was for nothing. Well then, does God supply you with the Spirit and work miracles among you by your doing the works of the law, or by your believing what you heard? (Galatians 3:2-5, NRSV)

The Unbearable Trinity

John 16: 12-15

Jesus says he has more to say to the disciples but they cannot bear it now. When the Spirit comes, he will lead them into all truth and speak what he hears. All the Father has is Christ's so whatever the Spirit declares is Christ's word.

The following is an excerpt from the prayer "Eternal Trinity, Deep Mystery" by St. Catherine of Siena, Doctor of the Church:

O Eternal Trinity, I have tasted and seen the depth of your mystery and the beauty of your creation with the light of my understanding. I have clothed myself with your likeness and have seen what I shall be. Eternal Father, you have given me a share in your power and the wisdom that Christ claims as his own, and your Holy Spirit has given me the desire to love you. You are my Creator, eternal Trinity, and I am your creature. You have made of me a new creation in the blood of your Son, and I know that you are moved with love at the beauty of your creation, for you have enlightened me.

Wherever the Trinity is, there is spaciousness and graciousness. The Trinity is far bigger on the inside than it appears on the outside and should you ever enter into the 'tower' where True Self dwells with the Trinity, you will begin to discover light and life that the Wounded Warrior would find unbearable.

Why unbearable? What could Jesus have said to his Disciples that they would not have been able to bear before the Spirit came to them to lead them to their real and true selves, and to open a door revealing (declaring) all that belongs to the Father and the Son? Jesus didn't say, "I still have many things to say to you, but you cannot *understand* them now." He said, "...but you cannot *bear* it now."

When we live with the Wounded Warrior we have little capacity to bear the reality of the light inside the circle of the Trinity, because the Warrior is self-oriented, self-defined and self-circling, even though in its spiritual quest it tries to be otherwise. However, no matter how hard it tries, everything comes back to its Self and the question of how it is succeeding or failing. Even the disciples, who lived with Jesus for three years, needed the Holy Spirit to break through the defensive walls of their flesh and create within each of them the capacity to see a circle of light much larger and more powerful than they could ever have imagined. Without the Spirit, they would have shut down in the face of it.

Can anything be too big, too free, too delightful, too powerful, too abundant or too loving for us to be able to bear? Absolutely. The inside of the Trinity will always be too much for us to bear if our image of God is a dark reflection of our own insecurities, fears, self-doubts and our ineffable need to be right. Not only do we always want to be right when we are challenged by other people but we are continually scrambling to make sure we are right with God and that we have the right beliefs, the right faith, the right prayer system, the right directions, the right track, a right mind...

All these things have to do with the Warrior's security system and very little to do with life inside the Trinity. For us, being right means being safe and safe is good, even if it means living in cramped and dark quarters. If we 'get it right' then nobody can blame us for whatever, especially and hopefully not God. Meanwhile, the Trinity constantly invites us to live in the light of a relationship where rejoicing is the first language and 'blame' is a word from an ancient dead language.

In the second reading for this Sunday, Paul says, *"Since we are justified by faith, we have peace with God through our Lord Jesus Christ, through whom we have obtained access to this grace in which we stand..."*

Have you ever noticed that the Wounded Warrior, the false self, never ever feels spiritually justified? So, then it concludes that its faith is faulty. It determines that when it doesn't feel at peace with God or with itself (which is most of the time), it's because it hasn't done all the right things.

True Self, at home with the Trinity, has let go of the need to be right and righteous. It knows that in itself it has absolutely no capacity to form itself into something that deserves the unbearable freedom of the Trinity. It knows that the only thing left to do is rejoice in the Resurrection that opened the portals of the Kingdom to all who desire to walk through. True Self allows itself to be soaked by the Spirit's anointing so that it can bear all that Trinitarian love which, to the Warrior, is unbearable and unimaginable. It is unbearable to the Warrior because to fully receive it means letting go and losing control. It is unimaginable because letting go and losing control of everything it thinks is 'right' is frightening.

In the last reflection I spoke of being with your True Self and allowing the Trinitarian light to shine on the Warrior by recognizing and observing, through and with the Trinity, the Warrior's struggles and challenges. This is truly "dying to self" for it always feels like death and crucifixion to choose to leave the Warrior and seek out the dwelling place of True Self. Even when one has experienced the peace and healing that comes from allowing the Trinity to shine its compassionate light on the Warrior, it is still difficult to stay in the Tower and allow the Warrior to be diminished by the light. We are all addicted to our Warriors' needs, perceptions, battles and control systems and once we allow ourselves to go back to the war zone, we forget who we really are. We forget that we have a choice. We forget that God's Truth, in the person of Christ, came through the power of the Spirit to set us free. We forget that the Warrior can *never* gain us that freedom. We forget the reality of True Self and we settle back into a life of aching and yearning for more than we have while strenuously defending the little we think we have.

I am always amazed at how difficult I can find it to make the simple decision to move to the Tower and stay with my True Self and stay within the gentle, compassionate wideness of the Trinity. I am amazed at how easily I slip back to the Warrior's compound at the first sign of trouble in order to join the battle and add to the wounds and scars of my own self-rightness.

Is this not the original sin, the original and ongoing struggle, the original challenge and brokenness in us all? While the Trinity invites us to live and flourish within the warmth its freedom and love...

...we prefer to stay on the outside and shiver in the cold.

The Grace of Weakness

Luke 9: 11-17
The feeding of the Five thousand.

"Most assuredly, I say to you, unless a grain of wheat falls into the ground and dies, it remains alone; but if it dies, it produces much grain." (John 12:24, NKJV)

And He said to me, "My grace is sufficient for you, for my strength is made perfect in weakness." Therefore most gladly I will rather boast in my infirmities, that the power of Christ may rest upon me. Therefore I take pleasure in infirmities, in reproaches, in needs, in persecutions, in distresses, for Christ's sake. For when I am weak, then I am strong. (2 Corinthians 12: 9-11, NKJV)

For God's foolishness is wiser than human wisdom, and God's weakness is stronger than human strength. (1 Corinthians 1:25, NRSV)

This foolish plan of God is wiser than the wisest of human plans, and God's weakness is stronger than the greatest of human strength. (1 Corinthians 1:27 NLT)

"Do you know, daughter, who you are and who I am? If you know these two things you will have beatitude within your grasp. You are she who is not, and I AM HE WHO IS." (The Lord speaking to St. Catherine of Siena)

God always takes what is small, weak, empty and foolish and transforms it into a receptacle of his greatness, strength, abundance and wisdom. This was a consistent principle in Christ's life whether he was choosing disciples, changing water to wine, taking a few fish and some loaves of bread to feed a multitude or anointing the humble elements of bread and wine to contain his whole substance and being.

The most radical choice he made to transform what was weak in order to display his power was his choice to become a human being, subjecting himself to the inherent weaknesses of that state, including death, which is often experienced violently in this world. When he was resurrected and awesomely transformed, he went from being *a* body with blood to being *The* Body and Blood – the life source and resurrection power for the whole world.

The Warrior cannot get this. Oh, it definitely tries to grasp it but it struggles mightily with the whole concept of being weak in order to be strong. Its intellectual belief in this principle may be firm but the whole concept is one of anguish. It cries out, "I am weak! Help me Lord!" only to feel like it's calling out to an empty universe. It asks, "Lord, how weak do I have to become before you will step in with resurrection power? How can I make myself any weaker?" It doesn't realize that the very question it is asking indicates that it hasn't grasped the true essence of weakness at all.

To the Warrior, weakness means the point it comes to when it has already tried everything in its power to change a situation, itself or another person. It has tried every prayer, every change of attitude it can muster and every method that promises relief. To the Warrior, weakness is the failure of its own strength. If God does come to it in this "last resort weakness" (and he often does because of his compassion), the Warrior easily forgets how inept its own strength is to resolve anything and it fairly quickly returns to its own strength and control systems.

But the weakness the scripture speaks of is beyond the Warrior. It's beyond the Warrior's capability because the weakness that

God values is a state where there has been a revelation that the old wineskin is too small to be able to hold the new life being sought. It is a state completely open to transformation.

Transform: to go to the other side of a visible shape or configuration of something. The real transformation of people in the Gospel came when they realized the absolute uselessness of the Warrior to get them across the divide. Like Peter, what they ultimately grasped was that their inner Warrior's strength was futile and more likely to take them further away from Christ than closer to him. Because the Warrior can't even conceive of a life of real weakness, it ends up using its own strength to make Christ into its own image rather than being transformed into the image of Christ.

What the Warrior works with is untransformed strength. Just as bread and wine in their natural states have no transforming power, our Warriors' natural strengths cannot change us from one shape to another. Our Warriors cannot reconfigure our inner beings. Only when Christ is the substance of power does transformation become available but when the Warrior's faulty and static strength is filling the cup, there is no room for Christ's dynamic strength. Only those who embrace their own weakness with joy will be able to fully experience it.

Embracing your weakness means reveling in it. It means rejoicing in being "he or she who is not" so that Christ can be the "I AM WHO IS". Weakness is not simply coming to the end of your rope. Weakness is a full recognition that there is *nothing* one can do on one's own to attain transformation – even before there's a rope to come to the end of. In fact, as long as a person receives the Eucharist with the mistaken idea that the body and blood of Christ will make self stronger, there will be no transformation. It never was intended build anyone's self-strength. It was intended to be the source of resurrection power for the lonely grain of wheat that falls to the ground and dies.

Remember the Pharisee and the publican? The Pharisee was full of his own Warrior strength and righteousness. He was not open to the transformative power of God; all he wanted was justification and maybe a little gratitude from God. He felt his cup was already full. The publican was the one who went home justified. He wasn't justified because of his words but because he didn't try to be any more than what he was: weak. He was empty and ready to be resurrected and transformed.

The True Self gets this. True Self doesn't need to be strong. It doesn't strive for approval and self-justification because it lives in communion with Christ. It feasts on the transformative power of the resurrected Body and is infused with divine Blood.

What a life!

10th Sunday Ordinary C

The Resurrection Man

Luke 7: 11-17
Jesus raises the dead son of the widow of Nain.

I have been intrigued with resurrection lately. Whenever I look at the world of nature, it feels like God is whispering, "I am the Resurrection." Everywhere in the natural realm of life, something is always dying, dead or being resurrected.

"Unless a grain of wheat falls to the ground and dies it remains a single grain."

To us, the prospect of dying is scary and the idea of the death of our physical bodies is frightening. It is the ultimate sign that we are not in control. We may do everything in our power to stave off dying and death, but in the end we have no control over the inevitable. Dying, death and resurrection are the rhythm of the universe and they are in our genetic code.

This process is pure gift. If God engineered the whole world to move through this life rhythm over and over from the beginning, there must be something phenomenally God-like about it. To God, death is not failure and death is not even the end, as we perceive the end to be. Death is a transformative state; it is a necessary bridge to resurrection and to life that is more abundant than it was before.

Our spiritual lives also encompass this natural and super natural rhythm of life. At any given point you are either dying, dead or rising again. You can't avoid it. But you can prolong the dying part. Though we all agree theoretically with the idea that we are called to die to the False Self in the spiritual life, we generally resist that dying process, because when it happens and situations are out of our Wounded Warrior's control, it feels more like failure. When we are ill, temporarily or chronically, when relationships crumble, when our children make unhealthy choices, when we are deeply disappointed because our plans don't work out, when life spins out of our hands, we resist the dying. It feels more like something is faulty or we are guilty of gross inadequacy than it feels like clean spiritual dying.

While I was writing this reflection a friend of mine sent me this quote: "When God shuts one door, he opens another – but sometimes it is hell in the hallway!" It is absolutely true. Sometimes spiritual dying and death feel like hell in the hallway.

To Christ, death, whether it's physical or spiritual, is not the end of the world or the end of anything. It is the beginning. It is not a process that is outside of him. He is the dying. He is the death. And he is the Resurrection! In his incarnation he completely embraced the whole rhythm of life to death to life and infused it with his own body and blood. He is not only the Master of the process; he *is* the process. To live in Christ is to be continually soaked in the process of dying and rising again.

In the Gospel, it was on the mother that Jesus had pity – not the dead son. Death is not failure. In fact, the son may have been a little upset to be brought back to life. He had been on his way to major transformation but Jesus beheld the widow, took pity on her and said to the son, "Not yet. I know you'd love to go but I'm calling you back for a little while." Then he resurrected the son. Even before Jesus died on the cross and rose again, he was the Resurrection. The whole world existed within him and was dependent on the rhythmic heartbeat of his love. In Christ, dying is transformation. There is no other way to get to the Resurrection.

You go to Mass and you partake in the Eucharist. Among other things, your reception of the Body and Blood is an "Amen!" to being absorbed into the dying, death and resurrection process of your life and the life of the whole world. You are not just ingesting the Body and Blood in the way you put gas in your car. You are saying, "My Lord...Yes!" to being one with the universal mystery of dying, death and resurrection. To the world, dying and loss is failure but Christ came to show that dying and loss is part of a full abundant life. He saved us from the sting of dying and loss by showing us that he *is* the Resurrection. In his lifeblood, no pain is useless and no loss represents failure. It is all his Body and Blood.

The Word breathes into the universe, "I am the Resurrection."

We must breathe with him.

The Nonsense of God

Luke 7: 36 - 8:3

A Pharisee invites Jesus to dine with him. While there, a woman who is recognized as a sinner, comes and bathes his feet in her tears, then anoints them with oil and kisses. The Pharisee thinks that if Jesus were a prophet he would know the woman is a sinner. Jesus asks the Pharisee a question: if a creditor forgave one man a debt of five hundred denarii and another of fifty denarii, which of the debtors would be more grateful? The Pharisee answers that it would be the one who owed more. Jesus points out that the Pharisee didn't give Jesus any water for his feet but the woman bathed his feet with her tears and he says that her sins, which are many, are forgiven.

One of the biggest challenges in the spiritual life is that God is not like us and we are continually trying to define him and form relationships with him based on common sense. So many times in your life you have heard, "Well, it's just common sense," or "Use your common sense." Common sense is an understanding held by the majority of people and in many areas, common sense just makes...sense. The place where common sense often breaks down is in the spiritual life. In understanding the Lord, what we need to rely on is uncommon sense and quite often nonsense.

Let's look at some of the world's common sense. As a child, you learned that when you were polite, didn't fight with your siblings, ate all your food and kept your room tidy, Mom and Dad were pleased with you. At school you learned that if you studied hard, did your homework and handed in assignments on time, the teacher was pleased with you and your parents as well as the teacher were even happier when you made high grades. In life in general, you learned that you should keep the speed limit, not steal, pay your bills, be honest and not hurt anyone. All this is common sense or what our society has deemed to be acceptable behavior necessary for a healthy society and the common sense is usually right.

Common sense in the spiritual life is good too, up to a point. Common sense helps individuals and communities, whether it's families, parishes or the whole church, function in an orderly way. The place where common sense breaks down is when we attempt to fit God into our common sense about love. When it comes to his love, he's all nonsense. He doesn't fit the mold. We are challenged to leave behind all common sense – otherwise we'll never fully grasp how loved we are.

It's very easy to miss a key word in this week's Gospel. It's in verse 47 where Jesus says, *"Therefore, I tell you, her sins, which were many, have been forgiven; hence she has shown great love."* The word that makes all the difference is "hence" or, in modern language, "therefore".

This woman is weeping, her tears anointing Jesus' feet as she pours expensive ointment on them. This woman has come *knowing already that she has been forgiven her many sins*. Jesus said that her sins, which were many, "have been forgiven" not "will be forgiven". How did she know that? Well, it wasn't through common sense, that's for sure. Common sense would have told her to stay away from that house. Common sense would have told her that as a sinful woman, most likely a prostitute, she was worthy of being stoned or, at the very least, judged, scorned and thrown out. That was the religious common sense of the Jewish society in those days. We don't know if she entered that house in fear and trembling, knowing the kind of reception common sense almost guaranteed she would receive from the Pharisee. However, something had penetrated common sense. It was the nonsense of God. She came in knowing that

Jesus had forgiven her. She came with the uncommon sense that she was a beautiful beloved child of God. She came in love, knowing she was loved and that Jesus was the full manifestation of the nonsense of God.

Common sense would have us read that sentence as *"her many sins have been forgiven **because** she has shown great love"*. There is a very subtle difference but it's one that keeps us from the nonsense of God. We interpret it to mean that Jesus pronounced her sins forgiven *because* she had come in and anointed his feet with tears and ointment. This makes sense to us because of all our natural common sense. If I am good to Jesus, he will forgive my sins and love me. Certainly, we are called to express awareness of and repentance for our sins but in this gospel, the woman had already come face to face with her own weakness and had already encountered the forgiveness of God. She was ministering to Jesus in pure love. It wasn't because she wanted to earn his love but because she could not keep her gratitude 'sensible'.

The nonsense of God is that we are completely and utterly loved even though everything is broken within us, even though we fail and react in unhealthy ways and even though we make poor decisions in our lives. We can do absolutely nothing to make ourselves more loved. The act of repentance is not so that God will love us more, it is so that we can move past our own walls, be healed of our inner distortions and be freed from our blindness so that we can open ourselves to transformation. We repent so that we can find our True Selves, see and experience his inconceivably wild love and fall in love with him in return.

The woman came into the Pharisee's home with her ointment and tears because she had fallen in love with God, not in order to make God love her. She wasn't looking for a pat on the head, a high religious grade or a certificate of merit. She came in knowing that she had been forgiven much and, though she had very little to offer in return, she offered what she had: overwhelming gratitude, tears of love and fragrant ointment. Perhaps she was inspired by Song of Songs 1:3 where the beloved said, "Your oils have a pleasing fragrance. Your Name is like ointment poured out; therefore (hence) the maidens love you."

In our world, common sense tells us we need to do and accomplish in order to earn and deserve anything.

God is not like us.

Thank God!

Saving Life

Luke 9: 18-24
Jesus instructs his disciples that if any want to become his disciple, they must pick up their cross daily, for those who lose their life for his sake will save it and those who want to save their life will lose it.

The False Self, or the Wounded Warrior, is the part of you that is continually scrambling to save its own life and it's often easy to identify when the Warrior is saving its own life. That's when you begin to give in to self-pity, experience offended pride rearing up inside or when you feel anger, resentment, heavy anxiety or fear of loss, and you react strongly in order to manipulate or modify the circumstances. These kinds of life saving mechanisms are not hard to identify even though it's extremely difficult to become disentangled from them.

The place where recognition is more problematic is where the Warrior is trying to save its own life on a spiritual level. The Warrior is not always recognizably selfish. In fact, very often the Warrior seems outwardly deeply selfless in its goals and apparent desires. It's not the goals and desires that are flawed; it is its own inherent need to be in control and to make things go the way it thinks things should go. Underneath its seemingly great motivation to serve God, the continuous and unhealthy motivation is to keep itself from blame, guilt and further wounds. This motivation is unhealthy because it totally distorts the essential message of the Good News.

"For those who want to save their life will lose it..." Save their life. Who's doing the saving here? Not Jesus. Jesus is saying that no one has the ability to save his or her own life. Later in scripture

Paul states that no one has the ability to follow the law perfectly (self-salvation) and even if they could it couldn't save them. Last week's second reading is a great example:

Yet we know that a person is made right with God by faith in Jesus Christ, not by obeying the law. And we have believed in Christ Jesus, so that we might be made right with God because of our faith in Christ, not because we have obeyed the law. For no one will ever be made right with God by obeying the law.
My old self has been crucified with Christ. It is no longer I who live, but Christ lives in me. So I live in this earthly body by trusting in the Son of God, who loved me and gave himself for me. I do not treat the grace of God as meaningless. For if keeping the law could make us right with God, then there was no need for Christ to die. (Galatians 2: 16, 19-21, NLT)

It is interesting that alternate translations of the above speak of the faith *of* Christ, not faith *in* Christ. It would seem that we aren't even capable of faith; we are completely dependent on Christ's faith. The cross and self-denial that Jesus speaks of is accepting that spiritually, you just don't have a leg to stand on and that total surrender is the only thing that's left for you to do.

Jesus says to pick up your cross daily but what the Warrior wants to do is fashion its own crosses. The reason that it wants to create its own crosses is because the daily cross is not under its control. This cross is whatever is happening in the moment. It is your life. It is your simple and broken humanity. It is the broken humanity of everyone around you. It's the messy chaos that makes up your life. The cross is the core or the central meeting point of life, death and resurrection and it is not within anyone's control. If you are spending your time trying to manufacture other crosses that feel more acceptable or finding a way to get the cross of the present moment under control whether it's through prayer, repentance, good deeds or by trying to manipulate and direct everything in the way you think it should go, you are trying to save your own life. The Warrior is in control. The Warrior has made a judgement that life should not be the way it is, that the spiritual life should be something entirely different, and it will do everything it can to make life conform to the way it thinks it should be.

And Jesus simply says, "Pick up the cross of your day and understand that you have no control and cannot save yourself. Just follow me." As I have quoted before, he also said, "The flesh is useless. It is the Spirit that brings life." These words of Jesus are often confusing and threatening to the Warrior. Sometimes it seems like Christ is saying that you've got to do it all yourself and other times like he's saying there's no way you can do any of it. What's the deal here?

True Self has no problem with understanding 'the deal'. True Self is so aware of and comfortable with its own inability to be spiritually effective that all it wants to do is turn its face toward the sun, soak up the energizing and healing rays and become a sponge that is saturated by the whole nature of Jesus.

The Greek word for 'deny' means, "utterly refusing to recognize the original source involved." Your True Self, by staying with Christ and keeping its face turned toward Christ in full openness and acceptance, is utterly refusing to recognize your original perceived source of power, love, life and control: ego, False Self or the Warrior. Turning away from the striving of the Warrior can feel like dying and loss because you are letting go of control, but True Self knows that authentic life will never be found in the Warrior's camp.

Who do you say Jesus is? If you say he is the Messiah, the Christ of God, then you must stop allowing your Warrior to be your original source, the one who has your program of self-salvation all worked out. The Warrior loves programs and plans. But there is no program. There is only the daily cross and following Jesus through that cross to new life.

Jesus is the True Self of all True Selves, the Name above all names. The love, life and power he possessed when he was on earth sprang from the fact that he had gone completely past the Wounded Warrior muddying his waters and dragging him into a self-serving circle of defense, control and self justification. Christ knew exactly *who* he was, the Beloved of God, and he knew exactly *what* he was, the Messiah who had come to free his people and take them back to their real home.

And that's what he calls us to follow. Brilliant, isn't it?

Travelers – Not Settlers

Luke 9: 51-62
Someone says to Jesus that they will follow him wherever he goes but Jesus replies that the foxes have holes and the birds of the air have nests but the Son of Man has nowhere to lay his head.

I have always loved the passage: "...but the Son of Man has nowhere to lay his head." Even as a child those words fascinated me and I remember drawing a picture of it, but it wasn't until I was well into adulthood that I began to get a glimmer of how profound the words were. What started to seep into my consciousness was that this world was not Christ's true home – and it isn't my true home either. It was Peter who said, "Beloved, I urge you as *aliens* and *exiles* to abstain from the desires of the flesh (false self) that wage war against the soul (true self)." (1 Peter 2:11)

Aliens and exiles. Strangers in a strange land. This world is not where we came from or where we belong and somewhere along the way it is imperative that every Christian grasps this. What we possess and accomplish in this world is not ultimately who we are. We are not here to settle, to make our mark, to carve out a niche, to find security and be comfortable; we are pilgrims and nomads passing through on the way back to the place where we belong. As we traverse over the desert terrain and help others along the way to get home too, the question isn't what we gain; it's what we lose.

Not too many people would argue with me when I say it's a difficult and often lonely journey, but there are certain things that make it even more difficult and lonelier than it already is. Picture two people walking through the desert. The first has prepared for an arduous and long journey. The packsack on the shoulders is immense, full of all sorts of clothing, heavy boots, equipment, shelter and tools that might possibly be helpful on such a trek. Not only did this person start out with an impressive array of equipment but all along the way, helpful people have added to the load: arcane maps, unusual compasses, special water bottles, nutritious food, journals full of explicit dire warnings...so much 'stuff'. Watching the pilgrim, you notice that the weight of what is being carried makes it very difficult to achieve much movement through the deep sand. If one could peer into the thoughts of this traveler one would notice a lot of frustration, regret, fear and innate weariness. The traveler would constantly be trying to drink from the mirage pools of the future while trying gain sustenance from chewing on the dead past, the good and the bad. This pilgrim is actually not traveling much at all. He just thinks he is because he thinks he's got the appropriate load for a journey. Even though he struggles mightily with the load, he likes it because it's a familiar load. It's a load he calls his own and on which he rests his head.

The second pilgrim has very little – no packsack and no huge loads of food and equipment, preferring instead to trust the desert to provide what is needed when it is needed. The feet are shod with light sandals. To this pilgrim or nomad, the desert is alive with vital life signs. Food and water appear in unexpected places and the pilgrim knows that it is crucial to be paying attention because it's so easy to miss the ruah wind whispering directions for the moment and pointing out the subtle but awe inspiring signs of God's presence everywhere. This traveler steps lightly over the sand and, though the journey certainly has its difficulties, an unnecessary load does not bring him to a standstill.

Jesus had no possessions. I'm not talking now about just material possessions. He did not lay claim to or hold onto anything in the past nor did he grasp for assurances for the future. He did not need anyone to recognize him as someone important and worthy of respect. He ministered to people because he loved them not because he had a need to show off his value. He had no need to rain fire down upon a people who did not approve of him or support his mission. He set his face toward Jerusalem to embrace his death, not just for those who were committed to him and supported his mission but also for the unreceptive, the unbelieving and the closed off people of the world.

Christ didn't reach for a secure spot to call his own but walked in unburdened trust that he would be sheltered when he was in need of shelter and would be fed when he was in need of food. "My food, my tools and my shelter – my home – is to do the will of the one who sent me on this desert journey."

This is an incredibly tough journey but it's a thousand times more difficult when you're conflicted about who you really are, what you really need or want and where your home really is. When Jesus said, "Let the dead bury their own dead," he wasn't being harsh and uncaring. I suspect he knew that the man who said, "First let me go bury my father," was not wholly committed and, once back home, would most likely lose the inspiration he had found in Christ's presence. The man would bury his father but then maybe decide he should plow his fields, get married as was expected of him, raise some children and generally take care of business. He would always mean to get back to Jesus and would always tell himself, "When this stage of life is over I can be more committed and have more time to serve the Lord." Eventually, though, the clamors of normal life would make him mostly forget about that charismatic man he ran into on the road to Jerusalem. He would become one of the dead busy dealing with the dead and burying himself in a dead life.

Life has a way of doing that. It burdens us with false ideas of what is essential to the journey. It makes us forget our True Selves and forget that this world is not our real home, even though we're called to care for it with respect and love. It's so easy to gather far more than is needed and feel needy for far more than is gathered until the journey becomes a treadmill in the sand.

God doesn't want your money or your busyness so much as he wants you. *You.* Simply you. The unloaded, unsettled you. Who are you? What are all the perceptions, expectations and things you have accumulated in your life that seem to define you but actually only bog you down in the desert sand? What is the part of you that is absolutely alien to this world? Who is the you that will cross over that final horizon to your true home when everything in this world falls away? There is no doubt about it; it will all fall away like a pile of debris. All your accomplishments, doctrines, set-in-stone opinions, defenses, frames of reference and self-definitions will be like ashes in the wind. Only one thing can accompany you back home: love.

The choice is whether you are going to settle down with a load of heavy debris on which you can lay your head or whether you will travel light with love...

...like Jesus.

Rejoicing In True Power

Luke 10: 1-12, 17-20

Jesus sends out seventy of his disciples ahead of him to minster to people in every town and place he intends to go. He gives them detailed instructions about what to take and how to respond when people reject them. When the disciples return they are filled with joy because even the demons obeyed them. Jesus tells them to rejoice because their names are written in heaven, not because the spirits submit to them.

This scripture bothers me for the simple fact that if it is not read prayerfully, carefully and in context with the culture of the times, it could easily be used as a foundational scripture for an "Us against Them" mentality. If I came away from reading that scripture, thinking that anyone who has rejected my Christian testimony is a pagan doomed to hell, I would be one terrible Christian. This is not scripture that gives us a right to judge others who don't believe the way we do or condemn those who struggle with the Gospel message.

In fact, it is my contention that most people who seemingly reject Christ are not rejecting Christ at all. They are rejecting a lot of exceedingly poor representations of Christ. Most of them have never encountered the real Christ at all – just some other people's ideas of Christ and they have made judgments based on many unhealthy acts committed in the name of Christ. The Good News of Jesus is often not communicated authentically or effectively.

Having said that, there are two things I want to focus on in this Gospel passage that are important and could easily be missed in a quick reading.

The first is the fact that the disciples *returned with joy, saying, 'Lord, in your name even the demons submit to us!'* They did not return discouraged, frustrated and upset because they had been rejected over and over. It doesn't sound to me like they came back with sore ankles from shaking dust off their feet. They came back full of joy. Their excitement that even the demons had submitted to them suggests that Christ sent those disciples out with the Holy Spirit of authentic power and love, a power so effective that those who had the greatest potential to reject the message were healed of their bondage to the lies of the evil one. By love and the power of the Spirit, people were released to receive healing and hear the truth.

"See, I have given you authority to tread on snakes and scorpions, and over all the power of the enemy." Both Isaiah and Jesus proclaimed, *"The Spirit of the Lord is upon me...to set the captives free."* Christ did not send those disciples out to condemn or to speak words of doom; he sent them out to heal and to liberate prisoners through the mighty power of love.

This leads to the second point which is the last line of this week's Gospel passage: *'In any case, do not rejoice that the spirits submit to you, but rejoice that your names are written in heaven.'* Jesus was saying, "Right. You've experienced what can happen when I empower you. Now...detach. What the Spirit does through you doesn't make you more important or bigger in God's eyes. Don't start getting all full of yourselves. Just rejoice that you are fully loved and that you were loved even before you did anything. This is true power. This is the power of True Self."

There was a fellow who had a music ministry. He was a good musician and had a trained voice and he had been invited to give a mission at a parish I was involved in at the time. Before the first evening's service began, the parish priest asked me to come and meet this man. When I was introduced, the musician was obviously not in the least bit interested in meeting anyone. His whole attitude was, "Yeah, yeah...whatever."

His music and his talk were the main part of the mission but parish lectors and choirs were also involved in the liturgy with different choirs taking turns each evening of the mission. In front of the people, he came across as warm, humorous, very spiritual and a good speaker. At the end of the first evening, however, when coffee was served, perhaps because he had already met me, he sat down with me. He then proceeded to criticize certain aspects of the evening that the parish had been responsible for, especially the performance of the choir. It was as if he felt like his ministry had been diminished by the participation of non-professionals. I was appalled.

This man was very aware of how good he was at what he did. He was so aware of this that he had forgotten that, as far as the Lord is concerned, it's not what you do that should be a cause for rejoicing; it's who you are. And who you are has very little to do with what you do. Your ministries, your roles, your appointed tasks or your service to the community means diddlysquat if you don't know who you are. What you do does not define your importance in the kingdom, even if you are casting out demons, healing the sick or are the absolute greatest at whatever it is that you do.

Your name is written in heaven. Would you know who you are even if you were suddenly incapacitated for the rest of your life and couldn't raise a finger to accomplish anything? If that happened, would you feel like your whole definition and purpose in life had just been completely wiped out? Would you understand that before everything else you are the Beloved of God and that the only place where you can find your identity and approval is in the center of his humble heart? Would you know in your spirit that love is the only thing that matters and what you do after that is just bonus? Would you be peaceful in knowing that God doesn't *need* you – he just *wants* you? God wants to share the joy of his creative power with you and he invites you to participate in that creative power but your mission is not to be busy, important and effective. Your whole mission is to be loved and to be a conduit of the love that created you.

Your name is written in heaven and written in love. The Holy Trinity, the whole universe, all the angels and archangels, all the saints and all the companies of heaven know your name and know who you are.

Do you?

Mercy Without Borders

Luke 10: 25-37

A lawyer asks Jesus, "Who is my neighbor?" and Jesus tells him parable of the Good Samaritan.

There was Franciscan, Brother Andrew, who was on a journey, accompanied by a man who consistently tested the humble brother by insulting him and being derogatory and disparaging in response to everything Brother Andrew said. Every day for three days, whenever Brother Andrew spoke, his fellow traveler responded by calling him a fool and ridiculing him in some arrogant fashion. Finally, at the end of the third day, the fellow could stand it no more. He asked Brother Andrew, "How is it that you are able to be so loving and kind when all I've done for the past three days is dishonor and offend you? Each time I insult you, you respond lovingly. How is this possible?"

The Brother Andrew responded with a question of his own for the traveler. "If someone offers you a gift and you do not accept that gift, to whom does the gift belong?" His question provided his fellow traveler with a new insight. When someone offers you the gift of their insults and you refuse to accept them, they obviously still belong to the original giver.

What has this story got to do with the parable of the Good Samaritan? Not much. Except I changed the story a little from the original. In the original story it wasn't a Franciscan brother who was so loving and wise.

It was the Buddha.

Depending on where you are in your spiritual journey, if I had told this story and used the Buddha as the wise, loving man instead of the Franciscan brother, you might have experienced a bit of inner discomfort that I used the Buddha to illustrate a very Christian principle rather than a recognizably holy Christian of some sort. It's a fact that people of other faiths, who do not recognize Christ as the Messiah, often act in ways that truly reflect God's heart and do so in ways that could teach us Christians a thing or two. That can be disconcerting for some people.

We need to realize that when Jesus told the parable of the Good Samaritan, he deliberately used a Samaritan as the protagonist of the story rather than a good practicing Jew. To the Jews, using a Samaritan to illustrate mercy and the importance of caring for our neighbor would have been about the same as anyone using the actions of the Buddha to demonstrate to a group of good orthodox Catholics what God desires of them. The reaction of the Jews listening to Jesus would have ranged from mild discomfort to full outrage and complete rejection of Jesus and his teachings.

In his parable, Jesus didn't even have the Samaritan suddenly convert to Judaism before he so generously helped someone who was his spiritual enemy. Imagine if I had retold the parable and the cast of characters consisted of a Catholic priest, a renowned Catholic theologian and the Buddha – with the Buddha being the one who cared for the man who was beaten and left to die while the priest and the theologian avoided him. I think there would be many who would not be happy with me. No doubt, the lawyer was less than impressed with Jesus and his parable.

"And who is my neighbor?" Because it says that the lawyer was testing Jesus, it would be safe to assume that the lawyer asked this question because Jesus had given the right answer to the first question and the lawyer was pushing the envelope to see if

he could still get Jesus to walk into a trap. It wasn't an innocent question. The Pharisees, scribes and lawyers were always debating the finer points of the law and Jesus once scolded them that they would strain at gnats and swallow camels. They would adhere devoutly to insignificant points of the law while ignoring God's beloved laws of love and mercy. To even ask who is a neighbor indicated a bit of 'gnat straining'. So, I guess Jesus decided to give him a real camel to swallow.

The parable was certainly an uncomfortable surprise for the lawyer but Jesus' disciples experienced their own uncomfortable surprise as well. Just previous to this scripture passage, the Samaritans had denied hospitality to Jesus because 'his face was turned to Jerusalem'. The whole town rejected Christ because the people would not acknowledge that the temple in Jerusalem where Jesus was headed was the true temple. You may recall that the disciples offered to call down fire on the town to pay it back for refusing to put them up for the night.

Yet, here was Jesus telling a parable where the Samaritan was the hero. That must have been a shock for the disciples. Even though a whole community had overtly rejected Jesus as the Messiah, he let it be known that love and mercy are not the products of correct laws and belief systems. Love and mercy are the fruit of a heart that yearns for God and seeks to serve him. Jesus said to the Samaritan woman at the well, in relation to the proper place to worship God, *"But the hour is coming, and is now here, when the true worshippers will worship the Father in spirit and truth, for the Father seeks such as these to worship him."* God sees the heart, not the brand name.

This isn't a reflection on inter-faith respect, though that's a very good thing. My point is that God is so serious about his law of love and mercy that he made it a universal precept, not just a Christian tenet. No matter where mercy is displayed, God is there in fullness. One act of mercy is an open invitation to God to come and manifest his entire being to both the one being shown mercy and the one being merciful and he doesn't look at whether either of them belong to the proper group. There is no space between God and mercy. When we withhold mercy, we withhold God and we make a mockery of the gift we have been given.

It's actually not a choice.

Shakespeare said it beautifully:

"The quality of mercy is not strained.
It droppeth as the gentle rain from heaven
Upon the place beneath. It is twice blessed:
It blesseth him that gives and him that takes.
'Tis mightiest in the mightiest. It becomes
The thronèd monarch better than his crown.
His scepter shows the force of temporal power,
The attribute to awe and majesty
Wherein doth sit the dread and fear of kings,
But mercy is above this sceptered sway.
It is enthronèd in the hearts of kings.
It is an attribute to God himself.
And earthly power doth then show likest God's
When mercy seasons justice. Therefore, Jew, though justice be
thy plea, consider this-
That in the course of justice none of us
Should see salvation. We do pray for mercy,
And that same prayer doth teach us all to render
The deeds of mercy." (Merchant of Venice)

The One Thing

Luke 10: 38-42

Jesus visits Martha and Mary. Martha is upset because Mary is not helping. Jesus tells Martha that Mary has chosen the better part.

It's always been my thought that if there hadn't been any sibling rivalry between Mary and Martha before Jesus' visit, there sure would have been after.

I think we all secretly empathize with Martha even though we think we understand what Jesus is saying to her. We empathize because we know that when the pressure is on we are more likely to be running around, worried and distracted rather than sitting peacefully at the feet of Christ. If we were overburdened and there was someone around who could give a hand and ease the load but they chose to slip off to the chapel for some 'quiet time', we would not be impressed.

But this is not a story of two people, really. It's the story of the two sides of all of us. It is an analogy of the nature of False Self versus True Self, and our innate empathy for Martha illustrates how much we live within the confines of our False Selves and are utterly familiar with its actions, attitudes and emotions.

It wasn't so much that Martha was busy that was the problem; it was her attitudes and the fact that she was so worried and distracted. She was also obviously full of resentment, which led her to make judgments. She not only judged Mary; she judged Jesus as well. "Lord, do you not care...?" That was a judgment carefully couched in a question. Today we would call that question, "Passive Aggressive". What she was really saying was, "All the responsibility is on my shoulders. I am doing all the work while you and Mary sit around and chat. Neither of you has offered to help and neither of you cares if we have a fire or a meal at all. If it wasn't for me this place would be a mess."

The false self or the Wounded Warrior is a pro at being a martyr. The Warrior easily finds reasons for resentment and uses them to stoke the smoldering fires within. But if Jesus and Mary had said, "Martha! You're doing all the work...what can we do to help?" she most likely would have told them that she was fine and not to bother or else she might have given them some tasks but then critically micromanaged them. The Warrior has territories and defensive mechanisms and can't easily allow others, even the Lord, to share the burden unless full control is in its hands.

Martha may not have even particularly wanted help; she may have just wanted Jesus to notice her, approve of her busyness and praise her for carrying such a full load under such difficult circumstances. I've always assumed she was preparing a meal for Jesus but it doesn't say that. It just says she was distracted by many tasks. She welcomed Jesus into her home but she failed to make him the focus of her life when he was there. So much to do. So many expectations. So much depending on her and her alone.

Meanwhile, Mary sits at Jesus' feet completely focused on him. She hears his words, watches his eyes, delights in his smile and feels his whole nature of peace washing over her. This is True Self. True Self is at rest because it knows that this is where it belongs. This is what it was made for – to dwell within the circle of his love. The Wounded Warrior has somewhat to say about that. "You can't just sit around! You have to be productive and effective. Nothing will get done if all you do is have quiet times with the Lord." Wounded Warrior can't sit. It feels too much guilt and pressure. It feels like everything is depending on it being in control and efficient.

That doesn't mean that True Self is never active. It is often very active. But when True Self moves into action, it does so under God's direction. It moves within the Lord's nature. It goes out with grace, mercy, faith, justice, insight and wisdom, and in power and effectiveness. True Self does not get busy for the sake of being busy or because there are heavy outside expectations and pressures. When True Self does go into action, the power of God is available to change people and situations but True Self isn't overly concerned about measuring success and results. True Self simply desires to participate in the Kingdom dance with the Lord. What freedom comes from being a Mary! What incredible grace is available to those who find the still point within.

The Lord can really only consistently manifest himself through us when we have discovered the Mary Point within ourselves. All the busyness, activity and efforts to be productive can never replace the beauty and power of a soul who has learned to sit at the feet of the Lord, to gaze at him while inquiring, "What do *you* ask of me, Lord? Where do *you* want me to go? If you want me to go, I'll go. If you want me to stay, I'll stay."

The Martha, the Warrior within, welcomes the Lord into the house and works *for* the Lord but not *with* the Lord. The toiling Martha within often feels lonely and never realizes the companionship and warmth waiting at the still and silent Mary Point within. When I think of the difference it makes to know the peace of sitting at the Lord's feet, it makes me think of Psalm 84 (NKJV):

How lovely is your tabernacle,
O Lord of hosts!
My soul longs, yes, even faints
For the courts of the Lord;
My heart and my flesh cry out for the living God.

Even the sparrow has found a home,
And the swallow a nest for herself,
Where she may lay her young—
Even Your altars, O Lord of hosts,
My King and my God.
Blessed are those who dwell in Your house;
They will still be praising You. Selah!
For a day in your courts is better than a thousand elsewhere.

When Jesus entered Martha and Mary's home and welcomed Mary to sit in his presence, it would have been like she had come to the Temple, the Tower, the home she had yearned for all her life. His presence immediately healed all the thousands of days she had spent elsewhere.

It's good to go home. Go to your Mary Point.

A Letter Home

Luke 11:1-13

The disciples ask Jesus to teach them to pray so he teaches them the Our Father. Then he teaches them about praying confidently to the Father, saying that whoever searches, finds, and to whomever knocks the door will be opened. He says that if those who are evil know how to give good gifts to their children, how much more will the Father give the Holy Spirit to those who ask him.

Dear Father,

Jesus said we could talk to you just like you are our Abba. It is still hard for me to believe that I can talk to you using the name 'Father'. What a blessed name that is! After what seems like eons of believing we were separated from you and not worthy enough to even be in your presence, the name 'Father' speaks relief and peace to my heart. I can't begin to tell you how profoundly grateful I am – how grateful we all are – for our brother Jesus. Until we met him, none of us knew that we had totally forgotten who you really are. We had forgotten your face and we had forgotten what home looks like. Actually, before Jesus came, I would have said that none of us ever knew these things at all but now, every time he speaks to us I feel this familiarity stirring inside as if I always knew there was something more.

Jesus says he is like you and there is something in me that recognizes the truth of this. In fact, having him here is like home has come to us. It's difficult to explain because so much of the time all of us are trying to grasp exactly who he is and what his words mean, but late at night, when we're sleeping under the silent stars, I look up at the heavens and I'm overwhelmed with the sense that 'out there' has become 'in here'. Then I look over to where Jesus is lying and see that he is awake too. He'll turn his head and gaze at me with a knowing smile. In that moment I know the Kingdom of God has truly come to us, and Jesus knows exactly what I'm sensing. Imagine … your Kingdom vibrating and alive in the middle of a scrubby desert. It's not 'out there' anymore, not somewhere unreachable and inconceivable, but here and now. It has come. It has *come*!

If I had to explain to someone what this Kingdom is, the only word I could give it is Love. But it's not love in any sense that I knew it before the Lord came. He has shown to us dimensions of love we could never have comprehended on our own. Looking back, I can see how any love I had for anyone or anything was more of a reaching for someone, or something, to fill up the emptiness inside. I gave a little love but only in order to try to receive something I was missing. I loved you but it was a love filled with rituals that were designed to deliver me from evil, keep me safe and keep me on your good side. There was an underlying anxiety about my love for you. But the love that Jesus shows us has turned my whole idea of love upside down. I watch him and I can see that he is entirely filled with the knowledge that you love him. He's so complete within you that it is intriguing just to observe him. Even in simply walking down a road, he exudes the joy of being completely loved. Evil cannot touch him. Even when evil is challenging him and sneering in his face, the core of him remains solid and at peace.

Then he tells us we are loved in exactly the same way and all we have to do is believe it. "Everything I have is yours," he says over and over. "All you need to do is ask. Would you give your children a snake if they asked for fish? Of course not! Our Father just wants to give you everything he has given to me. Ask for it. Seek it out continually. Don't settle for less than what is your inheritance and has always been yours. Don't decide you're not worth it, good enough or not important enough. Speak to the one who is the Father of us all and ask for the Spirit. The Holy Spirit is the one who will lead you and open you up to who you really are and all that is yours. Never stop asking or seeking." It is obvious that he badly wants us to experience the same love that he is immersed in.

The love he shows us is overwhelming. It's not just because it is astonishing to believe that we could be loved so deeply and so strongly but also because it's clearly a love that cannot flourish where anger, hatred or resentment are welcomed in and entertained. It has always been a matter of pride with our people to hold on to the wrongs done to us. To us, it's always been "an eye for an eye and a tooth for a tooth," and we have no problem remembering every single eye and tooth that has suffered injury, personally and as a nation. But it became clear to me one night under those peaceable, silent and humble stars that your love cannot co-exist with anger or resentment. Where there is one, the other is not. Simple. If we choose to harbor even tiny seeds of resentment, we have chosen against love. When love is chosen, evil cannot prevail.

And when we choose love, we choose a different world. We choose your kingdom and our choice makes your Kingdom present in power, truth and healing right in that moment of choosing. Why would we ever choose to lurk in the dark places of resentment and anger when we could be alive in the brightness of the Kingdom? Still, before I know it, I often find myself chewing on thoughts of those who have wished me ill or done me harm. Then I realize what I'm doing. I kick myself and feel like such a failure until Jesus comes to me in my pain and says, "Peace. Just let it all go. Ask and the Kingdom will come back to you. The more you choose the Kingdom, ask for it and experience its light, the less you will find yourself choosing evil and all its lies. Take it one day at a time and in every moment of each day turn to our Father and ask for the bread of the Kingdom. This is the filling bread of love, forgiveness and grace. This is the food that you need right now. Don't ask for this bread for tomorrow and don't worry about tomorrow. The Father doesn't require that you are able perceive all the trials and evils that tomorrow might bring so you can pray for all of those like the pagans do. He doesn't require you to make any projections, not even about your own failures and limitations. The only moment that the Father cares about is this moment right now. Where are you right now? What are you choosing...*right now*?"

My Father...my holy and gracious Father. Right now I choose you. You are my heaven and you are here right now. I choose you in this moment. I choose your love. I ask for the Spirit of Light to give me the power to fully believe how much I am loved and to give me the strength to love and forgive my brothers and sisters the same way you love and forgive me. I want to be capable of loving like Jesus, who loves to the degree of how much he is loved.

Father, through my relationship with you, form me into one who makes the Kingdom of Love present and real to this weary hurting world. Father, fill all of us with your Spirit. Make us the same as your son – make us as lights that shine in the darkness so the darkness can never overcome us. Make us shine with your grace and truth.

As you will, so let it be. Amen and amen.

Your son,

John

What's In Your Storehouse?

Luke 12: 13-21

Some Jews were asking him to arbitrate between them so Jesus tells the story of the rich man whose lands produced abundant crops but he had no room to store all the crops. He decided to pull down the old barns and build larger ones, feeling that he would be able then to relax, eat, drink and be merry. But that night he died and all his abundance was of no use to him. Jesus says that it is the same for those who store up treasures for themselves but are not rich towards God.

Shocking!

Jesus was not only saying his mission was not to take sides in conflicts of who is right and who is wrong, he was also telling those listening to him that the possession of an abundance of material goods did not guarantee salvation and that God did not necessarily favor anyone who was rich. That would have been scandalously upsetting for his audience who had been taught that material abundance indicated God's approval and blessing.

We all need to sit up and pay attention here. This isn't really about whether we should have money or not; it's about what spiritual laws and ideas we perceive are critical to our own spiritual health. If Jesus walked into your parish next Sunday, in what way could he upset your carved in stone ideas about what God wants from his people? Could Jesus totally shock you? I don't mean just make you feel a little guilty because there are areas where you fail to do what you know is right. I'm talking about him saying something that would rock your foundations and maybe even make you angry and question his authority?

The problem that Jesus was pointing out in this week's Gospel was not that someone desired what he felt was his rightful share or that the man in the parable had lots of money. It was that, in both cases, the crux of the Kingdom of God was missing: love and trust. In one instance there was a question of what could perhaps be called a moral right and in the other, Jesus gave an illustration of someone actually living and acting according to a completely accepted spiritual precept of the day. In both cases, Jesus implied there was such a lack of awareness of what he deemed so critical to life that he even brought one fellow's salvation into question. Time and time again throughout the Gospels, Jesus openly told the people that laws and precepts are not what open the doors of the Kingdom to us. They're not what save us. It is love and trust. It is caring for the needs, spiritual, emotional and material, of others before we care for our own needs, and trusting in God to give us everything we need when we need it.

And here we are two thousand years later still struggling with those concepts, especially the idea of what it means to love. We are still a people that fall into rights and laws. We keep forgetting what Jesus taught. How we do this so easily and then feel so totally justified I don't know - but we do.

For instance, read this quote from Pope Francis:

"In our ecclesiastical region there are priests who don't baptize the children of single mothers because they weren't conceived in the sanctity of marriage. These are today's hypocrites. Those who clericalize the church. Those who separate the people of God from salvation. And this poor girl who, rather than returning the child to sender, had the courage to carry it into the world, must wander from parish to parish so that it's baptized!"

We honestly don't have to look too far to know that we have observed injustices performed in the name of Church law. We probably don't have to struggle too much to remember times when we personally felt obligated to follow a spiritual law rather than offer complete acceptance, respect, love and support to someone who was definitely on the wrong side of that law. There have been times when we operated out of our 'full storehouse' of the law and felt justified.

Jesus actually taught by his words and actions that he wasn't terribly concerned about morality and legality in the way the authorities had come to interpret morality and legality. I believe that as a Christian people we have come a long way in the journey of becoming a people who base acceptance of other people on love rather than on legality or morality. I think we're starting to 'get it' but it's still so easy to fall into the trap.

It feels a bit dangerous to us to simply love and accept rather than make sure the transgressor knows our righteous stands about everything and knows that we disapprove. You don't think this is a common struggle? Talk to any parent of older teenagers and young adults. There's at least one child in almost every family who in some way completely challenges the parents' sensibility of moral and spiritual rightness. And most parents I know, who have come through this difficult period, have come out with the understanding that love is far more important than legalistic stances. Legality shatters the fragile heart. Love mends it. At the same time, love mends the egotistical hardness, brittleness and selfishness of our own hearts. It creates in us a fuller awareness of how God loves us. The more we know how loved we are, the more we learn to trust deeply in God's provision for our needs rather than trusting in our own scrambling to stock up and maintain our own impoverished storehouses.

If there ever comes a time when God asks us about our pilgrimage here on earth, he won't ask if we were morally or legally correct. No, he won't. He will ask, "Did you love her? Did you respect him? Did you open your door and welcome them in with love and laughter? Or did you grudgingly allow them into your space and make sure they knew you weren't comfortable with their lifestyles, their failures, their struggles, their dreams and ambitions? Did you have to make sure they understood that they were mistaken?"

It's not just material wealth that can lull us into thinking we are secure. A certain kind of spiritual wealth can do the same. Remember the parable of the Pharisee and the publican? *The Pharisee, standing by himself, prayed: 'God, thank you that I am not like other men, extortioners, unjust, adulterers, or even like this tax collector. I fast twice a week; I give tithes of all that I get.'* He did not go home justified. This was a man with a full religious storehouse but it meant nothing to God because he had no love.

Listen! Jesus *doesn't care* if you are totally right. He *doesn't care* if your storehouse is overflowing with righteous deeds. He only cares that you love.

If we all really understood that, the whole church would be turned upside down. It would cease to be a storehouse and become what it was always meant to be:

Sanctuary.

19th Sunday Ordinary C

Where Is Your Heart? Where Is Your Home?

Luke 12: 32-48

Jesus teaches his followers not to be afraid and to trust that it is God's good pleasure to give them the Kingdom. He then exhorts them to be dressed for action and have the right priorities. He tells a parable and says blessed are the servants who are awake and ready to serve when the master of a house goes to a wedding banquet and arrives back in the middle of the night. Jesus warns against servants who take advantage of the master's absence to eat and drink and beat the other servants.

Perhaps it's time for a present moment reminder.

There's a tendency to hear this week's scripture as a reference to the end times. Since nobody knows when Christ will return, we'd better be doing what we're called to do because he could reappear at any moment. However, it's difficult to find real motivation in the possibility of Christ's return in glory after 2000 years of waiting. We have indeed gotten into a "My Master is delayed in coming," mentality.

The reality is, the Master has already come. We are the ones who are usually absent.

And where are we? Probably out beating on our slaves.

We slide over the parts of the scripture that mention slaves because slavery is not part of our sophisticated culture any longer. Or is it? A slave is someone that is under another person's complete control or ownership and it doesn't take much to bring to mind people we endeavor to maintain control over. Even making private judgments in your mind is a control mechanism.

609

Are you absent to the Master because you are spending most of your time keeping your life, and everyone else's life, under control and making sure other people are up to speed with your program and your agenda? Are you manipulating situations and circumstances to conform to your visions and your sense of what's right? Would these be the modern day 'slaves' that you continually beat upon in your mind and in reality?

Meanwhile, the Master waits at your house.

He has come with great pleasure to give you his Kingdom but you are not there. You are consumed with beating on past slaves - all those people and situations that wounded you and diminished your sense of control or power. You are busy anticipating future people and situations that will need to be beaten into submission so that life doesn't spin out of your control. You may even be beating up on yourself for not being able to maintain heavy self-control.

Meanwhile, the Master waits at your house.

When you chew over past circumstances you are away from home. When you develop all sorts of possible future scenarios, you have left home. When you worry, when you are offended, when you beat up on yourself, when you are anxious about maintaining control and when your thoughts are wrapped up in your own or others' needs and failures, you are absent from home. When you live with the Wounded Warrior (false self), you may feel you're at home but you aren't.

Just prior to this Sunday's reading, Jesus was telling his disciples not to worry about their needs in the familiar passage that includes, *"And by worrying, can you add a single hour to your life span? If then you can't to do so small a thing as that, why do you worry about the rest? Consider the lilies, how they grow: they don't work or spin; yet, even Solomon in all his glory was not clothed like one of these."* (Luke 12: 25-27)

Where is this Kingdom that is God's great pleasure to give you? Where is this realm of abundance and hope? Where is the Master who arrived unexpectedly, totally prepared to serve *you* at the table only to find you gone? He is in the here and now. The kingdom is here and it is now. The Master is in the present moment waiting for you to return. He waits for you to stop beating on slaves and on yourself, to stop regretting the past and to stop anticipating the future. He is in the peaceable Tower of the Present Moment waiting for you with all his Kingdom gifts and provision.

Waiting for *you*.

We know that Jesus commonly used hyperbole to get his point across, so we can rest assured that God will not cast us out and cut us to pieces. We are quite capable of doing that to ourselves. When we cast ourselves outside the present moment and outside of the Kingdom, our spirits can never be whole and healthy. We will remain fragmented, battered and scattered, and we will become the enslaved as we continually seek control and dominance. If we do not come home to our Master, there will be very little difference in the end between us and the unfaithful – between us and those who do not have the gift of faith and don't know any better. Now there's a humbling thought.

It's time to pay attention to the unsettled uneasiness that forms the background music of your life and get back to where you belong. As St. Augustine wrote, "You have formed us for yourself, and our hearts are restless till they find rest in you." Beating on our slaves is not an activity of rest or peace. It is not a kingdom activity.

Now is the Kingdom. *Now* is the time to come home.

The Seeds Within

Luke 12: 49-53

Jesus says that he came to bring fire to the earth and that he wishes it were already kindled. He did not come to bring peace to the earth but division. Households will be divided against each other.

Dangerous stuff, this Christianity.

Jesus was prophesying that anyone who chose The Way after his death and resurrection was going to be in for some great challenges and we only need to read the Acts of the Apostles to know how accurate Jesus was. It's incredible how religion has been, and still is, a point of huge conflict and anger.

Even many of us living in the Western Hemisphere, though not facing dangerous persecution, have experienced the conflict and fear that a different set of belief systems can arouse between individuals, groups and communities. Was Jesus saying, "This is the purpose of my coming," or was he actually expressing deep sorrow that it would be so? We know from everything Jesus said in the Gospels that he didn't come to establish a religious power base in order to create chaos, war and political and human grief, but the history of Christianity, sadly, has been one of immense division, struggle and pain. Sometimes it was the Christians who were being persecuted and sometimes the Christians were doing the persecuting – often persecuting people who were of their own faith group. Is this what Christ intended to be the result of his coming? Or was he just saying that this is how human nature reacts when the status quo is threatened or when people have a choice between love and power?

Let's bring this on home. But instead of recalling times such as when someone from another faith group or someone of no faith at all challenged your beliefs, let's talk about your own inner world of faith and religion and how you deal with threats to your own status quo. It's no good being critical of how the major religions of the world still cannot live peaceably together if we cannot look inside ourselves and see those same seeds of angry conflict, defensiveness and divisiveness in our own psyches.

Scenario: a new person in your faith community gets the ear of the pastor and begins to institute changes to the liturgy or to how the parish is run on a day-to-day basis. The people of the community are not consulted about the changes; they are simply told this is how it will be from now on. What is the reaction of the people? Violence. Guns and bombs aren't the weapons; words and judgments are. The new person and the pastor are torn apart by everyone's words. Groups form defended territories. People are up in verbal arms. Those who agree with the changes are pitted against those who disagree. The rancor and rage is huge and the community is split.

The seeds of violence have sprouted and division is the harvest.

Scenario: Your child becomes a rebellious teenager and one day tells you that you are a hypocrite, all religion sucks and she doesn't want to attend Mass anymore. You are hurt and you also fear for your child's spiritual welfare so you decide that she is not old enough to make that decision. You angrily tell her that as long as she is a part of the family she will attend Mass. She continues to go to Mass but her seething sulkiness places a huge damper on family unity and on any chance that church could be a pleasant occasion. Usually the drive to or from Mass ends up with you yelling at her because she's being so snotty and her yelling back because she's so resentful.

The seeds of violence have sprouted and division is the harvest.

Scenario: a person in your spiritual small group comes to group one evening all excited because he's been reading a new book. When he describes the message of the book, you feel that it is way off center and could be deemed dangerous to orthodox spirituality. It could also confuse some of the younger members of the group and lead them astray. In front of everyone, you immediately point out the errors in the book's theology and insist he shouldn't read any more of it nor share any more with the group. The fellow shuts up, is obviously hurt and humiliated and never comes back to the small group, but you feel justified because it's necessary to keep the majority on a safe spiritual path. You are also secretly relieved because he had always been a bit of a loose cannon anyway.

The seeds of violence have sprouted and division is the harvest.

The question is not whether someone is right or wrong. We always feel completely right when we allow the seeds of violence to grow. Wherever there is division there are always at least two parties who are each convinced they are completely right and the other is completely wrong. In our concern we may sense a threat or a danger. We may feel our authority is on the line. We may sense that someone else is acting in an inappropriate manner or is not exercising proper discernment. We feel absolutely right and completely justified in taking action.

However, consider this: Jesus was inappropriate. He was off center from a lot of commonly accepted laws. He was a loose cannon. He didn't seem to be discerning or orthodox and was leading a lot of young and inexperienced Jews astray. He challenged the status quo. He was totally divisive. The authorities felt they were absolutely right and completely justified – in crucifying him.

No, Jesus did not come to establish another power base. He did not come to institute yet another religion where people could claim to be right and throw stones, literally or figuratively, at those who disagree with them. This week's Gospel must be read in context with the last few readings as well as the verses not included in the liturgical readings. Jesus is saying, *"Trust me. Trust your Father. Do not trust in power, money or possessions. Don't find your security in all those things the world finds security in – including being in the right group following the right theology. Don't follow me because you think I'll make everything peaceful, secure and easy. Look at me. I came to bring the fire of love and I am about to be baptized in a fire of hatred kindled by the righteous; I will be crucified because they think I am a threat and you will be thought of as threats as well. But trust in my love. Trust in our Father's love. Don't allow the seeds of violence to grow in your hearts but rather, let love take root. I have overcome the world not by power or by superiority or by fear. I have overcome it through love, opening the door for you to do the same."*

Walk through the door of love. Plant the seeds of respect and acceptance. Heal the division in yourself, in your home and in your faith community. Let God take care of the question of who's right and who's wrong.

Because we haven't done such a great job of that so far.

That Narrow Door

Luke 13: 22-30
Someone asks Jesus if only a few will be saved. He says to strive to enter through the narrow door for once the owner has shut the door, many will knock and say, "Lord, open the door for us; we ate and drank with you in the streets," and the owner will say, "I do not know where you come from. Go away from me." Then Jesus adds that people will come from the east, west, north and south and will eat in the Kingdom of God. Some are last who will be first, and some are first who will be last.

"Lord, will only a few be saved?" This question caught my attention because the Jews actually don't focus on the afterlife and personal salvation but, instead, consider salvation a national or corporate concern. The salvation of the individual Jew is connected to the salvation of the entire people and Messianic salvation is the liberation of the nation of Israel from political bondage plus a number of other benefits that come with the freedom of a nation. Neither do many Jews believe in the concept of everyone being born in original sin. Every individual is expected to act according to the precepts of the Torah and it is accepted that everyone sins (misses the mark). The remedy for missing the mark is atonement through repentance, prayer, good deeds and sacrifice. Individual goodness is desirable because it benefits the nation as a whole and the good of the community is considered more important than the good of the individual.

So, perhaps the questioner was confused since Christ was teaching that salvation was a personal matter. Or he could have been thinking about the Jewish belief that the Messiah would come to save the remnant of Israel, a precept taught by Old

Testament prophets who believed that God would separate the evildoers from the good people of Israel. Those left in God's care would be the remnant and perhaps there were some who were thinking that if Christ really was the Messiah, then the good would be separated from the evildoers. If this were so, Christ would only save the few – the Remnant.

"The process by which this remnant is separated is likened to the gathering of grapes or the shaking of an olive-tree, the result being that some of the fruit is left. But though those who survive will be few in number, they shall be called holy... Many, even the greater part, of Israel will fall or be carried away. The remnant will be saved and will return. (Jewish Encyclopedia)

Whatever the questioner was thinking, Jesus' answer indicates that he understood that the question pertained more to the Jewish national religious mindset rather than to the personal need of redemption. In the story Jesus tells, notice that the owner of the house is responding to a group of people. When he says, "I do not know where you come from," the reply is *"We* ate and drank with you." This is not the reply of a single individual knocking on heaven's door; it is a company of people saying, "Let us in.".

So, what was Jesus saying? He was saying that simply belonging to a nation or a particular religious group was not enough anymore. The point wasn't that the owner of the house was so mean that he wouldn't open the door to latecomers; it was that all those who were truly in sync with the owner were already in the house and they were there not because of a corporate identity or even because they were pretty good people. They were there because they had a close relationship with the Master of the house. They knew him and he knew them. They had intimate knowledge of each other.

In other words, it wasn't just that they had come to the owner's house early enough – they actually *lived* there. The master's house was their home. They not only identified themselves outwardly with the master, they were personally involved with him. They loved him, spoke with him, laughed with him, struggled with him, asked questions, listened to the answers and then acted upon what they heard.

The prophets and prophetesses of Israel were men and women who went beyond simply knowing the Torah and following its precepts. They had had 'face to face' encounters with the Lord. They weren't always terribly pure of heart. They considered themselves poor material to become prophets. But they talked to God and listened to him; they heard his still small voice and allowed his immense passion to inflame their own hearts.

Jesus' mission was to bring all people into intimate relationship with God, not just a few prophets and the occasional high priest. All of us are invited to become priests, prophets and royalty in the Kingdom of God. All are invited to the banquet table. All are invited to come home to the Father. Just because we are called Jew or Christian or Muslim etc. and have hung out wherever God is supposed to be found, doesn't necessarily mean we have accepted the invitation to enter into close relationship or to come home and live intimately with the master of the house.

In another scripture, Jesus said to the Chief Priests, *'The truth is, the tax-collectors and the prostitutes are going into the kingdom of God ahead of you.'* (Matt. 21:31) Those who consider themselves members of 'The Chosen' group or 'The Most Acceptable To God' crowd, whether it's a whole faith community or positions of authority within that faith community, may be *'the first who will be last'* and many whom we would not consider acceptable on any level because they are of a different faith or seem morally weak could very well be the *'last who will be first'* in the house of the Lord. We can presume upon nothing except moving toward being deeply in love with a God who is full of grace and is in love with us.

Paul quotes Jeremiah in Hebrews 8: 8-12 (ESV)
"Behold, the days are coming, declares the Lord,
when I will establish a new covenant with the house of Israel
and with the house of Judah,
not like the covenant that I made with their fathers
on the day when I took them by the hand to bring them out of the
land of Egypt.
For they did not continue in my covenant,
and so I showed no concern for them, declares the Lord.
For this is the covenant that I will make with the house of Israel
after those days, declares the Lord:
I will put my laws into their minds,
and write them on their hearts,
and I will be their God,
and they shall be my people.
And they shall not teach, each one his neighbor
and each one his brother, saying, 'Know the Lord,'
for they shall all know me,
from the least of them to the greatest.
For I will be merciful toward their iniquities,
and I will remember their sins no more."

Do you hear the yearning in God's voice? Talk to him. Listen for him. Talk to him more than you talk to your spouse, your children and your friends. Works, faith identity or proximity is not what will bring you home. Only relationship brings you home and a true relationship cannot be developed if you are rarely consciously present to the one who yearns for you.

Relationship is everything.

The Place Of Being Beyond Place

Luke 14: 1, 7-14

Jesus is invited to a meal at a Pharisees house and he noticed how the invited guests chose the places of honor. He tells them that when they go to a meal they should choose the lowest place so that the host may honor them by encouraging them to move to the place of honor. All who exalt themselves shall be humbled and all who humble themselves will be exalted.

This is a gospel that, sadly, has often been reduced to 'doormat theology'. In other words, God is only pleased when you put yourself last, never assert yourself, always think of other people's needs and never your own. "Blessed are those who let other people walk all over them." And don't you ever think too highly of your own gifts!

Many people struggle often with the challenge of how to be a servant without being a slave. There are those who choose the lowest place because they don't feel they deserve anything else or they are fearful that God will judge them to be lacking in humility and holiness if they even come close to appreciating themselves. Once having placed themselves in a lowly position and becoming accustomed to being last and not first, serving but not being served, giving but not demanding or receiving, they find themselves unable to accept any other position. Even if honor were offered it would likely be refused. It's too risky. God might be displeased.

Consciously placing oneself in the lowest place is often perceived as the ultimate way of kingdom spirituality. If that were so, Jesus would have come to earth as a lowly carpenter, died on the cross, gone to the grave - and he would have refused to be resurrected.

"No, thanks. I'll just stay here in the dark loneliness of death. Don't worry about me. I'm fine."

In the gospel, Jesus is not saying the lowest place is the best place. He's not saying the place of honor is a place bereft of holiness and goodness. He's simply saying, *"The kingdom of God is not defined by position. It is defined by Love. Don't make the mistake of thinking that being honored means you're of greater value than others to the community and the Kingdom and neither should you think that refusing to be honored makes you holy."* Being honored by others does not define our relationship to God or indicate spiritual worth but neither does being in the lowest place give anyone a free pass into God's affections and approval. Humility is not a state of believing yourself to be less deserving than anyone else. Humility is knowing and accepting the whole truth about *who* you are and by doing so, finding the freedom to serve in love without worrying about *where* you are or *what* you are.

Certainly, you are a person with faults, failings, weaknesses and little ugly spots but if that is all you see then you have not accepted the whole truth about yourself. Conversely, you may be an extremely gifted person in a multitude of areas with a talent for doing an incredible job no matter what task you undertake but if that is all you see then you have not accepted the whole truth about yourself. The truth about each one of us is that we are broken vessels and the truth about each one of us is that we are outrageously beautiful works of art created by an awesome God. Each one of us is worthy only of the lowest place and each of us is worthy of the highest honor that comes from being a baptized child of the Father, a sister or brother of the Holy One of God and a vessel of his mighty Spirit.

So, what do we do? What are we called to believe about ourselves? How do we walk humbly? Well, think of Christ, the purest example of humility there is. He became a poor carpenter's son in a backwater town but he allowed a woman to anoint him with the finest of oils. He dined with sinners, pub owners, prostitutes and tax collectors but he also attended banquets in the homes of the rich and well to do. He died as a criminal but was resurrected into awesome glory.

Did he define himself as worthy or unworthy? Did he act as a nothing slave or was he full of his own importance, lording his position over people? Did he allow people to walk all over him or did he demand full respect and become miffed when he didn't get it?

None of the above.

The fact is, Jesus simply knew exactly who he was to the Father and he loved and served out of the fullness of that knowledge. He didn't serve out of a need for others to see him in a certain light and appreciate him or realize how important he was. There was no inner pressure on him to choose the lowest place or the highest place. He didn't need to be perceived as lowly nor did he need the respect of others. If he was given the lowest place, fine. If he was taken to the place of honor, that was fine too. It didn't matter. He could minister to his people no matter where he was. Jesus was beyond place and position. Those weren't the things that defined him and they weren't the things that facilitated his ministry. What defined him was that he was the Beloved of God and what gave him the power to minister was Love. He knew the Father loved him and that's all he needed to be who he was, and to do what he was called to do.

You, too, are loved by the Father. If you can fully accept that and enter into the joy of that, then you won't be particularly concerned one way or the other whether you are high, low or in between. When you walk in true humility, within the truth of yourself or within True Self, there will be times when you will find yourself serving in places that are lower than low and there will be times when you will be the guest of honor at the banquet table and your gifts and abilities will shine for all to see. Whatever. As long as you know in your heart how much the Father loves you, it will not matter in the least where you find yourself.

Be humble...be loved. And go from there.

And Again I say, "Sna!"

Luke 14: 25-33

Jesus warns the crowds, saying that whoever doesn't hate family and life itself, cannot be his disciple. He says to not start what can't be finished and uses the examples of someone building a tower without seeing if he has enough money to complete it, or a king waging a war against another king without considering if he has enough men to win the war. Jesus ends with the admonition that unless you give up all your possessions, you cannot become his disciple.

(In a Year A reflection I wrote about looking up the Aramaic word for the word 'hate', which was used in a different Gospel. Parts of the first few paragraphs of the reflection below are taken from that first reflection to remind you of what I discovered about the word 'hate' as it is used in scripture.)

It is a shock to our spiritual systems when Jesus uses the word 'hate'. In this day and age where hate can be a legal crime and we are so aware of the terrible consequences of hate in society and in our personal lives, to read about Jesus encouraging us to hate our fathers, mothers, husbands, children, brothers and sisters feels terribly harsh and wrong. It doesn't seem very Christ-like and it is difficult to know how to respond to it.

Knowing that the modern English translations of some words in the bible end up to be not exactly true to the original meaning and intention of the speaker, especially if the speaker was of a completely different time and culture, I decided to see if I could find the original Aramaic word for 'hate' and see if our modern definitions square up with what Jesus was really saying. What I discovered was that the Aramaic word for hate is 'sna'.

I have no idea as to the pronunciation of the word 'sna', but what I discovered about this word is that it has five meanings and the only meaning that made any sense at all in the context of what Jesus is saying in this Gospel was the definition, "to put to one side". Within that definition, Jesus is not urging us to despise and shun the people who are closest to us, or anyone at all. In the context of this whole Gospel passage, Jesus is speaking about priorities and explaining that if we choose to follow him, it's not a choice that allows for a halfhearted commitment to be complied with only if it's convenient or if it doesn't cost too much. It's also a choice that calls for much clarity and lightness of being. By lightness of being, I mean not being so burdened with possessions that it's impossible to move when the Spirit says move.

In the last verse, Jesus says, *"So therefore, none of you can become my disciple if you do not give up all your possessions."* Give up. Sna. Set to one side. I love the image of setting something to one side because it feels like gentle detachment. It's not an act of loathing or of throwing something in the garbage or of complete rejection; it is simply an act of saying, "Excuse me. My attachment to you is in my way and I can't see Jesus. I'm just going to move you over here." Either it's a matter of moving someone or something just off to the side or else moving ourselves into a position so we can keep the Master in sight. It's detaching from an obsessive focus on the possessions we have, human or otherwise, in order to behold Jesus more clearly. Detachment is an ongoing exercise of simply keeping our sight lines clear. It doesn't mean not caring about people or situations; it means making sure we can see Christ first.

The definition of what we possess and hang onto in a way that blocks our view of Jesus is going to be different for each one of us and a continual discernment is important to a vibrant spiritual life. This discernment, by the way, will take the rest of your life.

Detachment is a journey, not a one-time act, and as you grow in the spiritual life, you will find that you detach yourself from one thing and suddenly find yourself too attached to something else. We are all a bit like possession magnets.

For some, the vision blocker will be material possessions that require constant maintenance and updating. Others might not be so concerned about material things but find that they have gradually taken possession of children, partners or friends in such an unhealthy way that peace and trust in God's provision and saving power is lost. Others are deeply possessive of their dogmas, rules and regulations. We all possess strong opinions on certain issues and it's a matter of pride that we won't give an inch, not one inch, even when compassion is called for, not righteousness or rightness. Many are very attached to their roles, ministries and territories within a parish community and aren't aware of the subtle moment when defending their territory has become more important to them than what they were originally called to do, or who it was that called them. Some people are deeply possessive of their fears or their disappointments and frustrations and find it difficult to let them go or forgive.

Everyone possesses dreams and desires – many of them worthy and good until they make the present moment lose its good taste. When we are trying to control everything in our lives, when we have plans, desires, dreams and expectations, and when we feel it is up to us to control people and circumstances to make everything fit into our visions, we will find that eventually we are bogged down, slogging along in a desert without making any headway. Even when the plans and desires seemed to be initiated by God, our innate tendency is to try to make it all happen the way *we* think it should all happen. The responsibility of creating, controlling and maintaining our own lives is a very heavy possession, one that obscures the vision of Christ. How can you follow him when you can't even see him?

In other words, there is nothing in our lives, spiritual or secular, that cannot become a possession that has the potential of getting in the way of beholding Jesus. Possessions complicate life and obscure the simplicity of love, and if we look very closely we will see that the one who grabs on to possessions and guards them fiercely is the false self. It needs control and possessions make it feel in control.

What Jesus knew when he told us to 'sna' our possessions was that once we lose sight of him and lose a sense of our relationship to him, false self becomes aggressively afraid and then spiritual understanding becomes distorted. When false self's spiritual understanding becomes distorted it's hard for us to know who we are and, more importantly, we forget who Christ really is. We forget the full beauty of his love. We spend more time with words of fear, resentment, complaint, discouragement and dissatisfaction than we do with words of trust, gratitude, praise and love.

"...none of you can become my disciple if you do not give up all your possessions." That sounds like a strict and cold ultimatum but try hearing it this way: *"Beloved, if you are weighed down by all that you cling to and all that clings to you, it will be impossible for you to follow me because you won't be able to see me and you will forget what I look like. Eventually you won't be quite so eager to come close to my heart because you'll be afraid of me, afraid of my love and afraid that letting go will cause you to bleed more than you already do. When you're burdened by possessions, the evil one tells you that I am to be feared, that you are not valuable, that you are unlovable, a failure and unlikable and that your life is a mess. When you cannot see my eyes, you will believe him. Yes, it costs much to follow me and to keep me close to you but it will cost far more to lose sight of me. If you cannot see my face and see the love pouring out of me for you, you have nothing at all and all your possessions are like dust in the hot, dry wind."*

The wondrous thing is he never goes ahead and leaves us alone to struggle in isolation with all our possessions. He is there, patiently waiting to help us unload and set aside our burdens so that we can behold him and he can behold us, face to face, in freedom and love. He wants us to detach simply because he is lonely for our love and because he knows that we will die without his.

There is no God like him.

Again, the Suscipe, the prayer of St. Ignatius, says it all:

Take, Lord, and receive all my liberty,
my memory, my understanding
and my entire will,
All I have and call my own.
 You have given all to me.
To you, Lord, I return it.
 Everything is yours; do with it what you will.
Give me only your love and your grace.
That is enough for me.

Waste Management

Luke 15: 1-32

The parable of the Prodigal Son – especially the last part where the elder son is resentful.

This gospel emphasizes the supremely generous nature of our God who welcomes the lost and brings them out of the cold darkness into the warm light of home. But what does this scripture have to say to the vast majority who have remained committed to the faith and have never even considered tossing it aside for the emptiness of living solely for the gratification of self?

I'm inviting you to relate to the feelings of the elder brother, but I would be very surprised if any of my readers are guilty of deep feelings of huge resentment toward those who have chosen to return to the church or toward those adults who are received into the Church at Easter. It's not the feelings of the older son toward the younger son that need examination in our lives. It's the attitude of the older son toward his father that is problematic.

The word prodigal means "recklessly spending resources; wastefully extravagant" and when we hear the word, it naturally brings to mind the younger son but could not the older son have been prodigal as well?

That's not how he has traditionally been defined in the context of this parable but when I read that Gospel and hear his resentment and observe his reaction to his Father's joyful generosity, I have to conclude that this older son was also prodigal and that he, too, had a problem with being wasteful and cavalier with the resources he had available to him. His waste was different than his younger brother's obvious and measurable waste. It was more subtle and harder to identify because it was disguised within surface obedience to the rules and conformity to expected behavior. Did the elder son stay at home and work hard because he loved his Father, had a close father/son relationship and enjoyed spending time with his Father or was it because he was afraid not to or because had his sights on his own future inheritance? Had he left the present moment behind and begun living for more than he had?

What did he waste? What were the resources he squandered away? He wasted a chance to appreciate extravagant love. He squandered away the opportunity for close relationship. He threw away the wisdom that comes from being close to, listening to and learning from someone who only desired his happiness. He misused time that could have been spent discovering the joy that can easily be found in sharing a simple meal or singing a psalm together. It was all there for him in the present moment but he wasted those moments. Even when he was terribly upset with his father, he did not seek his father out to discuss it with him. Instead, he asked the servants what was going on. His father actually came to *him* to find out why he was upset. Even at that point the son did not realize that he was so loved by his father that his father went out of his way to seek him out. All the older son could see was the injustice of so much love being lavished on his younger brother.

It's easy to look at that older brother and dislike him but, as it is with most hearts that are wounded, there is more to the wound than what we can see on the surface. It would be easy to point a finger and in pointing that finger, we would completely miss a poignant lesson of what happens when we take for granted, or stop being mindful of, all that is already ours.

The older brother is all of us who have ever lapsed, without meaning to, into doing all the right things, having all the right perspectives and praying all the right prayers but forgetting that there is more to the spiritual life than just right actions. The full spiritual life is a right heart dwelling in the right place. It is a Kingdom mystery that as God's people we are on our way home while at the same time we already *are* home. We are a pilgrim people who travel best when we stay still and dwell in God. Not just near him. In him.

When was the last time you simply gave thanks for what is? I mean outside of those times when God answered a prayer in the way you hoped he would. How often do you bring yourself back to the present moment to just be with him, even for 15 seconds? That's hard to do sometimes, especially when the present moment is chaotic, hurtful or dry and unappealing – we'd far rather live in the past, dwelling on what life seemingly stripped us of, or in the future with all the images of the way we think things should be. The present moment can seem so empty of God and of our inheritance. Yet that is where God is. God completely surrounds us, upholds us and is in every breath we take. God is totally there but we are not at home. Our bodies are there but our hearts and spirits are somewhere else.

We are prodigal without ever leaving home.

There's an old adage that says, "Familiarity breeds contempt." Many good people would be offended if someone suggested they have contempt for God and his blessings but for ten minutes just try staying in the present moment where God dwells. If one is not used to being there, it is so easy to immediately get frustrated in that present moment. If peace, an answer, joy or some sort of sense of God's presence doesn't make itself known very soon, our whole desire is to leave and go somewhere else that is more appealing, even if it's just somewhere in our heads. If we really respected and honored God in the present moment we wouldn't throw up our hands and head off into the past or future. There is a certain amount of contempt in our refusal to stay in the moment. We are saying to God that we prefer to go where our senses are titillated, even in negative ways, than stay wherever he is. Just like the younger brother.

We are prodigal without ever leaving home.

If we spend all our inner time guiltily chastising ourselves for our own perceived failures, we are being seriously wasteful of something extremely precious: the rich, lavish forgiveness and love of God which is always ours and always available. If we get all wrapped up in judgment over the failures of others we are not only wasting forgiveness, we are being contemptuous of it.

We are prodigal without ever leaving home.

If we've ever reviewed all the things we've done for the Lord – all the people we've helped, all the ministries we've participated in, all the prayers we've prayed, all the money we've given, all the times we denied ourselves – and have held that list up to the Lord as a reason for him to fulfill our desires and answer our prayers, we are brushing aside all that we have already been given and labeling it 'not enough'. We are telling God that only the fatted calf will prove that he loves us, forgetting that he gave us the slaughtered lamb.

We are prodigal without ever leaving home.

The parable of the prodigal son can be a very comforting one when we see how generous God is with his gracious love but it can also be a very uncomfortable one if we realize that as older brothers and sisters we all have the capacity to put God on trial and find him lacking. Even if you've never overtly rejected God and would never even consider doing so, perhaps it's time to rediscover and fully appreciate what has already been lavished upon you and to humbly ask forgiveness for being a stay-at-home prodigal. God will shout, laugh, run to you and welcome you with open arms.

We might be prodigal but our God is prodigious.

The Shrewd and the Faithful

Luke 16: 1-13

Jesus tells the parable of the rich man who threatens to fire his manager for squandering his property. The manager, concerned about his future, goes to his master's debtors and reduces their debts so that they will be amenable to him when he loses his job. When the master discovers what the manager has done, he commends the manager for being so shrewd. Jesus says that the children of this age are shrewder in dealing with their own generation than are the children of light. He also states that no slave can serve two masters; you cannot serve God and wealth.

In reading this parable we can make a very confusing mistake by assuming that the rich man represents God. He's not God. He's just a rich man who was shrewd enough to recognize and appreciate shrewdness in another. It takes one to know one, sort of thing. It doesn't say that the manager was completely let off the hook; it just says that the rich man commended him for his astuteness and Jesus points out that people in the world are more shrewd in dealing with the world than the children of God are in dealing with the world – and the spiritual life. If you can't be faithful to the Gospel at every point in your life even if you're interacting with those who only care about their own gain, then you will not be able to be faithful when it comes to true inner riches. *"And if you have not been faithful (to Christ) with what belongs to another, who will give you what is your own?"*

This week's gospel once again brings us to a place where there needs to be some healthy self-examination. We all need to understand that simply shifting around one's attitude towards money and wealth isn't necessarily going to procure the kind of faithfulness Christ is talking about. It's the relationship with God that needs to be diligently sought after. It is what will bring everything else into line, and what is needed to recognize this principle is kingdom shrewdness.

Fr. Pedro Arrupe, S.J., was the General of the Society of Jesus from 1965 to 1983. As a priest in Japan he experienced imprisonment, deprivation and suffering, and was a man who deeply identified with the poor. He wrote the following:

"Nothing is more practical than finding God, than falling in love in an absolute final way. What you are in love with, what seizes your imagination, will affect everything.
It will decide what will get you out of bed in the morning, what you will do with your evening, how you spend your weekends, what you read, whom you know, what breaks your heart and what amazes you with joy and gratitude. Fall in love, stay in love, and it will decide everything."

When visiting a Jesuit province in Latin America, Fr. Arrupe celebrated the Mass in a suburban slum, the poorest in the region. Fr. Arrupe was moved by the attentiveness, respect and gratitude with which the people celebrated the Mass. His hands trembled as he distributed communion and watched the tears fall from the faces of the communicants.

Afterwards, one especially large man invited Fr. Arrupe to his home, a shack that was half falling down. The man seated him in a rickety chair and invited Fr. Arrupe to observe the setting sun with him. After the sun went down, the man explained that he was so grateful for what Arrupe had brought to the community that he wanted to share the only gift he had, the opportunity to share in the beautiful setting sun.

Arrupe reflected, "He gave me his hand. As I was leaving, I thought: 'I have met very few hearts that are so kind.'"

The poor man was a shrewd man and Fr. Arrupe knew it. It takes one to know one. It takes a person who knows God deeply to be able to recognize another heart that has discovered true wealth. The man in Fr. Arrupe's story lived in a falling down shack yet he had a deeply grateful heart and was intensely aware of who it was that authored the magnificent gift of the Eucharist and of a sunset. He shared with Fr. Arrupe all the wealth he had – and what wealth it was!

We who are relatively rich in material possessions and who walk daily in religious freedom and choice, are often guilty of squandering and being unfaithful to the immense wealth God has given us, wealth such as an easily accessible Eucharist or a setting sun.

Kingdom shrewdness is a gift but we need to ask for it and practice it. It is a heart that astutely watches and waits for the presence of God always and everywhere. It is a heart that has the ability to recognize true wealth and to recognize what will bring peaceful security and what will create an unhealthy avaricious longing for more and more. It is a spirit so wise that it yearns for the riches of God's grace and love and so finds God's grace and love in unexpected places.

Challenge: look at the most confrontational or wounding problem in your life right now. Are you simply hoping it will all work itself out in a way that gets you off the hook? Are you wrangling with self-defensiveness and endeavoring to control everything and everyone according to your agenda? Are you tempted to blame other people or things for your problem?

Or are you desiring, praying for and actively seeking a creative, Spirit led solution that will bring forth a deeper and more gracious understanding of who God is and who you really are, as well as bless everyone involved in the problem?

Jean Allen

Now that's kingdom shrewdness.

638

Getting Into The Heart Of It

Luke 16: 19-31
The parable of Lazarus and the rich man.

Just to back up a tad, Jesus was telling this parable to the Pharisees who were "lovers of money and were ridiculing him" after listening to his parable of the dishonest manager (verse 14). The interesting thing about this is that the Pharisees of all people should have been very familiar with God's concern for the poor. One could pull out verse after verse from the Old Testament with messages like this one from Isaiah 58 (NKJV):

"Is this not the fast that I have chosen:
Is it not to share your bread with the hungry,
And that you bring to your house the poor who are cast out;
When you see the naked, that you cover him,
And not hide yourself from your own kin?"

Somehow, even with clear guidance like the above, the religious authorities had determined that wealth was an explicit indication of God's blessing. If you were wealthy it meant you were a very righteous person and on your way to heaven, and if you lived in poverty it was a sign that you were a sinner and maybe even that you were 'unrighteous', which would mean you were to be avoided and you were on your way to hell with no hope of salvation.

In this parable, Jesus is not simply reaffirming that God has a heart for the poor and expects us to have the same heart; he is also being very pointed about the fact that the religious law of the day had moved very far from the original heart of the Law of Moses and the prophets.

In the story, Lazarus, the poor man, went to heaven while the rich man went to Hades, but Jesus didn't say that Lazarus was not a sinner. He was not indicating that poverty always implies righteousness. What Jesus was saying was that the assumption that being wealthy plus being absolutely scrupulous about every minor interpretation of the law, as the Pharisees generally were, was *not* a sign of righteousness and *not* a guarantee that they were pleasing to God.

We may not believe anymore that wealth is a sign of righteousness but I'm afraid we can still easily fall into the misconception that being scrupulous will win God's blessing or at least keep us safe from his anger. Some of the priests, Pharisees and scribes were corrupt and power hungry, but a huge number of them were simply totally convinced that the Romans were in power because the Israelites had somehow failed to keep God's law to his satisfaction. Therefore, they thought that being absolutely scrupulous in being obedient to every last tenet of the Mosaic law as well as to the multitude of minor interpretations of those tenets would bring them back into God's favor and on into freedom from the Romans.

Then along came Jesus telling them that the Law would not save them nor set them free and it could not guarantee their salvation. Can you imagine their consternation when Jesus said in his story that the sinner went to heaven while the rich man went to Hades? The truth is that all of us should be filled with some of the same consternation because we all have a human tendency to place our trust in the wrong things. In endeavoring to adhere meticulously to the tenets of the law, the Pharisees completely forgot the heart of the law, which was, is and always will be love.

We, too, forget.

In last week's Gospel Jesus said, "You can't serve God and mammon too." Everyone thinks 'mammon' just means money. Translated, mammon means, "That in which we trust." Under that definition, even righteous works such as feeding the poor could be labeled 'mammon' if the person performing the works is depending on those works to make him or her righteous in God's eyes. That's not action born of love. That's actually action that keeps God at a safe distance. I've mentioned before how all of us can fall into keeping little lists of all our righteous deeds, hoping that God is impressed and hoping that we've done enough to merit his approval. And very often when things aren't going well we wonder if it's because we haven't been 'good enough'. It's very subtle but one reason it's so difficult to let go of this merit based spirituality is because the false self gains a sense of control when it feels there are actions and deeds it can do to make itself right in God's eyes. The idea that there is nothing we can do to be right and that we can only be loved by God, love him back and then freely share that love with our brothers and sisters makes false self feel far too vulnerable and out of control.

Abraham said *"If they do not listen to Moses and the prophets, neither will they be convinced even if someone rises from the dead."* Sure enough, not even Christ rising from the dead was enough to shift the inner perceptions of most of the Jewish religious authorities and sometimes, the fact that Christ died and rose from the dead is not enough to pull *us* out of our scrupulous fears and our dependence on our actions to assure ourselves that we deserve approval.

What is the greatest of the commandments? You shall love the Lord your God with all your heart, with all your soul and with all your mind - and the second greatest commandment is like it: love your neighbor as you love yourself. On these two commandments hang all the law and the prophets. Jesus was saying to the Pharisees that if they never understood the true core of the law, not even the miracle of resurrected love would penetrate their hearts of stone.

Has your heart been penetrated?

27ᵗʰ Sunday Ordinary C

A Breath Of Fresh Air

Luke 17: 5-10

The apostles ask Jesus to increase their faith and Jesus replies that if they had faith the size of a mustard seed they would be able to say to the mulberry tree to be uprooted and planted in the sea. The he asks who among them would welcome a slave to his table after the slave has just done what he was required to do. Jesus says that we, too, when we have done all that is commanded, should say that we just worthless servants and we have just done what we ought to have done.

"Increase our faith, Lord!" That seems like such an appropriate thing for the disciples to ask of Jesus but the reply Jesus gave them almost sounds like a bit of a put down. Wouldn't a request like that be one that would bless Christ's heart and make him feel that his message about Kingdom priorities was actually getting through to them?

Maybe.

The thing about Jesus is that he is a heart reader; he always knows the deeper motivations behind the prayers we pray and the requests we make. He would have known exactly why the disciples were asking him to increase their faith and my guess is that their inner motivations were not what he was looking for. Perhaps it was necessary for him to immediately set them straight and make them understand that spiritual riches can, like material riches, can be coveted for the wrong reasons and end up being abused.

The disciples may have been asking for an increase of faith because it was so amazing when Jesus said, "Be healed," to an ill

643

person or commanded a storm to be still and those orders were instantly obeyed. What power! They sure wouldn't mind having that kind of faith. Think of what they could do with it! Think of the status they would attain if they had the power to command physical bodies, trees, waves and mountains. Think of the respect they would receive. If any of those thoughts were even on the periphery of their minds, Jesus needed to immediately let them know that the desires for power and status are not kingdom desires. As Habakkuk said in this week's first reading, *"Look at the proud person! Their spirit is not right within them, but the righteous person lives by their faith."*

The disciples may also have been asking for an increase of faith because they were still having trouble believing that Jesus was who he said he was. In spite of all his teachings and miracles, they still had confusions, questions and doubts. It could well have been a combination of both motivations: the temptation to seek power and status as well as the hardness of their hearts that made it difficult for them to believe, even in the face of all the evidence, that Jesus was the Messiah, the Son of God. Wrong motivations plus a lack of basic trust creates very rocky soil for the planting of true faith. In this week's psalm, God exhorts us not to harden our hearts like his people did at Meribah and Massah, when they tested him and put him to the proof even though the people had seen his works.

Jesus' reply was not intended to knock them off their high horses by telling them their faith was so puny it wasn't even as big as a mustard seed and that they were just worthless slaves as far as he was concerned. He was actually opening up to them a beautiful kingdom mystery: true faith permeates the heart of the humble one who knows the power of being a servant of the Lord. Only in God's kingdom can the word 'power' be yoked with the word 'servant' and make complete sense.

Mind you, it does nothing for you to go around saying, "I am worthless, a big nothing and a lowly worm," and think that this is what is pleasing to God – unless you realize that God created worms and thinks they are an awesome work of immense beauty and worth. Only then may you call yourself a worm. What is actually pleasing to God is the heart that does not demand compensation for service rendered. God owes you nothing – but he gives you everything. Why is it so difficult for all of us to rest in that? We always want to say to him, "I did this and this for you. I gave up my time, I left behind possessions, I accepted the difficult situation, I was generous with my money, I built up this and tore down that, I spoke your truth when it was unpopular to do so..." and the expectation is that we should be rewarded at least by increased faith, if not all sorts of other little bonuses and blessings. It's difficult to comprehend a God who does not operate on the worldly reward system of 'I'll do this for you if you do that for me.' This kind of attitude keeps a person on the surface of a true spiritual life, and it creates a vulnerability to being continually knocked off balance when things don't go right or when one finds oneself in a spiritual desert. It's easy to feel punished and abandoned and wonder why it's deserved.

Jesus wants you to live on a deeper level than that. He urges you to move onto a level of faith that doesn't look for rewards or compensation. He's not asking you to engage in self-abnegation or to completely reject your worth and value; he's inviting you to live in a place of total security based on the knowledge that before you ever tried to do something for God you were utterly loved by him and your value to him was complete. It is impossible to make him love or value you more than he already does. Living Faith comes from dwelling in a resting place where power, status and recognition cease to be important because you have found your status and recognition in God and he holds all the power.

Walking in faith means seeking and discovering his face in every moment and in every person you encounter. Walking in Faith is knowing that God has done it all and is in all. He has done the work and completed the story. Walking in faith is knowing that all that's left for you to do is to love and serve him, not for a reward but because the gratitude of your faith gives you wings and makes you desire more than anything to fly close to him. It won't matter to you how you serve, who you serve or where you serve because you will know that he can move mountains and reveal himself whether you are cleaning toilets or speaking to thousands.

Christ wants us all to understand that faith is not a thing we can possess and it's not a just a power that makes things happen; it's an environment. It's where we are called to live, move and have our being. The disciples asking for their faith to be increased was like them asking to be given more air to breathe. They didn't need more air. They just needed to stop holding their breath.

We all need to be less aware of how we think things should be going, accept that we are the beloved of God and abandon ourselves to being a servant of the Lord by being a servant of the ones he loves - which means every single person we encounter each day, whether they are Christian or not. We must serve them as if they are Christ himself.

If we can do that, we will be living in the heady atmosphere of the Kingdom and we will have more faith than we will know what to do with.

Just breathe.

Get Changed Before You Go

Luke 17: 11-19

Jesus heals ten lepers and send s them to show themselves to the priests, but only one, a Samaritan, turns back to give thanks.

The readings for this Sunday are about gratitude and conversion and Catholics are a Thanksgiving people, a Eucharistic people: every time we participate in the Eucharist, we are engaging in a communal act of huge thanksgiving. Every day is Thanksgiving as far as the Church is concerned because gratitude is foundational to who we are and to everything we do – or it should be.

But when was the last time you were converted?

Of the ten lepers, only one returned to give thanks and to show that he recognized Jesus as God. The fact that he was a Samaritan, who knew the Jews despised him, made his gratitude even more poignant. He obviously sensed that Jesus was in no way concerned about his religious background. He simply returned praising God while prostrating himself at Jesus' feet in a true act of conversion, and Jesus assured him his faith had made him well. That meant spiritual healing as well as physical. The other nine lepers clearly did not feel the need to be converted. They were of the Jewish faith and, in their understanding, that was the one true faith and they felt absolutely no need to turn around and acknowledge Jesus, even though it was he who healed them. They were on their way to be obedient to the law by showing themselves to the priests in order to be pronounced officially well so they could regain their status in the community. What more did they need?

Were they grateful? Who knows? Certainly they would have been experiencing huge relief and their minds would have been racing, thinking of the lives they could return to as normal and acceptable people. They would have been filled with joy as they thought of going back to their families, their friends and their jobs. However, relieved and joyful does not always equal truly grateful. Those nine healed lepers chose to stay within their old way of understanding God and completely missed the opportunity to be introduced to an incredible new life. They thought that by being law abiding Jews they had all that was spiritually necessary.

We can be in the right place doing all the right things and still be in deep need of conversion. If we do not seek conversion constantly, we will become static and stagnant believers. We will be maintaining, not growing.

As I have noted before, 'Conversion' is a Latin term: con (altogether) and vertere (turn) meaning "to completely turn around", or "to change in form". Reconciliation is one point of conversion. It's an act of recognizing the things we've done wrong, turning around, confessing them and receiving cleansing forgiveness, which can lead to gratitude and healing. But what about conversion in the midst of all that we do *right*? Sometimes we can be so familiar with the spiritual routines, beliefs and rituals that are so foundational to our lives that we lose the urgent consciousness that the spiritual life is not a life of simply maintaining faithfully what we have, but one of continually seeking out and going deeper into new discoveries of who God is and who we are. Whenever we can't conceive of anything deeper or different, we tend to stop seeking.

"Turn to me and be saved, all you ends of the earth, for I am God, and there is no other," said God in Isaiah 45:22(NIV)

It doesn't matter who you are or how committed you have been to the Lord, every morning, from the moment you open your eyes to a new day and in every moment throughout that day, God is saying to you, *"Turn to me and be saved, for I am God. There is no other."* Being 'saved' is not just being pulled away from the clutches of the Evil One or from the power of death; being saved is also being pulled away from the dangers of the status quo and 'good enough' religion. Being saved is being lifted out of the quagmire of cynicism and criticism. Being saved is being freed from a heart of stone and being given a spirit of gratitude and a tender heart of flesh. Being saved is knowing that you can never get to the bottom of a heart like God's and that you will never fully comprehend him but you're willing to die trying. Being saved is coming to know your Name, your True Self, and entering into the joyful revelation that it was never about you – and yet, it was always about you.

In the last reflection, I said that gratitude within our faith gives us wings and makes us want to fly close to the heart of God. This time I'm adding that gratitude helps us to be open to the Godwinds of grace, the grace that causes us to be changed in form. That means transformed or *not being the same as you were before*. Something else that aids us in conversion is a willingness to say, "Maybe I don't know it all. Maybe I have only been seeing part of the picture. Maybe I've been trying to create myself and make myself righteous and holy. Maybe I've been holding on too hard to creating myself and not allowing God to create me according to the name by which he and he alone calls me."

Conversion is a risk. Always has been and always will be. It's a risk of not being the one who's got the plan, learned the rules, totally knows the score and is in control. The kingdom journey is not a game plan; it's an adventure into the 'known unknown', meaning we can listen to what others have to say about the spiritual journey but in the end we need to go ourselves and find out that it's completely different than what we assumed it would be. Conversion doesn't necessarily mean that all that we have been up to the present moment was wrong; it just means we accept the fact that we're never ever finished with being radically changed. Note that I didn't say we're never finished with just being made nicer, more pliant, more obedient or more irreproachable. I'm talking about being Changed. Capital 'C'. The Samaritan leper, rather than just asking for and experiencing a change in his circumstances, allowed Christ and the circumstances to change him.

Conversion, indeed, is risky and it may also involve suffering because suffering strips us of control and self-sufficiency. In turning back to give thanks to Jesus after knowing the suffering of illness and of isolation, the Samaritan leper risked everything. He was given his heart's desire and he could have gone off like the others and returned to the old spiritual life he had always known, physically healed but spiritually static. In turning back to Jesus, he was opening himself to a future where it would be necessary to examine all his religious assumptions and attitudes to see how a poor carpenter with the power to heal would fit into his life. From then on, even if he never saw the Lord in person again, Christ would always be there in spirit and in truth, challenging him and changing him.

May Christ do that to us all.

And In This Corner...

Luke 18: 1-8

Jesus is encouraging his followers to pray always and not to lose heart and he tells them the parable of the widow who kept coming to an unjust judge to ask for justice against her opponent. The judge finally gives the widow justice so she will stop coming and bothering him. Jesus asks if an unjust judge responds to continual petition, will not God grant justice to those who ask? The Jesus queries as to whether he will find faith on earth when he returns.

A few years ago, Fr. William Hann, who is, at this writing, pastor of St. Joseph the Worker in Victoria, spoke about Habakkuk crying out to God and challenging God because God just didn't seem to be listening to his pleas and his prayers. Fr. Hann, who had been going through some extremely difficult and painful circumstances, had this to say:

"The beauty of the prophet Habakkuk is that he dares to give voice to his fear and frustration and that he dares to put it on God's desk. I wonder sometimes whether we dare to be as honest with God as that prophet is. The suggestion is often made that you don't speak to God that way.
I would like to suggest that in a life of faith there is room for speaking to God in the way Habakkuk does. God can handle our anger and our emotional outbursts when we must come to terms with the shattering of our dreams or betrayal in any of its ugly forms.
These past months I know I have cried out to God and asked him for answers, for an explanation, to ask him for something to hold on to, for fear that I might otherwise go under." (Quoted with permission.)

When I heard that homily, I thanked God for a priest who's not only transparent about his own struggles but is also one who knows the immense value of wrestling with God.

This week's gospel is about praying without ceasing but it is also about spiritual honesty. In the lectionary's translation of this gospel passage, the judge says, *"I will grant her justice, so that she may not wear me out by continually coming."* (NRSV) An alternate translation to that is, *"...so that she will not slap me in the face."* That widow must have been displaying a huge amount of anger and frustration if the judge was afraid of being slapped in the face!

We can be too nice in our prayers – a niceness that blocks us from really coming face to face with the Living God and discovering that he loves it when we wrestle with him in complete naked honesty. Indeed, this pounding on God's door is absolutely necessary for our spiritual growth. God is not fooled by our nice safe prayers – but we are blinded by them.

Remember the story of Jacob where Jacob wrestled with God in the form of an angel in the desert? He wrestled through the night and he wouldn't let go until God blessed him. God not only blessed Jacob but he gave him a new Name: Israel. Before the wrestling match, Jacob would not have been ready to hear his true Name. Jacob was too full of himself. I'm not saying he was an arrogant or egotistical man. He may have been, I don't know, but when I say 'full of himself' I mean that even though he was afraid and in danger, he was still depending on his own thinking, ability, might and power to handle his circumstances. During the wrestling match, God dislocated Jacob's hip but then he blessed and gave him a new Name, one that expressed everything God was calling him to be.

Scripture is full of examples of holy men and women who have dared to speak their minds to God, to desperately ask him why things are the way they are, to demand justice or a change in plan. This has probably confused more than a few Christians down through the ages who have wondered how God could have a plan and then change it just because some ordinary person asked him to. This can bring on an uncomfortable insecurity about the constancy of God's plans. If we can pray and challenge God's plan and his ways and then he actually listens to us, is that not giving us too much power? Are we not called to just humbly say, "Thy will be done," and then meekly shoulder the burden of whatever cross we've been given? If we pray, ask for something that's bad for us, and God gives in, isn't that making us into spoiled brats? Isn't it dangerous to question God's directions and plans?

These questions are all based on the idea that God is just like us only he's the boss. He's the Dictator, a benevolent one but a dictator none-the-less, and wrestling with a dictator has never been perceived as a smart idea. Lightening bolts and punishment may be involved. Better to just give in immediately rather than chance offending God. Don't misunderstand me. Saying, "Thy will be done," is a beautiful prayer, but please note that Jesus prayed that prayer of exquisite submission *after* struggling mightily with his Father, *after* asking that the cup be taken away and *after* sweating blood. Something dynamic and intimate happened between him and the Father that we are not privy to but, whatever it was, it took Jesus to the next level of a love revelation that brought him the strength of grace he required, a renewed vision of what was at stake and the courage to do what needed to be done to bring us all home. Thank God he wrestled and was not the least bit concerned that he would offend his Father.

Listen. If you ever seem to change God's mind about anything it's because that was his desire in the first place and he wanted you to engage in the *only* kind of relationship dialog that could ever change the mind of anyone: Questions. Honesty to the point of being utterly naked. Spilling the guts. Laying it all out on the floor until there is nothing left to hide. Refusing to walk away until there's resolution or revolution. Not being silent just because you're afraid of being wrong or in case the other will get mad at you. Waiting and listening without fear.

It's messy all right. The blood and guts all over the floor will be all yours but the difference between doing this with God as opposed to doing it with another person is that God gently and lovingly cleanses the blood and guts and puts them all back in right order and then he heals the wounds and gives you a new Name and a new way of walking.

Don't just be O.K. with asking God nicely for things or answers. Get right in there and wrestle with him. Challenge him. Question him. Honestly lay out your fears and frustrations. It's the only way to learn who he really is because if you are like the insistent widow and you keep at it, he will respond by revealing his nature and showing you aspects of himself you never suspected were there. He reveals himself to those who want to know him so badly that they're willing to struggle through the night for that ultimate blessing. He wants us to wrestle through the darkness with desire, because that's how his real face becomes planted deeply in our hearts. I cannot tell you how many people pray without looking God in the face because they are so convinced that what they will see in his face are disassociation, condemnation, disappointment and sadness. What are actually there are connectedness, joyful love and fierce desire. No one can desire God as much as he desires us.

There have no doubt been times in your life when God has answered a prayer of yours after a not particularly challenging struggle. Think back on all the prayers he has quickly answered in your life – so many little prayers prayed, answered and forgotten. But the ones that really moved you forward in your spirit in a way you could never have done yourself were those prayers prayed through the night in great anguish, prayers where you cried out in distress or prayers that were prayed for so long that you thought God had forgotten you. These are the kind of prayers that transform us and bring us to a new understanding of who he is and who we are.

Don't lose heart. Go ahead and wrestle with God, the same God that Jacob and Jesus wrestled with. Then get ready to be dislocated...

      blessed...

            and renamed.

The Exchange

Luke 18: 9-14
The parable of the Pharisee and the Publican.

The question I tend to ask when reading scripture is not "What?" but rather, "Why?" In this particular reading, it would seem to be obvious as to why the tax collector went home justified rather than the Pharisee. Nobody enjoys being around someone who is a self satisfied, self-righteous prig and is arrogant about his or her accomplishments, so why would God? We all agree that being self-righteous is not a 'nice' way to be and that it is much more pleasant to hang out with someone who doesn't act like he or she is the epitome of virtuous behavior that everyone else should emulate. Naturally, God would like the humble tax collector better than he would like the self-satisfied Pharisee. Anyone would. End of story. Lesson: don't think too highly of yourself.

That doesn't satisfy me. Yes, I agree that we should strive to not be self righteous, but I believe Jesus told this parable, and others like it, not only to wake people up to the fact that God isn't impressed by our own manufactured acts of righteousness but also to teach us something about God's desire to walk with his people in relationship. The lesson here is not that God *won't* walk with you when you are self-sufficient; the lesson is that he *can't*. There's no room for him.

The tax collector went home justified or made righteous in the sight of God but the justification had nothing to do with what he did or did not do. It had everything to do with the capacity he had to receive the fullness of God into his heart. His actions were not what made him righteous; God was his righteousness. Scripture confirms this:

*But God chose what is foolish in the world to shame the wise; God chose what is weak in the world to shame the strong; God chose what is low and despised in the world, things that are not, to reduce to nothing things that are, so that no one might boast in the presence of God. He is the source of your life in Christ Jesus, **who became for us wisdom from God, and righteousness and sanctification and redemption**, in order that, as it is written, 'Let the one who boasts, boast in the Lord.' (1 Corinthians 1:29,30, NRSV)*

In the last reflection, I wrote that before Jacob wrestled with God, he could not receive God's blessing because he was too full of himself and I specified that this did not necessarily mean that he was arrogant; it just meant that he relied too much on himself. We all do that to some degree or other and even being anxious about whether we're doing all the right things is placing ourselves just inside the cramped ring of self-sufficiency. When things aren't going well for us we have inner checklists of all that we are doing right, wondering if we are missing something. We wonder if it's something we are doing or not doing that is blocking God. If God is not answering our prayers, it's got to be our fault, right?

"Maybe if I went to reconciliation more often... Maybe if I prayed for half an hour instead of fifteen minutes... Maybe it's because I lose my temper a lot or because I didn't put as much in the collection plate as I normally do... Maybe it's because I have inner criticisms of some people... Maybe, maybe, maybe..."

It is good to be good. But being good and doing good is not what makes us righteous or justified before God and it's not what makes God respond to our prayers or makes him want to have relationship with us. The tax collector went home justified because he was empty enough, open enough and humble enough to receive God's righteousness. The Pharisee, on the other hand, had all the justification he felt he needed – his own. He knew the Mosaic Law and adhered to it faithfully. According to the law, he was clean, morally and ritually. He was 'Spiritually Responsible' and he was certain this was what procured God's approval and made him righteous. But remember the parable Jesus told about the servant who did all he was supposed to do? He couldn't claim a place at the Master's table simply because he had done his job.

This gives us an idea of the amazing graciousness of God. He doesn't fill us with his righteousness because we do all the right things but because he loves us so much that he desires to fill us with himself. *He* is our gift, our righteousness and our justification. Everything he gives us is pure gift given out of love, not out of obligation or as payment in kind.

There is a huge amount of relief in this understanding if one can grasp it. The idea that we do something in order to receive justification is putting the cart before the horse. We need to receive first and then our actions will flow naturally and beautifully from a heart full of gratitude. We need to understand there is nothing we could ever do to merit the gift of God's righteousness. All he wants is for us to come to his table, poor, empty and hungry for him.

Listen to this passage from Isaiah 61 (NKJV): *(The Spirit of the Lord is upon me) ... to comfort all who mourn, to provide for them that mourn in Zion, to give to them beauty for ashes, the oil of joy for mourning, the garment of praise for the spirit of heaviness; that they might be called **trees of righteousness**, the planting of the Lord, that he might be glorified.*

He is glorified when we are poor enough and empty enough to receive him - and sometimes that means admitting before God that we have absolutely no capacity to do any of what we have been feeling responsible for doing: letting go of the past, forgiving, trusting, serving, understanding or believing. We can only be open and empty. We can only wait on him and be willing to participate in the mystic love exchange, which is ashes, grief and despondency for his beauty, joy and a spirit of praise.

Do you get it? *He* is our righteousness - everything he is and has is available to us just because he loves us and all we're required to do is to show up, give up, let go, be empty and revel in our poverty.

If ever there was a reason to celebrate, this is it.

Risk Assessment

Luke 19: 1-10
The story of Zacchaeus climbing a tree to see Jesus.

Do you ever feel that in the spiritual life everyone else is grasping something important but you're just a small person whose vision is blocked? Everybody talks about this Jesus person but all you can see are crowds of people who are talking about him, defining him, discussing him and parsing his every word and action. Sure, you could just listen to all the words and homilies being spoken about him but everybody seems to have a different take on who he is, what he is doing and why he is doing it, and something inside of you wants more than that. You want to experience him for yourself. Even if you could just behold him from a distance with your own eyes, it would be better than what you're getting now. Your heart is crying out, "I want to see Jesus!"

What are you willing to do to see him?

Zacchaeus was the chief tax collector in Jericho and he was a rich man. He was short but I'm willing to bet he wasn't the only short person in Jericho. The difference between Zacchaeus and others who couldn't see Jesus because of the crowds was that Zacchaeus was willing to take a risk in order to see him with his own eyes. In his case, it was a huge risk because he was willing to risk his pride. He would have known that the people of Jericho did not hold him in high esteem. Tax collectors were employed by the Roman occupation, and tax collectors, as far as the Jewish people were concerned, were traitors to their people and cheats because they often overcharged and pocketed the extra shekels. By climbing a tree in order to see Jesus he would have been opening himself to a lot of ridicule and scorn but something in his heart cried out, "I want to see Jesus!"

Jesus didn't stop and call Zacchaeus down to eat with him just because he was a rich tax collector; Jesus called him down because Zacchaeus had literally gone out on a limb in order to see him. I've said before that Jesus is a heart reader and what he read in Zacchaeus' heart was more than just idle curiosity. Zacchaeus had risked a lot in order to see Jesus. There was unfulfilled desire there and perhaps Zacchaeus understood that his riches and possessions were not making him happy in the way he had hoped. Jesus called Zacchaeus down because Zacchaeus had capacity. Did Jesus say, "...Zacchaeus too is a son of Abraham," simply because Zacchaeus was a Jew, or because within Zacchaeus there was the same seed of desire that Abraham had possessed, a kind of desire that moved Abraham to risk much in order to walk with God?

We can stand before the Lord and profess that we are poor, that we have nothing to offer him and that we depend on him for all we need to live, but sometimes we need to go a little further than that. Going further does not prove anything to God who knows exactly who we are but it moves us beyond our ingrained self-images, beyond who we think we are and what we think we are capable of. Going further stretches our little boxes of small definitions, and that always requires taking a risk.

I want to emphasize that taking a risk is not an exercise in trying to gain God's approval by what we do. Rather, it is a widening and deepening of our inner capacity to see and receive Jesus. We have to keep in mind that what is a risk for one person may not be a risk at all for another so this is a very personal journey and we must not get caught up in comparing ourselves to other people and finding ourselves lacking – or comparing them to ourselves and making judgments when they find it difficult to do what is relatively simple to us. This is definitely a 'mind your own business' part of the spiritual journey. God does not compare us to anyone else so we should be very careful about doing it ourselves.

The kinds of risks that can challenge us are many and varied. They are rarely dangerous except to our egos or our false selves. Sometimes the risk is to take on a task we don't feel is within our skill set or is one we're not certain we're able to do well. Sometimes the risk is to allow someone else to be in control or to allow someone to take on a task when we feel we'd do a much better job. There is a risk in allowing others to misjudge us. There is a lot of risk in receiving when we're used to being the ones who give. For some, the risk is to be silent when everything inside wants to rebut and disprove. Some need to take the risk of being more transparent while others need to know the risk of not being the center of attention. So many kinds of risks to choose from.

What we are all called to risk is our pride and our fear of being vulnerable and imperfect. This is exactly what Zacchaeus risked by climbing the tree. His desire to see Jesus pushed him beyond protecting his self-image and when Jesus spied him in the tree, Jesus knew he had encountered someone who could receive his Word. Still, there was one more thing Zacchaeus needed to do before he committed himself to the risky acts of repentance and reparation.

Zacchaeus had to first decide to come down out of the tree.

That, too, was a risk. He could have said, "No. I'll stay here, thanks very much. I've caught a glimpse of you, Jesus, and that's good enough for me. If I come down, I will be fully committed. It will mean that I am willing to go the whole way with you and risk far more than I've risked so far. If I come down, my life will be in your hands; nothing will ever be the same again. All my inner perceptions are going to be challenged and every day I will be called to take Kingdom risks." Zacchaeus would be facing far more changes in more than just his outward actions if he really wanted to engage with Jesus.

Zacchaeus took a risk, came down and participated in the love exchange: beauty for ashes, the oil of joy for mourning and a garment of praise for a spirit of heaviness. After coming down from the tree of risk, he became grafted to 'The Tree' - the Tree of Righteousness. He had been lost but now he was found. Salvation in the person of Jesus had come to his house. I particularly like the fact that Jesus said salvation had come to Zacchaeus' house, not just his home. By saying 'house', Jesus was promising salvation not just for Zacchaeus but also for his family and his servants – his household. By taking a risk in order to see Jesus, we will be affecting many more people than just ourselves.

By the way, there is another person in scripture who took a risk, climbed a tree, came down, was utterly transformed and brought salvation to his house:

Jesus, the King of Kingdom risk takers.

Unknowing

Luke 20: 27-28

Some Sadducees who did not believe in resurrection ask Jesus about who would a widow of seven men, be married to in the afterlife.

In the longer version of this Gospel, the Sadducees went through a whole rigmarole about 7 brothers, each one marrying the same widow as the previous brother died. They were asking to which brother would the widow be married in the resurrection? They were obviously trying to trap Jesus because they didn't even believe in the resurrection. There is a whole wonderful message in this Gospel about life and resurrection but I'm going to look at something a bit more obscure, yet is something that does have an impact on our present resurrected lives and on how we relate to God.

The Sadducees may not have believed in life after death but many others of the Jewish leadership did and there would have been many debates amongst themselves over questions such as the one the Sadducees posed to Jesus. It made me wonder how the Pharisees would have answered the question, a question that rose out of the human proclivity to make God – and therefore the afterlife – look a lot like a reflection of our experience of life here on earth.

The following is a favorite little folk tale of mine:

A saint was once given the gift of speaking the language of the ants. He approached one ant, who seemed the scholarly type, and asked, "What is the Almighty like? Is he in any way similar to the ant?"

Said the ant scholar, "The Almighty? Certainly not! We ants, you see, have only one sting. But the Almighty, he has two!" When the saint asked the ant scholar what heaven was like, he solemnly replied, "There we shall be just like him, having two stings each, only smaller ones."
A bitter controversy rages among ant religious schools of thought as to where exactly the second sting will be located in the heavenly body of the ant.

The first time I heard this I laughed out loud because I know that in the past I have been as certain of the Almighty's characteristics as that little scholarly ant was.

Be honest with yourself. Do you not believe deep down that God has much the same opinions as you do? When you think about your perceptions of God, of the spiritual life and of what will happen in the afterlife, do you not see God as a lot like us only bigger – maybe with two stings instead of one? If you were to accept that you actually have no idea what God is like, where would you be? If you suddenly said to yourself, "I have no clue. *We* have no clue," what would you be left with? Most of what we surmise about God is based on what we know about ourselves and on our experiences of the world, and when we understand that even all of humanity's vast history of experience is about as useful in personally knowing who God really is as an ant's experience, it's a little overwhelming to realize how small we really are and how little we really know.

But we carry on like the ants believing in a God that is just like us only a bit bigger and more powerful. It would seem that according to common perception, God has an ego that needs to be right, needs to be respected, needs to be continually validated by our recognition and praise and needs to be in full control. Just like us.

God doesn't *need* any of these things. Anytime in scripture that we are called to offer praise, recognition, obedience, respect and love to God it is for *our* benefit, not his. The call to trust and to live and grow in faith is not a call to a subservience that will keep us safe from a hard task-master; it is a call for us to enter through a gateway to a place called the Kingdom, a place that is wider, deeper, higher and more full of life than we could ever imagine. It is a call to discover that our God is not just 'out there'; he is 'in here'. It is a call to understand that Christ's birth, death, resurrection and new life wasn't just a one time event that brought us to salvation; it is the full journey of every present moment of every committed follower of the Good News. There is no separation between our lives and Christ's.

We need to stop making God look just like us, shake off all those limiting human attributes we assign to God (especially the part that assigns God an ego or a false self) and begin a journey of unknowing. Really, not knowing anything is the absolute best place to start. We spend much of our lives accumulating knowledge about God, and this is a good foundation, but at some point we need to let all that head knowledge go and begin to seek the gates of the Kingdom, gates that only exist in the heart. Words and head knowledge will not move us through those gates. Only love and desire will open those gates and usher us into the Kingdom where God waits to dance with us.

That's right. *Dance.* Think of a waltz with two individuals meshed together into one graceful and flowing movement. It looks like each one is fully aware of what the next step should be, but there is always one who is leading. In a good dance relationship, the partner who is being led has such trust in the one leading and follows so well that the two might as well be a single entity.

How can we dance with God if we keep a distance between him and us? How can we dance in full partnership if we insist on seeing ourselves as related to him but completely separated from him? How can we dance if we don't see ourselves as worthy enough to be held by him?

Those Sadducees were very learned men. Jesus was saying to them that all their knowledge and surmising would, in the end, not take them through the door to resurrected life. God is not the God of the dead but of the living and we are the children of the resurrection. God is unknowable by our limited minds.

But he is completely danceable in our hearts.

We're On Our Way Home

Luke 21:5-19
Jesus is speaking about the signs of the end times.

The subject of the end times is pretty frightening but at the same time has a strange fascination for people. Throughout history, lot of people have seemed pretty willing to be convinced that the end is near. The fact is, when the end times will take place is not something we are called to focus on. The Church does not bring these scriptures to our attention to scare us or make us start looking around for obscure, or not so obscure, signs that the world is in a complete downward spiral and God is pretty much winding things up. We need to remember that *"...this world is not our permanent home; we are looking forward to a home yet to come."* (Heb. 13:14) and in 1 Peter, chapter 2, right after he tells us that we are a royal priesthood, Peter says that we are *'visitors and pilgrims'.*

In other words, we don't belong here. I've said it before. We're visitors. Don't get too settled.

In Philippians 3, Paul says, *"But our citizenship is in heaven and it is from there that we are expecting a Savior, the Lord Jesus Christ."* We need to understand that we are citizens from another country and it is from that country that our Savior came, comes and will come again. We don't belong here and perhaps that's why the subject of the end times fascinates us. We are naturalized citizens in this world but we yearn to go home. That deeper yearning is the reason why there is always a hole within that wants to be filled, no matter what we do and accomplish. Whether we recognize it or not, everything within us aches for Jesus to come and take us back to where we belong, where we fit, where we are loved and valued simply for who we are, not for what we do and accomplish.

Do we have to wait until death frees us from this world in order to find out who we really are? Absolutely not. Jesus is always coming to us and calling us by our true names but we are too often listening to other strident voices that give us false names and we miss his subtle voice. It's hard not to allow the values and expectations of the others to name us and define us. We are encouraged to seek our identities in our roles, vocations, natural talents and accomplishments, and the concept that God does not value us for what we do but for who he created each of us to be is completely contrary to how we've been taught to think. It's difficult to wrap our heads around that idea when all our lives we have been taught that our value depends on fitting into the norm, whatever that norm may be.

It is good to be responsible citizens of this world and loving members of the Church. It is good to strive to use our gifts and develop our capabilities for the benefit of the larger community. It's good and right to discern our vocations. Finding our true value doesn't mean dispensing with these things. It means going beyond them. It means going higher, deeper and wider. If we do not discover our individual spiritual identity in God's eyes, the rest of it will never satisfy and it will never ever feel like we've done enough. You could be totally called to be a dedicated single, a spouse, a parent, a deacon, a priest or a Religious but these vocations will not fill up all the chasms in your heart until you know your real Name - the name God calls you by – and until you come face to face with Love himself.

I need to emphasize this: if you don't know who you are, you will always feel like there must be more, that you're not quite measuring up and that you haven't quite gotten 'there'. No matter how much you try to do and accomplish what you feel you've been called to do and accomplish, it will never feel like you've done enough or that you've received enough. You can avoid facing these feelings of lack and inner hunger by keeping really busy doing everything you feel is expected of you, and more, but eventually when you stop – or when something like illness stops you – you will still come face to face with the knowledge that all you have done and everything you thought was validating you and defining you was not enough and never will be enough. And at those times, all you will want to do is leave and go home.

Stop! Stop and take time to ponder that not only did Christ come into the world and not only will he be coming again, but also that he is coming every moment of every day. He is coming NOW. There may one day be a day of worldly apocalypse where Christ will come riding on the clouds one last time but before that time we are all going through our own large and small apocalyptic-like events where we are wounded, where our insecurity is uncovered and we are threatened, when our inner temples are leveled, when we are confronted, exposed and made to feel we are not good enough. These upheavals in our lives make us cry out for some place where we really belong.

And Jesus comes. He comes from Home and as he comes, he calls you by your real name. He never comes to punish. He comes with vindication that the world can never give. He comes to say, "Take heart. You're on your way back home. I know you lost your way because you're alien to this world and it's so easy to get disoriented, but I know who you are and I haven't lost you. You are in my sight and in my grip. You are not alone."

You do not belong here. You do not 'fit'. But Jesus came and showed us all how to make it through as a stranger in a very strange and harsh land. He knew all of his True Names, so he knew exactly who he was and who was the source of his total worth. He had nothing to prove or accomplish, except to get us all back. He simply knew love, received love and desired to share love. Now it is his desire to come and share his love with you as well as share with you the ultimate joy and the full satisfaction of knowing your own name. Every moment he is coming to bring home to you until it's time to come and bring you home. When you actually hear him call your real name it will be like receiving a piece of the homeland to carry with you in your spirit to the ends of the earth and until the end of your world.

And it will be enough.

The King of Grace

Luke 23: 35-43

The leaders and the soldiers mock Jesus on the cross and hang an inscription over him that says, "This is the King of the Jews." One criminal on one side of him taunts him, saying, "Save yourself and us!" But another criminal on the other side rebukes the first criminal and asks Jesus to remember him when Jesus comes into his Kingdom. Jesus says, "This day you will be with me in paradise."

We have such a gracious King.

When celebrating the kingship of Jesus, we come face to face with the tension between the worldly definition of Kingly power and the heavenly definition, because Jesus turned all the definitions upside down and redefined what it means to be King. One of the most powerful examples of his brand of kingship was his response to the thief on the cross beside him. Gracious. He was gracious beyond what we can fathom. He was nailed to the one place where not even the Father would have faulted him for being completely swallowed up by his own agony but Jesus still remembered who he was and what he was called to be: an incarnation of the Grace of God.

I'm sure all of you have encountered a gracious person at least once in your life. Have you ever stopped to analyze what made that person seem gracious to you? What did they do? How did they act that made you appreciate just being in their presence? What was their response to you and others that made them so attractive?

We appreciate graciousness wherever we find it but one place where we are really blessed is when we encounter gracious behavior in our priests. The priest in the parish we belong to is a very gracious man and there are many gracious priests in our diocese – as well as in your diocese, wherever that may be. However, priests who failed to reflect God's gracious love have disappointed all of us at one time or another, and the body has sustained many wounds. My response to that is: yes, but how many people have been wounded by the same lack of graciousness in *us*?

I have written this before, but it's so important that it is worth repeating. We, the Royal Priesthood, have exactly the same responsibility as ministerial priests to be beautiful and accurate reflections of God's graciousness. We are called to be People of Grace and we are called to be a Gracious People. We are dignified daughters and sons of God and Christ the King is our brother. It behooves us to become a little more familiar with royal behavior as it was and is defined by Jesus, and then ask ourselves if we exhibit the kind of behavior that makes others feel worthwhile and blessed in our presence.

Note how Jesus responded to the thief. He did not make the thief go through a full account of his sins. The thief was already suffering the natural consequences of his failures and that was enough. Jesus, engulfed in exactly the same suffering as the thief even though he didn't deserve it, did not respond to the thief or to the situation with judgments of good versus bad or right versus wrong. Jesus did not lecture, reprimand, demand restitution or require a complete change of character before he welcomed the thief. And he didn't harbor any resentment whatsoever that as a good person he was suffering just as much as this bad person. What he did was immediately become the thief's best friend. *"Today you will be with me in paradise."*

Gracious.

The gracious person is not hung up on appearances and does not make judgments. In the welcoming heart of a gracious person it is not a shock that a thief can enter paradise on the arm of the king. Gracious people are free of the self-judgment that says, "I'm pretty good" or "I'm very bad" but instead, focus on appreciating the beauty and value that God sees in them and which allows them to appreciate the immense beauty and value of others – even those who don't meet the accepted criteria of goodness or value.

We say off the top of our heads that others certainly have value because our Christian theology teaches that Christ died for the whole world. But generally what we *really* mean when talking about the value of those who do not meet our standards of goodness or right thinking is that they have 'potential value' or that they have not yet reached 'full value'. Presumably they will reach full value when they meet certain criteria such as recognizing the error of their ways, apologizing, changing their behavior or their belief system or coming back to church. The problem with this attitude, besides that it doesn't reflect the nature of our King, is that we get caught up in the necessity of having to watch and strictly maintain our own righteousness, something we have no capacity to do. It's a jagged and weary circle of judgment and somehow the King of unconditional love gets left out of the loop.

Truly gracious people have experienced true grace, know they are loved and therefore assume that everyone they meet is a co-receptor of God's full love and is worthy of utter respect, attention and appreciation. This is why you enjoy being with a gracious person. You feel special. You feel as if that person really sees you. You feel valued and respected for who you are, as you are.

It is good to practice being gracious toward everyone you

encounter but it will be a struggle to maintain a consistently gracious manner unless you have consistent encounters with our gracious King. I think we often think of grace as a thing, either something God gives to us in order to overcome a specific struggle (actual grace) or what we receive in baptism, the divine life that infuses our souls (sanctifying grace). Grace is all of that, but it's pretty dry theology until you experience the utter beauty of being in the presence of a gracious King who only has eyes for you, who is delighted that you have come as you are and tells you that he wants to sit with you at the banquet. When you have personally spent time being the focal point of gracious and joyful love, that's when you begin to understand the fullness and wideness of true grace. That's when you fall deeply in love with your King. That's when you fall in love with how the King sees you and others, and that's when you begin to yearn to emulate the gracious dignity of your King. Then grace becomes an overflow from loved received rather than an outer action that can easily break down, allowing you to get caught up again in self-judgment and in the judgment of others.

St. John of the Cross wrote:

When you regarded me
Your eyes imprinted your grace in me,
In this, you loved me again,
And thus my eyes merited
To also love what you see in me….
Let us go forth together to see ourselves in your beauty.
(Spiritual Canticle, 32, 33)

Be regarded by the King. Be imprinted by Grace.

Appendix

The Good Child

There are a lot of annoying and genuinely disturbing things about the Advent/Christmas season in the secular world today. There's a lot of materialism and merchants put people under a huge amount of pressure to spend much more than they can afford. Political correctness is rampant and many stores and institutions now refuse to use the word 'Christmas' at all. Radio stations and stores start playing Christmas music in November and by the time Christmas comes, you feel like if you hear, "Have a Holly Jolly Christmas" one more time you'll throw something. All the business promotions make a person feel like Christmas should be so peaceful, warm, positive and fun. Song lyrics and advertising images emphasize the joy and comfort of coming home to family, which causes a disconnect in the hearts of many because 'home and family' to them has always meant discord and pain – and Christmas doesn't change that at all. It often exacerbates the situation. Once you start seeing the all the hype, materialism, pain and empty promises, it's easy to feel like the spirituality of Christmas is in danger of being completely lost.

So, as we move through the last days of Advent, let's turn our focus to something that is beautiful and astounding. Have you ever realized that no other faith has a religious celebration that has affected the world the way the birth of Christ has done and still does? Certainly, the secular world goes to a lot of effort to subvert the real meaning of Christmas but in spite of its best efforts, it fails. It fails because "bonum diffusivum sui" which means, "It is the nature of goodness to diffuse itself." When Jesus was born, goodness and light took up residence in the world and, as John 1:5 says, *"The light shines in the darkness, and the darkness did not overcome it."* It still hasn't. Never will.

No matter how the world tries to cash in on the Christmas season and no matter how much those who are politically correct try to deflect attention away from the name of Christ or from the reason we celebrate, light emitting goodness saturates the whole season. This is God's glow of goodness because good cannot exist outside of him. And at Christmas, it seems like he is especially exuberant in the diffusion of his goodness. Every act of giving whether it's based in Christian values or not comes from the goodness of God and every person, company or institution that gives in any way, is an instrument of God whether they know it or not. It's as if the light of Christ's birth cannot be overcome no matter how much the secular world shies away from acknowledging it.

When I listen to the radio, watch television, read the newspapers and scan the Internet, I am boggled by the efforts of so many to minister to the poor during Advent and Christmas. There are empty stocking funds, penny drives, charity concerts and a multitude of Christmas meals being offered to those who can't afford one. Food bank drives abound. Radio stations have contests to see which station can get the most food items collected. Local businesses invite people to come by with food and gifts to try to fill up the back of a trailer truck. Even municipal garbage collectors have food drives. Individuals are doing random acts of great kindness. People volunteer to stand outside in the cold to ring bells and collect money for the poor and all who can generously tip coins into the kettle on their way past.

We have a choice. We can look at the negative. We can cry foul because we feel like Jesus is being left out. We can be cynical about a corporation's motivations in providing a meal or collecting items for the food bank. We can shake our heads at how Santa is better known than Christ. We can focus on the darkness. It's so easy to do that and it's very addictive.

Or we can start seeing that when a holy infant was born into the world, the world lost the battle against the light. The Light could not and cannot be kept down. Christmas could be outlawed completely and the light would still shine. Goodness would still come bubbling up through the cracks because darkness cannot overcome the light.

"The Word became flesh and made his dwelling among us. We have seen his glory, the glory of the one and only Son, who came from the Father, full of grace and truth." (John 1:14 NIV)

Rejoice, people of God! There is good news of great joy for all of you: to you is born this day a Savior, who is the Messiah, the Lord. The world will try to shut him up. It will nail him to a cross. It will twist his words and subvert his truths. It will try to make money off of him. It will attempt to replace him, negate him, eliminate him and make him into a myth.

But the world cannot do it. It is fighting a losing battle. So, lift up your hearts and seek the face of the infant in every act of goodness and generosity you come across. Soon you will see him everywhere and you will know: The child has won.

Because you just can't keep a good God down.

Mary, Mother of God A, B and C

Woman Of Grace

First reading Num. 6: 22-27
The Priestly Benediction:
The Lord bless you and keep you;
the Lord make his face to shine upon you, and be gracious to you;
the Lord lift up his countenance upon you, and give you peace.

Responsorial Psalm 66
Response:
O God, be gracious and bless us.

I have written before about how much I love the word 'gracious' and how I believe it is a super natural and necessary characteristic of a priestly people. Here's where it all started:

I had been ill for a long while, was in recovery but was at that stage where my physical energy was still very low and my emotional energy was even lower. I was depressed and having a difficult time finding joy in anything. Thinking about heading out to New Year's Eve Mass was a difficult thought and I was scanning the Mass readings, desperate for something that would lift the heavy, enervating sense that the world was a cold, cold place.

The first thing I read was, *"...the Lord make his face to shine on you and be gracious to you."* The instant I read the word 'gracious', something stirred within me. Then I read it again in the Responsorial Psalm. Gracious. Nothing major happened within me at that moment but it was as though a single clear drop of pure water fell in my cold wasteland. I held it like a fragile treasure and just repeated the word 'gracious' over and over to myself. Every time I repeated it, the droplet seemed to grow a little bigger and a little stronger. During the Mass, the Feast of Mary, the Mother of God, I was filled, little by little, with a sense of wonder at the graciousness of God and Mary appeared to me to be the epitome of that grace. Over the next few days, the droplets became a pool and the pool overflowed to become a stream. My wasteland started to absorb the clean living water. Eventually the stream became a river, one that has never stopped flowing and one that I have often dipped my aching heart into over the years.

Having discovered Mary to be not only full of grace but also beautifully gracious within that fullness, I began to watch her. She became my mentor on the mystical journey to God. I observed her pondering and storing up treasure in her heart. I observed a peaceful patience that went beyond simple trust and became a power in itself. I observed quiet compassion that knew what was necessary when people were in need. I saw her in agony at the foot of the cross, but somehow I always saw her also being mindful of the needs of the younger ones who accompanied her. I saw her stand with John, the disciple that Jesus loved, the one who followed hungrily after Jesus and understood most intuitively what Jesus was saying. How appropriate that Jesus would grace Mary and John with each other. They would be able to communicate without words. They would just know: The Word is with us, the Word is Love and the Word is Grace.

I also saw her in the locked room with the disciples and by her very presence she kept those men from completely disintegrating in fear with her gracious words of wisdom and peace.

Mary...the first mystic of the New Testament. She watched and waited, and then waited some more and watched some more. She absorbed and contemplated and asked, "What is this?" It wasn't a question of frustration but one of deep spiritual exploration. "Where will this go? How will this all play out? Who are you? Who am I?"

She was full of grace and grew strong in graciousness. She was supremely human and became an icon of everything we can be.

Yes, we can.

May the grace of God be with you all. May Mary lead you to the river.

Amen

Inhaling For Joy

- …according to your abundant mercy blot out my transgressions. Wash me thoroughly from my iniquity, and cleanse me from my sin.

- …therefore teach me wisdom in my secret heart. Purge me with hyssop, and I shall be clean; wash me, and I shall be whiter than snow.

- Create in me a clean heart, O God, and put a new and right spirit within me.

- Restore to me the joy of your salvation, and sustain in me a willing spirit.

- O Lord, open my lips, and my mouth will declare your praise. For you have no delight in sacrifice; if I were to give a burnt offering, you would not be pleased.

- The sacrifice acceptable to God is a broken spirit; a broken and contrite heart, O God, you will not despise.

(Excerpts from Psalm 51, NRSV. Ash Wednesday Liturgy)

Ash Wednesday sometimes creeps up on us quickly. It doesn't feel like it's been that long since we put the Christmas decorations away and suddenly it's time to think about what we can do during Lent to prepare ourselves for the great celebration of Easter. It's actually a good idea to reflect on Lent a week or so before Ash Wednesday so that we can ponder on what it is exactly that God may be calling each of us to focus on during the Lenten Season, the season of deepening self awareness and of drawing closer to the heart of our God.

I chose certain excerpts from the Ash Wednesday psalm because they illustrate a crucial spiritual truth that is often overlooked by God's people, especially in times such as Lent. The truth is that even though we may sincerely practice self denial, offer sacrifices and experience heartfelt moments of sorrow over our sinfulness, we have absolutely no capacity to make ourselves uncontaminated and worthy of the Father's Love. What's more, the Father knows that we are completely disabled and helpless when it comes to cleaning ourselves up.

When he tells us to come to him with weeping and fasting, he is not saying that before we come to him we have to make sure we are all clean and pure and that we have made ourselves spotless inside and out. What he is saying is, *"Come. Come with the awareness that you are small and I am the All in All. Come with the sorrow of knowing that you have tried to accomplish things that only I can accomplish. Come with the knowledge that you have tried too hard, have cried too much, have crumbled under too many burdens, felt too lost, for too long and still have made so little progress. Come with the understanding that looking on the Cross of my Son is not for your condemnation but is what should bring you tremendous joyful relief because he has accomplished everything that you never could and never will be able to accomplish, especially when it comes to making yourself whole and worthy. Come because you are so loved, not because you are so good."*

If we really approached Lent with true understanding and were able to fully receive its inherent gifts, we would rename it "The Season of Breathing." Can you recall a time in your life when you were carrying a huge emotional burden of some sort and suddenly everything worked out beautifully? Can you remember the unexpected sense of being able to breathe freely and how it felt like you hadn't really been breathing for a very long time? If we really understood the full impact of all that happened at the first Easter, we would become giddy with the delicious freedom to breathe.

What really struck me about the Ash Wednesday psalm was that the one who was being expected to perform all the action was not the psalmist but the Lord himself. Listen:

...**blot out** my transgressions...**wash me** from my iniquity ... **cleanse me** from my sin... **teach me** wisdom...**purge me** with hyssop...**wash me**, and I shall be whiter than snow...**create in me** a clean heart... **put within me** a new and right spirit...**restore to me** the joy of your salvation...**sustain in me** a willing spirit... **open my lips**...

Obviously, the psalmist understood something we seem to forget. The ball is in the Lord's court. He alone is the source, the power and the action. When we try to wash, cleanse, teach, purge, create, restore, sustain or open ourselves in order to make ourselves acceptable to the Lord, we are leaving out the key part of our salvation: *why* Jesus died on the cross. We need to grasp, once and for all, that we cannot accomplish our own salvation. We are absolutely, totally and irrevocably incapable of healing ourselves of our sins, failures, wounds and disabilities. It is this understanding – and the grateful acceptance of it – that is pleasing to the Lord.

"The sacrifice acceptable to God is a broken spirit; a broken and contrite heart, O God, you will not despise."

What is a broken spirit? It is the spirit of one who knows he has no capacity to be whole, knows he is not God. This broken spirit knows that no one, not herself nor anyone else, can expect her to be capable of something only God is capable of. "Blessed are the poor in Spirit for theirs is the Kingdom of God." Those who are so busy trying to heal themselves and make themselves clean and pure and worthy are certainly not barred from the Kingdom; it's just that it's hard for them to allow themselves entry because it's so difficult to accept that the Kingdom is completely available to those who are incapable and needy. The door is wide open to the poor in spirit because Jesus, knowing our inadequacies and disabilities, did it all for us. He paid the full price of admission.

If God is the only one capable of creating and cleaning us, then what is our responsibility in the equation?

To show up.

That sounds simple and simplistic but, in reality, in spite of all our spiritual activity, all our services to our parish community, all our prayers, devotions and all our good intentions, sitting as empty broken vessels before the Lord is not an easy place for anyone to be. 'Human Beings' is a misnomer. We should be called 'Human Doings' because we prefer to do rather than be. We 'do' because we feel much more in control – until we discover that all our 'doings' haven't done much for us in the depths of our beings and we start to see that we have existed on the surface of all our needs.

Lent should be a time of consciously showing up, a time of being there and being aware. Whatever your chosen Lenten sacrifices and offerings are, they should be more than just something you do; they should act as reminders, not only of your spiritual poverty but also, most importantly, as reminders of the awesome beauty and wonder of Christ's sacrifice. If all you do is focus on how much of a failure you are or how bad you are but never allow yourself to face full on the incredible fact that Jesus did it all and because of what he did, you are forgiven, blessed, loved, healed and set free, then there might as well not be an Easter. The cross was not for our condemnation; the law already did that and still does that. The Cross was for our freedom and healing –

for freedom from guilt and shame and for the healing of all the wounds we have sustained from our own sins, failures and inadequacies.

This Lent, may I suggest that whenever you go to prayer, practice self-denial or practice whatever practice you choose to increase your spiritual awareness, remind yourself that without Easter, Lent has no meaning. Then ponder on this line from the Easter Exultet:

"O happy fault, O necessary sin of Adam, which gained for us so great a Redeemer!"

Be there and be aware. Breathe. And laugh with relief.

CPSIA information can be obtained at www.ICGtesting.com
Printed in the USA
LVOW11s1748300816

502494LV00007B/653/P